Augmented Reality

Berlin Studies in Knowledge Research

Edited by
Günter Abel and James Conant

Volume 11

Augmented Reality

Reflections on Its Contribution to Knowledge Formation

Edited by
José María Ariso

DE GRUYTER

Series Editors
Prof. Dr. Günter Abel
Technische Universität Berlin
Institut für Philosophie
Straße des 17. Juni 135
10623 Berlin
Germany
e-mail: abel@tu-berlin.de

Prof. Dr. James Conant
The University of Chicago
Dept. of Philosophy
1115 E. 58th Street
Chicago IL 60637
USA
e-mail: jconant@uchicago.edu

ISBN 978-3-11-049700-7
e-ISBN (PDF) 978-3-11-049765-6
e-ISBN (EPUB) 978-3-11-049583-6

Library of Congress Cataloging-in-Publication Data
A CIP catalog record for this book has been applied for at the Library of Congress.

Bibliographic information published by the Deutsche Nationalbibliothek
The Deutsche Nationalbibliothek lists this publication in the Deutsche Nationalbibliografie; detailed bibliographic data are available on the Internet at http://dnb.dnb.de.

Printing and binding: CPI books GmbH, Leck
♾ Printing on acid free paper
Printed in Germany

www.degruyter.com.

Table of Contents

Part 3: The Epistemology of Augmented Reality

Part 4: Negative Knowledge Through Augmented Reality

Part 5: Educational Applications and Implications of Augmented Reality

Introduction

José María Ariso

Is Critical Thinking Particularly Necessary when Using Augmented Reality in Knowledge Society? An Introductory Paradox

The growth of Information and Communication Technology has delivered such a vast amount of information that the term 'information society' was created to refer to a society characterized, above all, by the global and massive scale in which raw data are created and disseminated. But the mere fact of receiving information must not be confused with knowledge creation. As David and Foray (2002) pointed out, information 'takes the shape of structured and formatted data-sets that remain passive and inert until used by those with the knowledge needed to interpret and process them' (p. 12). Indeed, the term 'knowledge society' represents progress in relation to 'information society' just because information becomes valuable inasmuch as it is processed and transformed into knowledge. In other words, information is valuable for a knowledge society if and only if people are able to convert it into resources to improve the human condition. According to UNESCO (2005), in knowledge societies everyone must be able 'to develop cognitive and critical thinking skills to distinguish between "useful" and "useless" information' (p. 19). Yet even though distinguishing whether a piece of information is useful or useless constitutes a critical initial step for knowledge creation, such distinction is not sufficient to generate it: to this end, it is necessary to take a further step and find meaning as well as develop understanding. Only in this way will information be transformed into knowledge which can be applied in diverse contexts for improving our quality of life.

Bearing this in mind, Augmented Reality can be regarded as a technological resource that may contribute to facilitate the transition from information society to knowledge society. Let us see why. To begin with, Augmented Reality consists in 'overlaying virtual imagery onto a physical world scene' (Li/Been-Lirn 2013, p. 109). Hence, 'Augmented Reality allows the user to see the real world, with virtual objects superimposed upon or composited with the real world. Therefore, AR [Augmented Reality] supplements reality, rather than completely replacing it' (Kipper/Rampolla 2013). As shown by the large number of new Augmented Reality applications which emerge daily in fields as diverse as robotics, engineering, education, entertainment, manufacturing, medicine, archeology, tourism, the military or urban modeling, among others, this technological resource allows

DOI 10.1515/9783110497656-001

users to transmit a great deal of information, but at the same time it usually shows to a great extent how such information can be applied in diverse circumstances. Augmented Reality thus involves a qualitative change in information handling and knowledge formation. It is true that, during the last years, there were major technological developments of a quantitative nature, like growing mobile connectivity and higher bandwidths. But Augmented Reality entails a revolution in the presentation of information. Virtual Reality technologies had already generated a substantial progress in this regard by completely immersing the user inside a synthetic environment, so that he 'cannot see the real world around him' (Kipper/Rampolla 2013). However, the information provided by Augmented Reality – and often also the very application of such information – is added to our perception of the real world.

Of course, basic formation is needed to interpret some pieces of information and transform them into knowledge. For instance, the information provided in Augmented Reality guided neurosurgery through image projection techniques, whose clinical feasibility and reliability has been proved in a clinical setting (Besharati/Mahvash 2015, Meola *et al.* 2016), will be absolutely useless for the layman, while it will enable surgeons to know tumor status, basic effects that their operation is having, and steps to be taken. Therefore, the fact that virtual imagery is superimposed upon world scenes should not lead to think that the mere presentation of information involves knowledge formation, but there are cases in which this may happen in a greater or lesser degree. To shed more light on this point, I would like to draw attention to the two poles of a continuum. In the first pole, information is presented verbally, with the unique particularity that it appears associated spatially and temporally to the object to which it refers. This may happen, for instance, when a smartphone is focused on a building and an Augmented Reality application adds two pieces of information to the view of the edifice: let us suppose that, on the one hand, it can be read that the building is a museum which offers an exhibition of Gustav Klimt's main paintings, while, on the other hand, there is a sophisticated explanation – either textually or via audio – of Klimt's symbolism. If such information could be transformed by a user into knowledge, he should be able to do a number of things with what he has learned, such as clearly expressing it in his own words or applying it in a variety of contexts – for example, by comparing how Klimt and other painters used specific symbols. Since it is verbal information of considerable complexity, Augmented Reality technology can obviously not ensure that any user will be prepared to understand it. This case strongly resembles the use of traditional tourist guides published in paper form, yet the next two examples show how AR technology may contribute to facilitate the transition from information society to knowledge society. Firstly, in the middle part of the continuum we can find many instances of school eLearning which consist in superimposing images and words through markers upon physical world scenes. By way of example, teachers may illustrate on a real arm not only the names and appearance of the muscles and bones involved in the arm contraction movement, but also how these elements interact to generate the mentioned movement while the real arm is being contracted (LearnAR 2010). Secondly, at the opposite pole there is not information to be processed, but information – usually in the form of images – which in a sense has already been applied. Thus, when someone turns on a tablet or a smartphone at home to buy a suit through an Augmented Reality application, he can watch not only diverse suits, but also how they suit him over his own image. In this way, information is not restricted to the mere visualization of a suit and its features, as it also allows users to know whether a specific suit fits them well. Hence, it can be stated that this information has been applied or presented in such a perfectly understandable way for the user that he will know how each suit looks on him, so that he will be able to do things like deciding whether he will buy one suit or another.

As can be seen, Augmented Reality technology creates possibilities that until recently still sounded like the stuff of science-fiction: a clear example of this is the possibility of checking out comfortably at home the fit of a suit which may be stored in a shopping centre from another continent. The extraordinary possibilities offered by Augmented Reality may even lead some people to ascribe to this technology the Midas touch, according to which it will figuratively convert into gold anything it touches. After all, one of the major attractions of Augmented Reality is that it often seems to show clearly and directly how to apply some pieces of information without requiring the slightest effort from the user, that is, without any need for critical thinking. It is important to keep in mind that, when this technology is used for gaming, critical thinking often turns out to be a nuisance because the game's appeal lies just in letting oneself go without resisting immersion in it. Admittedly, it might be objected that critical thinking is an essential element of gaming in new technologies like Augmented Reality, as a good dose of ingenuity is often required to overcome specific challenges and, thus, get to the next level. There is a major aspect, however, that we should not forget. The reflection demanded by this kind of games can be and often is expressed through a more or less random process of trial and error, as such games are designed to be played at a high – and sometimes frenetic – pace, so that the player's tension and interest do not diminish. That is why the limited reflection carried out during the game turns out to be exciting and is bound to the challenge faced at that very moment, without considering aspects which are external to the game, e. g. those related to the technology used. It is therefore expected that the player unhesitatingly welcomes all the conditioning factors of the game, whatever these may be, as not for nothing are games designed so that the player submerges into action without being distracted by thinking. This lack of critical attitude may persist in contexts other than gaming, as Augmented Reality technology presents a certain playful character: we only need to notice the immediacy with which our perception of reality may be supplemented with multiple virtual objects that can be manipulated at will in very different ways. This playful nature is characteristic of the majority of new technologies, whose design is intended above all to enable us to carry out the most varied activities easily and pleasantly, which for most people –and thus also for designers – entails avoiding critical thinking as much as possible. Nevertheless, the playful character inherent in the use of Augmented Reality hides a paradox, as critical thinking is particularly necessary in order to avoid blind reliance on the information provided by this technology. Indeed, the fact that Augmented Reality technology presents information attractively overlaid onto physical world scenes – and that such information may include contents as basic and indisputable as the day's date or the names of the surrounding streets, among many others – may lead some people to accept without any reservation other contents as well as most of their applications.

As I will thereupon show, there are at the very least three reasons as to why it is particularly necessary to implement critical thinking when using Augmented Reality. First of all, Augmented Reality may condition knowledge formation to a great extent by prioritizing a specific way of using or projecting information at the expense of other or others. Augmented Reality technology enables users to monitor the results of choosing different alternatives, but it can also be employed to hide one or several options in order to favor specific interests which perhaps do not coincide with those of the user. In this regard, the Augmented Reality user may think that the right choice – even in cases where there are no correct alternatives but simply different ones – is the first one offered by the application; moreover, he may also take for granted that the only possible options are those shown in the application, which is not necessarily the case. Secondly, it is important to note that, even though the information provided by Augmented Reality is often really useful, it may occasionally be offered in the wrong place and/or at the wrong time. Furthermore, such information might be unwanted, unnecessary, or could even consist in mere creations elaborated without a particular purpose or with an expired one. In fact, it is also possible that the Augmented Reality user is monitored or manipulated when using this technology. To return to previous examples, when a user looks for information on a building through Augmented Reality, he should consider the extent to which he is reading reliable information or mere propaganda. Regarding the user who tries on a suit through an Augmented Reality application, he would do well to reflect upon the extent to which such suit seems to look as wonderful as the seller would wish to make him believe. Thirdly, it may in certain cases be very difficult to distinguish fact from fiction, for, as already pointed out, in Augmented Reality virtual imagery is added to our perception of the real world. Most uses for this technology intend virtual objects to stand out so clearly that they can be distinguished without any doubt from the world scene; but there may be people interested in misleading us by creating virtual objects which are disguised in the world scene as if they were real objects.

Of course, there are many valuable uses of Augmented Reality, making it a clear example of Positive Technology inasmuch as it contributes to raise the quality of life by increasing emotional, psychological and social well-being (Riva *et al.* 2012, Argenton *et al.* 2014). But as we have just seen, it is also possible to make a perverse use of this technology, from which it follows a number of important ethical questions in relation to issues such as lack of privacy (Schmalstieg *et al.* 2002). Furthermore, Augmented Reality technology can be used for aesthetic purposes, as experienced in the exhibitions displayed in 2010 at the Museum of Modern Art in New York, and in 2011 at the Venice and Istanbul Biennials (Thiel 2014). This reference to ethical and aesthetical issues constitutes a first approach to the philosophical field and its relation to Augmented Reality. Nevertheless, this volume does not deal with ethical or aesthetical issues, but with other philosophical ones, related, on the one hand, to diverse possibilities, consequences and applications of Augmented Reality, and on the other, to the way in which this technology serves as a touchstone for tackling philosophical problems of key importance and with a long tradition. In order to provide a more detailed approach, I have divided the volume into five parts. The first one addresses three questions that are characterized, in different ways, by their historical relevance: specifically, this first part tackles issues as diverse as paradigm shifts regarding digital innovation dynamics, the epistemic potential of virtual realities for the historical sciences, and the description of grammatical clarifications which consider Augmented Reality as the crowning of a long process of increasing epistemic and existential access to reality. The variety of these issues reveals that it was not my intention to place the authors into a strait jacket by asking them to address a very specific issue. Instead, the aim was that authors should feel free to choose a philosophical topic related to Augmented Reality, because the volume would thus allow a glimpse of a greater variety of very interesting and innovative issues and approaches, with the added incentive that today we can still tackle those questions from the perspective of an epoch in which Augmented Reality technologies are in full development stage, so that their use is not yet so widespread and frequent as it is expected to be before long.

There is no doubt that the very expression 'Augmented Reality' already includes ontological enigmas of great interest, as it represents a significant challenge to clarify in which sense reality is augmented, or which notion of reality is entailed here. That is why the second part of the volume is dedicated to analyzing ontological problems related to Augmented Reality. Specifically, this part will address issues as basic as the alleged existence of virtual objects and the notion of 'reality' implicit in Augmented Reality, but also others as original as Hegel's identification of real reality with reason by taking it as conceptually Augmented Reality. The third part focuses on epistemic issues, as not for nothing does the subtitle of the volume indicate that it deals above all with knowledge formation. Hence, this part tackles such problems as the epistemic salience of roles played by Augmented Reality applications across the dimensions of Augmented Reality content and interaction, the alleged informational augmentation of perception provided by Augmented Reality technologies, and the challenge that some instances of Augmented Reality can generate to extended knowledge and even to our very knowledge of the external world. The fourth part also delves into epistemic concerns, as it concentrates on negative knowledge and its links with Augmented Reality. The three chapters of this part outline the potential of Augmented Reality to promote ignorance in urban settings, the way negative knowledge and the learning processes through which it is developed are affected in virtual environments, and a proposal to apply cognitive restructuring through Augmented Reality glasses in order to foster a patient's negative self-knowledge. This chapter is clearly interdisciplinary, as it shows how Augmented Reality technologies could be applied in psychopathology while presenting a new philosophical concept. Yet, as has been shown, this is by no means the only interdisciplinary chapter. Furthermore, the fifth and last part of the volume looks at the educational applications and implications of Augmented Reality. This part focuses on the use of Augmented Reality in the different educational stages as well as its advantages and disadvantages, the consequences of Augmented Reality on pedagogical anthropology, and the way in which the planning of the subject 'Augmented Reality and Accessibility' has evolved at a Spanish university in accordance with the technology's evolution and the needs of users of Augmented Reality applications.

Having said this, I will now explain each chapter in greater detail. The first part, which tackles issues characterized by their historical significance, begins with the chapter "From Augmented Reality to the Internet of Things: Paradigm Shifts in Digital Innovation Dynamics", in which Klaus Mainzer notes that Virtual Reality, Augmented Reality and the Internet of Things constitute three different paradigms which followed one another. While VR consisted in replacing the real world with a computationally simulated one, AR supplemented our real-world environment with digital instruments which are equipped with sensor interfaces. Yet the new paradigm is the “Internet of Things”, in which billions of objects are intercommunicated through sensors: a clear example of this can be found in mobility networks, where cars are communicated with one another and their technical infrastructure regardless of human drivers. Mainzer focuses on the paradigm shift between Augmented Reality and the Internet of Things and remarks that Augmented Reality applications revolve around the embodied mind; however, the Internet of Things-world is developing together with large-scale infrastructures of society. These infrastructures are cyberphysical systems which obtain information from their physical environment through sensors, process it, and influence their environment. Thus, cyberphysical systems use some Augmented Reality technologies, but they overcome mere Augmented Reality applications by creating new integrative platforms with increasing levels of self-organization. According to Mainzer, this means that Internet of Things technology does not merely “augment” reality, but transforms it into a new kind of self-organizing superorganism characterized by the swarm intelligence derived from the technical co-evolution of mankind with technical infrastructures.

In the chapter “Abstract Entities and Augmented Reality: A Pragma-Linguistic Approach", Javier Vilanova carries out a clarification of the main concepts and expressions related to Augmented Reality. Specifically, Vilanova starts from a pragmalinguistic conception of language and grammar bearing in mind, above all, the work of Ludwig Wittgenstein and John Austin. Thus, Vilanova describes a number of examples of uses of the expressions in diverse situations by comparing not only the different examples themselves, but also examples of the use of other expressions looking for similarities, analogies and differences. In this way, he tries to offer a synoptic view that can be of great help to become conscious of the features of the phenomena and, by extension, to reach a deeper and better understanding of puzzling uses of the expressions. In this way, Vilanova aims to shed light on ontological puzzles regarding the nature of entities generated by new technologies. After analyzing the terms ‘virtual’, ‘reality’, ‘extension’ and ‘augmentation’ from a grammatical point of view, Vilanova compares Augmented Reality with four kinds of arguably abstract entities (universals, fiction, mathematics and social phenomena) by recalling what everyday language and common sense can tell us about them and discerning whether and how that can be applied to cases of Augmented Reality. This series of comparisons leads him to three conclusions. First, Augmented Reality is constructed through linguistic procedures. Second, entities produced by the technological devices involved in Augmented Reality must be considered as abstract entities: in other words, Augmented Reality augments reality because it produces new entities that allow the properties of pre-existing entities and situations to unfold.

And last but not least, Vilanova begins by stating that Augmented Reality constitutes the clearest example of abstraction, but then he realizes that Augmented Reality should be regarded as the main model for our notion of abstraction. For Vilanova contemplates Augmented Reality as the culmination of a process which began when language was created, and was further developed through some instruments like science that allowed us both to augment reality with new types of objects and situations, so that our epistemic and existential access to reality was also extended.

The third chapter has been written by Stefan Weinzierl and Steffen Lepa, and is entitled "On the Epistemic Potential of Virtual Realities for the Historical Sciences. A Methodological Framework". Although immersive media environments like virtual or augmented audio-visual ones have often been used to provide historical knowledge, few attempts have been made to generate new knowledge through the virtual reconstruction of historical scenarios. Regarding this kind of practice, however, the scientific community has reservations that are due, above all, to the extent to which virtual environments can be considered as a form of scientific evidence, the way in which such environments – which are necessarily based on historical evidence that is already known – may provide new knowledge, and the role that could be played by virtual or augmented realities within an epistemological concept of historical research. To answer these questions, Weinzierl and Lepa offer a methodological framework which is illustrated by dealing with three questions related to the Forum Romanum, i.e. which was the maximum audience size reached by a speaker on this Forum, how the size of this audience varied because of the modifications and relocations of the Rostra, and whether these changes were made to improve the acoustics, or rather due to political and symbolic reasons. After combining ideas and procedures from virtual reality research, media psychology, communication science and ethnology in order to develop their methodological framework, Weinzierl and Lepa highlight three possibilities for new knowledge to arise from virtual or augmented historical environments. First of all, they point out that new information can be extracted from the historical evidence by bringing into relation specific bits of information which had not been previously combined. Second, virtual or augmented environments are able to transform numerical models of historical circumstances into sensory signals. Hence, they provide information regarding the perceptual impression of historical environments, which are in turn easier to understand for non-experts. In this way, virtual historical environments are very useful for exploring the actual perceptual meaning of coefficients obtained from mere numerical simulations. Last but not least, virtual historic environments might become a further example of interdisciplinary cooperation which shows how new knowledge can arise from cooperation between disciplines far apart from each other.

The second part is dedicated to ontological problems related to Augmented Reality. To begin with, in the chapter "Scientific Truth as Augmented Reality. On the Contrast Between '*Wirklichkeit*' and Actuality" Pirmin Stekeler-Weithofer draws attention to the augmentation of reality that takes place in virtual reality by adding possibilities. To shed light on this idea, he brings up Hegel's modal notion of reality ('*Wirklichkeit*') – or 'real reality', according to Stekeler's contextual translation – as a kind of possibility and its difference with actuality ('*empirische Realität*'). Since appearances constitute only a sign for those real objects that produce them, that is, since an underlying reality must be inferred from the appearances in the mode of abduction, objective statements about *real reality* are necessarily fallible. This indicates in which sense real reality should be considered in itself as Augmented Reality. Stekeler analyzes some features of the 'augmentation' of actuality by reason that turns actuality into 'real reality'. As only humans have access to – non-present – possibilities due to their faculty of thinking, Hegel's formula "reality is a possibility" invites us to distinguish between what is actually perceived by someone and what can count as objectively real ("*wirklich*"). Yet what is real cannot be perceived without modal or conceptual mediation, so that we cannot access objective reality by mere sense-perception. Indeed, reality claims are rarely immediate, for what we count as real is usually dependent from propositions with trans-personal inferential impact and truth conditions that go beyond the realm in which truth can be evaluated by mere perception. That is why non-tautological empirical truths are fallible. Hence, we must always judge whether a given possibility-judgment should be regarded as telling us what really exists. Bearing this in mind, Hegel's insight is far from being a bizarre theory about real reality which we can access – as it corresponds to mere possibilities – through thinking and not by perception, for we perceive actual appearances instead of their real or objective causes. In short, Stekeler presents Hegel's identification of real reality with reason by taking it as conceptually Augmented Reality, applied to empirical experience.

According to Thomas Gil, technological development has not sufficed to reject traditional philosophical responses to the ontological question of what there is, as the main component elements of reality are still individual things, qualities, classes and facts. In fact, Gil offers a brief review of the history of philosophy in the chapter "Existence and Ontological Commitments" to remind us of some of the main answers to the question of what reality is made of. Thus, he takes into account Plato's theory of abstract Forms, Aristotle's rejection of this theory and further consideration of substantial beings, Ockham's reduction of Aristotle's categories from ten to two by admitting only substance and quality,

Wittgenstein's conception of the world as made of facts, and Quine's language- and theory-relative ontology in which the status of being an existing entity is denied to intensional entities. After his review, Gil describes the main lines of what Floridi calls "Fourth Revolution", whose impact would be comparable with the Copernican, the Darwinian and the Freudian revolution. From Floridi's point of view, we have become informational organisms closely connected with each other and embedded in informational environments which we share with a number of natural and artificial informational agents: indeed, our practical world actually includes informatized entities or "ITentities" which mutually interact to bring us multiple benefits in our daily lives. Nevertheless, Gil points out that, although it is currently possible to distinguish more types of objects in the world, the traditional ontological vocabulary is not affected at all, as they ultimately go on being objects. Taking literary fictions as a reference, Gil also warns that fictional objects or characters exist only ideally in such texts without being contained in reality: thus, these objects or characters exist just because literary fictions exist. Finally, Gil states that this idea would also be applicable to the alleged existence of those objects created by new technologies, above all Augmented Reality.

"What Actually is Augmented Reality". The title of Juan Antonio Valor's chapter already indicates the question he tries to answer, for which he bases himself on the notion of reality as developed in prior philosophical conceptions. Thus, Valor follows two distinct philosophical strands. On the one hand, he starts by describing Locke's theory of knowledge, in which it is discussed whether Ideas can faithfully represent what exists in extra-mental reality, as well as Newton's empiricism, for Newton presupposes that the repeated permanence of the simple ideas of primary qualities is due to the constant action of the primary qualities belonging to the extra-mental reality. Valor brings up both strands because, although they emerged in the 17th century, they are somehow at the basis of what we still mean by reality. Hence, in the 17th century a notion of reality is defined according to which the material reality that exists beyond our minds as well as our ideas consists of solid atoms moving and resting in space and time. This leads Valor to state that, if we ended up not recognizing the mediation of technical devices between the material reality and our senses, Augmented Reality would become everyday reality, even though both of them would convey an appearance generated within our mind due to the action of extra-mental material reality. On the other hand, he also exposes the main lines of the pragmatic conception of reality developed by Dewey, whose anti-dualism places emphasis on the correlation of organism and environment in the situation, and Rorty, who attributes reality to centers of descriptive gravity which vary depending on our descriptions and the languages we use. Bearing all this in mind, Valor concludes that, from the standpoint of empiricism, Augmented Reality is only an appearance caused by the action on our senses of material reality, whereas according to pragmatism the reality we grant to Augmented Reality will depend on the problems it allows us to solve.

The third part, devoted to the epistemology of Augmented Reality, begins with the chapter "Augmented Skepticism: The Epistemological Design of Augmented Reality", in which Spyridon Orestis Palermos draws attention to the danger of our everyday epistemic practices being easily disrupted by Augmented Reality technologies. As Palermos points out, it has been argued that when agents and their artifacts operate in a mutually interdependent way that imitates the cooperative interaction and thereby integrated nature of our organismic cognitive faculties, we may speak of extended cognitive systems that can generate extended knowledge – i.e., knowledge that is responsibly held on the basis of the mutual interactions of the corresponding human-machine coupled systems. Bearing in mind how Augmented Reality systems work, they are remarkable candidates for giving rise to extended cognitive systems and extended knowledge. Yet some instances of Augmented Reality can generate a challenge to extended knowledge and, more worryingly, to our knowledge of the external world at large. Indeed, their users may be exposed to the danger of being unable to distinguish between reality and Augmented Reality. It is true that the integrated nature of our cognitive systems allows us to single out reality augmentations that cannot be easily confused as parts of physical reality, yet there are other aspects of Augmented Reality which might turn out to be very confusing for the user. According to Palermos, this danger generates a form of future 'augmented skepticism' which should not be neglected, to the extent that significant measures should be taken not only to design future Augmented Reality systems, but also to teach users how to employ this technology in order to avoid this epistemic threat. Palermos therefore raises two points regarding the future use and design of Augmented Reality. Either people will have to learn how to develop new epistemic skills in order to safely integrate and employ Augmented Reality; or Augmented Reality holograms should be specifically designed so as to clearly and in all instances stand out from the real elements of the physical world (for example by being delineated with fluorescent borders); or, preferably, both.

The question tackled by Boleslaw Czarnecki and Tadeusz Czarnecki appears in the very title of their chapter: "Is Augmented Reality a Source of New Types of Knowledge?" Bearing in mind that knowledge emerges only if the conditions of agency and contact with reality are fulfilled, Czarnecki and Czarnecki wonder what type of environment could generate a new kind of experience which, in turn, could provide a new type of knowledge. In this sense, Augmented Reality seems to be a very interesting option as it offers scenarios which are compatible with cognitive agencies, yet they also contain Virtual Reality overlay cut off from reality. To face this problem, Czarnecki and Czarnecki suggest that Augmented Reality technology provides ontologically heterogeneous scenarios in which experiences of individuals and experiences of models are mixed. Furthermore, they not only analyze whether Virtual Reality experiences of inner screens may suffice to create new manual skills, but also enquire whether fully augmented simulations can generate such skills. According to Czarnecki and Czarnecki, our cognitive contact with simulations may be at least as good as the current contact with reality, above all if simulations serve to reduce the risk of failure when aiming for useful information or manual skill. Provided that problems are prior to the knowledge which is expected to solve them, simulations may be even better than fully veridical experience in solving problems. Lastly, Czarnecki and Czarnecki conclude that Mixed Reality visualizations cannot provide any new kind of knowledge-*that* unless the visualized models are registered with reality. Yet such registration should take a number of forms in order to qualitatively enhance new knowledge. In addition, it is not clear at all which forms of registration could be actualized and, even more importantly, whether it would really make sense to actualize those that could be.

In order to show in which sense it is not only misleading but maybe also harmful to think that Augmented Reality informationally allows us to augment our perception, Karsten Schoellner starts the chapter "Augmented Reality and Augmented Perception" by describing three philosophical phenomena that could be considered as varieties of 'Augmented Reality'. First, he brings up Wallace Stevens' notion of how the poetic imagination can enrich our reality by providing something beyond plain reality but without ceasing to be real, that is, a transformed or Augmented Reality. Second, he describes the "sensibility theory" of moral and aesthetic value developed by McDowell and Wiggins in order to explain how what they call "anthropocentric properties" – i.e. properties that are real and objective although they are somehow dependent upon human sensibilities – can emerge from human culture and enter into a naturalistic world. Third, he refers to Wittgenstein's distinction between the world of the happy and that of the unhappy, so that the individual whose world enlarges will feel that his sense of reality has been augmented, even though reality itself remains unchanged. After having exposed these related notions of what 'augmenting reality' might consist in, Schoellner draws attention to the use of the word 'reality' in the expression 'Augmented Reality', which is fundamental to clarify to what extent this technology entails an augmentation of reality. When contrasting Augmented Reality technologies with the three varieties mentioned above, he realizes that these technologies, paradoxically as it may seem, threaten to diminish our reality. For Stevens, McDowell, Wiggins and Wittgenstein already warned that, in order to augment reality, we should go beyond our need to possess and control; yet inasmuch as Augmented Reality technologies are used to increase our control over our own experience, they may contribute – and indeed already contribute – to our getting out of the present moment.

The fourth part of the volume is intended to analyze how negative knowledge can be fostered through Augmented Reality. Jaana Parviainen begins the chapter "'Imagine Never not Knowing': An Epistemological Framework for Understanding Negative Knowledge in Augmented Reality" by noting that there has been much debate in recent years about the extent to which the use of computers embedded everywhere, not only in our environments but also in our bodies, would overburden our cognition in our everyday lives. As might have been expected, such a use of ubiquitous computing has generated a number of ethical and social concerns. In order to provide a broader approach to the use of Augmented Reality in the context of the smart city, Parviainen addresses questions of information materialism related to social epistemology and the phenomenology of the body. Although the interaction of embodied beings, things, and technology determines what thoughts and actions are possible, she considers Augmented Reality as an embodied medium bearing in mind technological unconsciousness. This means that we are often unaware that we are using multiple systems of computers and devices, so that the task of shedding light on such infrastructure and its dynamics is of utmost importance. In order to foster a broader look at the epistemological implications of Augmented Reality, Parviainen discusses negative knowledge in terms of Augmented Reality. From her point of view, it is impossible to access directly from ignorance – understood as the situation in which one is not aware that he does not know – to positive knowledge without negative knowledge, that is, without acknowledging and being aware that we don't know something. After showing how Karin Knorr Cetina's notion of liminality helps to understand how augmented technologies provide contextual information by supplementing or even replacing human senses, Parviainen explains how her discussion of negative knowledge in terms of Augmented Reality is related to our embodiment, kinesthesia, movement, and transition in space. But although Augmented Reality technologies offer advantages such as liberating individuals from their normative and traditional use of spaces to develop instead deeper and more personalized ways to attain their environment, and educational potentials of Augmented Reality may also promote new or "extended knowledge", Parviainen points out that our use of Augmented Reality has also potential to promote ignorance, as people tend to interact in urban settings with a mundane knowledge infrastructure whose function they often do not understand. For instance, there are a number of systems which collect large amounts of data about the users – e.g. their locations, intentions or desires –

in such a way that the user is not aware at all of the information gathered by these systems, and for which purpose. In fact, Augmented Reality technologies may provide us with hidden information in which we are not interested, or it may also erase relevant objects and information. Hence, Augmented Reality can generate new ways of revealing, distracting, and imperiling people. In short, the technologies of Augmented Reality can be regarded as filters which provide new information – which is sometimes irrelevant about our physical world – while at the same time concealing from us information regarding the kind of data collected, as well as how and why they are processed. In this sense, there is a part of our perceptual world which remains in shadow.

Negative knowledge is experiential knowledge focused on what is wrong and what not to do in given situations to avoid errors, but also on limitations in one's own knowledge, skills or cognition. Bearing in mind, on the one hand, that negative knowledge is acquired above all by learning from errors, and on the other, that virtual environments generate altered conditions for what constitutes errors and for how and why learning from errors takes place, Martin Gartmeier, Charlotte Jonasson and Maria Solomou wonder in the chapter "Negative Knowledge in Virtual and Game-Based Environments" how negative knowledge and the learning processes through which it is developed are affected in virtual environments. From a pragmatic standpoint, they focus on four points and reach the following conclusions. First, simulations – e. g. flight simulators – provide optimal conditions for practicing error-prone tasks while developing relevant negative knowledge, as learners may reflect upon errors and memorize which situations should be avoided in the future as well as which actions lead to such situations. Moreover, learners can pose relevant and challenging problems, which require that they develop negative knowledge about their limitations in problem-solving abilities. Second, computer games provide an extraordinary access to immersive possibilities, to the extent that players are liberated from physical and even from moral boundaries which are characteristic of the real world. The goal of these games often consists in committing acts of great violence and cruelty, that is, in showing fictionally immoral attitudes. Negative knowledge is therefore developed inasmuch as the player imaginatively adopts an immoral attitude, which might deepen his understanding of how he would feel when freely acting in such a way and, by extension, he might acknowledge his responsibility for those actions. Third, the player must learn for mistakes in order to make progress through the game. After having failed several times, negative knowledge is enhanced regarding what not to do the next time, although he still does not know how to master that challenge. As computer games often allow only one correct way to solve certain problems but many options which lead the player to failure, these games are full of negative knowledge which must be continuously transformed into positive knowledge. Fourth, game-based environments often contain far fewer options and rules than real life, which entails a drastic reduction of complexity. According to Gartmeier, Jonasson and Salomou, this reduction may be perceived by players as liberation and relief from challenges and ambiguities inherent in real-world contexts. However, game designers should be careful in regulating the learning from errors-aspect of games, as the facilitation of the performatory mode of action does not require the player to develop as much negative knowledge to deal with the limits of his own skills.

José María Ariso proposes in the chapter "How to Increase Negative Self-Knowledge by Using Cognitive Restructuring Through Augmented Reality: A Proposal and Analysis" a new kind of negative self-knowledge by taking as a reference the concepts 'self-knowledge' and 'negative knowledge'. Specifically, Ariso's notion of negative self-knowledge consists in the knowledge that someone has of what he or she is not like. This kind of knowledge is promoted when applying cognitive restructuring, as this technique has been employed in the last few decades to help patients identify and dismantle wrong thoughts about themselves. Ariso's contribution consists in showing how Augmented Reality may contribute to improve the use of cognitive restructuring. At first sight, this peculiar combination may appear attractive, for it suggests a new use of a technology as groundbreaking as Augmented Reality. Yet it would be a grave mistake, as previously stated, to ascribe to this technology the Midas touch, as if it could convert into gold whatever it touches. That is why Ariso explains the advantages of an Augmented Reality application for overcoming the resistances shown by clients when employing cognitive restructuring: for instance, by beginning to use this technique whenever disturbing thoughts are perceived, by maintaining concentration while such thoughts are identified and dismantled, and by re-evaluating whether the wrong thought is still perceived as true. Moreover, this application has the advantage of supporting the patient *in situ*, that is, in those situations outside the office in which he could otherwise not count on the therapist's support. By the way, it is also explained how the therapist's role would vary if he used the application described in this chapter: though he would go on performing his previous functions, now he should also become a specialist in adapting the application to each patient's needs and characteristics. Nevertheless, the ultimate aim will still be that the patient masters the technique to the point of becoming able to apply it spontaneously in his daily life without the support of therapist or Augmented Reality glasses.

The fifth and final part of the volume is dedicated to shedding light on some educational applications and implications of Augmented Reality. In the chapter "Augmented Reality and pedagogical anthropology: reflections from the philosophy of education", Juan Luis Fuentes begins by pointing out that educational thought has always been linked to anthropological thought. Indeed, education would not be possible if human beings did not have some specific traits, a group of characteristics that allows us to talk about a transforming influence on the reality of an individual or a group of individuals. Hence, the concept of education is not attributed to other species, but to humans. In those cases, instruction or training are commonly used. In this chapter, Fuentes analyzes some of the challenges and contributions of Augmented Reality to philosophy of education, paying special attention to its consequences in one of its basic areas: pedagogical anthropology. He points out some of the more relevant anthropological traits related to the modern technology. For that, he follows the proposals of some important authors in pedagogical anthropology, a discipline that has been studied by philosophy since it was born, but which was not systematically developed from an educational perspective until the second half of the twentieth century, specifically in Germany and United States. In particular, Fuentes studies the human quality of non-instinctivity and its influence on the development of initiative, which in the current technological model has a basic role because it gives us an open space for human singularization. To sit before a screen that sends the same information to every spectator responds to a closed and predefined anthropological conception, without space for the needed initiative. On the contrary, participation through technology extends the possibilities of human mediation and its answer to the stimulation, and it also increases its election and creation capacities, not only as mere variations of a melody but also as the possibility to produce a new one, making possible its realization as an 'acting being'. On the other hand, Fuentes stresses human precariousness and the ability to adapt. This can be peculiarly observed in Augmented Reality because the environment is barely modified when a mixed reality is created, and provides a privileged look and hypersensitivity, which has a feedback effect on intellectual capacity. Moreover, Augmented Reality devices allow us to go deep into the ontological knowledge of reality, through transmediation, and into Zubiri's concept that defines a human being as a 'being of realities', in that it increases the possibilities to take over remote situations far from the closest environment. Finally, Fuentes analyzes the leisure understood as human but not vital need, which is revalorized in the technological context, which in turn could benefit education as a consequence of its contribution to an integral vision of the human being, less utilitarian and more ethical.

In the chapter "New Challenge in Education: Enhancing Student's Knowledge Through Augmented Reality", Almudena Castellanos and Carlota Pérez reflect on the use of Augmented Reality in the educational field. They focus on the analysis of the point to which Augmented Reality technology is useful to generate meaningful learning or, in short, to improve the learning process. According to Castellanos and Pérez, recent studies have shown that the appropriate use of Augmented Reality facilitates constructivist and enquiry-based learning, increases student's motivation and academic performance, allows the manipulation and relation of very small or very large elements – like molecules or celestial bodies – which could otherwise not be manipulated by students, and helps treat people with autism or physical disabilities. Yet even though Augmented Reality offers these and other advantages for teachers and students, it has not yet become a mainstream technology in education. Castellanos and Pérez state that this is due to a number of factors: the difficulty of accepting innovations that entail changes in habits, parents' resistance to the use of Augmented Reality as a vehicle for knowledge, the information overload that could be undergone by students, and the lack of technical means and knowledge to use this technology. To address the latter problem, Castellanos and Pérez present a number of tools which make it possible to create Augmented Reality applications very quickly, so that there is no need to be a programmer or an expert in computers in order to enjoy this technology. Furthermore, they describe in detail a large number of uses made of Augmented Reality in infant education, primary education, high school and professional development, as well as university education. Lastly, Castellanos and Pérez conclude that, although Augmented Reality is not yet widespread extended to pupils in schools, it is in a full process of expansion, so that it is expected that this technology will acquire more significance in the teaching-learning processes with the benefits outlined above.

Even though Castellanos and Pérez indicated in the previous chapter that Augmented Reality technology can be operated without the need for specialist knowledge, it is obvious that this technology is possible due to the work of highly qualified professionals. To shed light on the training of these experts, María Elena Alva, Teobaldo Hernán Sagastegui, Vicente García, Jordán Pascual and Rubén González explain in the chapter "Teaching Augmented Reality" what kind of knowledge must be acquired by students of the degree of Computer Engineering at the University of Oviedo (Spain) within the subject of 'Augmented Reality and Accessibility'. To start with, authors point out that this subject constitutes a clear example of the developments undergone during the last decades by the education plan in accordance with technology's evolution. In other words, the structural knowledge, as well as the elements of associated knowledge, imparted on this subject depends on the needs of the Augmented Reality applications' users – including those users with physical and/or cognitive limitations –, that is, on what they wish to know and the way in which they want to know it when using such applications. Indeed, the goal of the course is not only that students acquire long-lasting knowledge about the fundamentals of the course, but also that they acquire skills to manage tools and technologies that help them to develop projects planned to facilitate the access to additional information. Thus, students should be acquainted with the user's needs to adapt processes and techniques by adding computer-generated elements which allow them to easily access additional information and, by extension, to reach a sense of coexistence of the real environment with the virtual world. Drawing on Bloom's model and Krathwohl's proposals, Alva, Sagastegui, García, Pascual and González therefore describe the methodological, individual, systematic and common competencies as well as the learning results that should be acquired by students to reach the proposed goals of the course by participating in seminar, workshop, practical, evaluation and tutorial sessions. In this way, students are expected to achieve a series of objectives in the cognitive, affective and psychomotor domain of knowledge. Furthermore, Alva, Sagastegui, García, Pascual and González present the model they use for the evaluation process, which combines both individual and group assessment activities with cooperative evaluation from the teacher and the students.

Lastly, it is important to highlight that this volume was not meant to provide final conclusions or definitive findings, but to propose ideas and standpoints that provoke readers into reflecting from an interdisciplinary point of view on philosophical issues related to Augmented Reality when this technology is still at a development and expansion process. In fact, I would be satisfied if this volume encouraged further discussions, as this is the highest praise for a philosophical work. Thus, it only remains for me to thank Günter Abel and James Conant, the series editors of the *Berlin Studies in Knowledge Research*, as well as the De Gruyter Publishing House for this opportunity to foster academic reflection.

References

Argenton, L./Schek, E./Mantovani, F. (2014): "Serious Games as Positive Technologies". In: Schumaker, R./Lackey, S. (eds.), *Virtual, Augmented and Mixed Reality. Applications of Virtual and Augmented Reality*, New York: Springer, 169 – 177.

Besharati, L./Mahvash, M. (2015): "Augmented-Reality Guided Neurosurgery: Accuracy and Intraoperative Application of an Image Projection Technique." In: *Journal of Neurosurgery* 123(1), 206 – 211.

David, P. A./Foray, D. (2002): "An Introduction to The Economy of the Knowledge Society." In: *International Social Science Journal* 171, 9 – 24.

Kipper, G./Rampolla, J. (2013): *Augmented Reality. An Emerging Technologies Guide to AR*, Amsterdam: Elsevier.

LearnAR (2010): "Learn AR – eLearning with Augmented Reality". https://www.youtube.com/watch?v=7G3H3lmCWlE, visited on 8 May 2016.

Li, N./Been-Lirn, H. (2013): "Cognitive Issues in Mobile Augmented Reality: An Embodied Perspective". In: Huang, W./Alem, L./Livingston, M. A. (eds.), *Human Factors in Augmented Reality Environments*, New York: Springer, 109 – 135.

Meola, A./Cutolo, F./Carbone, M./Cagnazzo, F./Ferrari, M./Ferrari, V. (2016): "Augmented Reality in Neurosurgery: a Systematic Review." In: *Neurosurgical Review*. DOI: 10.1007/s10143-016-0732-9.

Riva, G./Baños, R. M./Botella, C./Wiederhold, B. K./Gaggioli, A. (2012): "Positive Technology: Using Interactive Technologies to Promote Positive funCtioning." In: *Cyberpsychology, Behavior and Social Networking* 15, 69 – 77.

Schmalstieg, D./Fuhrmann, A./Hesina, G./Szalavári, Z./Encarnaçao, L. M./Gervautz, M./Purgathofer, W. (2002): "The *Studierstube* Augmented Reality Project." In: *Presence* 11(1), 33 – 54.

Thiel, T. (2014): "Critical Interventions into Canonical Spaces: Augmented Reality at the 2011 Venice and Istanbul Biennials". In: Geroimenko, V. (ed.), *Augmented Reality Art. From an Emerging Technology to a Novel Creative Medium*, New York: Springer, 31 – 60.

UNESCO (2005). *Towards Knowledge Societies*. http://unesdoc.unesco.org/images/0014/001418/141843e.pdf., visited on 3 November 2015.

Part 1: **Augmented Reality and Historical Issues**

Klaus Mainzer

From Augmented Reality to the Internet of Things: Paradigm Shifts in Digital Innovation Dynamics

Abstract: In the past, "Augmented Reality" only meant that our real-world environment is extended by digital instruments which are equipped with sensor interfaces (sound, video, touching) to enhance men-machine communication. An even elder paradigm was "virtual reality" replacing the real world with a computationally simulated one. But, nowadays, exponential growth of computer capacities, Big Data and fast algorithms lead to a new paradigm with is called the "Internet of Things" (IoT) with dramatic change of our living world. Billions of objects ("things") are equipped with trillions of sensors to communicate with one-another. This kind of machine-to-machine communication enables self-organizing IT-networks growing together with global technical and societal infrastructures: Smart cities, smart grids, smart mobility, and the industrial internet (Industry 4.0) are examples of cyberphysical systems. Reality is no longer only "augmented" by IT-technology. It is changed into a new kind of self-organizing superorganism controlled by fast Big Data algorithms as nervous system.

Keywords: Augmented Reality, Internet of Things, embodied robotics, cyberphysical systems, complex systems dynamics, paradigm shift, innovation dynamics, self-organization.

1. From AR Systems to Embodied Mind

1.1 What are AR Systems?

Classical computers are isolated to their physical environment. They only need electrical power and instructions given by human operators on keyboards. Humans and animals communicate with their physical environment by sensors of hearing, seeing, and feeling. In the history of technology, human abilities were enforced and extended by technical instruments and machines. Augmented Reality continues this development with computer-generated sensory input such as sound, video, graphics, and any kind of sensitive signal (Azuma 1997, Metz 2012). Augmentation also means enhancement of human abilities.

DOI 10.1515/9783110497656-002

Many Augmented Reality-Systems are already worn on the human body. Eyeglasses are enhanced by Augmented Reality displays with cameras. Head-mounted displays take images according to the user's head movements. Tracking technologies incorporate digital cameras, optical sensors, accelerators, GPS, RFID and wireless sensors. Augmented Reality platforms are applied to medical, industrial, and military applications. A huge market of Augmented Reality is nowadays entertainment.

Augmented Reality came up with technical breakthroughs of processors, displays, sensors, and input devices. Modern sensor technology is more and more inspired by biological evolution. Natural organisms are full of sensors which support controlling and self-organization of motor processes. All kinds of sensations are realized by specialized sensor cells. Even cognitive abilities like consciousness depend on self-awareness by organic sensors. In general, a sensor can be defined as a converter of a system that receives an input signal from the system's environment which is converted into an internal signal of the system. In the case of biological organisms, analog physical signals such as light, sound, temperature, pressure etc. are converted into digital neural pulses which are understood by the nervous systems. But signal converters are not only sensor cells, but also signal molecules such as hormones or neurotransmitters. Even proteins can be considered as signal converters of an organism to detect toxins, hostile or alien substances. Thus, in nature, we can distinguish a scaling hierarchy from molecular to cellular and organic sensors which make life as self-organizing systems possible.

Like natural sensors, the abilities of technical sensors are determined by their resolution of received signals. Very small signals must correspond to very high sensitivity of sensors. In engineering sciences, sensor technology started with macroscopic devices which are miniaturized to MEMS (microelectromechanical systems) and NEMS (nanoelectromechanical systems). Nanoelectronics follow Richard Feynman's visionary statement "There's plenty of Room at the Bottom". According to Moore's law, computational capacity is not only doubled in a period of 18 months: the computational instruments are simultaneously miniaturized with decreasing costs. But Moore's law runs into limitations of miniaturization with nano and atomic scaling. Traditional semiconductor technology (CMOS) must be improved and overcome by integration of "More-than-Moore" technologies with HF, analog/mixed signals, biochips, and interactions with the environment by sensors and actuators.

1.2 Augmented Reality and Embodied Behavior

Augmented Reality technology is closely adapted to the human body. It is an embodied technology. Therefore, the success of Augmented Reality-technology depends on our knowledge of the human body and its interaction with the physical environment. Even our feeling and mind cannot be separated from bodily experience. What do we know about the embodied mind?

Organisms are a subclass of information systems which can be found in nature, technology, and society (Mainzer 2016b). There are different examples of information systems – animals, primates and humans, populations and societies, computers and robots, and communication networks. They all are distinguished by different kinds and degrees of abilities, sometimes in interaction and in dependence of humans. But with increasing autonomy of agents and robots in self-organizing information and communication networks, we observe a technical development of abilities surpassing natural evolution of organisms and populations. There are increasing abilities to solve complex problems. Complexity degrees can be measured by the algorithmic tools of computational complexity, i.e. time or size of the procedures to solve a problem. The distinction of natural and artificial systems is only justified by the fact that "artificial" systems were once initiated by human technology. In the future, originally "artificial" systems may reproduce and organize themselves in an automated evolution (Mainzer 2003, 2010).

But, how can a robot prevent incomplete knowledge in an open environment? How can it distinguish between reality and its restricted perspective? Situated agents like human beings need no symbolic representations and updating. They look, talk, and interact bodily, for example, by pointing to things. Even rational acting in sudden situations does not depend on symbolic representations and logical inferences, but on bodily interactions with a situation (for example, looking, feeling, and reacting).

Thus, we distinguish formal and embodied acting in games with more or less similarity to real life: Chess is a formal game with complete representations, precisely defined states, board positions, and formal operations. Soccer is a non-formal game with skills depending on bodily interactions, without complete representations of situations and operations which are never exactly identical. According to the French philosopher Merleau-Ponty, intentional human skills do not need any symbolic representation, but they are trained, learnt, and embodied by the organism (Merleau-Ponty 1962, Dreyfus 1982). An athlete like a pole-vaulter cannot repeat her successful jump like a machine generating the same product. The embodied mind is no mystery. Modern biology, neural, and cognitive science give many insights into its origin during the evolution of life.

1.3 Embodied Mind and Brain Dynamics

The coordination of the complex cellular and organic interactions in an organism needs a new kind of self-organizing controlling. Their development was made possible by the evolution of nervous systems that also enabled organisms to adapt to changing living conditions and to learn bodily from experiences with its environment. We call it the emergence of the embodied mind (Mainzer 2009). The hierarchy of anatomical organizations varies over different scales of magnitude, from molecular dimensions to that of the entire central nervous system (CNS). The research perspectives on these hierarchical levels may concern questions, for example, of how signals are integrated in dendrites, how neurons interact in a network, how networks interact in a system like vision, how systems interact in the CNS, or how the CNS interact with its environment.

In the complex systems approach, the microscopic level of interacting neurons can be modeled by coupled differential equations modelling the transmission of nerve impulses by each neuron. The Hodgekin-Huxley equation is an example of a nonlinear reaction diffusion equation of a travelling wave of action potentials which give a precise prediction of the speed and shape of the nerve impulse of electric voltage. In general, nerve impulses emerge as new dynamical entities like the concentric waves in chemical reactions or fluid patterns in non-equilibrium dynamics.

But, local activity of a single nerve impulse is not sufficient to understand the complex brain dynamics and the emergence of cognitive and mental abilities. The neocortex with its more than 10^{11} neurons can be considered a huge nonlinear lattice, where any two points (neurons) can interact with neural impulses. How can we bridge the gap between the neurophysiology of local neural activities and the psychology of mental states? A single neuron can neither think nor feel, but only fire or not fire. They are the "atoms" of the complex neural dynamics.

In his famous book *The organization of Behavior*, Donald Hebb (1949) suggested that learning must be understood as a kind of self-organization in a complex brain model. As in the evolution of living organisms, the belief in organizing "demons" could be dropped and replaced by the self-organizing procedures of the self-organizing procedures of the complex systems approach. Historically, it was the first explicit statement of the physiological learning rule for synaptic modification. Hebb used the word "connectionism" in the context of a complex brain model. He introduced the concept of the Hebbian synapse where the connection between two neurons should be strengthened if both neurons fired at the same time (Hebb 1949, 50).

Hebb's statement is not a mathematically precise model. But, later on, it was used to introduce Hebb-like rules tending to sharpen up a neuron's predisposition "without a teacher" from outside. For example, a simple mathematical version of Hebb's rule demands that the change Δw_{BA} of a weight w_{BA} between a neuron A projecting to neuron B is proportional to the average firing rate ν_A of A and ν_B of B, i.e., $\Delta w_{BA} = \varepsilon\, \nu_B \nu_A$ with constant ε. In 1949, the "Hebbian synapse" could only be a hypothetical entity. Nowadays, its neurophysiological existence is empirically confirmed.

On the macroscopic level, Hebb-like interacting neurons generate a cell assembly with a certain macrodynamics (Haken 1996). Mental activities are correlated with cell assemblies of synchronously firing cells. For example, a synchronously firing cell-assembly represents a plant perceptually which is not only the sum of its perceived pixels, but characterized by some typical macroscopic features like form, background or foreground. On the next level, cell assemblies of several perceptions interact in a complex scenario. In this case, each cell-assembly is a firing unit, generating a cell assembly of cell assemblies whose macrodynamics is characterized by some order parameters. The order parameters may represent similar properties of the perceived objects.

There is no "mother neuron" which can feel, think, or at least coordinate the appropriate neurons. The binding problem of pixels and features in a perception is explained by cell assemblies of synchronously firing neurons dominated by learnt attractors of brain dynamics. The binding problem asked: How can the perception of entire objects be conceived without decay into millions of unconnected pixels and signals of firing neurons? Wolf Singer (1994) and others could confirm Donald Hebb's concept of synchronously firing neurons by observations and measurements.

In this way, we get a hierarchy of emerging levels of cognition, starting with the microdynamics of firing neurons representing a visual perception. On the following level, the observer becomes conscious of the perception. Then the cell assembly of perception is connected with the neural area that is responsible for states of consciousness. In a next step, a conscious perception can be the goal of planning activities. In this case, cell assemblies of cell assemblies are connected with neural areas in the planning cortex, and so on. Even high-level concepts like self-consciousness can be explained by self-reflections of self-reflections, connected with a personal memory which is represented in corresponding cell assemblies of the brain. Brain states emerge, persist for a small fraction of time, then disappear and are replaced by other states. It is the flexibility and creativeness of this process that makes a brain so successful in animals for their adaption to rapidly changing and unpredictable environments.

Cell assemblies behave like individual neurons. Thus, an assembly of randomly interconnected neurons has a threshold firing level for the onset of global activity. If this level is not attained, the assembly will not ignite, falling back to a quiescent state. If the threshold level is exceeded, firing activity of an assembly will rise rapidly to a maximum level. These two conditions ensure that assemblies of neurons can form assemblies of assemblies. Assemblies emerge from the nonlinear interactions of individual neurons. Assemblies of assemblies emerge from the nonlinear interaction of assemblies. Repeated several times, one gets the model of the brain as an emergent dynamic hierarchy.

In brain research, it is assumed that all mental states are correlated to cell assemblies. The corresponding cell assemblies must empirically be identified by observational and measuring instruments. In brain reading, for example, active cell assemblies correlated with words and corresponding objects can be identified. A single neuron is not decisive and may differ among different persons. There are typical distribution patterns with fuzzy shapes which are represented in computer simulations. Brain research is still far from observing the activities of each neuron in a brain. Nevertheless, the formal hierarchical scheme of dynamics, at least, allows an explaining model of complex mental states like, for instance, consciousness. In this model, conscious states mean that persons are aware of their activities. Self-awareness is realized by additional brain areas monitoring the neural correlates of these human activities (e. g., perceptions, feeling, or thinking). This is a question of empirical tests, not of armchaired reflection (Chalmers 2010). For example, in medicine, physicians need clear criteria to determine different degrees of consciousness as mental states of patients, depending on states of their brain.

Thus, we aim at clear working hypotheses for certain applications and not at a "complete" understanding what "consciousness" means per se. Besides medicine, the assumption of different degrees of self-awareness opens new perspectives of technical applications. Robots with a certain degree of self-awareness can be realized by self-monitoring and self-control which are useful for self-protection and cooperation in robot teams. In technical terms, these robots have internal representations of their own body and states. They can also be equipped with internal representations of other robots or humans which can be changed and adapted by learning processes. Thus, they have their own "theory of mind" with perspectives of first and second person. In this sense, even consciousness is no mysterious event, but observable, measurable, and explainable in appropriate research frameworks. The formal hierarchical model offers the opportunity to build corresponding circuits and technical equipment for technical brains and robots with these abilities.

Obviously, patterns of cell assemblies in the brain are not identical with our perceptions, feeling, and thinking. But, it is well confirmed in modern brain research that neural patterns of firing cells are correlated with mental states. These correlates can be mathematically defined and modeled in state and parameter spaces with associated dynamical systems which allow us to test our models (Mainzer/Chua 2013). With the technology of brain reading, an analysis of cell assemblies was used to extract correlates of what is represented (e. g., pictures, words, phrases): Of course, there are only the first steps of research, but it seems to be possible at least in principle. Brain reading opens new avenues to Augmented Reality in neuropsychology: We learn to understand neural patterns of patients for better therapies.

Motor, cognitive, and mental abilities are stored in synaptic connections of cell assemblies. A hard core of synaptic network is already wired, when a mammal brain is born. But many synaptic connections are generated during growth, experience and learning phase of mammals. Firing states of neurons with repeated action potentials enforce synaptic connections. Thus, during a learning phase, a cell assembly of simultaneously firing neurons creates a synaptic network storing the learnt information. Learning phases can be modeled technically by learning algorithms (Mainzer 2007). As we all know, the learnt information can be forgotten, when learning is not repeated and the synaptic connections decay. Thus, on the micro level, brain dynamics is determined by billions of firing and not firing neurons, and, on the macro level, by emerging and changing cell assemblies of neural networks coding different neural information.

The efficiency of neural networks depends on their number of hierarchical layers. They enable the brain to connect different neural states of, e. g., visual, haptic, and auditory information. But, there are also layers monitoring perceptual procedures and generating visual consciousness: A person is aware and knows that she perceives something. Even our emotions depend on specified neural networks which are connected with all kinds of brain activity. It is a challenge of brain research to identify the involved layers and networks of the brain during all kinds of mental and cognitive activities by AR technologies.

Compared with human brains, technical systems may be restricted, but they are sometimes much more effective with their specific solutions of cognitive and intelligent tasks. In Augmented Reality- and AI-technology, semantic webs and i-phones can already understand questions to some extent and even answer in natural languages. The technology of applied (speech analysis) algorithms may be different from biological procedures which were developed during evolution. But, they solve the problem to some degree with their computer power, high speed, parallelism and storage which can be improved in the future.

These procedures can be illustrated by automated translations of two languages with Big Data algorithms (Mainzer 2014). A human translator must know grammar, vocabulary and the filigree meaning of both languages. The reason is the big number of words and phrases with multi-meaning depending on different contexts. Thus, a human translator must not only master all the nuances of both languages, but also the contents of texts. This task can be managed by statistical methods on a very high level. It is not necessary to speak or to understand both languages. Further on, you do not need a linguistic expert who, together with a programmer, feed a computer with linguistic knowledge or rules. You only need a mass of data in a pool with translated texts from a source language into a target language.

The Internet is an example of such a powerful store. In the meantime, nearly every group of words is translated by anyone and anywhere for several times. Parallel texts are the basis of this kind of translations. The probability that a translation is close to a text increases with the frequency that a group of words in the data pool is translated in a certain context in a certain way. The context of words can be determined quantitatively by a computer with statistical measure numbers. Thus, from a technical point of view, we must not understand what "understanding" means in all its filigree meaning. May be that cognitive science and brain research will be successful someday to do that. In the meantime, we are already mastering linguistic challenges by powerful data bases and algorithms in a better way than human linguistic experts ever did.

1.4 Augmented Reality and Embodied Robotics

Embodied computing applies the principles of evolution and life to technical systems (Mainzer 2009). The dominating principles in the complex world of evolution are self-organization and self-control. How can they be realized in technical systems? In many cases, there is no finite program, in order to forecast the development of complex systems. In general, there are three reasons for computational limits of system dynamics: 1) A system may be undecidable in a strict logical sense. 2) Further on, a system can be deterministic, but nonlinear and chaotic. In this case, the system depends sensitively on tiny changes of initial data in the sense of the butterfly effect. Long-term forecasting is restricted, and the computational costs of forecasting increase exponentially after some few steps of future predictions. 3) Finally, a system can be stochastic and nonlinear. In this case, pattern emergence can only be predicted probabilistically.

In complex dynamical systems of organisms, monitoring and controlling are realized on hierarchical levels. Thus, we must study the nonlinear dynamics of these systems in experimental situations, in order to find appropriate models and to prevent undesired emergent behavior as possible attractors. From the point of view of systems science, the challenge of embodied robotics is controlled emergence.

In the research project "Cognition in Technical Systems" (CoTeSys 2006–2012), cognitive and life sciences, information processing and mathematical sciences, engineering and robotics work systematically together to explore cognition for technical systems. Robotic agents cannot be fully programmed for every application (Shuji Kajita 2007). The program learns from experience where to stand when taking a glass out of a cupboard, how to best grab particular kitchen utensils, where to look for particular cutlery, et al. This requires the control system to know the parameters of control routines and to have models for how the parameters change the behavior. The sensor data of a robot's environment, which is the robot's "experience", are stored in a relational database system, the robot's "memory". According to the paradigm of probabilistic robotics (Thrun/Burgard/Fox 2005), the data in the database together with causal structure on domain relations imply a joint probability distribution over relations in the activity domain. This distribution is applied in Markov logic, which allows inferring the conditional probability of logical (first order) statements. In short: A robot can estimate the environmental situation probabilistically.

According to the paradigm of complex dynamical systems, a robot can be described at different levels, in which global properties at one level emerge from the interaction of a number of simple elements at lower levels. Global properties are emergent in the sense that they result from nothing else but local interactions among the elements. They cannot be predicted or inferred from knowledge of the elements or of the rules by which the elements locally interact, given the high nonlinearity of these interactions.

Simple examples of embodied robotics are reactive robots. They are controlled by simple neural networks, for example, fully connected perceptrons without internal layers and without any kind of internal organization. Nevertheless, these robots can display not only simple behaviors, such as obstacle avoidance, but also behaviors capable of solving complex problems involving perceptual aliasing, sensory ambiguity, and sequential organization of sub-behaviors. The question arises how far we can go with reactive sensory-motor coordination in Augmented Reality technology.

Not only "low level" motor abilities, but also "high level" cognition (for example, categorization) can emerge from complex bodily interaction with an environment by sensory-motor coordination without internal representation in symbolic syntax. We call it "embodied cognition": Developmental psychology shows that an infant learns to associate and categorize objects and to build up concepts by touching, grasping, manipulating, feeling, tasting, hearing, and looking at things, before it is able to use syntactical rules of linguistic symbols. The reason is that language acquisition follows a biological program (Friederici 2006): In the brains of babies, the three bundles of nervous fibers which are responsible for syntactic, semantic, and auditory language processing (cf. 2.3) do already exist. Only the circuits of semantic and auditory processing are developed and can be visualized in the brains of babies. But the 3rd bundle of fibers which enables the application of syntactic symbolic rules is not developed before the age of three years. The neural networks need more than eight years to realize their final efficiency of symbolic syntax processing.

These observations motivate embodied robotics. Symbolic representation refers to linguistic signs in natural languages or formal terms in programming languages. A conventional computer only works according to the symbolic instructions of a computer language. But embodied robots react and act by sensor inputs and haptic actuators with their environment. In an analogue way, the categories of human infants start with impressions and feelings based on sensor circuits which will be connected with linguistic representations in later stages of development. We have an innate disposition to construct and apply conceptual schemes and tools at a certain stage of development (Bellman 2005, Mainzer 2008a – b). In embodied robotics, robots are equipped with neural networks to recognize correlations and patterns of sensor data for their orientation.

The whole Internet can be used as big "memory" of robots which overcomes the limitations of human brains. We are far away from capturing all cognitive human abilities in technical systems. But, in some special fields, there are, again, technical strategies which are much more effective than our evolutionary equipment (e.g., pattern recognition of Big Data algorithms with the Internet). Their application are beyond Augmented Reality-technologies.

2. From Augmented Reality Systems to Cyberphysical Systems

2.1 Augmented Reality-Technology and Internet of Things (IoT)

In the past, the IT-world was separated from physical infrastructures. Augmented Reality-technologies were first bridges to physical environment to enhance single sensors of the human organism. The embodied mind is still in the center of Augmented Reality-applications. But, nowadays, the IT-world is growing together with large-scale infrastructures of society. In the Internet of things (IoT) billions of objects are equipped with sensors and RFID to communicate with one another. These are no longer only wearables like biosensors worn on the body as Augmented Reality-technologies. In mobility networks, for example, cars communicate with one another and their technical infrastructure independent of human drivers. They realize a kind of swarm intelligence which can be observed in insect populations (Wilson 2000).

These infrastructures are called "cyber-physical systems" (CPS). They observe their physical environment by sensors, process their information, and influence their environment with actuators according to communication devices. CPS are complex systems of many self-organizing net components, dramatically increasing the adaptability, autonomy, reliability and usability of automotive, aerospace, energy, healthcare, manufacturing, transportation, and consumer appliances. CPS integrates several Augmented Reality-technologies. But, CPS overcomes single Augmented Reality-applications and creates new integrative platforms with increasing degrees of self-organization.

An application of CPS is the industrial internet (industry 4.0). The 1st industrial revolution introduced the steam engine. The 2nd industrial revolution was Henry Ford's mass production, division of labor, and working on the assembly line. The 3rd industrial revolution additionally applied industrial robots for further automation of production. The 4th industrial revolution changes production on the basis of cyber-physical systems and internet of things. Production, marketing, and trade are transformed into a more or less self-organizing complex system which is only possible with massively applied sensor technology.

Augmented Reality-technology (e. g., videos, cameras, sensors) with industrial internet produces a huge amount of data with chances and risks: Fast computing networks, Big Data, and sensor technology open new avenues of fast data mining, pattern recognition, and profiling of products and persons in economy and society. In short: Big Data is the other side of the coin of accelerating technologies with sensors and fast computing networks. From an evolutionary point of view, organizations of companies must adapt to the exponential growth of technologies driven by Moore's law, distribution of sensors, and Big Data. Some technologists already propagate the transformation from "linear" to "exponential" companies.

In an accelerating world, small teams in decentralized organizations seem to be more flexible and adaptive than big and centralized dinosaurs of companies. In Silicon Valley, companies like Google and Facebook seem to have mastered the scaling of technology. They focus on sensor and information technology which seem to dematerialize technical equipment in daily life. Actually, physical equipment like cameras, libraries and music players are miniaturized to apps on smartphones. Companies producing this kind of physical equipment disappeared within a few years.

Without any doubt, the exponential growth of sensor distribution in our societies can support medical care, environmental monitoring, and security of life. Sensor technology and computing networks should improve human well-being by more secure and efficient, but less vulnerable human infrastructure. But, on the other side, totalitarian tendencies of a police state must be avoided by clearly legal and democratic rules of sensor and data application. Digital dignity is the primary ethical goal in a complex world with increasing automation by sensors and Big Data.

2.2 IoT and Robot Societies

A robot society is a group of robots with Augmented Reality-technologies which has the ability to communicate, interact, and to solve problems jointly. By that, a robot society can generate intelligent behavior like interacting ants of a population or interacting neurons of brains. A society is defined by its information and control structure which make possible common task planning and execution. In this case, a robot is a locally active agent driven by a battery and low input signals which are amplified and transformed into complex patterns of behavior.

Most of the autonomous mobile robots are operating in neither stabile nor structured environments (Bekey 2005). Therefore, a major trend in robotics is going towards multi-robot systems (Balch/Parker 2002). In many cases, the decomposing of a complex task into parallel subtasks is a possibility to speed up the performance (Mataric/Sukhatme/Ostergaard 2003). Sometimes, several robots work with the same subtask, increasing the redundancy of the system. Furthermore, there can be tasks where a successful completion of a task requires close cooperation among the robots. Such case is, for example, the carrying of a large object together. It requires some sort of interaction between robots, whether is a direct communication or some sort of indirect communication through sensing the forces in the object to be transported. These robots are equipped with Augmented Reality-technologies.

This kind of task as well as many other tasks normally related to multi-robot systems has clear analogy to biological systems (Wilson 2000). A group of ants solve their behavioral problems through sensing the forces and torque in the object. Based on this information they change the direction of forces accordingly or needed some ants change the position of their hold. Numerous similar examples can be found from nature. Tests by evolution during millions of years are proven to be feasible in dynamic and hostile environments and can thus provide valuable information and inspiration for similar type of engineering tasks.

A profound challenge of interdisciplinary importance is the question how can social intelligence emerge and evolve as a novel property in groups of social animals and robots. According to our definition of intelligence, robot societies have intelligence with a certain degree, if they can solve problems with a certain degree of complexity. The question can be solved by focusing the attention on the very early stages of the emergence and evolution of simple technical artefacts. Therefore, one should start by building an artificial society of embodied agents as real robots with Augmented Reality-technologies, creating an environment or artificial ecosystem and appropriate primitive behaviors for those robots, then free running the artificial society. Even with small populations of simple robots, a large number of interactions between robots can be generated (Brooks 1999, Braitenberg/Radermacher 2007, Pfeifer/Scheier 2001). The inherent heterogeneities of real robots, and the noise and uncertainty of the real world, increase the space of possibilities and the scope for unexpected emergence in the interactions between robots.

We aim at conditions in which a kind of proto-culture can emerge in a robot society. Robots can copy each other's behaviors and select which behaviors to copy. Behaviors will mutate because of the noise and uncertainty in the real robots' sensors and actuators. Successful types of behavior will undergo multiple cycles of copying (heredity), selection and variation (mutation). With evolutionary time, a genetic algorithm process to grow and evolve the robots' controllers so that the emerging patterns of behavior become hard-wired into the robots' controllers (Nolfi/Floreano 2001).

2.3 Cyberphysical Systems as Sociotechnical Systems

Social networks of more or less autonomous robots are only one possible development in a general trend of future technology. In a technical co-evolution, global information and communication networks are emerging with surprising similarity to self-organizing neural networks of the human brain. The increasing complexity of the World Wide Web (www) needs intelligent strategies of information retrieval and learning algorithms simulating the synaptic plasticity of a brain (Berners-Lee 1999). The Internet links computers and Augmented Reality-technologies with other telecommunication devices. At the router level, the nodes are the routers, and the edges are their physical connections. At the interdomain level, each domain of hundreds of routers is represented by a single node with at least one route as connection with other nodes. At both levels, the degree distribution follows a power law of scale-free network which can be compared with the networks in systems biology. Measurements of the clustering coefficient deliver values differing from random networks and significant clusters. The average paths at the domain level and the router level indicate the small-world property.

In the future, global information networks will grow together with societal infrastructure in cyberphysical systems (acatech 2011). Current examples are complex smart grids of energy. Many energy providers of central generators and decentralized renewable energy resources lead to power delivery networks with increasing complexity. Smart grids mean the integration of the power delivery infrastructure with a unified communication and control network, in order to provide the right information to the right entity at the right time to take the right action. It is a complex information, supply and delivery system, minimizing losses, self-healing and self-organizing.

Smart grids with integrated communication systems accomplish a dynamical regulation of energy supply. They are examples of large and complex real-time systems according to the principles of cyber-physical systems (Lee 2008). Traditionally, reserve energy which is used to balance peaks of consumption or voltage drops is stored by large power plants. The main problem of changing to renewable energies is the great number of constraints depending on questions of functionality as well as security, reliability, temporary availability, tolerance of failures, and adaptability (Wedde *et al.* 2008). Cyber-physical systems with local and bottom-up structures are the best answer to the increasing complexity of supply and communication systems (Cyber-Physical Systems 2008). In a technical co-evolution mankind is growing together with these technical infrastructures. Their collective abilities emerge like swarm intelligence of populations in evolution which are sometimes called "superorganisms".

Increasing computational power and acceleration of communication need improved consumption of energy, better batteries, miniaturization of appliances, and refinement of display and sensor technology (Weiser 1991, Hansmann 2001). Under these conditions, intelligent functions can be distributed in a complex network with many multimedia terminals. Together with satellite technology and global positioning systems (GPS), electronically connected societies are transformed into cyberphysical systems. They are a kind of symbiosis of man, society, and machine overcoming traditional Augmented Reality-technologies.

Communication is not only realized between human partners with natural languages, but with the things of this world. Cyberphysical systems also mean a transformation into an Internet of Things. Things in the Internet become locally active agents equipped with sensors, apps, and AI (Mainzer 2016a). From an ethical point of view, all these cyberphysical systems should be initiated and developed as service and assistant systems for human well-being and saving the Earth system. The ethical point of view makes the difference to technology-driven visions and distinguishes human dignity.

References

Acatech (ed.) (2011): *Cyberphysical Systems. Acatech Position* (acatech = National Academy of Science and Technology), Berlin: Springer.

Azuma, R. (1997): "Augmented Reality". In: *Presence: Teleoperators and Virtual Environments*, Vol. 6, N. 4. The whole title should be "A Survey of Augmented Reality", 355–385.

Balch, T./Parker, L. (eds.) (2002): *Robot Teams: From Diversity to Polymorphism*, Wellesley Ma: CRC Press.

Bekey, G.L. (2005): *Autonomous Robots. From Biological Inspiration to Implementation and Control*, Cambridge Ma.: MIT Press.

Bellman, K. L. (2005): "Self-Conscious Modeling". In: *it – Information Technology* 4, 188–194.

Berners-Lee, T. (1999): *Weaving the Web: The Original Design and Ultimate Destiny of the World Wide Web by the Inventor.* San Francisco Ca: Harper Business.

Braitenberg, V./Radermacher, F.J. (eds.) (2007): *Interdisciplinary Approaches to a New Understanding of Cognition and Consciousness*, Ulm: Universitätsverlag Ulm.

Brooks, R.A. (1999): *Cambrian Intelligence: The Early History of the New AI*, Cambridge MA: The MIT Press.

Chalmers, D. (2010): *The Character of Consciousness*, Oxford: Oxford University Press.

Cyber-Physical Systems. Program Announcements & Information. *The National Science Foundation*, 4201 Wilson Bouleward, Arlington, Virginia 22230, USA, 2008–09–30.

Dreyfus, H. L. (1982): *Husserl, Intentionality, and Cognitive Science*, Cambridge Ma.: MIT Press.

Friederici, A. D. (2006): "The Neural Basis of Language Development and Its Impairment". In: *Neuron* 52, 941–952.

Haken, H. (1996): *Principles of Brain Functioning. A Synergetic Approach to Brain Activity, Behaviour and Cognition*, Berlin: Springer.

Hansmann, U. (2001): *Pervasive Computing Handbook*, Berlin: Springer.

Hebb, D. O. (1949): *The Organization of the Behavior*, New York: Wiley.

Lee, E. (2008): "Cyber-Physical Systems: Design Challenges". In: *University of California, Berkeley Technical Report* No. UCB/EECS-2008-8.

Mainzer, K. (2003): *KI – Künstliche Intelligenz. Grundlagen intelligenter Systeme*, Darmstadt: Wissenschaftliche Buchgesellschaft.

Mainzer, K. (2007): *Thinking in Complexity. The Computational Dynamics of Matter, Mind, and Mankind*, New York: Fifth Edition Springer.

Mainzer, K. (2008a): "The Emergence of Mind and Brain: An Evolutionary, Computational, and Philosophical Approach". In: R. Banerjee / B. K. Chakrabarti (eds.), *Models of Brain and Mind. Physical, Computational and Psychological Approaches*, Amsterdam: Elsevier, 115–132.

Mainzer, K. (2008b): "Organic Computing and Complex Dynamical Systems. Conceptual Foundations and Interdisciplinary Perspectives". In: R. P. Würtz (ed.), *Organic Computing*, Berlin: Springer, 105 – 122.
Mainzer, K. (2009): "From Embodied Mind to Embodied Robotics: Humanities and System Theoretical Aspects". In: *Journal of Physiology* (Paris) 103, 296 – 304.
Mainzer, K. (2010): *Leben als Maschine? Von der Systembiologie zur Robotik und Künstlichen Intelligenz*, Paderborn: Mentis.
Mainzer, K./Chua, L. O. (2011): *The Universe as Automaton. From Simplicity and Symmetry to Complexity*, Berlin: Springer.
Mainzer, K./Chua, L. O. (2013): *Local Activity Principle*, London: Imperial College Press.
Mainzer, K. (2014): *Die Berechnung der Welt. Von der Weltformel zu Big Data*, Munich: C.H. Beck.
Mainzer, K. (2016a): *Künstliche Intelligenz – Wann übernehmen die Maschinen?*, Berlin: Springer.
Mainzer, K. (2016b): *Information: Algorithm – Probability – Complexity – Quantum computer – Life – Brain – Society*, Berlin: Berlin University Press.
Mataric, M./Sukhatme, G./Ostergaard, E. (2003): "Multi-robot Task Allocation in Uncertain Environments". In: *Autonomous Robots* 14(2 – 3), 253 – 261.
Merleau-Ponty, M. (1962): *Phenomenology of Perception*, London: Routledge & Kegan Paul.
Metz, R. (2012): "Augmented Reality Is Finally Getting Real". In: *Technology Review*, 2nd August.
Nolfi, S./Floreano, D. (2001): *Evolutionary Robotics. The Biology, Intelligence, and Technology of Self-Organizing Machines*, Cambridge Ma.: MIT Press.
Pfeifer, R./Scheier C. (2001): *Understanding Intelligence*, Cambridge Ma.: MIT Press.
Shuji Kajita (2007): *Humanoide Roboter. Theorie und Technik des Künstlichen Menschen*, Berlin: Aka GmbH.
Singer, W. (1994): "The Role of Synchrony in Neocortical Processing and Synaptic Plasticity". In: E. Domany/L. van Hemmen/K. Schulten (eds.), *Models of Neural Networks* II, Berlin: Springer.
Thrun, S./Burgard, W./Fox, D. (2005): *Probabilistic Robotics*, Cambridge Ma.: MIT Press.
Wedde, H. J./Lehnhoff, S./Rehtanz, C./Krause, O. (2008): "Von eingebetteten Systemen zu Cyber-Physical Systems. Eine neue Forschungsdimension für verteilte eingebettete Realzeitsysteme". In: *Pearl 2008 – Informatik Aktuell. Aktuelle Anwendungen in Technik und Wirtschaft* 2007, 12
Weiser, M. (1991): "The Computer for the 21st Century". In: *Scientific American* 9, 66 – 75.
Wilson, E. O. (2000): *Sociobiology: The New Synthesis*. 25th Anniversary Edition, Cambridge Ma.: Harvard University Press.

Javier Vilanova

Extended Reality and Abstract Objects: A pragmalinguistic approach

Abstract: In this paper I carry out a grammatical clarification of the main concepts and expressions commonly used when dealing with "Augmented Reality". I specifically focus on resolving ontological puzzles concerning the nature of entities produced by new technologies. I offer an analysis of the grammar of the terms "virtual", "reality", "extension" and "augmentation", and I compare Augmented Reality with other problematic domains of language (universals, fiction, mathematics and social phenomena). I conclude that: (i) Augmented Reality is constructed via linguistic procedures; (ii) entities within the realm of Augmented Reality belong to the family of abstract entities; and (iii) Augmented Reality is the ever-evolving culmination of a process that humans started when we created language and have continued to develop through science, engineering, art and other instruments that empower us both to expand reality through the inclusion of new kinds of objects, and to extend our epistemic and existential access to reality.

Keywords: Augmented Reality, extended reality, virtual, abstract, pragmalinguistic.

1. Introduction[1]

The 1980 South African movie *The Gods Must be Crazy* begins with an empty bottle of Coca-Cola being found by members of a *IKung* tribe in the Kalahari Dessert. Most of the film shows the efforts of members of the tribe, living in a pretechnological culture, to give meaning to (and find a use for) the completely alien object. I firmly believe that one of the main tasks of philosophers is to assist their fellow citizens in understanding such "completely new" objects or phenomena that invade our daily lives once in a while. I can find no better example of a puzzling alien phenomenon these days than the family of novelties that go

1 This work has been financed by the Spanish Ministry of Economy and Competitiveness (project FFI2013-41415-P and the Complutense University (research group 930664). I thank their members for their support and suggestions. I also thank the editors of this volume for their encouragement and kindness, José María Ariso for his invitation to think, and Christopher Evans for revising the English version of this text.

DOI 10.1515/9783110497656-003

under the name of “Augmented Reality”. This is not least because I believe that whenever we come across the next generation of gadgets, applications or video games for the first time, we feel the very same astonishment and confusion that the members of the San tribe felt. Even the expression itself, which is no newcomer to the realm of words (it seems it was used for the first time in 1992, by a pair of Boeing technicians when they were designing tools to assist in manufacturing processes), has *prima facie* a suspicious feel to it. To our ears and minds, it sounds almost contradictory: an oxymoron like “round square” or a category mistake such as “blue number”. It is also obvious, I hope, that these suspicions arise mainly from what we may call, in a very naïve sense, our “ontological commitments”: can something not belong to reality but belong to an augmentation of it? And what could an augmentation of reality be? Do things in such an augmentation exist or not?

My purpose in this paper is to clarify (or help to clarify) the use of the expression “Augmented Reality” and other related idioms (such as “virtual reality” and “extended reality” – henceforth ‘ER’). To do this, I focus on puzzles that naturally arise regarding the ontological status of the new kinds of entities we see on the screen or we hear through our headphones. I consider their nature, their relation to other entities, and the similarities and dissimilarities with ordinary, standard objects. In the next section, I provide and examine some examples; but before that, I would just like to make a few brief comments on the method I will follow.

The philosophical realm I am going to move through is what we can call, using neutral terminology, “linguistic philosophy”. By this, I mean that I am not going, for example, to examine what happens inside the head of a person who experiences Augmented Reality (I will not embark, for instance, on phenomenological research) or to attempt to deduce the conditions of possibility of the existence of Augmented Reality (there will be no transcendental deduction). Instead (and more humbly) I will examine the rules that the uses of the words involved can be seen as conforming to; what we may call the “grammar” of the expressions that are used when talking about Augmented Reality.

More specifically, I will move within a branch of linguistic philosophy which starts from a specific conception of language and grammar that we can call, again in neutral terminology, “pragmatic”, and whose roots are usually related to the work of Ludwig Wittgenstein and John Austin. According to that conception, we do not explain meaning by giving semantic definitions or describing syntactic rules (although this is not forbidden as an auxiliary tool), but rather by describing multiple and diverse examples of uses of the expressions in different situations. One important step in the methodology is comparison between the different examples themselves and also comparison with examples of the use of other expressions that are more or less akin to those considered, looking for similarities, analogies and differences. The aim is to obtain a holistic, synoptic perspective that allows us to become conscious of all the features of the phenomena, and consequently to understand puzzling uses of the expressions better. This is what I mean in the title of this paper, when I refer to "a pragmalinguistic approach".

2. An initial survey

I will take as my primary reference "The Bible" of Augmented Reality: the 2013 book by Kipper and Rampolla *Augmented Reality: an emerging technologies guide to AR*; although I will also take into account some texts from open access sources, such as Wikipedia. According to Kipper and Rampolla, Augmented Reality is a variation of a virtual environment or "virtual reality" (VR). In applications of VR, users are entirely immersed in a synthetic (computer-generated) environment: they cannot see the real environment around them. In Augmented Reality, in contrast, the computer-generated audio, video, tactile or haptic information is mixed with and overlaid on a real environment. Three characteristics are required for something to count as Augmented Reality:

1 (combination) Augmented Reality combines real and virtual information;
2 (interaction) Augmented Reality is interactive in real time;
3 (3D) Augmented Reality operates and is used in a 3D environment.

Although the "core" of Augmented Reality is the first characteristic (combination), I will place considerable value on the second (interaction). The third feature (3D), which Kipper and Rampolla use to differentiate Augmented Reality from Photoshop and other 2D combinations of real and virtual information, in my opinion is much less important, even incidental; although I will pay some attention to it towards the end of the paper. Kipper and Rampolla also apply the term Augmented Reality to other things (a field of research, an industry, a new medium for creative expression, etc.); but I prefer to see it here mainly as a technology, specifically as a computer technology with a wide range of applications: advertising, task support, navigation, art, domestic and industrial uses, sightseeing, social networking, education, translation, entertainment and games.

As for the functions of Augmented Reality (a key point for the pragmalinguistic approach, in which the meaning of an expression is "how it is used and what for"), those authors distinguish two categories. On the one hand, we have what they call "the augmented perception of reality" ("perceptive Augmented Reality" from now on), which *shows us reality and enhances what we can see and do*, or *enables objects or relations to be perceived*. Some examples of this category of Augmented Reality are:

- HUD, the heads-up display that gives the pilot of an airplane a digital overlay with an artificial horizon and selected flight information;
- Intelligent Eye, a smartphone app that automatically changes the text visible on the screen through translation into another language;
- and the popular Google Glass headset, a device that continuously feeds the user information on the environment, based on specific personalized preferences.

On the other hand, what they call "the creation of an artificial environment" (or "creative Augmented Reality"), *shows how what is not real allows us to see the imaginary, or allows us to see things that do not exist in the real world and to share that view with others*. Some examples are:

- Construct3D, a mathematical educational tool that allows students to build virtual 3D geometrical figures based on 2D descriptions;
- Magic Mirror, a shopping tool that allows the user to put on virtual glasses and clothes, and see how they look from different perspectives;
- and History Pin, a smartphone app that allows users to "integrate" their image into historic settings.

Kipper and Rampolla provide much information on the methods, support and development of Augmented Reality; but I think it is excessively technical, so I will not reproduce or use it for my analysis here.

I would just like to make one last observation regarding the place of Augmented Reality within the field of contemporary technologies. Although Kipper and Rampolla do not use the expression, Wikipedia includes Augmented Reality as a case of ER; which *refers to all real and virtual combined environments and human–machine interactions generated by computer technology and wearables* (see https://en.wikipedia.org/wiki/Extended_reality). Thus, ER includes Augmented Reality, VR and "augmented virtuality" (VR), that is, the merging of real objects into virtual environments. There is a fuzzy boundary between Augmented Reality and VR (it is not easy to say when the environment is too full of virtual objects to be properly called real) which, precisely because of its vagueness, I will not take into consideration here. What I will focus on is exploring what we mean when we say that something is an extension of reality (ER), when we say that the extension is virtual (VR) and when we say that the extension is an augmentation for the purpose of perceiving properties of real objects (perceptive Augmented Reality) or for the purpose of seeing the imaginary combined with real objects (creative Augmented Reality). This gives us four words to examine: “real” (as opposed to virtual), “reality”, “extension” and “augmentation”. So, let us begin.

Real (vs. virtual). The first thing that it is important to note is that, as John Austin famously pointed out, “real” is a highly exceptional word because *it does not have one single, specifiable always-the-same meaning* (Austin 1962, 64). According to Austin, this implies that the word is always used in combination with a (perhaps implicit) noun and usually in a negative form; so normally we do not say that something “is real”, but that something “is not a real X”, where X denotes a specific kind of things. If I say, for example, that the gun the main character in Woody Allen’s *Take the Money and Run* used when trying to escape from jail was not *real*, what I actually want to say is that it was not a *real gun:* it was like a real gun (it had the appearance of an actual gun) but it lacked some fundamental properties of genuine guns (it did not shoot bullets because it was made of soap!). Please note that I do not want to imply that there is also another thing (apart from the carved soap, in the previous case) that is not real or that is real and unreal at the same time; something like “gunness” or “virtual gunness”. Perhaps we can say that there is something like an “appearance of a gun”, but this is just a property, an aspect of the carved soap. Analogously, when I say that the objects in VR, or the objects added in Augmented Reality, are “not real”, what I mean is that they are not real people, or cats, or books; but they are like (they have the appearance of) real people, cats or books. Of course, I can say, for example, that the glasses added to my face in the Magic Mirror app are not real, meaning that they are not made of plastic as they appear to be or that I cannot wear them because they are not solid. We must not forget, however, that we are not looking at an unreal, inexistent thing; what we are looking at, some colored dots on the screen produced by electrical impulses, is as real as my flesh and bones. This, I think, is all that we need to be aware of in order to understand the use of “virtual” when talking of ER. “Virtual” is just one more member of a large family of words that deal with illusions (forgeries, mirages, magic tricks, *trompe l’oeils*, etc.) and I believe there is nothing entirely new in ER compared to the old cases of illusions (aside from the technical media that support the illusion): nothing that obliges us to change the grammar of “virtual” in order to accommodate the new cases.

Reality. In contrast to the constant use (and abuse) of the word by philosophers, in ordinary language “reality” is a word that we rarely use. Sometimes we talk about some specific domain of reality, the reality of business, or the reality of videogames, but these uses are figurative or they can easily be reduced to the use of the word “real” explained above. On the rare occasions when we use the word without specification, for example when someone says that witches do not exist in reality or that science tries to explain reality, “reality” is just a way of expressing the most general and universal set of things. In this sense, "reality" means almost the same as "everything" and I suspect it is derived from it. Usually we use "all" or "every" to specify some specific domain that determines the set referred to ("all people", "every bird", etc.). As a special case, when we do not specify the domain, the set we refer to through our use of "everything" is "reality"; and in this sense it follows, almost by definition, that nothing exists outside reality. Everything belongs to (unspecified) reality, because reality is the sum of everything. Of course, what is real and what is not can be discussed, but there is no space for an intermediate realm: there is no limbo of "not belonging to reality but belonging to ER". Once again, we can talk of virtual objects and situations in Augmented Reality, but we must not forget that, just as with fake guns or white rabbits in conjuring tricks, they are part of all-comprising reality.

Extended. So, if reality is the set of everything, how can it be extended? Well, let us take a look at the ways we extend ordinary things. We say that we extend our fingers to make them straight, for example, or that the cook extended the pizza dough over the table with a rolling pin. We also say that the public works will extend the cycle lane by two kilometers or that the match was extended by 5 minutes to compensate for lost playing time. Observing the examples, and leaving aside residual or unrelated uses, we can see that there are two related but different senses here. In what I will call the "increase" sense, one extends something by adding new stuff to a previous entity, sometimes building or manufacturing new things (e. g., the French army extended its armament with nuclear weapons), sometimes just by enlarging the scope of previously existing things (the Spanish government extended the limits of Lugo county). In the "unfold" sense, to extend something means to expand something to a greater length or to cover a greater area without adding new stuff, sometimes just straightening it out it to its full size (as with a finger), sometimes stretching it out (as with the dough). The first sense is clearly more akin to the nature of VR and what I have called "creative Augmented Reality": we extend reality by producing new entities that we add to the set of "everything". Please note, however, that in our common speech there is no shadow of an intermediate realm here: at the very same moment when we produce the new entity (the new visual configuration on the screen, for example), it becomes an element of the only reality there is. As for the second sense, in perceptive Augmented Reality we display some possibilities and aspects of our environment and in this sense I believe I am not twisting English too much if I say that we are "unfolding" them. When we see our environment though Google Glass, we unfold some previously existing but unavailable information, in the same way as we do when we unfold a map and use it to study the orography of a country.

Augmentation. Augmented Reality covers the more ordinary cases of ER, so there ought not to be many new aspects here and fortunately, there are not. In most ordinary uses of the word "augmentation", it can be interchanged with the word "extension". Usually this coincides with extension in the "increase" sense, as in "the UE has augmented its members in recent years"; but sometimes it can refer to the "unfold" sense, as when we say that we see things augmented when using a magnifying glass. Indeed, the magnifying glass can serve as a very good metaphor for what many Augmented Reality applications do: they do not physically augment the scene or the things in it, but they augment our image or in general our perception of them. In this sense, it explains better than the map metaphor how Augmented Reality applications can "extend" our perception of reality; in the same way the magnifying glass allows us to perceive details that were previously beyond our senses, the information provided by an Augmented Reality device allows the user to gain an awareness of aspects that would otherwise remain hidden.

We should not, in any case, take the difference between creative and perceptive Augmented Reality (or between the two senses of extend and augment) too strictly. Some perceptive-Augmented Reality applications, such as Goggle Glass, insert imaginary items into the visual field or change color and other visual properties; while Word Lens and HUD display very useful virtual banners and signals. So extension through unfolding always involves some extension through increasing. In the same way, some examples of creative Augmented Reality would also count as cases of perceptive Augmented Reality: Magic Mirror can be seen as an instrument for exploring the aesthetical properties of glasses or even for perceiving some aspects of my face (something like *how my face is suited to these glasses*); while History Pin allows us to perceive a historical site from a new perspective and discover unexpected aspects by mixing contemporary people and items with it.

This minimal analysis offers us, I believe, a promising route towards the solution of the ontological puzzles. If the main sense of "extended" in ER or "augmented" in Augmented Reality is the "unfolding" sense, if all apparent production of new entities is just an indirect form of exploration of the possibilities of a given situation, then the "limbo" between unextended reality and ER is just a mental illusion. The "new entities" are just complex (sometimes called "high-level") properties of physical, entirely material situations (in Augmented Reality those situations include the computer, the screen and other technological apparatus) that resemble or look like different kinds of properties or entities (they are fakes or simulacra in the sense described above). So, in experiencing Augmented Reality we are simply encountering an *unfolding* of the only reality there is. In cognitive applications, the aim of this unfolding through Augmented Reality is the apprehension and exploitation of properties of material objects; while in recreational applications, the aim is to produce fake objects for our aesthetic enjoyment and to stimulate our imagination.

So far I hope that we have obtained a clearer picture of Augmented Reality. However, there are two points that I have not taken into account yet that require further analysis in order to avoid confusion. I will address the now.

Instrumentality. So far I have concentrated on the first clause in Kipper and Rampolla's definition of Augmented Reality (combination), but the second clause (interaction) poses another issue that I should also take into account. It is not enough to say that what we perceive in Augmented Reality as virtual objects are complex properties of material objects, because not only do we *perceive* the virtual objects, we can also interact with them. In Construct3D and Magic Mirror, we can modify the objects we perceive with our hands. What is more, we can use them to interact with material objects, as in ARMAR: a program that assists mechanics in maintenance and repair tasks. This is not a feature of our common notion of perception. Clearly, perception is useful (even indispensable): perceptual information enables us to take good decisions and organize our behavior; but the instruments or media through which we obtain perceptual information (our senses) are not the same as those we use to act in our environment. How can we deal with this "instrumental" side of Augmented Reality?

Illusion and delusion. Another important point concerns the nature of the illusion produced by the technological device. It is not enough to say that in some cases our senses are "deceived" and we feel we are in the presence of something that does not exist. Unlike mirages and some optical illusions, we are not really *deceived* in Augmented Reality; on the contrary, we participate willingly in the imagination game, and we obtain some degree of pleasure or satisfaction from the experience. Moreover, here, there seems to be something exclusively human: a cat can be deceived by a fake mouse, it can even try to hunt it and perhaps play with it; but only humans have devised practices that essentially involve illusions. I need to clarify this point not only in relation to the distinction between perceptive and creative Augmented Reality, but also with a view to avoiding a skeptic doubt that sometimes appears when the difference between perception and action is lost. In some applications of Augmented Reality, some real objects that we cannot perceive directly are reproduced; this happens, for example, in some medical applications that "show" the fetus inside the pregnant mother or offer X-ray vision of a patient's arm. Is this indirect perception of something hidden, or just an illusion? Well, the computer has no access to the inside of the arm, and the recreation could be completely wrong (the patient could be wearing an orthopedic hand) so perhaps it is better to say that it is an illusion. However, if it is just an illusion, what stops us saying that in all cases of Augmented Reality (and even in all cases of normal perception) we are just dealing with illusions, perhaps delusions, and that the set of real properties, the "thing in itself", remains inaccessible?

3. Abstract Entities

When one has to deal with a completely new type of entity that defies our taxonomies, as with the bottle of Coke in the Kalahari, a good strategy (perhaps the only one we have at our disposal) is to compare it with more familiar types of entities that resemble it in some particular respect. Anyone who knows something of the history of philosophy will recognize the family resemblances between the discussion in the previous section and the traditional philosophical debate regarding abstract entities: a very old and frequently bitter dispute that has engaged philosophers for millennia. I am not going to immerse myself in that philosophical discussion here (something that I am afraid would produce more white noise than enlightenment); instead, I will compare Augmented Reality with different types of arguably abstract entities. I will recap what common sense or everyday language can tell us about such entities and consider whether this can be applied to cases of Augmented Reality; and if so, how.

3.1 Universals

Traditionally, universals are the archetypal abstract entities. "Redness", "mankind" and "beauty" were terms that gravely concerned Ancient Greek philosophers. Famously, Plato proposed that such references belong to an immaterial realm that is removed from time and space: the world of forms or ideas. In contrast, Aristotle proposed that they do belong to our ordinary spatiotemporal world, though not as things but rather as properties (whether structural or formal) of things. Medieval nominalists considered that such words were *flatus vocis:* not referring to any specific entity, and at most identifiable with sets of objects (the set of objects that are red, for example). Independently of the question of the place of universals within reality (if they have one), we should note that they are mainly related to our experience of material, physical entities. This constitutes, nonetheless, a complex and usually mediated relation, as we do not, in general, spontaneously perceive universals in our environment. We can see directly the color of a tomato in front of us, but to identify it as the same color as that of the carpet in my living room requires training, the use of memory, reflection and sometimes the possession of concepts. But ultimately we only see them in specific objects and situations, "redness" in a tomato, "beauty" in a seascape and "mankind" in the faces of those around us. Even if we prefer to reserve such words for some immaterial, supranatural beings (something that I do not recommend), it should be clear that: (i) epistemic access to universals is always obtained though particulars: we can only use the word "redness" properly as long as we can see and identify red things; (ii) the utility of universals in our daily language lies in their applicability to our dealings with the physical world: they enable us to organize, exploit and, more importantly, *share* perceptual information in a way that would be impossible without them (for example, to form and answer questions as *Which color is your car?* or *How many colors do I need to make this picture?*).

Many examples of Augmented Reality are analogous to or simply fall within the domain of universals in our natural language. Specially, perceptive Augmented Reality can be seen as an extension of the conceptual system of our natural language, allowing us to identify and make use of universals that are applicable to our environment. The most popular Augmented Reality app, Layar, can be seen as providing universals that are embedded in objects that form part of the scenario. Other applications, such as Magic Mirror or HUD, recognize and outline geometrical shapes, or identify shared properties of objects when assisting with classification tasks.

3.2 Institutions and Social Phenomena

At first glance, it could seem as if, here, we are in the exact opposite corner from universals. Rights and duties, institutional powers and social status are not to be found in nature but are created by us. If we can talk about them as existent, it is mainly and perhaps exclusively as conventions or as the result of conventions. It is a convention that the oldest legitimately recognized child of the reigning monarch of Spain is the Prince or Princess of Asturias; and it is only as a result of convention that Leonor de Borbón, the daughter of Felipe VI, will enjoy the privilege of being buried in the El Escorial pantheon and is to be addressed as "*Excelentísima Señora*" (Most Excellent). I think that the difference between institutional and non-institutional entities must not be neglected (particularly when it is deliberately erased as a step in the legitimization of a social injustice as "natural"). However, there are some important qualifications concerning what it means to say that "social phenomena are conventional" that we must not neglect. Firstly, "conventional" does not mean "arbitrary"; there are restrictions as to what we can decide by convention (we cannot decide by convention that the Prince or Princess of Asturias has the power to breathe under water) and there is always a reason to be found in our needs and goals: the purpose of the convention that justifies it (unjustified institutions tend to disappear). Secondly, the convention only exists as long as we follow it; so the convention requires, and in the long run converges with, our commitment to behave in certain ways (as John Searle has famously argued, every social fact hides a "collective intention"). Finally, there is gradation in the "conventionality" of social phenomena: from almost biological and directly intentional (for example, the preferential feeding of babies) to completely artificial and only indirectly intentional (for example, the raising of the interest rate by the IMF), and there are always genetic and constitutive dependence relations between them.

Many examples of Augmented Reality are related to the world of the social. The app Recognizr offers the user data about a person, including web and social network data, and allows the user to contact and communicate with that person. Furthermore, in many games and social networks, such as Second Life or Facebook, we assist and participate in the creation of a network of institutional status, power and duties as complex as any in the "real world" (and connected to it: virtual currency has been recognized by the European Central Bank since 2012).

3.3 Mathematics

The case of mathematical and other theoretical entities is intermediate between the "perceptual" basis of universals and the "intentional" basis of the social. Of course, there is also gradation here (whose importance will be revealed later). When I say that there were five pebbles in the sack, now I have added two more, and so there are seven, it looks as if I am giving a factual report. In contrast, when I say that zero factorials equals 1 or, even more clearly, that the degree of the zero polynomial equals $-\infty$ (or -1), it looks as if I am just describing a convention. In the middle of such gradation, we find many uses of mathematical expressions where it is impossible to distinguish the conventional from the factual. When a textbook on geometry presents a graph and some proof involving a square and a compass is provided, we cannot determine where the representation finishes and the stipulation begins. That there is a conventional element is clear: we use many concepts that we do not see at all (Π, $\sum$ or Δ); and, if we are strict, what is printed on the page can only be taken as a reference to the mathematical expression by convention (there are no "perfect circles" or "genuine triangles" in reality). It is nonetheless also obvious to readers of the textbook who follow the demonstration that they are learning something about the printed figures; something that can be applied to other physical objects. The same "hybrid" nature is experienced in Augmented Reality. As I said, Construct3D allows virtual objects that fit a specific geometrical concept to be "created"; while some recent apps allow us to see and manipulate the 3D shadows of hypercubes and other 4D objects.

It is worth stopping for a moment at this point, which I believe to be critical, and taking a closer look at where we are. Let us take definitions as an example, for the purpose of getting a closer look. It is traditional to distinguish two types of definitions: a *descriptive* (sometimes called "real") definition gives the characteristic features of a previously existing thing (for example, if I define water as H_2 O); while a *stipulative* definition (sometimes called "conventional") gives the criteria for applying a new word or a new use of an old word (for example, Goodman's definition of "grue" as "a property of an object that makes it appear green if observed before some future time t, and blue if observed afterwards"). There certainly is a contrast between them, as I have said, and it is important when demarcating discourse domains (for example, social from scientific discourse); but, as I have also been stressing, the difference is only one of degree and frequently both aspects are combined in the same definition. If the general formula for a descriptive definition is something like: "X is a Y if and only if it has properties P" (please do not take this too seriously; I give it just for the sake of the argument, as a general approximation and not as a theory); and the general formula for a stipulative definition is: "From now on, let every and only the Xes that have the properties P be Ys", then the hybrid definition that works in mathematics has the form: "From now on, let X, that has the properties P, be taken as a Y that has the properties Q".

If we pay attention to the way we use our definitions, we will see that not only in mathematics, but in all fields, the original format is the hybrid; and that both purely stipulative and purely descriptive definitions are degenerate cases of the hybrid. First, as I say above, any stipulative definition must fulfill some adequacy requirements. "To have the height of Chesterton's killer" fails to define anything, because Chesterton died a natural death; and it has been noted that even a definition of a logical constant, such as Prior's tonk operator, must fail. Meanwhile, every descriptive definition includes some conventional element, because some decisions are taken as to which cases we leave aside, which are considered prototypical, when it is better to distinguish two different kinds or to merge different cases into one kind, etc. Second (and this is an important point I will come back to later), no definition, description or declaration works in isolation, but only under the framework of a multitude of linguistic elements and movements; and very frequently it is in these other pieces of language that the element apparently absent from the literal definition hides ("imaginary numbers" or "i" may appear to be stipulatively defined, but when we look at the role they play when calculating the interest on a loan or the strength of a building, their factual nature immediately becomes apparent). If this were not enough, we must furthermore not forget the "what it is for" of the definition; a word came about to fulfill a function, to fill a gap in our language, which gives the word its *raison d'être*. So no definition is completely stipulative (there is a matter of fact as to whether it succeeds in filling the gap or not) and none is completely descriptive (its correctness is judged in accordance with pragmatic considerations).

This same hybrid nature appears in our speech acts. Following John Searle's taxonomy, we usually use universal words descriptively as defined in *assertives*; statements of the type: "John's house is white", which we use to report a matter of fact. In the domains constituted by stipulative definitions, such as the social, the typical speech act is a *declaration*, of the type: "I declare John and Mary to be married", which we use to confer new institutional status and in this way "change reality" in accordance with the proposition of the declaration. In the mathematical domain, as in general when we use hybrid defined words, the typical speech act is what Searle calls a *representative declaration*, such as when the soccer referee decrees "It is a penalty" or the judge gives the ruling "The accused is guilty". These contain a factual claim ("the defender touched the ball with their hand" or "the accused committed the crime") but they also change reality, producing new situations and events (the forthcoming penalty kick or the jail time to be served). Once again, if we observe what is happening carefully, not only mathematical statements but all our common speech acts have this hybrid nature. And it is always difficult to find a "pure assertive" because there are always factual considerations underlying the declaration.

3.4 Fiction

Other regular residents of the "House of Abstraction" are the characters, places and objects described in works of fiction: literature, cinema, painting and other arts. An initial contrast is that, unlike universals and the majority of mathematical entities, fictional creations are mostly particulars (I say "mostly" because a novelist can invent new types of things, as in science fiction, for example); this makes the use of "abstract" a bit different here. If in the case of universals we say that they are abstract mainly as opposed to "concrete" (and then we may disagree as to whether they are part of reality or not), in the case of fictional creations we call them abstract in contrast to "material", "really existent" or even "self-existing". In this aspect, the domain of fiction is a neighbor of institutional space; when we say that money is an abstraction, we are just saying that there is nothing in nature that is in itself money, and that euros, dollars and rupees exist only as long as we have the will for them to continue. This feature is perhaps a consequence of another: fictional creations are the best examples of mere stipulation; they are introduced freely by the author with almost no adequacy conditions (except maybe for some sophisticated and vague aesthetic criteria).

As I have said, however, there are no purely stipulative definitions when we consider the whole language game and not just the move performed by a declaration. In the case of fiction, we must once again bear in mind the "what it is used for" of the creation. Fictional declarations play an essential role in the game of imagination that the artistic or literary work triggers. Understanding the "definition" of Don Quixote or Shangri-La is not the end but the beginning of the literary practice. We have to use our minds to conceive the person behind the description and the deeds; trying to grasp a physical appearance, a personality, a pattern of behavior, a circumstance and even an ego. In short, we have to take the fictional character as *real*.

This trait of fiction, which traditionally is sometimes called the "fictional pact" and other times, in homage to Aristotle, the "mimetic pact", is just one facet of a profound and distinctive feature of humans. Moreover, we cannot understand human forms of life, and especially the importance of the symbolic in them, if we neglect this crucial point. That oh-so-human feature is our capacity for consciously treating things as different from what they are. This is, in a certain sense, natural and even innate to humans: a small child treats a teddy bear as a living thing; but it is also expanded and radically positioned at the center or our existence by education and other socialization processes. A different version of the fictional pact, not related to leisure and in which the factual consequences have an important value, is at work in the background when we take "as real" the process of baptizing a child. Yet another version, weak but indispensable, is at work whenever we call an irregular three-dimensional object a triangle or we say that the door and the window are the same color when in fact there are many slight differences between them. If I am not wrong, the literary fictional pact is just a modality of the pact that we tacitly sign up to whenever we participate in linguistic or symbolic practices: the compromise of treating conventions unconventionally, of taking definitions as not mere stipulation and adopting the same attitude towards them as we have to matters of fact. Without the fictional pact, creative Augmented Reality could not have been developed, because we could not make use of or even recognized "virtual" objects. Video games (VR or Augmented Reality) are, in this sense, a continuation of Greek drama, the performances of medieval minstrels and Hollywood movies.

As I hope I have demonstrated, "abstract" applies to a heterogeneous family of concepts; and abstraction works in such very different ways that it would be useless to try to provide a general definition. However, we can find a common trait; one that is not exclusive but is central in the cases of abstract notions and expressions: they are words whose grammar raises pertinent questions concerning the identification of references (they are categorematic), but we cannot identify the references with anything that we perceive directly with our senses. When we introduce the gradualistic and holistic features of our language, we can clearly recognize that abstract expressions are also related to experience; but in a complex way that involves not only straightforward perception but also the execution and acknowledgment of actions, intentions, dispositions and complex relations. Considering these two features of abstraction, holism and graduality (or hybridism), we can easily deal with the two perplexities I described at the end of section 2 above. On the one hand, in natural language there is a wide notion of "perception" that includes the use of memory, imagination, training and other skills and abilities, as well as the use of tools and instruments (indeed, I have been using it unproblematically in this paper every time I have talked of "seeing" or "perceiving" an aspect of a concept or a relation between words). Moreover, this notion fits perfectly with the sense of the extended perception of reality that Augmented Reality permits. On the other hand, there is no genuine "delusion" in AR and there is no genuine question about the veracity of Augmented Reality in general. In creative Augmented Reality, we play with illusions as we do in other linguistic games that exploit fictional pacts; the best examples of our symbolic capacity at work. In perceptive Augmented Reality, the veracity does not depend on being or not being a "real" thing that is represented by a device interface (or on what that thing is); it depends on the global success of the activity that is executed using Augmented Reality (for example, the surgical operation assisted by Augmented Reality).

4. Augmenting Reality

The set of results we have considered so far are, I believe, sufficient to allow me to summarize an initial conclusion of this grammatical study: we understand Augmented Reality better if we take the new entities produced by the technological devices involved as abstract entities. They bear some family resemblances to universal notions in our natural language and mathematical entities, and also to fictional and institutional entities. We can say that Augmented Reality "extends" (or augments) reality because it "makes it bigger", producing new entities that serve to "unfold" the properties of pre-existing entities and situations.

This cannot be the end of the story though. Although the examples I have given so far may be enough to allow us to perceive the analogies (and disanalogies) – that is certainly my hope – the reader may feel a bit disoriented by the comparisons. The term "abstract", in all the different usages I consider in the previous section, is always applied to phenomena, properties or entities that are not the direct objects of our perception; either because they are not concrete, or simple, or immediate, or because they just do not exist. But in Augmented Reality, as the first clause of Kipper and Rampolla's definition states, the new entities appear in front of us mixed with standard entities, and they look as concrete and physical as those standard entities. So, how is it that I can classify them together with those invisible things: numbers, marriages, unicorns and so on?

To answer this question we have to take a step forward in the analysis. My method so far has been to compare the new things with older, more familiar ones. This has a hidden advantage: sometimes it enables us not only to understand the new things better, but also to gain a new perspective (the one which arises from the comparison) on the old types of things; to see and understand them better. I will now try to convince you not only that traditional abstract entities belong tout court to the realm of everyday things, but also that Augmented Reality offers us the best proof that they belong there. I will begin by giving a description of the genealogy of the "mistake"; I mean, of course, the mistake of believing that abstract entities are not physical. First, I will consider two common errors that I believe the idea that abstract entities have an ontological realm of their own may stem from.

The "popular" mistake: not taking into account that the production of abstract entities is a linguistic process. We must not forget that a symbol is what it is through its reference to another thing that we do not have in front of our eyes when we are using it (it is intentional in Brentano's sense). Because of this, when we are using a symbol, we have the impression that it is hiding something from us; that it has a life of its own, as Wittgenstein famously pointed out. Usually we can find entities in our environment that more or less correspond to the things the "intention" of the symbol is directed towards. In the case of the expressions examined in the previous section, however, we have great, sometimes insurmountable difficulties finding those entities. So we may finally make the mistake of yielding to the temptation of postulating those other mysterious, invisible entities, abstract objects, and the ontological mess begins. But all the perplexities disappear if we realize from the beginning that the "intentionality" of symbols is just a consequence of their being meaningful, and that the "life" or the "soul" of the symbol is simply the meaning we assign to it.

The "philosophical" mistake. Once we have recognized the symbolic nature of abstract entities (that they are just meanings or parts of meanings), we have to take into account the pragmatic nature of meaning. If one is moving within the syntactic-semantic framework, if one insists on finding the sense and reference of the expression, then we make a mistake similar to the popular but even more severe, because now we have the endorsement of the theory which "obliges" us to produce the things that constitute the reference of all words, and accordingly "implies" that abstract entities exists. This produces a new set of problems and debates, such as the nominalist-conceptualist polemic or the indispensability of mathematics argument, that have occupied philosophers for centuries without a consensus being reached.

In order to avoid falling into these two errors, and in general to avoid postulating mysterious ontological domains, I next consider two features of the pragmatic conception of language that are extremely helpful.

(i) Meaning is not an entity that accompanies the symbol or that is hidden inside its material appearance; meaning lies in our use of the symbol. Once we attend to the practices, actions and attitudes (as in the fictional pact) that surround the symbol (and which belong to the everyday world), we see that the functions, goals and ends (those we fulfill and those we fail to fulfill) are the things that "give" objectivity and even factuality to the symbol, and that "insert" it into reality. The meaning becomes factual because it is a fact, or not, that in a given situation it is used rightly (or not), and that the expected consequences are obtained (or not) in that situation. We do not need any "object" to ensure the objectivity of the meaning, because it is the situation that chiefly determines which other possible situations are obtained when we use this or that other expression in this way or another.

(ii) Meaning is not something fixed or well delimited (it does not have the dimensions of an object in the non-philosophical sense of the word) because it is: (a) continuously changing (we adapt and sometimes modify usage according to the peculiarities of the situation); and (b) holistic (the actions and practices related to uses of the different symbols interpenetrate one another). The notion of "number", for example, is not "closed" by a definition; rather it is something that is constantly rebuilt through the interaction of a plethora of interwoven practices. There is not any "common property" shared by the many things we call "numbers" (so neither is there a "universal entity" in the traditional sense), or by the many things we call a "natural number", or by the many things we call "twenty"; but rather there is a tangle of changing praxis, belonging not only to mathematics but also to other theoretical domains (physics, economics, etc.) and to practical activities (law, art, etc.).

Note that there is nothing wrong with the old "reifying" discourse concerning abstract entities; just as long as we do not forget that it is only "a way of speaking". Such idioms also belong to language and they play their roles. Taking Othello and Desdemona "as real" helps us to immerse ourselves in and fully engage with Shakespeare's story; and the rigor of mathematical thought depends on taking numbers "as real" entities with intrinsic properties that can be characterized by a description. The mistake occurs when we take what is a linguistic convention as a matter of fact.

When we understand abstraction from within this pragmalinguistic framework (in general terms, as a linguistic recourse and not as some means of access to other ontological realms), then it is natural to take Augmented Reality as a process of abstraction. With Augmented Reality, technology has enhanced our ability to take advantage of situations, sometimes extending them (in the sense of increasing them) with new objects produced by us. In this way, Augmented Reality extends (in the sense of unfolding) properties and potentialities that otherwise we would not be able to grasp or exploit. We can take things a step further though. From within the pragmalinguistic approach, there are good reasons to claim that Augmented Reality is not only an example of abstraction, but the best example of it; and the one that best allows us to avoid the "reification" temptation. Indeed, as we have seen, that mistake stems from the fact that in many cases of abstraction we cannot perceive the alleged entities with our senses (for example, when reading a novel we do not see the characters with our eyes); but in Augmented Reality we can see, hear and even sometimes touch the entities.

Let us return to Kipper and Rampolla's definition, which is revealing in relation to this point. To begin with, Augmented Reality is a technology. Perhaps in the old conception this is a reason to consider it as non-linguistic; but in the new conception, where all components of language are taken as tools, being a technology is not an impediment but fulfills this necessary condition for being a symbol. Moreover, as a technology, it is more difficult for us to forget that it is something that does not come "out of nowhere", but in fact something that we make with our minds, and also with our hands.

I have said that the third clause in the definition is, in my opinion, less important; but the fact that the objects of Augmented Reality have the visual properties of physical 3D objects does prevent us for taking them as Platonic entities. In Augmented Reality, abstract entities are there in front of us (although in some cases we know that they are just simulacra of the things they appear to be, as we saw in section 2 above).

If we still feel the "Platonic temptation", we must take a look at the second clause of the definition. Something that was difficult to understand in terms of the old explanation was the "communication" between abstract and regular entities; something that looks impossible if they belong to different ontological realms (a problem that can be tracked through history, from Plato-Aristotle's Third Man to Wittgenstein-Kripke's On Following a Rule). But in Augmented Reality we handle abstract entities and, even more revealingly, through handling them we manipulate other things in our environment. This point confirms and clarifies a previous one: the factual element in abstraction comes from the things we can do with the abstract. Indeed, the best proof we have that abstract entities are just a kind of physical entities is that we can interact with them and that by interacting with them we also interact with other physical entities they are casually connected with. Even when we only use Augmented Reality to grasp aspects of our environment, as in Layar, we can do so because Augmented Reality entities are casually connected with the environment (changes in certain properties and relations cause changes in the icons and simulations). But we can also use Augmented Reality to produce variations in our environment; so there is causal connection in the opposite direction too. It is important here to pay attention not only to the changes in our environment, but also to the ways Augmented Reality affects our lives. It is very interesting and revealing that Kipper and Rampolla are deeply concerned with the social, ethical and legal issues raised by Augmented Reality. These include not only the ways in which Augmented Reality affects (or will affect in the future) our ways of life, in terms of some important aspects as public safety, health, education and personal relations, but also specific legal issues such as those concerning the right to privacy or when aggressive publicity is to be considered a criminal offence. This demonstrates not only the insertion of Augmented Reality within our overall system of linguistic practices, but also that in Augmented Reality, as in other abstract domains, nothing is completely virtual, fictive or ineffectual.

If that still is not enough, if any shadow of a doubt remains concerning the exact sense in which we are faced with something "real" in Augmented Reality (in the ordinary sense of the word, remember, including the cases in which we are just dealing with a "real falsification"), then we have the first clause in the definition to rely on: technological Augmented Reality entities and standard entities are mixed together within the same situation. That "virtual" and "real" elements overlap proves that we are not in two different contexts "at the same time", but in just one single context formed by different kinds of things including technological images and sounds.

At this point I am in a position to invert my initial thesis. I have tried to give good reasons to support the claim that Augmented Reality entities belong to the family of abstract entities; and when looking for similarities and differences, I have discovered that Augmented Reality is the best and clearest example of abstraction. It may be argued that although they appear later in our history, it is better to take Augmented Reality as the model, the archetype for our notion of abstraction. The point we are just now beginning to reach, thanks to new technologies, is the culmination of a process we started when we created language, and we have developed through science, engineering, art and other instruments that empower us both to expand reality with new kinds of objects and situations, and to extend our epistemic and existential access to reality. Therefore, I believe that it is better not to say that Augmented Reality is a case of abstraction, but quite the reverse: abstract entities (both the new and the old) belong to Augmented Reality.

References

Austin, John (1962): *Sense and Sensibilia*, London and New York: Clarendon Press.
Kipper, Gregory/Rampolla, Joseph (eds) (2013): *Augmented Reality: An Emerging Technologies Guide to AR*, Amsterdam and Boston: Syngress/Elsevier.

Stefan Weinzierl and Steffen Lepa

On the Epistemic Potential of Virtual Realities for the Historical Sciences. A Methodological Framework

Abstract: Virtual or augmented audio-visual environments can be employed not only for the impartment of knowledge to a wider audience, but also for the generation of knowledge within the historical sciences. In this context, the transformation of numerical models of historical circumstances into an immediate sensual experience may be used both in an exploratory manner as well as for testing specific hypotheses through subjective perceptual analysis. As with any other empirical approach, the new insights provided can be biased on different levels. In order to make virtual realities (VRs) a valuable tool for research, traditional quality criteria for empirical research need to be adapted to the specific setting created by observational fieldwork 'within' 3D audio-visual computer simulations. Two major causes for degradation in the credibility of VR-based historical research are related to the relationship between simulation and historical 'reality' as well as to the human agents experiencing the simulated environments and the conclusions drawn from their subjective impressions. Hence, our contribution attempts to outline procedures and methods for estimating and comparing the ecological validity of virtual environments as well as the level of intersubjectivity regarding the inferences drawn during and after experiencing them. For this purpose, we suggest to synthesize existing ideas and procedures originating from virtual reality research, media psychology, communication science and ethnology.

Keywords: Virtual Reality, Augmented Reality, Virtual Acoustic Reality, Virtual Historic Environment, Virtual Archaeology, Cyber Ethnography.

Immersive media environments have been used for quite some time for the *impartment* of historical knowledge to a wider audience (Mikropoulos/Natsis 2011). They have a long tradition reaching from panoramic paintings (Oettermann 1980) and diorama reconstructions of historical events (Gernsheim/Gernsheim 1969) to virtual environments using recent 3D technologies in museums (Stogner 2009, Bearman 2011), or cultural heritage projects (Bogdanovych *et al.* 2010, Pujol/Champion 2012). Examples include the virtual reconstruction of urban space and daily life in 13th-century Bologna, key historical theaters of

DOI 10.1515/9783110497656-004

18th-century Venice (Lercari 2016), or of audio-visual media installations such as the *Poème électronique* and the Philips pavilion by Le Corbusier and Edgard Varèse at the Brussels world fair in 1958 (Lombardo *et al.* 2009).

Less frequent are attempts to *generate new knowledge* from the virtual reconstruction of historical scenarios, and much greater are the reservations within the scientific community against this kind of scientific practice. These reservations may be differently motivated in each individual case. In their core, however, they are related a) to doubts regarding the credibility of virtual environments as a form of scientific evidence; b) to the question of how new knowledge may emerge from virtual environments, which are always based on already existing historical evidence; and c) what kind of role virtual or augmented realities could play within an epistemological concept of historical research. With the current text, we would like to sketch out a methodological framework that will attempt to provide answers to these questions.

This framework will be exemplified by a concrete problem drawn from the authors' own research. The open question concerned a) the maximum audience size reached by a speaker on the ancient Forum Romanum between ca. 500 BC and ca. 500 AD; b) how the size of this audience changed with the several modifications and relocations of the Rostra; and c) whether these modifications were carried out for reasons of acoustics, or rather for the political and symbolic motives usually invoked in the historiography of the Roman empire. This concrete problem was part of a larger project dedicated to the digital reconstruction of the ancient Forum Romanum[1] and worked on by a team of archeologists and acousticians.

In the following outline for a methodological approach towards the use of virtual realities for historical research, we will restrict ourselves to the acoustic domain, which was particularly important for the given problem, although all technical and methodological stages have an almost one-to-one equivalent in the visual domain. Since many of the methodological problems are closely related to the technical process of generating a virtual environment, we will first give a brief outline of binaural synthesis as the chosen approach for virtual acoustic reality (Fig. 2).

1 See http://www.digitales-forum-romanum.de/, accessed on 20 September 2016.

Fig. 1: Digital reconstruction of the ancient Forum Romanum. The model represents the conditions in 14 AD, the year of Augustus's death. View from southeast.

1. Virtual acoustic environments

Binaural synthesis is one approach for the generation of virtual acoustic environments. It is the acoustic equivalent of stereoscopic displays, in which one image is generated for each eye of a single observer. In binaural synthesis, one acoustic signal is generated for each ear of a single listener and presented by headphones. These signals are designed to excite the eardrum as an acoustic sensor in the same way as a corresponding real sound field.

For the synthesis of this signal, a 3D model of the desired environment is used together with a specification of the acoustic properties of the desired sound source and the desired receiver in order to numerically simulate the sound propagation from source to receiver. The result of this simulation, including both the direct sound as well as all sound reflections at the boundaries of an open or enclosed space, is encoded as binaural room impulse responses (BRIRs), which describe the transfer path between a sound source and a defined (e.g.: human) receiver. If these impulse responses are linked to a temporal source signal such as speech or music by a numerical process called *convolution*, the corresponding sound source will be perceived at the desired point in space encoded in the BRIR. This perception includes all spatial properties of both the source and the environment, such as the distance, the direction of the source and the size and reverberation of the surrounding space. In order to invoke this perception, the result of the convolution has to be applied to the ear canal of a listener by headphones. The generated *auralization* (Vorländer 2008) of an acoustic scene will only be perceived as immersive if the listener can naturally interact

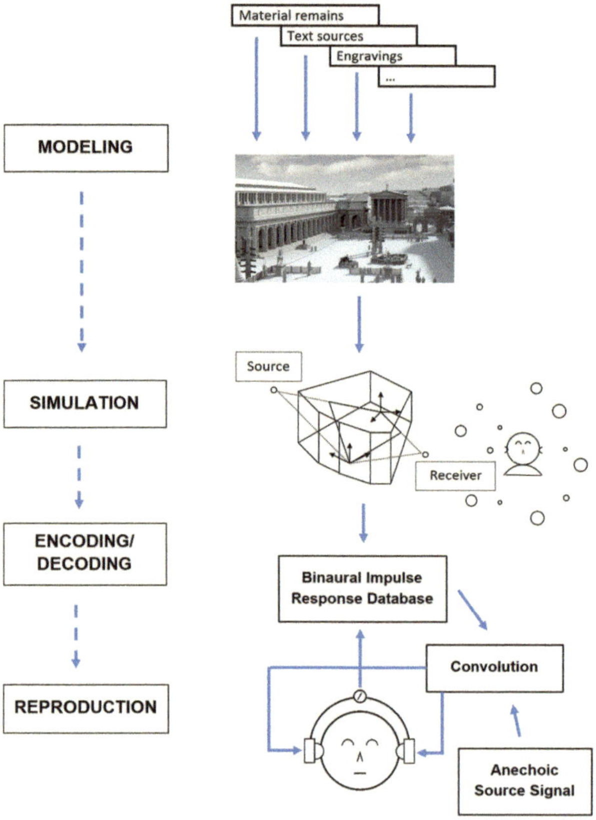

Fig. 2: Processing steps for the generation of virtual acoustic realities by binaural synthesis.

with the produced sound field, i.e. if the ear signals are re-calculated for different head orientations, so that the listener can move *within* the scene rather than the scene moving with the listener. This feature also has an equivalent in stereoscopic displays, in which the image has to be re-calculated in real-time whenever the observer changes his or her visual orientation. And just as with stereoscopic displays, it depends on the reproduction device, whether the simulation is presented as virtual or Augmented Reality. Headphones can exhibit different degrees of openness, ranging from closed headphones with a strong insulation against the external sound field, occasionally even supported by noise-cancelling algorithms, to open or even extra-aural headphones, which leave a gap of some centimeters between the ear and the headphone and constitute no significant obstacle for the external sound field. The latter are particularly suitable for simulations presented as Augmented Reality (see fig. 3).

Fig. 3: Violinist playing in an Augmented Reality with extra-aural headphones. The direct sound of his instrument, unobstructed by the open headphone design, is mixed with the simulation of a concert hall, generated by binaural synthesis.[2]

If the observations made within such a virtual acoustic reality shall be exploited as eyewitness reports about the corresponding historical scenery, the credibility of resulting inferences can be questioned at two levels. The first concerns the relationship between the simulation and the historical 'reality', the second concerns the reliability of the observations made by human observers inside the generated virtual or Augmented Reality. Both aspects will be considered more closely in the following.

2. Considering the uncertainty of virtual reconstructions

If virtual reconstructions are evaluated as a research tool, it is necessary to specify their epistemological function, since – as with any other tool – their adequacy

2 This setup was used to study how musicians adapt their way of playing to different room acoustic environments (cf. Schaerer Kalkandjiev/Weinzierl 2015).

can only be determined with respect to a desired goal. In the case of historical research, this requires a well-specified research question or hypothesis that can be answered of confirmed on the basis of qualitative or quantitative data retrieved from virtual historical environments. In the example discussed throughout this text, the question concerns the speech intelligibility in the ancient Forum Romanum, in other cases it might relate to the sound impression of historical concert halls, the visual impression of historical churches, the visual impression of paintings in museums before and after the introduction of electric light or other similar problems.

In the present discourse about the possibility of research in virtual environments, we think that the discussion is often overly focused on the question of whether simulations can replace the experience of a real, historical environment, or, more generally, whether virtual reality can fully replace 'real reality'. This question seems unproductive to the authors. This is less because it might be technically unfeasible in the foreseeable future to provide fully transparent virtual environments.[3] More relevant from a methodological point of view is that there is no criterion to answer this question without specifying the task, that an observer of (and listener 'in') the virtual or Augmented Reality has to perform. For most questions of mere perceptibility (e. g., speech intelligibility such in the present example), however, such criteria can be well-formulated and justified – based on theory or on empirical pretests – for a media system in order to fully convey the necessary cues for a listener confronted with this task.

Consequently, it might not always be necessary to generate virtual environments with a maximum level of realism and interactivity (whatever that implies). Simply with respect to efficiency and limited resources, it might be rather desirable to provide a virtual environment with only the features necessary to answer the question for which it was devised.

3. Reliability and bias I: The virtual environment

As far as the process of transforming historical evidence into the virtual reality presentation of a certain historical scenario is concerned, each step of the transformation can introduce uncertainties which affect the credibility of the final result. If we take a closer look at each of these steps in the order they have to be processed in practice (fig. 2), the first stage includes the establishment of an en-

3 The "perceptual illusion of non-mediation" was suggested as a criterion for completely transparent virtual realities providing an unrestricted sense of presence (Lombard/Ditton 1997, 9).

vironmental model of the desired scenario. In visual simulations this would include a 3D model incorporating the geometry of the space and the texturing of the surfaces. In acoustic simulations it would include a 3D model and the acoustic properties of all boundaries such as the absorption and scattering coefficients of the employed surfaces. The types of model parameters required at this stage depend on the subsequent simulation algorithm; while for wave-based numerical simulations of the sound propagation such as the finite element method (FEM) a complex impedance is required for each boundary element representing the amplitude and phase difference between the incoming and the outgoing sound wave, for ray-based acoustical simulations, often combining raytracing and image-source-method algorithms, only a real-valued reflection coefficient is required, as the phase of the acoustic wave is ignored in this simulation type.

No matter which simulation approach is selected, any of the required input parameters is subject to uncertainty which may result from insufficient knowledge of the historical conditions themselves or from insufficient knowledge of how to translate historical evidence into the required input parameters. In the case of the Forum Romanum, for example, there was insufficient knowledge about the material used for the walls of the surrounding buildings. Furthermore, also the absorption and scattering properties of Roman concrete (*opus caementicium*), which was introduced after 200 BC and used for many of the larger buildings of the forum, could only be estimated. The exact state of construction of the forum at a specific point in time was partly unknown, for there were contradictory information in different sources such as pictorial representations and textual sources. Further, while it was known that certain sound sources (speakers, horse-drawn vehicles, other sources of noise) were present in the investigated scenario, their exact acoustic radiation characteristics, i.e. the frequency-dependent directivity, might be unknown.

The uncertainties at this stage, which we suggest calling *modeling uncertainty*, result from the classical problem of incomplete or inconsistent historical evidence. They are not yet related to the computational processing of this evidence, but have to be understood and treated with a classical source-critical approach; the simulation method only defines the type of evidence required in order to generate a virtual representation. Historians might otherwise not be interested in the sound absorption of Roman concrete; for the acoustic simulation it is essential information.

At the second stage, the reliability of the numerical simulation itself may be questioned, i.e. the assumption that the sound propagation from the source to the receiver is correctly modeled by the selected numerical approach. We could term the uncertainties at this stage *simulation uncertainty*. Simulation uncertainty is an engineering problem inherent to any kind of numerical simulation of physical processes. It is usually addressed by using measurements conducted on real physical systems as a reference and by comparing these to simulations on the basis of specific dependent variables. These variables are selected according to a defined functional application. For example, if it is the function of an acoustic simulation to predict the reverberation of newly designed concert halls, measured reverberation times would constitute an appropriate reference for simulated reverberation times, as would other room acoustic parameters (Bork 2005a, 2005b). In the case of virtual realities intended to create a convincing sensory impression, the perceived difference to a corresponding real environment would be an appropriate reference for an evaluation of the simulation uncertainty. For the operationalization of the 'perceived difference', different measurable indicators have been proposed (see next section).

At the next stage, the results of a numerical simulation have to be encoded in a certain data format for storage or for live transmission, and decoded for reproduction. As with any communication channel, the information transmitted by encoding and decoding is overlaid by noise, which can have a multitude of sources. In the case of binaural synthesis, these include, for example, the spatial discretization of the sound field at the receiver. Whereas in a real sound field, listeners can introduce infinitesimally small modulations to the sound field by infinitesimally small head movements, BRIRs are available only for a predefined grid of head orientations. They have to be interpolated for head orientations in between. The simplest solution is a nearest-neighbor interpolation, i.e. the hard switching in the predefined grid; but even more advanced solutions are always error-prone approximations. Other encoding/decoding errors can be due to the fact that only initial parts of the impulse responses are exchanged dynamically to increase computational efficiency. They can also result from the audio signal format used or simply from the numerical resolution of the digital system used. The errors introduced by encoding and decoding could be summarized as *coding uncertainty.*

At a final stage, the accuracy of the optical or acoustic reproduction can be questioned, i.e. the extent to which the quality of the optical or acoustic signal presented to the eyes or the ears with respect to the desired reference is degraded by the employed reproduction system. Whereas coding uncertainty is introduced in the digital domain, for *reproduction* some kind of human-computer interface is required. In the case of binaural synthesis, degradations can relate to the headphones and the head tracking device used. The transfer function of the headphones, for example, can lead to timbral differences between the original and the technically reproduced sound source. Latencies in the acoustic adaption of the ear signals can lead to spatial instability of the reproduced sound source, latencies in the visual adaption in head mounted displays can even cause so-called simulator sickness if visual and vestibular motion cues are no longer consistent. Inaccuracies at this stage could be called *reproduction uncertainty.*

4. Characterizing the reliability of virtual environments

The uncertainties introduced at the modeling, simulation, coding and reproduction stage have to be indicated and quantified by appropriate means in order to convey a transparent overall picture of the reliability of the virtualization.

At the modeling stage, incomplete knowledge about the original spatial environment can, for example, be documented by alternative models representing different potential historical conditions, all of which can be plausible with respect to the archeological remains and historical knowledge in general. For modeling parameters such as the acoustic boundary conditions, an estimated range of possible values can be given according to expert knowledge. There are different ways to investigate the propagation of these uncertainties at the level of input parameters through the simulation to output parameters such as, in our example, speech intelligibility in the Forum Romanum. For discrete input parameters, such as different models representing different possible spatial configurations, a simulation can be run for every element of a set of models, giving a corresponding set of output parameters. For input parameters with a continuous estimated range of uncertainty, a sampling scheme may be applied, and then the simulation has to be run for this sample of input parameter values in order to estimate the output uncertainty. Finally, a statistically corroborated estimation of the uncertainties at the level of the output parameter would specify input parameters as probability distributions and use a sampling scheme that considers the probability of each parameter value. This can be achieved by random sampling (Monte Carlo strategies) or by dividing the range of each uncertain input parameter into equi-probable intervals and sampling accordingly (Rubinstein/Kroese 2008). The result is then a set of output values representing the probability distribution of the parameter of interest (cf. fig. 4).

The uncertainties arising from the numerical simulation algorithm itself are usually estimated by comparing simulations to measurements of the corresponding real physical systems. This is not as straightforward as it may seem, however, because the measurements used as references for the uncertainty of the simulation have a measurement uncertainty themselves. Moreover, it can be difficult to ensure that the input parameters used for the simulation will correspond exactly to the parameters of the real system. And, finally, benchmark tests between measurement and simulation are, at least in acoustics, based on considerable technical efforts. Hence, they can be conducted only for a small sample of physical systems and provide only a rough estimation of the reliability of the simulation algorithm without statistical information about the uncertainty distribution. Nevertheless, these benchmarks are common for most numerical simulation methods in the form of round-robin tests or competitions between alternative approaches and implementations.[4]

Encoding and decoding errors can be controlled by system design in order to keep them below a predefined technical or perceptual threshold. The spatial discretization of binaural simulations, for example, has been shown to be inaudible with a sampling grid of 2° for the horizontal, vertical and lateral discretization of BRIRs (Lindau/Weinzierl 2009). With respect to the dynamic exchange of these impulse responses for different head orientations, a prediction formula has been devised specifying the time window necessary for such a dynamic exchange in order for audible artifacts to be avoided (Lindau *et al.* 2012). The underlying test procedures are similar to those used for the encoding and decoding of audio signals with data compression (mp3), which determine a threshold of transparency, i.e. the data rate necessary for the differences between the encoded/decoded source material and a given reference to be inaudible or come with acceptable degradations.

At the reproduction stage, it is the established parameters for imaging devices or sound transducers that can be applied to evaluate the information loss between the computer model and the human user. These include the field of view or the image resolution of displays or the frequency bandwidth, the linearity of the transfer function or non-linear distortions caused by headphones. For interactive virtual environments, it includes the update rate or the system latency of the head tracking device. For all these parameters there is a large stock of research in the field of quality and usability research that can be used in order to assess the perceptual relevance of the intrinsic limitations of the systems and devices used.

For virtual acoustic environments as a whole, different degrees of distinctness of simulation and reality have been suggested as measures: The *plausibility* of a simulation (Lindau/Weinzierl 2012), measuring the ability of a subject to identify the simulation in a random, alternating presentation of simulation and reality, and the *authenticity* of a simulation (Brinkmann *et al.* 2014), measuring the ability of a subject to perceive *any* difference between simulation

4 For examples see http://rr.auralisation.net/ for room acoustic simulation and auralization, and Durante/Riedel (2008) for wind flow simulation.

and reality, even if the simulation cannot be identified as such. For a differential diagnosis of differences between simulation and real references, a taxonomy has been developed by qualitative research (Lindau *et al.* 2014). While these tests give no indication of the stage at which the virtualization degradations occurred, they give an overall picture of the quality provided.

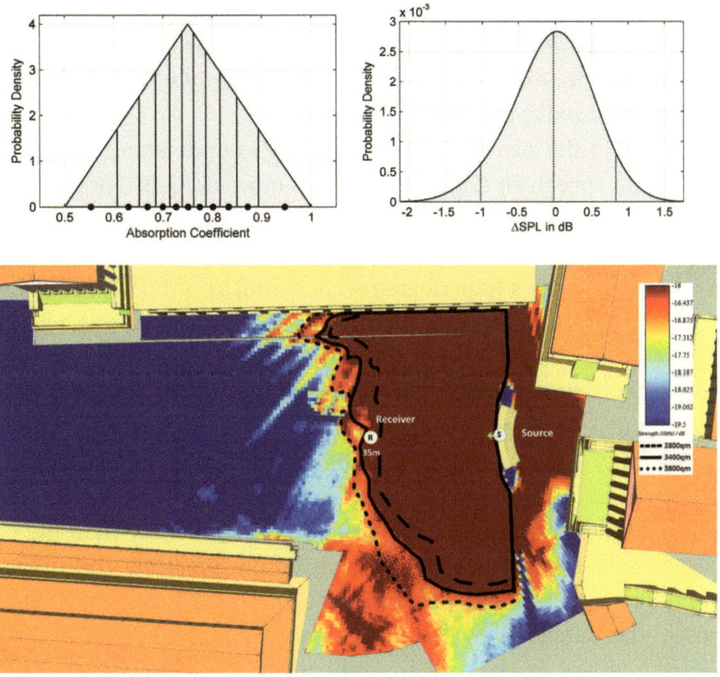

Fig. 4: Uncertainty propagation through the acoustic simulation. Top: Assuming that the absorption coefficient of the audience lies in an interval between 0.5 and 1.0 (with a triangular distribution, and 0.75 as the most probable value, top left), the resulting uncertainty of the sound power level at the border of intelligibility is ca. ±1 dB (5%/95% quantiles, indicated as dashed lines, top right). Bottom: The color map shows the regions of good (red) and poor (blue) speech intelligibility on the ancient Forum Romanum. The solid line indicates the border of intelligibility, with the dashed lines related to the uncertainty of ±1 dB sound power level calculated above. The corresponding size of the audience area that could be reached by a trained speaker is 3400 m² (2800 m²/3800 m²).

5. Reconstructing historical events vs. reconstructing historical *spaces of possibility*

The above mentioned uncertainties at the different stages of digital reconstructions will, as a result, lead to a corresponding range of uncertainty for the specified variables of interest, such as speech intelligibility in the described model study. Independent of this problem is the question of whether the generated virtual environment and the results derived from it are supposed to represent one specific historical scenario, or whether they aim at a *range of possibilities* related to a certain historical situation.

Are we interested in the size of the audience able to understand Marcus Tullius Cicero during his speech *In Catilinam* on November 8, 63 BC, or are we interested in how many persons could *typically* understand speeches given by different orators on different occasions during a given historical period? For the first problem, there will usually be a high degree of modeling uncertainty, because we do not know exactly how powerful the voice of this specific person was, what the rhetorical concept of his speech was, or how large and how attentive the crowd was on this specific occasion. Hence, we will be confronted with a high modeling uncertainty leading to a corresponding uncertainty about the level of the results on speech intelligibility. For the second problem, the historical scenario itself is described by a range of input parameters rather than a single model state, and the limits of this range can usually be determined more precisely than the conditions of one specific event. We can determine quite precisely the range in which the sound power of trained speakers lies (e.g. through empirical investigations on present-day subjects), by assuming that the size of the crowd could be something between virtually zero and an audience corresponding to the maximum density of standing persons possible in a public place, or by taking into account the fact that the level of attention of an audience at public speeches in terms of the background noise level can again be empirically determined, assuming that the noise level produced by a modern crowd is not substantially different from a crowd during the Roman period.

In order to describe a range of historical conditions corresponding to a state space of computer models instead of one specific historical occasion, similar strategies to those being used to describe a range of modeling uncertainties can be applied, i.e. by calculating the model for the limits of the range or by estimating a probability distribution for the respective input parameter and by letting a sampled version of this distribution propagate through the simulation in order to calculate the resulting uncertainty at the level of the parameter of interest (fig. 4). In practice, due to the limited information about single events and the empirically more substantiated knowledge about the range of historical conditions, there will often be a trade-off between modeling uncertainty and historical specificity. For the results that virtual reconstructions may provide for a defined range of historical events are usually much more reliable and thus scientifically more valuable than those for specific historical events.

6. Reliability and bias II: The observer

Unlike a merely numerical simulation, a virtual historical environment (VHE) encompasses interactive real-time sense data (sometimes also autonomous artificial agents) that are experienced and interpreted by human agents in order to make new knowledge claims about the historical circumstances under simulation. To legitimate such claims, even in the face of a technically perfect simulation of historical reality, scientists employing such a strategy should always follow established scientific quality criteria for conclusions drawn from systematic observations. After all, human agents tend to be unreliable, unique and autopoietic measurement instruments. They have constrained attention as well as different cognitive-perceptual capacities and they construct the identity of objects, events and their meaning from the background of their historical cultural upbringing and embeddedness. Furthermore, in interactive environments, different human agents may by definition perform different actions, thereby also arriving at idiosyncratic impressions of the very same simulated worlds. These epistemological problems are well known in research disciplines that have a tradition of dealing with subjective field observations, such as psychology, sociology and ethnography. Within these disciplines, several methodological answers have been developed to address these challenges. Even the problem of systematically performing social science in simulated virtual realities has been discussed for nearly 20 years now (Markham 1998). However, the type of systematic observation performed within VHEs differs radically from psychological *virtual reality experiments* (Veiling *et al.* 2013) as well as from *cyber ethnography* (Hallett/Barber 2014) in sociology or communication studies in that it is not directed at analyzing the actions or impressions of *other* human agents within virtual worlds or computer games but at analyzing a scholar's *own* subjective experience of being an actor within a simulated past cultural setting. Therefore, the methodological approach discussed here may be considered a new form of empirical inquiry that could be termed *cyber phenomenology.*[5] Nevertheless, we suggest building on

5 See Houliez/Gamble (2012) for a brief introduction into the phenomenological approach.

methodological techniques developed within the abovementioned fields, since, as we will try to show in the following, they help to improve and demonstrate the reliability and intersubjective validity of systematic scientific observations performed within VHEs.

7. Performing (semi-)structured phenomenological observations in VHEs to increase reliability

The most important challenge for cyber phenomenology from a *reliability perspective* appears to be the selectivity of human perception, regardless of cultural background and expertise. *Attention span*, cognitive *priming and halo effects* (Kochinka 2010), as well as the results of different actions performed in the same virtual environment by different actors may lead to very different subjective percepts. A straightforward methodological approach that is able to 'tame' the resulting idiosyncrasy of impressions with a long history of success in the social sciences is performing structured or semi-structured observations (Bryman 2008b). Again, these require a well-specified research question and a clearly specified range of phenomena of interest at the outset, which are then used to create an observation form (or category sheet) that formulates different activities a researcher has to perform (e. g. visiting certain places within the VHE) and leaves empty slots in the table to be filled out during or after the experience. These could be used to describe the subjectively experienced *mere existence* or the experienced *qualities or intensities* of certain a-priori expected phenomena. In the fully structured variant, all phenomena and their subcategories are already specified at the outset of the fieldwork, turning the table form into a multiple-choice questionnaire. In the semi-structured version, the categories for phenomena to look out for tend to be rather broad and the subcategories are open-ended, which leaves their creation to the field-observer, and thereby introduces an interpretive-integrative step in the later analysis (Gehrau 2002). Regardless of which of the two approaches has been adopted, due to their degree of standardization, both procedures principally allow the observations to be converted into numerical variables in a later step and thereby enable a quantitative comparison between the impressions of a larger sample of different historical researchers. This paves the way for systematic mathematical reliability checks, as well as for performing scale building and statistical hypothesis tests (Bryman 2008b). While internal validity and reliability are improved considerably when performing such structured observations, a drawback of these procedures is that they are only able to deal with a-priori expected phenomena, thereby imposing a deductive inferential style of inquiry with the typical tradeoff in external validity. Taken together, structured observation techniques appear well suited for quasi-experimental historical studies using VHEs that try to test specific hypotheses.

8. Employing open-ended ethnographic techniques in VHEs to increase intersubjective validity

The most important challenge for cyber phenomenology from a *validity perspective* appears to be the cultural-historical situatedness of human perception: every observational act is laden with implicit culturally-specific assumptions that structure the kind of entities, qualities, actors, relationships and events constructed by the human mind during perception (Bogen 2014). This problem even increases when research questions are of an exploratory nature. Therefore, from the standpoint of validity it appears important in these cases to employ a form of inquiry that maximizes the intersubjective traceability of subjective interpretations in order to 'tame' perception's cultural boundedness. Obviously, this is only possible if not the experienced phenomena alone, but also their subjective interpretations and the way they were reached are analyzed and compared qualitatively between different researchers with different backgrounds and areas of expertise. However, this is not possible with standardized observation forms (Bryman 2008a). Hence, when dealing with more open-ended research questions or when expecting a possible cultural-historical bias on the part of the scientific observer, it seems reasonable to accept drawbacks in reliability and to try to improve intersubjective validity by drawing on more 'qualitative' ethnographic techniques developed in cultural studies and ethnography instead of performing structured observations (Hallett/Barber 2014). Typical examples would be historical research projects that are not only interested in questions of the mere perceptibility or intensity of phenomena, but also in certain forms of aesthetic, emotional or social judgments. Hence, to ensure the intersubjectivity of the phenomenological findings from these scenarios, we recommend that researchers try to formulate "thick descriptions" (Geertz 1973) of their subjective impressions in the form of extensive written field notes or by employing think-aloud techniques (Bryman 2008a). To increase traceability of this subjective interpretive data, it should be enriched by locative data (positions, distances and actual movement in the VHE) and audiovisual-field recordings (screenshots, short movies and audio renderings) which would help other scholars to understand and trace the personal interpretations and conclusions. Furthermore, researchers performing cyber phenomenology in this way should explicitly disclose the stocks of historical cultural knowledge that they actively employ when trying to put themselves into the hermeneutic position of a contemporary observer. By triangulating these different forms of data in an interpretive analysis, which may also compare the field notes of a smaller number of researchers visiting the same scenario, a *grounded theory* (Bryant/Charmaz 2011) about previously unknown mechanisms and phenomena in the field may then be developed. Taken together, qualitative ethnographic techniques appear well suited for more open-ended, explorative historical studies using VHEs that try to arrive at new hypotheses.

9. Combining structured observations and ethnographic techniques

Obviously, ethnographic techniques and structured observations can also be combined in a complementary way to accommodate for each of their tradeoffs. Taking the research example discussed above, a historical scientist could have first ethnographically explored several VHEs with different historical versions of the Forum Romanum to arrive subsequently at the grounded theory that some of the positional changes of the Rostra must have been related to acoustic problems. This could give rise to an additional study employing structured observations in the same VHE in order to test this hypothesis statistically.

10. New knowledge based on existing evidence?

A final remark will be made on the possible future role of virtual environments and the related observation techniques we envision within an epistemological model of historiographical research. If the empirical material collected by historians is regarded as material traces of historical events that give rise to collective inferences regarding 'common causes' (Tucker 2004), one still has to explain the additional value of virtual environments, when these can only be based on evidence that is already known. Every aspect of the example simulation of the virtual Forum Romanum discussed in this article, from the forum's architecture and the surrounding buildings to the location of the Rostra was based on previous knowledge in classical archeology, and the computer model did not bring to light any new historical evidence.

Nevertheless, we see three ways in which new knowledge could emerge from virtual or augmented historical environments. First, by systematically relating together scattered bits of information (about the architecture, the architectural materials used, the location of the Rostra, the text of the speech) within a model of sound or light propagation, new information can be derived that was already embedded in the historical evidence available but had not been combined before. Thus, the scientific theories about sound or light propagation take on the role of *nomic regularities,* which carry "nested information" about the source of information, i.e. the original historical events (Tucker 2004, 18 f.).[6] This is similar to the application of natural laws about the ageing of materials in order to extrapolate the original appearance of the materials from the existing remains together with knowledge about the climatic conditions of the past. Since disciplines such as geology, meteorology, the material sciences or acoustics are currently intensively involved with the development of computer models for the dynamic, i.e. time-related, behavior of physical systems, the historical sciences would do well to exploit the wealth of nomic regularities inherent in these models.

Second, since virtual or augmented environments are able to lift the numerical variables of computer models to the level of sensory signals, they not only convey more comprehensive information on questions concerning the perceptual impression of historical environments; these are also easier to access explanatorily for non-experts in the respective scientific domain. A prediction of the speech intelligibility in the ancient Forum Romanum could, in principle, already be made based on information about the sound power of trained speakers, the distance between speaker and audience, the reverberation time of the place and the noise level generated by the audience. However, the analytical relations involved are themselves derived from psychophysical experiments. As statistical correlations, they have only limited accuracy when predicting the intelligibility of presentations of texts in a specific language with a specific rhetorical strategy from several listening perspectives. And it is one thing to know that the predicted speech transmission index (STI) at a certain place in the audience has a value of 0.7 and another thing to be able to listen to the virtualization of the speech in different places in the audience – at least for listeners who are not familiar with the meaning of STI values. Insofar, VHEs help to explore the actual perceptual meaning of coefficients derived from mere numerical simulations.

6 At this point, Tucker applies Dretske's information theoretical concept of knowledge and knowledge production to the historical sciences (cf. Dretske 1981, 71 f).

And finally, the integration of knowledge stocks from different academic disciplines, required for the empirically substantiated design of virtual historic environments, might make these a focal point of interdisciplinary cooperation, where scientific knowledge from areas as far apart as classical archeology, architectural and building history, the history of rhetoric, room acoustics and speech acoustics converge at one common point. And the history of science is full of examples of new knowledge emerging from a new and unusual cooperation between different disciplines.

References

Bearman, D. (2011): "3D Representations in Museums." In: *Curator: The Museum Journal* 54 (1), 55–61.

Bogdanovych, A./Rodriguez-Aguilar, J. A./Simoff, S./Cohen, A. (2010): "Authentic Interactive Reenactment of Cultural Heritage with 3D Virtual Worlds and Artificial Intelligence." In: *Applied Artificial Intelligence* 24(6), 617–647.

Bogen, J. (2014): "Theory and Observation in Science." In: E. N. Zalta (ed.), *The Stanford Encyclopedia of Philosophy* (Summer 2014). http://plato.stanford.edu/archives/sum2014/entries/science-theory-observation/ (accessed 10.1.2016).

Bork, I. (2005a): "Report on the 3rd Round Robin on Room Acoustical Computer Simulation, Part I: Measurements." In: *Acta Acustica united with Acustica* 91(4), 740–752.

Bork, I. (2005b): "Report on the 3rd Round Robin on Room Acoustical Computer Simulation, Part II: Calculations." In: *Acta Acustica united with Acustica* 91(4), 753–763.

Brinkmann, F./Lindau, A./Vrhovnik, M./Weinzierl, S. (2014). "Assessing the Authenticity of Individual Dynamic Binaural Synthesis." In: *Proc. of the EAA Joint Symposium on Auralization and Ambisonics, Berlin*, 62–68.

Bryant, A./Charmaz, K. (2011): "Grounded Theory." In: M. Williams/W. P. Vogt (ed.), *The SAGE Handbook of Innovation in Social Research METHODS*, Los Angeles et al.: SAGE, 205–227.

Bryman, A. (2008a): "Ethnography and Participant Observation." In: *Social Research Methods. 3rd Edition*, Oxford: Oxford University Press, 400–434.

Bryman, A. (2008b): "Structured Observation." In: *Social Research Methods. 3rd Edition.* Oxford: Oxford University Press, 253–272.

Dretske, F. I. (1981): *Knowledge and the Flow of Information*, Cambridge, MA: MIT Press.

Durante, F./Riedel, V. (2008): *Round Robin Numerical Flow Simulation in Wind Energy. Final Report.* http://www.dewi.de/dewi/fileadmin/pdf/publications/Studies/Round%20Robin/round-robin-flowsimulation-final-report.pdf (accessed 10.1.2016).

Geertz, C. (1973): "Thick Description: Toward an Interpretive Theory of Culture." In: *The Interpretation of Cultures: Selected Essays*, New York: Basic Books, 3–30.

Gehrau, V. (2002): *Die Beobachtung in der Kommunikationswissenschaft: Methodische Ansätze und Beispielstudien*, Konstanz: UTB GmbH.

Gernsheim, H./Gernsheim, A. (1969): *L.J.M. Daguerre: The History of the Diorama and the Daguerreotype*, Dover: Dover Publications.

Hallett, R. E./Barber, K. (2014): “Ethnographic Research in a Cyber Era.” In: *Journal of Contemporary Ethnography* 43(3), 306–330. DOI: 10.1177/0891241613497749.
Houliez, C./Gamble, E. (2012): “Dwelling in Second Life? A phenomenological evaluation of online virtual worlds.” In: *Virtual Reality* 17(4), 263–278, DOI: 10.1007/s10055-012-0218-1.
Kochinka, A. (2010): “Beobachtung.” In: G. Mey/K. Mruck (eds.), *Handbuch Qualitative Forschung in der Psychologie*, Berlin: Springer, 449–461, http://link.springer.com/chapter/10.1007/978-3-531-92052-8_32 (accessed 10.1.2016).
Lercari, N. (2016): “Simulating History in Virtual Worlds.” In: Y. Sivan (ed.), *Handbook on 3D3C Platforms*, Berlin: Springer, 337–352.
Lindau, A./Erbes, V./Lepa, S./Maempel, H.-J./Brinkmann, F./Weinzierl, S. (2014): “A Spatial Audio Quality Inventory for Virtual Acoustic Environments (SAQI).” In: *Acta Acustica United with Acustica* 100, 984–994.
Lindau, A./Weinzierl, S. (2012): “Assessing the Plausibility of Virtual Acoustic Environments.” In: *Acta Acustica United with Acustica* 98, 804–810.
Lindau, A./Kosanke, L./Weinzierl, S. (2012): “Perceptual Evaluation of Model- and Signal-based Predictors of the Mixing time in Binaural Room Impulse Responses.” In: *Journal of the Audio Engineering Society* 60(11), 887–898.
Lindau, A./Weinzierl, S. (2009): “On the Spatial Resolution of Virtual Acoustic Environments for Head Movements in Horizontal, Vertical and Lateral Direction.” In: *EAA Symposium on Auralization*, Helsinki, 1–6.
Lombard, M./Ditton, T. (1997): “At the Heart of It All: The Concept of Presence.” In: *Journal of Computer-Mediated Communication* 3(2). DOI: 10.1111/j.1083–6101.1997.tb00072.x.
Lombardo, V./Valle, A./Fitch, J./Tazelaar, K./Weinzierl, S./Borczyk, W. (2009): “A Virtual-Reality Reconstruction of Poéme Électronique Based on Philological Research.” In: *Computer Music Journal* 33(2), 24–47.
Markham, A. N. (1998): *Life Online: Researching Real Experience in Virtual Space*, Lanham: Rowman Altamira.
Mikropoulos, T. A./Natsis, A. (2011): “Educational virtual environments: A ten-year review of empirical research (1999–2009).” In: *Computers & Education* 56(3), 769–780.
Oettermann, S. (1980): *Das Panorama. Die Geschichte eines Massenmediums,* Frankfurt on Main: Syndikat.
Pujol, L./Champion, E. (2012): “Evaluating Presence in Cultural Heritage Projects.” In: *International Journal of Heritage Studies* 18(1), 83–102.
Rubinstein, R. Y./Kroese, D. P. (2008): *Simulation and the Monte Carlo Method*, New York: Wiley.
Schaerer Kalkandjiev, Z./Weinzierl, S. (2015): “The Influence of Room Acoustics on Solo Music Performance: An Experimental Study.” In: *Psychomusicology: Music, Mind & Brain* 25(3), 195–207.
Stogner, M. B. (2009): “The Media-enhanced Museum Experience: Debating the use of Media Technology in Cultural Exhibitions.” In: *Curator: The Museum Journal* 52(4), 385–397.
Tucker, A. (2004): *Our Knowledge of the Past. A Philosophy of Historiography*, Cambridge: Cambridge University Press.
Veling, W./Brinkman, W.-P./Dorrestijn, E./van der Gaag, M. (2013): “Virtual Reality Experiments Linking Social Environment and Psychosis: A Pilot Study.” In: *Cyberpsychology, Behavior, and Social Networking* 17(3), 191–195. DOI: 10.1089/cyber.2012.0497.

Vorländer, M. (2008): *Auralization: Fundamentals of Acoustics, Modelling, Simulation, Algorithms and Acoustic Virtual Reality*, Berlin: Springer.

Part 2: Ontological Problems in Augmented Reality

Pirmin Stekeler-Weithofer

Scientific Truth as Augmented Reality: On the Contrast between '*Wirklichkeit*' and 'Actuality'

Abstract: There is an empiricist prejudice deeply entrenched in the vagueness of English as a language for reflections on experience and cognition, knowledge and science, truth and reality. It results in a parochial way of contemporary 'international' philosophy. One of its core problems consists in a suitable understanding of the notions of forces and causes, dispositions and faculties. In recollection of Ancient and Kantian terminology, we can learn from Hegel, the great foe of immediacy, that real reality is a modal notion. It is conceptually Augmented Reality and, as such, a theoretically articulated possibility, which is in addition, on the ground of good reasons, evaluated as '*wirklich*'.

Keywords: actuality, *Wirklichkeit*, real reality, appearance, empirical cognition, conceptualized knowledge, evaluated possibility

1. Reality and reason

Reality is appearance augmented by reason. This gnomic thesis talks about a different augmentation of reality than we have it in virtual reality. Nevertheless, there is an important similarity or even an identical feature. In virtual reality, too, the augmentation consists in adding possibilities. This is the reason why a reflection on Hegel's insight that reality is a modal notion can be illuminating in our context of reflection.

One of the most notorious oracles of philosophy is Hegel's statement that the real is reasonable and the reasonable real. Hegel himself complains in the foreword of his *Philosophy of Right* that an author, who has written two books on the topic, could hope that the learned public would be in a position to interpret a gnomic formula like this in its intended meaning. This precludes arbitrary connotations, which a naïve reader might have when he first meets a formula like "reality and reason are the same". Unfortunately, a whole tradition of interpretations read the corresponding sentences in Hegel's oeuvre in a mystical way and identify Hegel's philosophy with a kind of spiritualism ('*Geistphilosophie*'). It is, however, not too easy to show that these readings are wrong – and even obviously so, if one has undertaken the labour to really read Hegel's texts and not

DOI 10.1515/9783110497656-005

just to muse about some of his Heraclitean aphorisms, which turn his work into a kind of Wagnerian drama with few lights in a complex and therefore seemingly dark texture.

However, I am not concerned here with an interpretation of Hegel's work as a whole, not even of particular parts, rather with a systematic background that lies at the bottom of its problems. This background concerns the notion of reality ('*Wirklichkeit*') in its contrast to actuality ('*empirische Realität*'). Hegel's approach reconstructs the contrast in the context of a radical project. It is the project of reframing the distinctions between empirical and conceptual (time-general, generic) propositions. Empirical propositions are (the contents of) statements about present or historical states of affairs a posteriori. They rest on qualitative differentiations, checked on the ground of sensation and perception, and say that something is a fact, for example that it is raining here and now – whereas yesterday in Berlin the weather was fine. Obviously, empirical statements presuppose a time and space of a speaker or at least a determination of a time and place from our perspective as in the case of naming the dates ('*anno domini*'). We also often need a determination of the spatial domain where an event has taken place or still is taking place – according to the corresponding ascertainment. In short, empirical statements are heavily indexical, historical. Their truth is always evaluated ex post, namely by us here and now. The qualitative distinctions that define the fulfilment- or truth- conditions refer in some way to actual situations.

We always actually make some differences. Even animals do this; but humans always already invest some generic knowledge in the form of conceptual commentaries or 'eidetic' sentences that tell us 'in general' something about the type or genus of what we refer to and how we distinguish it from other things. This means, in turn, that a person's actual perceptions always already stand in some definite relation to indefinitely many other possible perceptions as different ways of access to the very same object from other perspectives, for example yours at other times or theirs in the future. If I say, for example, that there is milk in the fridge, we presuppose to know what milk is. We also assume that milk as such is not poisonous. Such knowledge tells us something about the genus or species of the thing about which we empirically talk. Generic truths about milk as such or 'in itself' already 'transcend' in quite some important sense the presence of its empirical appearance in some way or other.

Hegel's basic observation now is this. The traditional notion of empirical knowledge in its contrast to eternal truth is conceptual blunder. This is so because there are no eternal substances like atomic matter at all – not to speak of souls, angels and gods. Everything in the world is finite. It has a beginning and an end, just as any living being has. This holds also good for any bodily thing and, of course, for any limited process and event. It holds for atoms just as for subatomic particles. It holds for suns and stars just as for individual persons and animals, even species and families of living creatures. The only time-general things and truths are generic, pure, and abstract. Such things are forms. Pure knowledge is knowledge about forms. Such knowledge is conceptually presupposed a priori in a relative sense when the corresponding concepts or words are applied to some or many empirical cases. The generic status of the sentences provides the reason why mathematics is so important for philosophy. We find here the paradigm case of pure knowledge as knowledge about ideal objects or forms that are applied in empirical knowledge. Philosophy is also (only) concerned with knowledge about forms, but not just with the ideal forms of mathematics. Philosophy reflects on the real forms of knowledge about the world and about ourselves.

Our question concerning the difference between empirical actuality and objective reality now runs already at its start into some formidable terminological problems. This is so because the Latin and English translations of Greek differentiations produce internal inconsistencies. One of it had already appeared above, where I 'translated' the word "actuality" by the German-Latin word "*Realität*" and the German word "*Wirklichkeit*" by the English-Latin expression "(real) reality". The problem here is this: "actuality" is thought to correspond to Greek "*energeia*". Therefore, its correct translation into German is "*Wirklichkeit*". For the German word expresses the actualizing *work* of some dynamic power, force, 'dunamis', which *produces* some *phenomena* (*Erscheinungen*). From the appearances we 'infer' their underlying 'causes', the real reality behind the merely *actual appearances*. The problem is that the word "actuality" refers much more to the empirical appearances here and now than to the mode of being of lasting objects. These objects are addressed as the causes of their appearances. As such, they are said to have forces and dispositions that can produce stimuli with certain responses. And they are already classified, sortal objects. The domain of the objects is a genus, species or type. Corresponding generic dispositions, faculties, possibilities belong to what Aristotle had called *energeia* and what still is understood in the German terms *wirklich* and *Wirklichkeit* – such that I will translate the latter by *real reality* in a kind of contextual terminology, proposed for our purpose. In fact, at least the everyday understanding of the word "actuality" refers to *present* appearances and *not* to its underlying 'real' or 'objective' reality. Precisely this fact leads to some confusions as they already have appeared above. The English word "actuality" has changed its logical place from the realm of causes and forces that explain or produce actual appearances to the empirical domain of appearances. But the appearances are a mere 'sign' for the real objects that produce them, or rather, we must infer an underlying reality from the appearances in the mode of abduction, by a principle of best explanation, which was made explicit and famous by Charles Sanders Peirce. This mode of abductive inference is the very reason for the conceptually necessary 'fallibility' of objective statements about *real reality.*

This shows already in which sense real reality is already in itself augmented reality. In the following, we shall explore some of the features of the 'augmentation' of actuality by reason that turns it into 'real reality'. And we shall see in which sense Hegel's insight is not at all a spooky and extravagant 'theory' about the real world – another word for real reality – as the object of *thinking* and not just of *perceiving.* For what we perceive are actual appearances, not their real, objective, causes.

Actuality is Hegel's "*Realität*" – in the sense of Kant's "*realitas phaenomenon*". As such, it belongs to the domain of qualitative distinctions, which we make partly individually, partly together in present situations. We invest, of course, subjectively and jointly accessible appearances, for example on the ground of deictical observations and collectively learned qualitative distinctions, which can be as primitive as that between 'it's raining', 'it's snowing' and 'the sun shines' – taken as a holophrastic expressions for fine weather. In fact, nobody really thinks already of the sun as a star that produces heat when he says that the sun shines in contrast to stormy or foggy weather. And if a child says "mama", "papa" or, later, "uncle", she often does not yet make distinctions between her real father or uncle and what looks as a father or uncle. In the case of "mama", the toddler perhaps does not do more than distinguish *practically* between situations in which mama is there and cases when she misses her. Even though the toddler certainly already can distinguish between her real mother and mother-substitutes, she does not yet use the word "mama" as 'naming an object with properties'. We do this only later after we have learnt the differences between grammatical roles, for example the special function of the word "mama" in a context like "mama is the best mother of the world". Here, "mama" has turned into a (local, relativized) 'proper name' – as we can see by the identification with the (local, relativized) definite description "the best mother" (from the point of view of the speaker).

2. Presence in its absolute position

Talking about objects in real reality already transcends actuality. This is so because the object does not have to be here – whereas qualitative distinctions work only in present actuality, in deictical contexts and situations. The Eiffel-

Tower in Paris, for example, is an object in the real world, but not in my actual surrounding here and now.

By the way, there is only one world, the real world of real reality. Talking about possible worlds is talking about the content of possible stories or state descriptions that never add up to a whole world. We therefore prefer talking about possible things, events, states of affairs or objects in the world and not about 'the actual' world in contrast to some 'possible worlds' – which are in possible-world-semantics anyway nothing but mathematical models.

In any case, qualitative distinctions rest on some 'showing', which includes non-visual ways of producing some joint distinctions on the ground of our five or six senses (seeing, hearing, touching, smelling, tasting and having a holistic bodily proprioception). The '6th' sense is often unhappily neglected, as the example of producing joint feelings of horror, fear, surprise can show as well as all kinds of depressing or hilarious moods. The unquestionable point however is this: Qualitative distinctions cannot surpass the domain of some more or less spatially and temporally limited *present processes* which we distinguish practically, in enactive perception. This happens in a way similar to how animals live in a limited presence. It is important, though, not to reduce presence to a mere moment (Nietzsche's *Augenblick*). Presence always is extended relative to ongoing processes in the near future. But presence never extends to merely possible events in the distant future (or past, or to fictional 'worlds').

The distinction between present actuality and mere possibilities is absolutely crucial for any correct understanding of the difference between the life form of animal and the life of human persons. For we have access to non-present possibilities only by some mediation or re-presentation. The most import means for such re-presentations is language. It is the easiest and 'cheapest' form of producing arbitrary representations aloud or silently. Drawing pictures and sketches or 'representing' them silently in mute 'thinking' or 'imagining' is already more 'expensive'. The differential and inferential conditions of fulfilment for pictures and images are much less 'precise' than the already 'digitalized' forms of language with its normalized or canonized conceptual criteria of differentiation and default forms of dispositional inferences, conditioned by further differentiations.

In contrast to qualitative differentiations together with corresponding verbal signs and signals (which we already find in the animal kingdom in a rudimentary way, too) humans can refer to non-present possibilities by 'thinking', i.e. by using language silently or publicly. Lewis Carroll would have said that one would need very sharp eyes to 'see' possibilities. And Hegel adds to this truism the insight that the only access to a mere possibility is indeed by *thinking*, i.e. by *representing* a possible state of affairs by some present linguistic act, for example by a description. In order to neglect inessential differentiations – like any structural analysis should do – I incorporate the cases of representations that use images or pictures into a broad notion of 'language'. Then, silent 'representations' of images, diagrams, sketches, writings, sequences of films and so on also count as silent production of 'language'. We represent, for example, a piece of music not only by silently 'hearing it' but also by some 'tacit' visual 'representation' of its musical notation. The notation helps a lot to 'represent' some complex piece of music – as the example of pianists show who certainly 'represent' in some tacit way or other the notes they play. Tacit thinking is therefore not more mysterious then reading a book silently. In fact, the cases are identical in form. As a result, we obviously must distinguish two different uses of the word "representation", the representation of possible states of affairs by some language and the inner, silent, representation of some sequences of language in tacit 'thinking'. There is no special language of thought as Jerry Fodor holds, tacitly suggesting a relation like that between a higher and lower computer language like Fortran and Assembler, where the latter is closer to the so called machine-language of the hardware.

We now slowly approach the core insight of Hegel's 'identification' of real reality with *reason* by reading it as conceptually augmented reality. In the contrast between 'experience' in the sense of 'actuality' and 'real causes', the latter are assumed as 'real objects' that 'produce' appearances via certain sensual stimuli causally. Hegel's word for actuality is, at first, *Dasein*, which we could translate as *presence*. In presence, all our practical, perhaps already joint, distinctions of qualities take place. If we look at the differences made from a logical point of view, the causes of the appearances, so called, are, in a sense, mere possibilities.

In classical empiricism, one jumps right into a speculative, metaphysical, theory according to which the qualitative differentiations are *prompted* by physical causations. The things are said to *produce* impressions (Locke, Hume), sense data (Russell, Ayer) or stimulus meanings (Quine). However, talking like this is just forgetting the logical analysis of perceptual judgments that are no automatic reactions triggered by sensations at all. Rather, the objective things as they are mystified in empiricism are in a sense 'absent' from the sheer presence of appearances. This is so because they are already generic things, typified and abstract. Such a thing is a thing in itself, but in the sense of Hegel, not in the sense of Kant. Kant uses the expression in order to talk about things totally beyond the reach of human knowledge. Such a use is incoherent, as Hegel shows in quite some details.

However, we need an immanent distinction between generic things as such and concrete things in-an-for-themselves, as Hegel labels the case of some reference to real objects in real reality. The word "concrete" comes from Latin "*con-*

crescere" and says that the generic properties that are necessarily fulfilled if the thing falls under the species in question and the individual object we refer to are 'grown together'. Only such concrete objects are real things in real reality. They are always already specified and typified objects, laden with dispositions and therefore dependent on 'their' concept. This concept, in turn, depends on a whole system of concepts, i.e. on a whole theory, as we today would say. Talking about the lion as such or in itself is speaking about the genus or species of lions in precisely this sense. Saying that this animal over there is a lioness means claiming that she is a female animal of the corresponding species with the corresponding faculties and dispositions. We would or could already evaluate the claim as wrong if the animal were dead, not only if it is only a fake lion.

We usually do not realize these logical facts about our talk about things as causes of appearances in the way we should. It should be clear that we have to take them into account in order to understand what we do when we say, e.g., that we *see* a green shirt in the department store and say, nevertheless, that 'in reality' the shirt is blue or bluish. 'Immediately' we might see a 'bent stick' in the water; but we might assume – and even fishing birds do similar things enactively – that the stick is nevertheless straight. What we see – and even distinguish together in the yellow light of the store – is, obviously, not the *blue* shirt, but a *green* shirt; and the *bent* stick appears to us as 'objectively' as a fata morgana in the desert. Only by *thinking*, i.e. by reference to a possible future, can we say that the stick as such is *not* bent and that, what we see as an oasis, is *only* an optical illusion.

Of course, while acknowledging that real reality is a modal concept, a kind of possibility, we do not have already explained the difference between mere possible cases and real cases. In fact, this is the crucial point. While nobody denies, if she is sane, that we cannot have access to possibilities if not by thinking, imagining, story-telling, or picturing, the very contrast between possibilities and reality misleads people, first, *not* to accept the insight that reality *is* a kind of possibility and, second, to confuse reality with actuality. The latter confusion lies at the ground of the whole tradition of empiricism and its illusions of immediacy.

Empiricism is, all in all, a speculative 'theory' of knowledge that reconstructs 'knowing' as a slightly developed kind of animal cognition. This is the deep reason why Berkeley, Hume and the empiricists cannot make sense of science at all – as Kant has realized and Hegel, the great foe of immediacy (Wilfrid Sellars) has convincingly shown. No wonder that Russell, the logical atomist and arch-logical empiricist, did not agree – and declared in his History of Western Philosophy that he believed that everything is wrong what Hegel has said. It is up to us to decide the implications of this statement for what Russell himself believes as true.

In any case, Hegel's reframing of the debate has quite important consequences. The first point is that we have access to real reality – just as to mere possibilities – only mediated by thinking, not just by perception. The second point is that evaluating a possibility as a *real* possibility in contrast to a *mere* possibility says that we should count with the possibility in our actions and plans. This is the crucial difference to merely counterfactual states of affairs told in fairy tales or divine myths. We do not and should not count with them in the world. They tell us what is not the case; but we may use them to represent *ex negativo* most general features of our world. If we talk, for example, about an almighty or all-knowing god, we just represent in a *negative* way some most general facts. According to Hegel, our talks about a utopian, non-existent, god show in a negative way the perspectival limitations of human faculties to act or to know things. These faculties are finite, but real. For example, we cannot travel into the past or into the future. Nobody can. However, we can make this fact and its limitations explicit by augmenting real reality by some *utopian and speculative* image of a god beyond all appearances. In fact, this is the very function of speculative sentences. Only negative theology is true theology; and only negative philosophy is true philosophy.

The problem of a more radical approach to avoid *any* 'speculative' talk as Hume famously has proposed consists in the fact that it makes reflections on whole domains of discourse in the world impossible. As a result, empiricism is the attitude to behave rationally without self- consciousness. Even if there is no god who could be in a position to wind 'the film' of the world back and forth – and this in no time, the image helps to see what it means to look at the world as a limited whole *sub specie aeterni*, as Wittgenstein does in his *Tractatus*. Once again, the situation is related to the games and films of virtual reality.

But how to reconstruct the more narrow distinction between a merely real *possibility* and real *reality?* The distinction is crucial because it is the distinction between well-justified belief in a real possibility and world-related empirical knowledge about real things and not only generic normal conditions. However, in empirical knowledge about what we really perceive, singular empirical observations and perceptions are already grown together with generic judgments and expectations. Hegel's deepest insight is here that the truth conditions not only of generic truths about a whole species of things in general but also about concrete objects go far beyond descriptions of 'merely subjective' appearances and involve judgements of the form of *dialectical reason*. We shall see what this means in our further consideration.

Any real possibility is represented by its generic description. It is evaluated as *real* by the judgment that it is *reasonable* to *count* with it. When, for example, a reliable weather-forecast tells us that in the evening there is a high probability of rain or even of a thunder-storm, hikers in the mountains are well advised to count with the corresponding possibilities, despite the fact that in the morning there might have been fine weather and no immediate sign for the possible tempest. Here, the above explanation seems to be obviously correct: A claim that says that a possibility is real says that we reasonably should *count* with it. *One should*, for example, *not* count with the merely formal, verbal, possibility that one will not die, not to mention other weird possibilities as 'traveling' to King's Arthur's court. There are many other fairy tales which we should not consider as representing real possibilities, for example in science fictions in which the content of a brain is 'copied' into an 'avatar' or other nice but counter factual analogies between humans and robots.

3. Dilemmas of epistemology

How do we, or how can we, now *sharpen* the notion of a *real possibility* and turn it into *real reality?* Hegel's answer seems to most of his readers still a mystery and much more to non-readers. For the answer uses words like "dialectical" and "sublation" (*Aufhebung*), which are even less understood than words like "actual", "empirical" and "real". It is not too difficult to explain them, though, if we realize that it is always *us* (no angel and no god) who have to evaluate what counts as 'real', 'objective' and 'true'. This holds even for our own explanations corresponding assurances. If we join Hegel's approach and look 'realistically' at what we 'really' do when evaluating the objectivity and truth of some world-related knowledge claim, we must acknowledge the following:

1) I as a person claim that some of my statements about some real state of affairs are true. My claim is, at first sight, only an expression of my 'belief', 'contention', 'opinion', *doxa*, even when I produces already more or less 'good' evidence or justifications for my 'belief'.

2) As a result, I as an individual subject alone cannot distinguish between my certainty about what I *hold* true or believe to be real and count as my *knowledge* – in some contrast to what I count only as my belief in a real possibility. This is the reason for the most famous, and most misunderstood, gnomic oracle of Socrates, who did not say, according to Plato "I know that I know nothing", but "I know that I do *not know*". In other words, Socrates knows that the declaration of a sentence of the form "I know that p" (for example "I know that there is milk in the fridge, I have checked") can express *only* a more or less well-justified belief.

After the writings of Edmund Gettier, there is a wide-spread discussion about Plato's 'definition' of *knowledge* as *true* belief with *good* arguments. However, we better deepen our reconstruction of Plato's arguments and try to read his formula "*alethes doxa meta logou*" as "true judgment with *sufficient proof*" – just as Theaitetos has a true belief about the fact that the roots of natural numbers that are irrational if they are no whole numbers – and a totally general and sufficient proof. In world-related judgments (like about the milk in the fridge) it is not too clear what a sufficient proof is or how we possibly can attain one. This is so because world-related knowledge is fallible. It is fallible because it can turn out wrong by chance. It can turn our wrong by accident since its very contents surpass systematically what we can control from our limited point of perspective. It surpasses immediate perceptival control by its conceptual form. This conceptual form consists in the fact that judgements about the objects perceived are generically thick, inferentially and dispositionally laden.

Moreover, exactly for these cases and not for the cases of mathematics Socrates' laconic gnomon applies, that he has learned on the ground of his logical and philosophical reflections (from Heraclit, by the way) that from the mere standpoint of the subjective speaker there is no 'absolute' fulfilment of the condition of knowledge. The result is that the "I know that there is mild in the fridge" always remains, in a sense, a well justified judgment about a real possibility. It does not yet count as knowledge about real reality. This is so because we know about contingent possibilities of errors. This leads many readers to assume that Socrates was the father of Scepticism and that Plato 'abuses' the figure for his 'Platonist dogmatism'. Even though I think that this is wrong, the problem and task is to overcome scepticism in a 'realist' reconstruction of a concept of knowledge. How do we know something about real reality? How does it relate to appearances? How does it surpass or transcend the too meagre notion of "well-justified belief" – evaluated as true by some third party?

One of these parties is the narrator of a Gettier-story, who tells us what allegedly is or was wrong, what true. Think, for example, of Alvin Goldman's case of a Potemkin village built around a barn: In this case Goldman, knows that his figure does not 'know' that she stands in front of a barn even though it is true and she has very good reasons to believe that the façade she looks at is the façade of a barn.

4. From believing in possibilities to knowledge of reality

Real reality is theoretically augmented reality, applied to empirical experience. This means that real reality is not just a real possibility defined by merely qualitative terms and distinctions as they are reconstructed in a 'Tractarian' picture of logically complex empirical propositions. They rather contain already theoretically 'thick' concepts and 'entities' which cannot be directly 'perceived' as such like 'forces' (energies) and 'dispositions' (as the content of conditional inferences or rational expectations).

Again, Lewis Carroll would have said that we would need *very* strong eyes to 'see' forces, powers, energies, causes and the like, by which we *augment* the mere actuality of present qualities by their real explanations. How turn causes, forces, powers and dispositions into 'objects of dialectical reason'? Before we answer this crucial question, we should point out that no empiricist ever can provide us with a sufficient account of what forces and causes are. Even though I can only state the point here, everybody who nevertheless is convinced of some empiricist account has a poor taste for what is a sufficiently good explanation. This holds, for example, for Hume's transposition of 'causes' from a 'deeper' level of theoretical thick explanations to the 'surface level' of merely regular sequences of present events. This seemingly 'critical' move, directed against allegedly metaphysical entities 'behind' the phenomena, destroys in the end any scientific explanations. Russell realizes this, even though he himself falls prey to the empiricist illusion of an immediate access to the real world by perception and cannot give an account for the logical *difference* of talking about forces and causes and talking about empirical events and sequences of events. The same holds for the early Wittgenstein, who defended, in the *Tractatus*, a variant of Russell's world view of logical atomism and, *therefore*, joins Hume in the claim that the 'belief in a causal nexus is the superstition'. This is driving the Devil out with Beelzebub, or rather, an overkill-argument against *any* causal explanations, produced on the ground of the wrong idea, all sentence of the 'natural sciences' were 'empirical sentences' about some 'many or all 'empirical events' and 'states of affairs' here or there, now or then. However, not *one* scientific sentence has the *indexical* and *temporal* form of *empirical* statements. All of them are *generic* sentences or rules that apply to prototypical cases, to a genus of things and processes, to stereotypes or ideal types. All these sentences are, in their very logical form, time-general, as Sebastian Rödl calls it.

What are the truth conditions of such *generic* statements? What kind of 'knowledge' is it that we produce in the sciences? This is, indeed, a deep question in Hegel's *Science of Logic*. The answer is that the truth conditions of the sentences of the sciences, including the sciences about human institutions called "*Geisteswissenschaften*", are the result of a worldwide *work on the concept. The concept* is, in turn, a generic label for the overall system of canonized default dispositions and inferences grounded on generic distinctions that govern reasonable expectations and reasonable judgments not only about real possibilities, but also about real realities, by which we explain actual qualities generically. In other words, we set our actual, qualitative, distinctions into a larger framework of theoretical generalities. And we say that what appears to us in actual perception (empirical 'experience') as an A is a real A only if A shows a whole system of features that are generically attributed to a thing of the generic kind of a particular kind exemplified by the individual (empirical) case (at present). What must be true about A such goes far beyond the mere judgment that this or that *appears* to me or you to be an A.

In our case of the milk in the fridge, I can err, even when I have checked if there is milk in the fridge, for example if the white liquid is say milk, or if it has already gone off or if it poisoned stuff. As we can see, the very truth of the claim "There is milk in the fridge" depends on *normal* conditions just like the truth of "this shirt is green". The fallibility of my knowledge in the store if the shirt is really green corresponds in a sense to the fallibility of my knowledge if there is really real milk in the fridge – which depends, in turn, on the relevant 'level' of 'sufficient proof'. Unfortunately the very notion of sufficient proof and, hence, the very notions of real (not merely ideal, utopian, divine) knowledge and truth behave like a moving target, as Plato already knew. The problem is that generic truths explicating conceptual conditions are ideal and indefinite. As a result, we can always add further conditions in such a way that no individual and no limited *group* of individuals can ever *finally* determine the fulfilment of *all* such conditions. The case is clear for geometrical ideas or ideal forms like circles or straight lines. It is a conceptual truism that in the real world there are no real, i.e. ideal circles – as empiricists like Protagoras and Hume have stressed. This should not lead us to sceptical relativism but to a relational reading of ideal concepts as Plato already has developed it. Assume, for example, that we two have agreed that there is milk in the fridge, for we went there, took it and drank it and were pleased with it as (normal) milk. In such a case it still 'can' happen, that we two are dead in the evening and the coroner determines form the content of our stomach that it was *no* (normal, healthy) milk.

Since all systems of conceptual fulfilment are indefinite, ideal, and no real case fulfils all ideal condition of a concept, just as no real figure is a perfect circle. We therefore always need realistic 'measures' or 'thresholds' A_c of the following pragmatic form: If something is 'better' than A_c, it is already a *good enough* C in the real world. Plato's refutation of scepticism and his relativization of fallibilism uses in fact this insight: Just as Kebes is tall only with respect to Socrates, but small with respect to Simmias, any one-place predicate stems from *relations* and needs the fixation of *appropriate* relevant 'measures' or 'parameters'. Moreover, any evaluation of truth and knowledge, i.e. of *sufficient proof*, refers to a *relevant generic* we-group. Therefore, it is not true that only *God* knows anything, as Heraclitus still seems to say and as many readers believe that Socrates had followed him. Rather, there is always a formally indefinite, ideally infinite progress of evaluation of evaluations … of truth and knowledge of individuals and groups. This is a general form defining truth and knowledge. There is nothing to complain about the indefinite regress, just as there is nothing to complain about the fact that in 'empirical reality', i.e. mere actuality, there are no ideal circles, angles, straight lines and the like. This general feature *appears* to the naïve thinker, not introduced into the mysteries of logical semantics, to be a sufficient reason for scepticism, at least fallibilism. The position says that there is no clear distinction between the pragmatic notion of real possibility and real reality. However, we all work with the contrast. It is not only a possibility that you will find the Eiffel-Tower in Paris if you go there.

The problem is, of course, that we do not take in every situation all the relevant parameters into account – and deal correspondingly with counterfactual conditions. In *normal* cases, the question if there is milk in the fridge and if I know it is settled, for example if you confirm my knowledge by your score-keeping and undertaking my 'proof' – and this "you" can be narrow or wide, even generic. It just has to be wide enough. It should not remain limited to a too small we-group.

In any case, only because of the indefinite possibility to turn real reality into a *mere* possibility it *seems* as if we do *not* know anything. Nevertheless, we *know* many things, as well and perfect, as any knowing of truths can be, namely when we evaluate the *relevant* proof conditions as sufficiently fulfilled. In mathematics, this is the case when the difference between true and false sufficient a demonstration and a *wrong* demonstration is as clear and distinct as between A and B – or between the mere assumption that there are infinite prime twins x and x+1 and a proof that inductive procedures show some truths for all numbers.

In the processual world of 'becoming' this level of a merely 'static' (geometrical) knowledge of mathematics cannot be attained, just because here all *contentful* conditions inferences always already *contain* dispositional inferences with respect to future behaviour of the thing or, also, some possible future knowledge about its past. This is the very reason why world-related concept or material concepts and their truth-conditions are heavily indeterminate, indefinite, especially if we abstract form the task of adjusting in concrete applications the relevant 'parameters'. If we do this, then there is no clear distinction between *true* world-related though inferentially thick propositions and wrong ones and sufficiently *proven* claims versus merely reasonable beliefs. However, even though we can often distinguish between well-proven truths and mere beliefs, there is by no means a clear-cut demarcation. There is no general 'either-or', much less a total time-independence.

The latter fact leads us to the insight into the very concept of the concept, the theory-dependence of the very notion of empirical truths that goes beyond mere appearances. In the domain of appearances, we only have apparent qualitative distinctions that tell us how something looks, i.e. how we qualify a Gestalt from our (joint!) perspective *without* any augmentation by conceptual default inference and any evaluation of 'normal expectation'. In real reality, appearances are augmented by objective causes.

It is clear that even animals can err. This is so because their perceptions are also already enactively connected to normal expectations that, by some chances, can fail to become fulfilled. In *this* aspect, our connections of qualitative distinctions at presence and dispositional expectations of normal behaviour of things (objects) is, in fact, similar to animals – and the empirical cognitive sciences are correct to investigate similarities and differences in some form of differential anthropology. However, the relevant differences concern the notion of non-present possibilities and real reality.

As a result, Hume's *autodafé* of the allegedly 'metaphysical' analysis of real reality 'behind' empirical appearances unfortunately throws the child of human knowledge and science out with the bathwater. It is crucial to see how colour-blind this attitude is. The criticism does not apply only to the metaphysical ideology of empiricism. It applies also to the self-misunderstanding of present days cognitive science, if they neglect the fact that language as it is taught is the core medium for storing, spreading and developing generic knowledge, codified in so called theories, that are nothing else than material-conceptual systems, the result of our scientific 'work in the concept' (*Arbeit am Begriff*).

As a result, philosophy and logic are *not* the disciplines to develop the concepts, but the *sciences* and their theories are here in charge. Philosophy and logic are 'only' metareflections on the development of theoretical, generic knowledge, but this is quite important for the very understanding of what science, generic knowledge, and conceptually informed empirical (perceptual) cognition is. Philosophy is the methodological self-consciousness of knowledge, *noēsis noēseōs*, without which there inner *science* (*Wissenschaft*) at all, but only traditional teachings of self-declared school-teachers, which were already ridiculed by Plato as 'sophists', i.e. as self-declared scientists that do not know what real science and knowledge is and this means what it ideally should be.

5. Reality as evaluated possibility

Only humans have access to possibilities. To be human even means to have the faculty of thinking, i.e. to have access to non-present possibilities. Hegel's title-sentence "reality is a possibility" says, accordingly, that we should distinguish between what is merely actually sensed or perceived (here and now) by singular individuals, such that it can be a reliable or a deceptive appearance of what there really is, on the one hand, and what can count as (objectively, hence at least trans-subjectively) real ("*wirklich*") on the other. We never perceive what is real without modal, hence conceptual, mediation. That is, we never have access to objective reality by mere sensation (*Empfindung*) or sense-perception, not even to the realities of our own bodily existence. This does not mean, however, that the actuality of, say, my headaches is questioned. Nor does it mean that we do not perceive with sufficient certainty that there is, for example, a chair in front of us. The only point is this: Talking about an objective thing like a chair already presupposes that we can expect that some possible things can be done with the object, e. g. that we can sit on it – which we cannot do if it is only a painted chair. Access to reality thus always requires a differentiation between merely 'seeming' appearances and how some specific reality shows itself, as we are inclined to say. This very fact gives the considerations of Hegel's *Logic of Essence* its importance and depth.

All this can be nicely shown at concrete cases, as, for example, when we look at a hilarious French mock-documentary on Stanley Kubrick and the race to the moon. In this film, Alexander Haig, Henry Kissinger, Donald Rumsfeld, some real CIA-grands and the widow of Kubrick discuss the notorious story that no man has even been to the moon. The scenes that show Neil Armstrong's first steps on the moon were filmed by Kubrick in a studio on earth – in order to get some appropriate propaganda material against the Russians on TV. Obviously, we have to evaluate at least the following three possibilities: What was shown in TV was the real thing (1). What was shown in TV was produced in a studio but the crew was really on the moon (2). The whole business was a hoax (3). In such an evaluation, we (should) accept something as 'real' ('*wirklich*') if, but only if, we have 'sufficient reasons' or 'satisfying grounds' for declaring that the possibility expressed in a judgment is no mere possibility but, as we say, reality.

In fact we say that something is really so and so, when we undertake such a reality claim and deny that it is a mere possibility. Hegel's most notorious phrase articulates precisely this fact: "what is real is reasonable and what is reasonable is real". The formula does not only mean, as Hegel himself sometimes says, that what is reasonable eventually comes (or, even more defensively: 'should come') into being. It rather says something about the logical status of reality-claims.

The basic insight is that reality claims are (almost) never immediate, that is, that we (almost) never 'immediately see' or 'sense' or 'perceive' what is real. This is so because what we count as real is (almost) never independent from sentences or propositions with trans-personal inferential impact and truth conditions that are constituted in such a way that they systematically surpass the domain in which we can evaluate truth merely subjectively by 'mere perception' or 'mere intuition'. This logical fact and nothing else is the reason why any non-tautological empirical truth is fallible. In other words, we always have to judge if a possibility-judgment can be viewed as telling us what really exists.

This shows the further reason why Hegel also claims that he has 'neutralised' scepticism by incorporating the problems that it articulates. Hegel uses the phrase "sublation" or *Aufhebung* for such a logical analysis. He speaks of a self-refutation or self-consummation of scepticism in this context. He thus refutes any dogmatism or 'rationalism' as well as any sweeping scepticism or subjectivism as in Humean 'empiricism'.

This does not mean that no-one knows anything for sure. It rather means that the quest for subjective certainty is not relevant for robust real knowledge in the sense of playing the game of giving responsible information about the world as accurate as possible and of assessing such informative acts in a control games of asking for and giving reasons. Almost no such reason will be 'absolutely' sufficient in the sense that there can be no further doubt. On the other hand, there is a truth in Cartesian self-consciousness. It consists in the 'absolute' fact that any judgment is my or your judgment, the judgment of hopefully responsible persons. The quest for subjective certainty holds philosophical epistemology still in its grip and results in a wrong alternative between dogmatic belief-philosophy and scepticism, which is, in the end, mere solipsism.

Now we can look back on Hegel's progress: The Logic of Being had been a deconstructive logical analysis of the naïve, naturalistic, point of view. It has shown that there is no 'immediate' talk about things and objects without presupposed norms and rules for what it means to make responsible claims or informative statements about them. Such statements are prima facie only possibly true. Insofar, we can understand the Logic of Being as a destruction of transcendent Pythagorean Platonism as we find it not only in theology and transcendent ('rationalistic') psychology, but also in scientism, i.e. in materialism and naturalism. The problem of Platonism is its 'reification' (*Verdinglichung*) of logical forms or of linguistic representations and explanations (of things and processes). Most prominent are reifications of causality and our talk about forces (1), but also of abstract objects like numbers (2), of abstract truths like mathematical truths (3), of mere possibilities as in any not merely formal theory of possible worlds (4), of theoretical entities like alleged rules wired in the brain as a computing machine in cognitive biology (5), and of institutional forms of actions and practices in economics (6).

Now we might understand at least in outline some of the most disturbing title-sentences of Hegel's *Logic of Essence*, as, for example, the following:

"What is possible is also impossible". "Real reality is a possibility", and, perhaps, the most contested of Hegel's logical oracles with which we have started: "What is real is reasonable and what is reasonable is real".

References

Brandom, Robert (1994): *Making It Explicit. Reasoning, Representing, and Discursive Commitment*, Cambridge, MA: Harvard University Press.
Brandom, Robert (2000): *Articulating Reasons. An Introduction to Inferentialism*, Cambridge, MA: Harvard University Press.
Brandom, Robert (2002): *Tales of the Mighty Dead*, Cambridge, MA: Harvard University Press.
Brandom, Robert (2007): "The Structure of Desire and Recognition: Self-Consciousness and Self-Constitution". In: R. Bubner/G. Hindrichs (eds.), *Von der Logik zur Sprache*, Stuttgarter Hegel-Kongress 2005, Stuttgart: Klett-Cotta.
Carnap, Rudolf (1928): *Der logische Aufbau der Welt*, Vienna: Springer.
Davidson, Donald (1980): *Essays on Actions and Events*, Oxford: Oxford University Press.
Engstrom, Stephen (2009): *The Form of Practical Knowledge. A Study of the Categorical Imperative*, Cambridge, Ma: Harvard University Press.
Gettier, Edmund (1963): "Is Justified True Belief Knowledge?" In: *Analysis* 23, 121–123.
Hennig, Boris (2006): *"Conscientia" bei Descartes*, Freiburg: Alber.
Hume, David (2001): *A Treatise of Human Nature, Being an Attempt to Introduce the Experimental Method of Reasoning into Moral Subjects*, Oxford: Oxford University Press.
Inwood, Michael J. (1983): *Hegel*, London: Routledge & Kegan Paul.
Longuenesse, Béatrice (1988): "Actuality in Hegel's Logic". In: *Graduate Faculty Philosophy Journal*, 13(1), 115–124.
Longuenesse, Béatrice (2007): *Hegel's Critique of Metaphysics*, Cambridge: Cambridge University Press.
McDowell, John (1994): *Mind and World*, Cambridge, MA: Harvard University Press.
Mill, John Stuart (1991): *On Liberty and Other Essays*, Oxford: Oxford University Press.
Mure, Geoffrey R. G. (1949): *An Introduction to Hegel*, Oxford: Clarendon Press.
Pinkard, Terry (1988): *Hegel's Dialectic: The Explanation of Possibility*, Philadelphia: Temple.
Pippin, Robert B. (1989): *Hegel's Idealism: The Satisfaction of Self-Consciousness*, New York: Cambridge University Press.
Quine, Willard Van Orman (1960): *Word and Object*, Cambridge, MA: MIT Press.
Quine, Willard Van Orman (1951): "Two Dogmas of Empiricism". In: *Philosophical Review* 60, 20–43.
Rödl, Sebastian (2005): *Kategorien des Zeitlichen. Eine Untersuchung der Formen des menschlichen Verstandes*, Frankfurt on Main: Suhrkamp.
Rosen, Stanley (1974): *G. W. F. Hegel: An Introduction to the Science of Wisdom*, New Haven, CT: Yale University Press.
Russell, Bertrand (1940): *A History of Western Philosophy*, London: Allen & Unwin.
Sellars, Wilfrid (1956): "Empiricism and the Philosophy of Mind". In: Herbert Feigl / Michael Scriven (eds.), *Minnesota Studies in the Philosophy of Science*, Vol 1, *The Foundations of*

Science and the Concepts of Psychology and Psychoanalysis, Minneapolis, MN: University of Minnesota Press, 253–329.
Stekeler, Pirmin (2014): *Hegels Phänomenologie des Geistes. Ein dialogischer Kommentar.* 2 vols, Hamburg: Meiner.
Stekeler, Pirmin (2016): *Hegels Wissenschaft der Logik. Ein dialogischer Kommentar.* Vol 1, Hamburg: Meiner.
Taylor, Charles (1975): *Hegel*, Cambridge: Cambridge University Press.
Tomasello, Michael (2014): *A Natural History of Human Thinking*, Cambridge, MA: Harvard Univ. Press.
Tomasello, Michael (1999): *The Cultural Origins of Human Cognition*, Cambridge, MA: Harvard Univ. Press.
Wallace, Robert M. (2005): *Hegel's Philosophy of Reality, Freedom, and God*, Cambridge: Cambridge University Press.
Wittgenstein, Ludwig (1922): *Tractatus logico-philosophicus*, London: Routledge.

Thomas Gil
Existence and Ontological Commitments

Abstract: Traditional (ontological) answers to the question concerning what there is have not lost their validity even if technological development has created higher-order informational devices, institutional facts due to collective intentionality keep on proliferating, and poetic imagination does not stop creating fictional entities. Individual things, qualities, classes and facts are still the main components of the reality which is relevant for human beings.

Keywords: Ontological commitments, higher-order technologies, Superhistory, informational objects, things, qualities, networks, institutional facts, the Fourth Revolution, fictional objects.

Nobody would have thought, two decades ago, that computers would accomplish certain tasks we used to conceive of as specifically human. Most of us assumed, without explicitly thinking too much about it, that there was a divide between human and digital labour, people and computers, difficult to eliminate. Self-driving cars were the stuff of science fiction, and not an imaginable daily reality. Today, cars without drivers exist that perform flawlessly. Improvement in robotics has created machines that can navigate and interact with existing objects in factories, warehouses, battlefields, and offices. And all such technological devices seem to be able to function not only in scientific research labs of leading software companies but also in the messy real world of persons and things. A huge and sudden progress has been accomplished, a progress that is exponential and combinatorial, so that almost everything seems today to be a potential object for the global process of digitization that is taking place in front of our astonished eyes. Think of the many smart phone applications available that help users to do whatever you can imagine a human being can do.

The terminology we choose to describe all these technological changes and developments is not that important. We may speak of a "second machine age" (Brynjolfsson/McAfee 2014) and contrast our epoch with the Industrial Revolution as that great sum of diverse developments in mechanical engineering, chemistry and metallurgy among many other disciplines that had such a huge impact on human culture and civilization. Computers and other digital engines are changing our world in such a way that we may choose to refer to such a transformation using the concept of a second machine revolution. Digital technologies (computers, software, and communication networks) have indeed revolutionized our daily lives. They change substantially the way we diagnose dis-

DOI 10.1515/9783110497656-006

eases, the way we talk and listen to what others have to say, the way we work and produce goods and services, the way we move around, and the way we enjoy life and the company of others when we don't work. Computers and other digital devices help us accomplish all our goals. Almost everything we used to do while living can now be digitized, that is, converted into bits that can be stored on a computer and sent over a network. What is important is not the terminology we use to speak about this new epoch in human history or "superhistory" (Floridi 2014). What is relevant is to understand what is really happening, and to examine critically what all these transformations justify us to affirm about reality as a whole. "Revolution 4.0" or the "Fourth Revolution", to use the concept preferred by Luciano Floridi, may be a revolution or simply the consequence of a continuous evolution.

1. What there is

The question about what reality is made of has been answered differently in the history of Western philosophy. It is the question about fundamental beings, existing things, or existing entities: the so-called ontological question.

For Plato, the real thing is not material, not what we perceive with our senses. In a strict sense, reality is for him ideal: a matter of forms that explain how the things we see and hear are possible. Studying mathematics holds, for Plato, the key to all understanding. And only objects as stable, constant and universal as the objects of mathematics can be the real objects of knowledge. Knowledge comes therefore from thinking, not looking. To escape from the naive view that concentrates on material things and takes them for the real things, the knowledge of pure mathematics and geometry is consequently for Plato the only way to go.

In Plato's philosophical school, in his Academy, many problems concerning the reality of Forms were however controversially discussed. How many Forms are there? Are there Forms for man-made objects? Are there Forms for nasty and unpleasant particulars? How is the relation between Particulars and Forms as Universals to be precisely conceived of? These and similar questions lead to several perplexities and difficulties Platonists could not easily get rid of.

Ultimate reality was for Plato and all those who accepted the theory of Forms a matter of abstract Universals on which the reality of everything else is somehow dependent. Not individual entities but abstract Forms constitute then the basic furniture of the real world. Such a theory was not easy to understand, let alone to accept. Aristotle (1963) did not accept it. He directed numerous efforts to develop an alternative theory of being, an alternative ontology. What are the real things science has to deal with? What are the fundamental items with which an explanatory science must concern itself? That is the question of ontology, the science of being, the question to which Aristotle devotes his early writing the *Categories* and the somehow obscure work the *Metaphysics*.

Aristotle's first insight is that "being" is said or predicated in many and different ways. "Being" can be said or predicated of certain things or entities which do not depend on others in order to exist. Aristotle calls such things "substances". Substances are "individuals" to which we refer with expressions like "this so-and-so". Substances are capable of being designated by a demonstrative phrase. They are separable items, things whose existence is not a matter of some other thing being modified in some way or other. But "being" can also be predicated in sentences that give an answer to questions like "What are its qualities?", "How large is it?", "How is it related to other things?", "Where is it?", and other similar questions. The "being" appearing in such sentences is according to Aristotle an accidental "being", an accidental way of being that presupposes the existence of a substantial "what" that it qualifies.

Substantial beings are ultimate subjects. They are separable. They are not parasitic. Accidental ways of being are parasitic. They are dependent on other beings, and they are not separable from them, that is, they are not separable from the substantial beings they are said of.

Ockham (1998) cuts Aristotle's list of categories from ten to two, admitting only substance and quality. Ockham's rejection of superfluous kinds of entities is known as "the principle of parsimony" or "Ockham's razor". Concerning the categories, the principle of parsimony helps us find out whether we have to admit distinct particulars falling under our universal terms in each of the ten categories.

In order to avoid unnecessary multiplication of beings in accordance with the multiplicity of terms it is necessary to show that many of the terms we use are "connotative" rather than "absolute". An "absolute" term is one that signifies things absolutely, whereas a "connotative" term is one that signifies things in relation to something or some things.

Ockham's eliminative strategy removes the assumption of essentiality of abstract terms in the accidental categories, showing that the Aristotelian doctrine of the categories does not entail an ontological commitment to ten mutually exclusive classes of entities. In Ockham's view, only substance and quality require such a commitment.

For Ludwig Wittgenstein (1981), the author of the *Tractatus Logico-Philosophicus*, the world consists of "facts". "Facts" are what makes propositions, that is, what we say or state about the world, true or false. Facts are not objects or things. Objects or things constitute the facts by being related to other objects or things in specific ways.

The nature of things consists in their possibility of occurring in facts. So when we think of things or objects, we think of the possibility of their connection with other things and objects. This means that knowing a thing or an object is to know the possibilities of its occurrence in facts when combined with or related to other things and objects.

Willard Van Orman Quine (1960, 1980, 1981) wants to know how our referential apparatus works. He is not only interested in ontological matters, in knowing what there is, but also in finding out how we refer to what there is, using different languages, and reacting properly to the information we get through our senses. How do we come to have knowledge at all? How can our thoughts be about the world? How does the mind come to be in contact with things other than the mental?

It is a long way from forms of energy impinging on the sensory surfaces of our bodies to our thought about the world and to the empirical content of our most sophisticated theories. And it is this long way that Quine tries to elucidate: from sensory stimulus to observational sentences, and from observational sentences to theoretical and scientific discourse.

For Quine, when we speak and say things, we are committed to there being objects that validate what we say. Therefore, Quine can assert: "To be is to be the value of a variable". And variables are positions to be occupied by objects and functions our sentences and theories provide.

Ontology is on Quine's account language-relative and theory-relative, because there is no language-independent sense in which we can say what there is or isn't. But Quine is not a relativist. He is a realist. For him all of our knowledge has the same aim: obtaining the best theory for predicting and understanding the course of events in the world. The idea of the "best theory" has for Quine to do with simplicity as well as with conformity with observation. Therefore, if it is part of our theory of the world that there are mountains, stars, atoms, electrons, and sets or classes, then we are committed to the idea that these things really exist. Quine as a realist takes the objects presupposed by our best ways of speaking and our best theories to be real.

In Quine's ontology there is a primacy of sentences. In Quine's ontology, more important than what there is, is what there is not, that is, what is resolutely denied the status of being an existent entity (properties, facts, meanings, ideas, sense-data, and many other so-called intensional entities). And in Quine's ontology the absolutely most important thing is the apt reconstruction of how we get to know what there really is.

2. Enlarging and transforming what there is

In advanced information societies information and communication technologies are transforming substantially the way people live, the way they work, the way they communicate, and the way they spend their free hours. The technological progress that has led to such a transformation has been considered by many as a Revolution. Luciano Floridi (2014) speaks about the "Fourth Revolution" and compares what is happening now with the Copernican, the Darwinian, and the Freudian revolution. What is happening now is revolutionary, according to Floridi, because the new information and communication technologies let us become informational organisms ("inforgs"), mutually connected and embedded in informational environments (the "infosphere") which we share with other natural and artificial informational agents. We keep on delegating and outsourcing to digital machines our memories, decisions, routine tasks, and get progressively integrated with them.

But what is really happening, and in what precise sense can we say that our reality is being nowadays enlarged and radically transformed?

2.1 Creating higher-order technologies

Digital engines are more than tools for interaction with the world and with each other. They change and reshape our mental and physical realities, modifying substantially how we relate to each other, and how we see ourselves and our world. They enable and empower us, and they make us think about the world informationally. Digital engines are becoming ubiquitous, penetrating almost everything and merging with it ("the Internet of Things", "web-augmented things", etc.). All sorts of artefacts and whole social environments get like that gradually informatized, and this due to the higher-order technologies we are creating.

Higher-order technologies come about when human agents delegate ever more tasks to technological devices till they get completely substituted by them in certain interacting networks. At first, human agents created technical artefacts to act upon material things. Such technical artefacts (like the plough or the wheel) are first-order technologies that enable and empower human agents to perform tasks they could not perform without them. Second-order technologies relate human agents no longer to natural, material objects but to other technologies. Screwdrivers, keys, vehicles are the artefacts we can think of to exemplify second-order technologies. Screwdrivers are technical artefacts that relate human agents with screws. Keys relate human users with locks, and vehicles human drivers with paved roads, another piece of technology.

Third-order technologies relate technological devices with other technological devices and artefacts. We, the human agents, enjoy or simply rely on such third-order technologies as beneficiaries or consumers, sometimes without even being aware of it, and without being part of the technological loop. In the "Internet of Things" as third-order technology, technological devices work independently of human users. Third-order technologies remove us, in a certain sense, off the loop. The expression "machine readable data" indicates the presence of such a generation of third-order technologies (barcodes, not created for eyes, but for deciphering machines; driverless cars; and so-called "domotic appliances", that are transforming our houses into smart environments by monitoring, regulating and fine-tuning the central heating system and the supply of hot water).

Whether a certain piece of technology is first-, second-, or third-order depends on the context. A pair of scissors is first-order when we use them to cut the stem of a rose. It is second-order when we use it to cut a piece of paper. If a robot uses it to cut a piece of cloth in a factory, the pair of scissors is then a third-order technology, human agents not being anymore present in the process. Modems and routers are quite good examples for third-order technologies. Something is going on then between technological devices and no human agent is involved in the happening. Human agents profit simply from such technological happenings.

Third-order technologies are becoming ever more indispensable in daily normal life. Ubiquitous as they may be, they are quite often invisible due to their user-friendly interfaces. More and more objects in our environments are third-order technologies: "ITentities" able to monitor, learn, interact, and communicate with each other.

We have grown up with technical artefacts like cars, buildings, furniture, clothes and all kinds of gadgets and machines that were not interactive or responsive. They were inert, incapable of interacting, communicating, learning, or memorizing. All such objects are becoming in many parts of the world fully interactive and responsive due to third-order technologies. Such a development changes substantially what there technically is. Our practical world contains now not only material objects (natural and artificial) and lifeless entities, but also digital, informational (informatized) entities, "ITentities", which interact and communicate not only with us but also with each other.

Luciano Floridi refers to societies, in which such ITentities proliferate and become ubiquitous: "hyperhistorical" societies. "Hyperhistorical" societies are highly dependent for their normal functioning and growth on information and communication technologies. The predominance of digital objects in advanced information societies contributes to a "dephysicalization" and "typification" of individuals as unique and irreplaceable entities. But such a passage from a world of unique material objects to a world of types of objects does not revolutionize at all the traditional ontological vocabulary. Digital objects and brilliant or intelligent machines are still objects and machines. And informational systems and networks are systems and networks. There is however a revolutionary change that comes about with them. Informational specialists are becoming increasingly powerful and influential the more we rely on higher-order technologies. New generational, geographic, socio-economic, and cultural divides are being generated and widened so that a new informational poor class and many informational slums could be the result of such a technological transformation.

2.2 Bringing about new institutional facts

In a world of brute physical facts it is possible for mental and social phenomena to exist. How institutional and social entities like nation-states, money, corporations, cocktail parties, ski clubs, summer vacations, and football games among many other things can come about in the physical world (hard sciences like physics, chemistry, and evolutionary biology help us understand), is what John R. Searle (2010) intends to explain in his social ontology. Two ideas are fundamental in Searle's social ontology: the idea of collective intentionality and the idea of constitutive rules of the form "x counts as y in c", that is, the idea of assigning functions.

For John R. Searle, respect for the basic fact that all kinds of intentionality have to exist in individual brains does not necessarily require that we reduce "We intend" statements to "I intend" statements. Intending to clean a room together with other people requires simply that I have in my head the thought "We are cleaning the room" and that the others have in their heads the thought "We are cleaning the room", not that each one of us has in his or her head the thought "I'm cleaning the room" plus that each one of us has additionally in his or her head mutual beliefs about the others' intentions.

There is indeed collective intentionality. And this collective intentionality happens when different individuals decide to do something together, collectively committing to coordinate their actions and doings. A specific application of such a cooperative self-commitment that characterizes collective intentionality leads to the creation of institutional facts or social institutions. Institutional facts or social institutions come about according to Searle on the basis of what he calls the collective assignment of functions.

The collective assignment of functions to people and objects is an important application of collective intentionality. Functions are always intentionality-relative. Institutional facts originate from their collective assignment. Assigning a function to someone or something consists in counting that someone or something, that is, a certain "x" as "y" in a specific context "c". Counting "x" as "y" in "c" confers a certain status. And that is precisely what it is to be an institutional fact, that is, to have a certain status, or to accomplish a specific function in a specific context.

The world in which we daily live is a "sea of institutionality" (J. R. Searle), full of institutional entanglements and facts. In such a world there are hospitals, schools, universities, trade unions, restaurants, theatres, churches, corporations, businesses, partnerships, money transactions, contracts, marriages, governments, friendships, families, parties, baseball teams, sporting clubs, real state agencies, politicians, policemen, professors, car owners, and convicted criminals among many other similar institutional facts. And as such a world develops and changes, many more institutional facts will come about that we will continue maintaining in their institutional reality.

A world of institutional facts is a world of rights, duties, obligations, requirements, and authorizations constituted all of them by language. Therefore, language is foundational for all institutional facts that make up the social world. Language may be considered to be a further institutional fact. Language is, however, more than that. It is the fundamental social institution required by all other institutional facts, those that already exist, and those that are yet to come.

2.3 Poetic imagination and its objects

In literary fictions, the authors present courses of events that are not descriptions of what has been, but possibilities of what could have been. Literary fictions use fiction operators that can make truth of what is not true, and so perhaps reveal in terms of truth what may be of some value. Frequently they reveal truths about passions, emotions, human attitudes and actions, and in general the human condition in an indirect fictional way.

We think mostly of novels when thinking of fiction. But if we want to clarify what fiction is in general terms, we ought to leave room for other genres like, for instance, plays and movies.

Fictions bring possible realities to mind. To be a work of fiction is to have been produced with a certain intention: the intention that it be appreciated as such by a potential audience. Therefore, it seems natural to conceive of it as the result of a game of make-believe. Games of make-believe bring with them a notion of fictional truth, of what is so according to the game.

Fictional objects do not occupy space in our world. We can never encounter them or visit them. They are materially non-existent. They exist only ideally in the literary texts they are part of. In other words, there are stories in which those objects are portrayed. Reality does not contain them. But they exist in stories as fictional characters. They exist thanks to the existence of stories (novels, plays, or movies).

Being a realist about fictional objects or characters in a novel seems to be a quite plausible position. If we affirm that "the Greeks worshipped Zeus", it is quite acceptable to believe that Zeus existed in a certain sense. The narrative text in which such an assertion is put forward makes us believe that the Greeks actually worshipped some (fictionally) existent thing or God they called Zeus. Zeus, like all fictional characters in novels, plays or movies, is the result of a creation process. Zeus and all fictional characters are somehow brought into existence, and then they keep on getting more additional properties in an incremental process for readers and authors. Those properties and details individuate them and are in the end the features that constitute each one of them as fictional individuals.

Strictly speaking, it would be better to avoid ontological commitments whenever possible. Paraphrasing what is said may be a good device according to Quine to enable us to talk conveniently about putative objects without being bound by ontological commitments. But such a paraphrasing strategy is not always convenient. Whenever possible we should substitute or replace then expressions like "There are fictional characters" by expressions like "In some fiction, specific characters are portrayed". On many occasions, however, paraphrasing substitutions and replacements do not seem to be desirable as they are cumbersome and even pedantic. The suitable specification of the ontological status of the objects in question as fictional objects would allow them to enter the realm of what there is. Those objects and characters do indeed exist in fictional texts that introduce, describe and refer properly to them.

References

Aristotle (1963): *Categories and De Interpretatione*, Oxford: Clarendon Press.

Brynjolfsson, E./McAfee, A. (2014): *The Second Machine Age. Work, Progress, and Prosperity in a Time of Brilliant Technologies*, New York: W. W. Norton & Company.

Floridi, L. (2014): *The 4th Revolution. How the Infosphere is Reshaping Human Reality*, Oxford: Oxford University Press.
Ockham, W. (1998): *Ockham's Theory of Terms. Part I of the Summa Logicae*, South Bend, Indiana: St. Augustine's Press.
Quine, W. V. O. (1960): *Word and Object*, Cambridge, Ma.: The M.I.T. Press.
Quine, W. V. O. (1980): *From a Logical Point of View. Nine Logico-Philosophical Essays*, Cambridge, Ma.: Harvard University Press.
Quine, W. V. O. (1981): *Theories and Things*, Cambridge, Ma.: The Belknap Press of Harvard University Press.
Searle, J. R. (2010): *Making the Social World. The Structure of Human Civilization*, Oxford: Oxford University Press.
Wittgenstein, L. (1981): *Tractatus Logico-Philosophicus*, London: Routledge.

Juan Antonio Valor

What Actually is Augmented Reality

Abstract: The answer to the question proposed in the title is complicated because what is meant by reality depends on prior philosophical conceptions. So, to respond rigorously, I should clarify the notion of reality by resorting to the history of philosophy. I shall offer two responses following two distinct philosophical stands. The first is the empiricism of Locke and Newton which I will take into account since although it emerges in the 17th century it somehow extends up to this day and is at the basis of what we mean by reality even today. The other position is the pragmatism of Dewey and Rorty, which openly criticizes the philosophical assumptions of classical empiricism and offers an alternative discourse upon which a new notion of reality is construed. What is real about Augmented Reality? Nothing, according to empiricism; it is mere appearance. And according to pragmatism the reality we grant it will depend on the problems it allows us to solve. In this paper I will explain both positions.

Keywords: Augmented Reality, appearance, situation, empiricism, pragmatism, representationalism, holism.

1. Experience by John Locke

In 1690 John Locke publishes *An Essay on Human Understanding.* Book I is a critique of the notions of evidence and certainty on which Descartes had based the new philosophy which had been studied in France for a few decades. In Book II, which is the one we consider central to this work, Locke systematizes his contribution and begins arguing that the starting point of all our knowledge is experience.

Experience consists of the observation of external sensitive objects or of internal operations of the mind. The instance that observes is the mind itself. In the first case it observes objects external to it and in the second case it observes itself. Thus *external and internal experiences* are respectively defined.

> Let us then suppose, the Mind to be, as we say, white Paper, void of all Characters, without any *Ideas*; How comes it to be furnished? Whence comes it by that vast store, which the busy and boundless Fancy of Man has painted on it, with an almost endless variety? Whence has it all the materials of Reason and Knowledge? To this I answer, in one word, From *Experience:* In that, all our Knowledge is founded; and from that it ultimately derives itself. Our Observation employ'd either about *external, sensible Objects; or about the*

DOI 10.1515/9783110497656-007

> *internal Operations of our Minds, perceived and reflected on by our selves, is that, which supplies our Understandings with all the materials of thinking.* These two are the Fountains of Knowledge, from whence all the *Ideas* we have, or can naturally have, do spring. (Locke 1991, 104)

It follows then that the notion of experience that Locke envisages assumes the acceptance of 1) an *instance* that is the mind, which is treated as "white Paper, void of all Characters"; 2) another instance beyond the mind which could be called extra-mental reality and which is formed by material objects; and 3) a cognitive relationship between the mind and the extra-mental reality. Points 1) and 2) place Locke's philosophy upon an ontological dualism, and 3) a cognitive relationship is understood as an epistemological representationalism that depends on a complex physical process:

> First, *Our Senses*, conversant about particular sensible Objects, do *convey into the Mind*, several distinct *Perceptions* of things, according to those various ways, wherein those Objects do affect them: And thus we come by those *Ideas*, we have of *Yellow, White, Heat, Cold, Soft, Hard, Bitter, Sweet*, and all those which we call sensible qualities, which when I say the senses convey into the mind, I mean, they from external Objects convey into the mind what produces there those *Perceptions*. (Locke 1991, 105)

The process begins by some senses being affected by external sensitive objects, which transmit to the mind not strictly "*Perceptions* of things, according to those various ways, wherein those Objects do affect them" but "they from external Objects convey into the mind what produces there those *Perceptions*". And what is "what produces there those Perceptions"? The cause is not the qualities of the bodies because "qualities ... in Bodies are, First such as are utterly inseparable from the Body, in what estate soever it be" (Locke 1991, 134); the cause is the affections that the qualities of the bodies produce on the senses. These are the affections which are transmitted to the mind and produce ideas in it. This explanation raises the following questions:

1) How do the qualities of bodies affect our senses?
2) How are the affections transmitted?
3) Understanding that affections are transmitted to the brain, how are they transmitted from the brain to the mind? Because we should bear in mind that the senses are material, the affections of the senses are material, the brain is material, but the mind is not material, but mental. Therefore, how are the affections transmitted from the material environment to the mental environment?
4) Placed in the mental realm, how do affections – now mental – produce ideas?

All these questions remain unresolved in the *Essay.* In fact, in the introduction to Book I Locke had already warned that they would be left unanswered. Thus he says:

> I shall not at present meddle with the Physical Consideration of the Mind; or trouble my self to examine, wherein its Essence consists, or by what Motions of our Spirits, or Alterations of our Bodies, we come to have any Sensation by our Organs, or any *Ideas* in our Understandings; and whether those *Ideas* do in their Formation, any, or all of them, depend on Matter, or no. These are Speculations, which, however curious and entertaining, I shall decline, as lying out of my Way, in the Design I am now upon. (Locke 1991, 43)

Although Locke has medical studies he does not want to enter into physical or physiological considerations. He just attempts to investigate "the Original, Certainty, and Extent of humane Knowledge; together, with the Grounds and Degrees of Belief, Opinion, and Assent." (Locke 1991, 43) And to that end he will use what he calls "this Historical, plain Method", which consists of studying exclusively the ideas of things that we have in the mind. (Locke 1991, 43–44) This is so stated in the introduction to Book I, but at the beginning of Chapter I of Book II we can read:

> I suppose, what I have said in the fore-going Book, will be much more easily admitted, when I have shewn, whence the Understanding may get all the *Ideas* it has, and by what ways and degrees they may come into the Mind … (Locke 1991, 104)

Therefore, he does not want to enter into physical or physiological considerations but he finally does, although in such a lax manner that he leaves unanswered the all-important referred questions. On such physical and physiological considerations are raised ontological dualism, epistemological representationalism and, for what concerns us the most here, a certain notion of reality that has survived to this day.

Before going any further, let us go back to the main thesis of Book II of the *Essay.* The mind has knowledge of itself to the extent it becomes aware that it thinks and of what it thinks, that is, of the ideas. It becomes aware of its own operations, such as "*Thinking, Doubting, Believing, Reasoning, Knowing,* Willing" (Locke 1991, 105), and also of the objects of these operations, which are the ideas. Interestingly, Locke asserts that the mind knows the ideas as ideas, that is, as signs or representations of objects external to the mind itself. The ideas expressed, for example, by the words "*Whiteness, Hardness, Sweetness, Thinking, Motion, Man, Elephant, Army, Drunkenness,* and others" (Locke 1991, 104), appear as representations and, to that extent, carry the news of the existence of something extra-mental which is mentally represented by them. This is so, says Locke at the beginning of Book II, and on this there is no possible doubt.

It is clear then that knowing is not like digesting food, that is, it does not consist of the introduction of external objects into the mind in the same way that food is introduced into the stomach, but in the emergence of ideas in the mind. To the question of how ideas arise, neither Locke nor anyone else has responded, in my opinion.

2. Simple and complex ideas

Ideas can also be divided into simple and complex. Simple ideas are the materials of all our knowledge and are characterized by the fact that the mind can neither make them nor destroy them. In other words, the mind proves itself totally passive at receiving them.

> These simple *Ideas*, the Materials of all our Knowledge, are suggested and furnished to the Mind, only by those two ways above mentioned, *viz. Sensation and Reflection.* When the Understanding is once stored with these simple *Ideas*, it has the Power to repeat, compare, and unite them even to an almost infinite Variety, and so can make at Pleasure new complex *Ideas.* But it is not in the Power of the most exalted Wit, or enlarged Understanding, by any quickness or variety of Thought, to *invent or frame one new simple* Idea in the mind, not taken in by the ways before mentioned: nor can any force of the Understanding, *destroy* those that are there. (Locke 1991, 119 – 120)

The examples of simple ideas that Locke himself provides are motion and color; softness and warmth in the same piece of wax; the coldness and hardness, which a man feels in a piece of ice; the smell and whiteness of a Lily; the taste of sugar and the smell of a Rose. (cf. Locke 1991, 119)

Complex ideas are formed by the mind through three of its own actions and using simple ideas as materials. These actions through which the mind exercises its power over simple ideas are combination, relationship and abstraction.

> 1. Combining several simple *Ideas* into one compound one, and thus all Complex *Ideas* are made. 2. The *2d.* is bringing two *Ideas*, whether simple or complex, together; and setting them by one another, so as to take a view of them at once, without uniting them into one; by which way it gets all its *Ideas* of Relations. 3. The *3d.* is separating them from all other *Ideas* that accompany them in their real existence; this is called *Abstraction:* And thus all its General *Ideas* are made. (Locke 1991, 163)

Locke enters into physical considerations of the mind because he understands that to attain the objectives of the *Essay* required a prior response to the question of whether ideas faithfully represent what exists in extra-mental reality. Since "*In this faculty of repeating and joining together its* Ideas, *the Mind has great power in varying and multiplying the Objects of its Thoughts, infinitely beyond what* Sensation *or* Reflection *funishedit whit*" (Locke 1991, 164), although complex ideas be justified both in the experience as well as in mental processes and not be mere arbitrary products, we cannot assure that what is represented by them should exist in the extra-mental reality. However, the absolute passivity the mind shows on reception of simple ideas could lead us to conclude that what is represented does exist in the extra-mental reality, in the same way that there is a seal which is represented by the impression on wax. Locke affirms that this way of thinking is common but cannot be maintained.

> ...that so we *may not* think (as perhaps usually is done) that they [our Ideas] are exactly the Images and *Resemblances* of something inherent in the subject; most of those of Sensation being in the Mind no more the likeness of something existing without us ... (Locke 1991, 134)

The argument he gives in order to understand that not all simple ideas are representations of something extra-mental, which he calls "*Quality*" (Locke 1991, 134), is the famous argument of the grain of wheat that we divide and whose resulting parts we divide again up to a point where the parts cannot be perceived (cf. Locke 1991, 134–135).Wheat had at the beginning a certain color, maybe a certain flavor, a certain smell, a certain strength, a certain shape, etc. Mistakenly we can understand that color, taste, etc., are qualities of the body; strictly we should say that they are simple ideas in our mind. The continued division of the grain makes us stop having the simple ideas of color, taste, smell, etc., but although the division continued further we would all have and will always have the ideas of strength, size, shape, movement, rest and number. How can we speak of strength, size, shape, etc., in the wheat powder? It would be a question of putting the wheat powder in a plunger, for example, to test its strength, size, shape, etc. At this point the issue is: why the continued division of the wheat grain into powder makes us stop having the ideas of color, taste, smell, etc., but cannot stop us from having the ideas of strength, size, shape, etc.? Locke's answer is that this happens because color, taste, smell, etc., are merely ideas in our mind and do not represent any quality of the extra-mental reality; instead, what is always maintained for everybody is the strength, size, shape, etc., because they are ideas that represent qualities which are always kept and strictly define the extra-mental reality.

The argument used by Locke is that the presence, under any changes or physical transformation, always and for all observers, of the ideas of strength, size, etc., makes us conclude that such ideas are not generated by the mind but that the mind behaves with absolute passivity before the extra-mental and permanent presence of the qualities of strength, size, shape, motion, rest and number, which he calls *primary qualities.* So that "the *Ideas of primary Qualities* of Bodies, are *Resemblances* of them, and their Patterns do really exist in the Bodies themselves." (Locke 1991, 137) However, the fact that the changes and physical transformations make the ideas of color, flavor, etc., modify or even disappear, being the mind, as it is, passive in receiving such simple ideas, leads us to conclude that what is referred to by those ideas, called *secondary Qualities* by Locke, "are nothing in the Objects themselves." (Locke 1991, 135) In short, the ideas of color, flavor, etc. are generated by the mind of the observers from the sensations produced by the primary qualities, but in the extra-mental reality there are no colors, flavors, sounds, etc.

Locke's argument is also used by Newton in the *Optics*. However, it can only be held on two assumptions that neither Newton nor Locke questioned. The first is that under any change or physical transformation it is always possible to experience the strength, size, shape, etc. of bodies. Experimentation can make us have to resort to a much more sophisticated instrument than a plunger, but it is assumed that with the appropriate tool the experience of the primary qualities of matter will always be possible. The second assumption is that the repeated permanence and for all observers of the simple ideas of primary qualities is only possible by the constant action of the primary qualities belonging to the extra-mental reality. But we could also assume, as Bishop Berkeley does, that such repeated presence is also possible by the action on our mind of a more powerful mind than ours.

3. The conception of reality in modernity

The most important thing is to understand that in this way a certain notion of reality is defined in the 17th century. The material reality that exists beyond our minds and our ideas consists of solid atoms, i.e. impenetrable, which have – precisely because they are impenetrable – a certain size and a certain shape and move and rest in space and time. The aforementioned idea of number refers to the existence of atomic units in all aspects but distinguishable by their spatial and/or temporal determination.

Newton refers very clearly to this conception of material reality in the following fragment of the *Optics:*

> All these things being consider'd, it seems probable to me, that God in the Beginning form'd Matter in solid, massy, hard, impenetrable, moveable Particles, of such Sizes and Figures, and with such other Properties, and in such Proportion to Space, as most conduced to the End for which he form'd them; and that these primitive Particles being Solids, are incomparably harder than any porous Bodies compounded of them; even so very hard, as never to wear or break in pieces; no ordinary Power being able to divide what God himself made one in the first Creation. While the Particles continue entire, they may compose Bodies of one and the same Nature and Texture in all Ages: But should they wear away, or break in pieces, the Nature of Things depending on them, would be changed. Water and Earth, composed of old worn Particles and Fragments of Particles, would not be of the same Nature and Texture now, with Water and Earth composed of entire Particles in the Beginning. And therefore, that Nature may be lasting, the Changes of corporeal Things are to be placed only in the various Separations and new Associations and Motions of these permanent Particles; compound Bodies being apt to break, not in the midst of solid Particles, but where those Particles are laid together, and only touch in a few Points. (Newton 1779, 260)

In view of this, what can we say about Augmented Reality? The answer is that Augmented Reality is only an appearance generated in the mind from certain physical activities of material reality that affect the senses not directly, but by means of a technical device (e.g., a smartphone, a Google Glass, an Oculus Rift, a Google Cardboard, etc.). The most amazing thing about the conception of reality that emerges nowadays is that it requires that the reality lived in the spontaneity of our daily life also be regarded as mere appearance. It is mere appearance generated in my mind the table on which I write, the computer I have in front of me, my hands resting on the keyboard or the trees I see through the window. Locke and Newton have convinced us that the material reality that creates all those complex ideas is just a set of atoms more or less stabilized in space and time by the action of given inertial and gravitational forces.

Then the question arises as to what is the difference between Augmented Reality and the reality of our daily lives? It may be that our everyday life was just a case of Augmented Reality. The movie *The Matrix*, directed by the Wachowski Brothers and released in 1999, describes daily life as a merely mental product generated by certain machines and certain software. We find a similar plot in movies like *Level 13*, by Josef Rusnak, released in 1999, and *Dark City*, by Alex Proyas, released in 1998. On the other hand, it could also happen that Augmented Reality was so incorporated into our daily lives that we completely lost awareness of its specificity. That is what happens when we wear glasses or introduce contact lenses into our eyes. It also happens when we use a microscope or a telescope. But in any case it is possible to recognize, if not directly, at least reflexively, the specificity of Augmented Reality. And this is because a mediation of a technical device is required between the material reality and our senses. We understand, however, that we are assuming the previous distinction between the natural and the artificial, and that such distinction appears increasingly diluted. If technological development made it impossible, Augmented Reality would simply become everyday reality. In any case, from our present day view, one and the other would convey an appearance generated within the limits of our mind from the action of extra-mental material reality.

4. Critique of modernity

In the Introduction to *Philosophy and the Mirror of Nature* Rorty points out that the conception of the world and reality of Locke and Newton has been maintained in one way or another until the 20th century, specifically up to the entry into the philosophical scene of Dewey, Wittgenstein and Heidegger.

> Wittgenstein, Heidegger, and Dewey are in agreement that the notion of knowledge as accurate representation, made possible by special mental processes, and intelligible through a general theory of representation, needs to be abandoned. For all three, the notions of "foundations of knowledge" and of philosophy as revolving around the Cartesian attempt to answer the epistemological skeptic are set aside. Further, they set aside the notion of "the mind" common to Descartes, Locke and Kant – as a special subject of study, located in inner space, containing elements or processes which make knowledge possible. (Rorty 1979, 6)

Rorty resorts to these authors to abandon the ontological dualism and epistemological representationalism of modernity and defend a behaviorist and materialistically oriented philosophy (cf. Rorty 1979, 379):

> Discussion in the philosophy of mind usually start off by assuming that everybody has always known how to divide the world into the mental and the physical – that this distinction is common-sensical and intuitive, even if that between two sorts of "stuff", material and immaterial, is philosophical and baffling. So when Ryle suggests that to talk of mental entities is to talk of dispositions to behave, or when Smart suggests that it is to talk of neural states, they have two strikes against them. For why, if anything like behaviorism or materialism is true, should there be anything like this intuitive distinction? (Rorty 1979, 17)

This post-modern and pragmatic philosophy brings in a new conception of reality. I want to account for it following Rorty's orientation and the references he makes to Dewey. From the pragmatic conception of reality that Dewey and Rorty propose I will try to understand Augmented Reality.

5. Notion of experience in Dewey's philosophy

In the article entitled *"The Reflex Arc Concept in Psychology"* Dewey criticizes the distinction proposed by Locke between mind and material reality for the consequences it has had for psychology. (cf. Dewey 1972, 96–109) Such dualism has allowed us to distinguish between two units, stimulus and response, and explain their connection from the repetition of the concurrence of both. Dewey analyzes the behavior of a child in front of a candle to conclude that such units cannot be maintained and that the starting point to be taken by psychology is the coordination between organism and environment. (cf. Shook 2000, 111–113)

Experience is to be understood as the interaction between an organism and an environment. But not in the sense that we usually say that an organism lives in an environment, assuming that both of them are already existent prior to the vital relationship established between them. Rather, it should be considered that the organism lives in virtue of the environment and that this stops being something indifferent and it becomes the environment of the organism inasmuch as being part of its vital functions. Thus, the environment of a locomotive animal differs from that of a sedentary plant because the land becomes part of their respective activities in a different way; the environment of a jellyfish differs from that of a fish because the water enters their bodily functions differently, etc. The organism and the environment are mutually defined through the vital relationship established between them. (cf. Dewey 1988a, 32) We may think that there is an independent nature of the organism, but this is environment only when it takes part of the organism's vital functions. And we can also think that organisms are part of nature; but they exist as organisms only when they are actively connected with the environment around them. (cf. Dewey 1988a, 40)

The complex system of interactions between organism and environment can be balanced. When this is the case Dewey insists that there is, in objective terms, *a unified environment.* (cf. Dewey 1988a, 32–33) Changes in the organism maintain their uniform integration in the environment, every activity paves the way for the next and all of them manage to occur not only in succession but also forming a well basted series.

However the balance can be broken, which happens when an excess or a defect appear in a given factor. In this case the need arises in the organism to recover the lost state and it starts making the necessary efforts to this end. Dewey calls *need* the state of disturbed equilibrium. The activity aimed to restore the balance is called *search and exploration.* The recovery of the balance is called *fulfillment or satisfaction.*

> The state of disturbed equilibration constitutes *need*. The movement towards its restoration is search and exploration. The recovery is fulfilment or satisfaction. (Dewey 1988a, 34)

Hunger, for example, is a state of imbalance. Various organic functions such as the digestive, circulatory, motor, etc. are no longer coordinated. At that time a real state arises (which is not mere sensation, insists Dewey) of unease, anxiety, necessity. (cf. Dewey 1988a, 34) From this moment the organism develops behaviors, such as lengthening limbs, opening the mouth, etc., designed to meet the need. Attaining this achievement allows the restoration of the state of balance, that is, the restoration of coordination between functions. When this is the case we say that the organism has given an adapted total response.

The efforts made by the organism to regain balance generate changes in the environment and at the same time, new environmental conditions involve a modified state of the organism. It is particularly true in the case of humans that activities carried out in order to meet their needs transform the environment, which creates new needs, which can only be met through changes in human activities, which in turn transform the environment, and so on and so forth.

The most important change that occurs in the organism is the conditioning of the subsequent behavior, i.e., the emergence of *habits*. (cf. Dewey 1988a, 39) Habit is the ability to repeat a certain behavior and it arises, according to Dewey, as the result of overcoming the state of necessity and the attainment of fulfilment or satisfaction. It is the satisfaction of the need which creates in the organisms an organic rearrangement that leads them to act similarly in similar conditions. The habit is not, in the case of higher organisms, completely rigid but the response operates with some flexibility regarding both the organism's actions as well as the environmental conditions. The habit does not arise therefore by a mere repetition but repetition is the result of a habit.

6. The situation

Dewey insists that our experience is not of isolated objects or events, but always of objects given in a context that is physical, biological and cultural. An object or event is a part in connection with the surrounding environment, which Dewey calls the *situation*. Sometimes, looking for certain purposes, it is possible to put the object in the foreground of attention and take it away from the complex environment that surrounds it, which is then blurred and relegated to the background. But this can be done because the experience is beforehand that of an object given in a contextual whole.

When the system of interactions between the organism and the environment is no longer in balance, that is, when the environment is no longer unified and each activity no longer paves the way to the next, then the doubt arises. In order to defend a radical empiricism Dewey affirms that it is the situation in which we are trapped and involved which is presented as being inherently dubious. In *Inquiry into Meaning and Truth*, the title of the publication of the William James Lectures that Russell taught at Harvard in 1940, he insists that you cannot believe that Dewey has ever meant there may be a doubtful situation without a personal doubter. (cf. Russell 1940, 407) To get Russell out of his astonishment, or perhaps to amaze him even more, in the article *"Propositions, Warranted Assertibility and Truth"* published in 1941, three years after the *Logic*, Dewey writes:

> When the term "doubtful situation" is taken in the meaning it possesses in the context of my general theory of experience, I do mean to say that it can exist without a personal doubter; and, moreover, that "personal states of doubt that are not evoked by, and are not relative to, some existential situation are pathological; when they are extreme they constitute the mania of doubting ... The habit of disposing of the doubtful as if it belonged only to us rather than to the existential situation in which we are caught and implicated is an inheritance from subjectivistic psychology". (Dewey 1988b, 184–185)

It is the situation itself which appears as being inherently doubtful, and that is why we are doubtful. Dewey also speaks of a situation which is indeterminate, unstable, troubled, complicated, ambiguous, confusing, full of conflicting tendencies, dark, painful, etc. (cf. Dewey 1988a, 109)

7. The inquiry

Both in the case of ordinary knowledge as in the case of scientific knowledge Dewey defines inquiry as follows:

> Inquiry is the controlled or directed transformation of an indeterminate situation into one that is so determinate in its constituent distinctions and relations as to convert the elements of the original situation into a unified whole. (Dewey 1988a, 108)

The starting point of the inquiry is an indeterminate, disturbed, unstable, uncertain situation. It is, in the first place, a situation that is objectively doubtful, that is, which itself is presented as having these traits. Given the correlation between organism and environment in the situation we can say that just because the situation is presented as being inherently doubtful we find ourselves doubtful. On the other hand, the same objectivity of the doubtful situation warrants its inter-subjectivity, i.e., the fact that the doubt is ours and of any organism living through it for finding itself in that given situation.

To account for the doubt as if it belonged to subjectivity and not to the situation itself is a legacy from the ontological dualism proposed by the subjectivist psychology of Lockean origin. This dualism explains the doubt from the existence of a material reality completely determined in its properties and relationships and of a mental reality that has an indeterminate knowledge of the material reality. Thus, from this point of view it is attributed to doubt a fully subjective character. Dewey resorts even to the interpretation of Copenhagen of Quantum Mechanics to explain that dualism cannot be maintained and that the indeterminacy belongs not to the knowledge of material reality, but to material reality itself. (cf. Dewey 1988a, 110) Therefore, it would be a mistake, a flight from reality, to try to get out of the doubt by simple manipulation of our mental states. Doubt is resolved by facing the situation and carrying out the necessary operations to change the existing conditions and restore the lost functional balance between organism and environment. (cf. Dewey 1988a, 110)

Secondly, doubt is not a general uncertainty, it does not affect the whole of life, but it belongs to a particular situation, which acquires special relevance on a vital horizon which is not questioned at this point.

Thirdly, it is the single and concrete doubt that exercises control over the necessary operations to get out of it. Not any solution is valid nor are there available beforehand some definitive criteria to determine a solution, but it is the concrete doubtful situation which provides the criteria and guide the operations leading to the restoration of the integrated situation.

Any action of the organism in the doubtful situation cannot be classified as inquiry. This requires both in ordinary knowledge as in scientific knowledge, a review of the environmental conditions, an anticipation of the consequences and a selection and ordering of the actions with respect to the specific features of the situation.

The doubtful situation is given; we come across it regardless of our will. At first what appears to us is an indeterminate situation characterized by the fact that, to our regret, there is an interruption in the events of life, in the fluid flow of the organisms' activities in their environment. There is nothing cognitive or intellectual at this time; we could say that the situation is precognitive. (cf. Dewey 1988a, 111)

The transformation of the indeterminate situation into a problematic one requires the implementation of the inquiry to achieve a minimum of determination in the situation. Such determination becomes all important because "without a problem there is only groping in the dark." (Dewey 1988a, 111) On the problematic situation will depend what is considered relevant and what is discarded as irrelevant and so will the selected data, the hypotheses or the suggested conceptual structures. Therefore to accept as a starting point for the inquiry an issue that does not belong to the given problematic situation renders the data, the hypotheses and the structure of the inquiry completely arbitrary.

The definition of the problem is not possible in an absolute indeterminacy, but it requires finding in the undetermined situation those constituent parts or contained ingredients *(constituents)* which are determined. These are taken as the constant factors of the particular situation. Its knowledge is obtained by observation. Dewey calls them *the facts of the case.* (Dewey 1988a, 113) They are the terms in which it is possible to formulate the problem and the conditions that must be taken into account when proposing any solution. That is why we say that the problem incorporates its solution.

One possible solution is then suggested by the facts of the case warranted by observation. The solution is presented as an *idea*, and is presented in the same way as the facts of the case are presented to observation. In Dewey's words:

> A *possible* relevant solution is then suggested by the determination of factual conditions which are secured by observation. The possible solution presents itself, therefore, as an *idea*, just as the terms of the problem (which are facts) are instituted by observation. (Dewey 1988a, 113)

The idea is not a representation in the Lockean sense, it is an anticipation of what can happen; it indicates a possibility referred to the resolution of the problematic situation. For this reason it is said that science is *predictive.* (cf. Dewey 1988a, 113) Since the idea indicates a possibility, its value is checked experimentally, that is, it must be put into practice, it must be put to work. This means bringing to light facts previously unobserved, called by Dewey *trial facts* (Dewey 1988a, 117), comparing them with the facts of the case and checking whether the idea allows for the interpretation and organization of all the facts into a coherent whole.

Since ideas point to something that is not present and existing here and now, they can be regarded as symbols that mean the non-present facts. A hypothesis is a symbol consisting of a general statement. Its meaning can be immediately relevant to the resolution of the problem. But it can also happen that such immediacy is not given and that it should be necessary to relate it to other intermediate meanings until the relevant meaning sought is reached. This is what is done when, through *reasoning*, ideas are put in relation with one another. (cf. Dewey 1988a, 115)

If finally the solution sought is not achieved we are forced either to change the ideas although keeping the facts of the case, or to change the facts of the case by changing the ideas accordingly, or, ultimately, to change the ways of reasoning. The validity of the facts, the ideas and the reasoning lies exclusively in the operational force to resolve the problematic situation.

On considering ideas as suggestions they seem to be reduced to mere mental constructs separate in principle from the scope of observation. In this case it should be explained, perhaps psychologically, how certain facts suggest certain ideas, and it should be explained, perhaps logically, why certain ideas, and not others, are solutions. The possibilities offered by reasoning should also be explained, that is, the fact that certain relationships between ideas allow for ideas that finally solve the problem. It is known that Kant's solution, presented by himself as the overcoming of rationalism and empiricism, resorts to the action of synthetic understanding to explain the relationship between the scope of sensitivity and the scope of understanding.

Dewey's solution diverges from the previous ones when considering that ideas as well as the facts of the case are operational. (cf. Dewey 1988a, 116) Ideas are operational because their content is a set of proposals and plans to act on the given situation in order to bring new facts to light. The facts of the case are operational because, unlike empiricism's assertions they are not determined units themselves, accessible through observation without any modification; they become relevant, they are selected and described in terms of the operational force they show to solve the given problematic situation. They are shown and backed, ultimately, when together with the suggested ideas they enable the exit from the problem situation and restore the fluid interaction with the environment. The operational nature leads Dewey to assert that the distinction between ideas and facts merely responds to a functional division of the inquiry work. (cf. Dewey 1988a, 116)

The described inquiry pattern is similar in both ordinary knowledge and scientific knowledge. The difference between them lies in the different subjects discussed and the various special techniques applied. The problematic situations with which common sense is faced have to do with activities of individual or collective use and enjoyment. The use and the enjoyment are the ways in which humans are directly related to the world around them. For the use and enjoyment, practical activities are carried out, such as living expenses, housing, defense, protection, etc., and objects such as planets or stars are of interest to the extent that they are connected with such practical activities. On the other hand, in the inquiry into common sense, those symbols contained in common language are used, which group members often employ to communicate with each other; and these symbols keep a direct reference to use and enjoyment activities.

Science is characterized for keeping an uninterested intellectual concern for matters of use and enjoyment. The problematic situation science faces has to do with objects that are not directly defined by activities of use and enjoyment, but by relationships. Therein lies its abstract and general nature. (cf. Dewey 1988a, 120) Scientific objects are strictly relational. The development of science has made us aware of this, as there has been a gradual interpretation of tertiary, secondary and primary qualities in terms of relationships. (cf. Dewey 1988a, 119–120) Accordingly, the language of science cannot be that of common sense, but it consists of a sign system that allows for the explanation of these relations from the connections that the signs establish with each other.

But with regard to the issue of objectivity the most important thing is that the solutions provided by the inquiry carried out both in ordinary knowledge and in scientific knowledge be solutions that organisms give themselves when, wanting to avoid pain and suffering, they select new data and new conceptual structures. Much of modern philosophy has attributed to pain a purely subjective nature and to the resulting inquiry, a remote utilitarian nature far from the standards required by objective knowledge. Dewey brings to light the ontological dualism that underlies this position and replaces it with an anti-dualism (cf. Shook 2000, 180–184) which claims as its starting point the correlation of organism and environment in the situation. Pain, doubt or problem thus acquire an objective character and become the criterion that guides the inquiry. And also the selected data and the conceptual structures that configure the solution acquire an objective character to the extent that their operational force should be able to transform the situation which, having been doubtful or problematic so far, now becomes fluid. The donation or imposition of the problematic situation warrants, in turn, the intersubjective character of the solution, that is, the fact that the solution, even when depending on the organism, not be so, exclusively, for this organism but for any other in the same situation.

8. Centers of descriptive gravity

All this discussion underlies Rorty's considerations around reality, which will serve us to understand what Augmented Reality is. To account for Rorty's proposal I will begin by Chapter IV of *Truth and Progress. Philosophical Papers, vol. 3* entitled "Charles Taylor on Truth" and will continue in Chapter V, entitled "Daniel Dennett on Intrinsicality".

To defend with Dewey that the validity of the facts, ideas and reasoning that are defined in a specific description of the world lies exclusively in the operational force to resolve a problematic situation leads to abandon what Rorty calls "the third dogma of empiricism, the distinction between scheme and content." (Rorty 1998, 87) This distinction refers to the existence of a world of things quite apart from how we describe it, that is, it refers to the "purportedly noncontroversial idea that things have intrinsic, non-description-relative features." (Rorty 1998, 87) Only abandoning this idea completely can we come to understand that the traits and relationships in the world, even causal relationships, arise precisely from within the descriptions we make. Therefore, we cannot say that the solar system was still, there, awaiting the arrival of Kepler, but rather that Kepler provides a re-description of the Copernican description and that Copernicus provides a re-description of the Ptolemaic description. (cf. Rorty 1998, 89–90)

You can defend the thesis that there are inherent traits in things if previously we defend the thesis that some descriptions made with some vocabularies manage to faithfully represent reality. If we defend, for example, that the vocabulary used by Newton allows a description that accurately represents reality while the vocabulary used by Aristotle fails to do so. We then say that the Newtonian description represents reality more accurately than the Aristotelian description thus assuming deep down a sort of linguistic representationalism. The question is whether such a statement makes sense, and Rorty thinks not. (cf. Rorty 1998, 86) He thinks not because he understands that the limits of language are the limits of the world and because he understands that what cannot be said cannot be thought. This philosophical position is identified with holism. (cf. Rorty 1998, 100–101)

Holists cannot speak of a reality formed by intrinsic features metaphysically understood as "property whose presence is necessary for the object being the object it is." (Rorty 1998, 103) The reality of objects, as Locke says, does not consist in a set of necessary properties "for the object's self-identity, a self-identity it possesses apart from any particular description of it by us" (Rorty 1998, 103), simply because outside description there are no objects. In short, Rorty says, "we must insist that *identity* is always identity under a description." (Rorty 1998, 103)

Consequently the objects must be considered as *centers of descriptive gravity*. (Rorty 1998, 105) With this expression it is meant that they are woven and rewoven by the descriptions we make and the languages we use, so that a change in the description entails a change in the objects because the descriptive gravity shifts, and new centers are generated. Rorty puts it as follows:

> Like heroines whose stories are told by novelists, and selves whose self-consciousness about their own past character results in the acquisition of a quite different future, objects change as our descriptions of them change. That is to say, their center of descriptive gravity shifts as inquiry proceeds. (Rorty 1998, 105)

There is, in short, no intrinsic character to grasp in the objects, no primary quality that defines their true reality beyond appearance. Objects are what they are in terms of the relationships they establish with other objects, and all this is evident and takes place in language. This leads us to abandon the distinction that Locke and modernity made between appearance and reality. There is no reality beyond the relations that appear in language. The reality of objects consists precisely in their appearing.

9. What is relevant

At this point it is inevitable to wonder whether they are real, to the same extent, the table on which I write, Sherlock Holmes, Middle-Earth, number 17, the rules of chess, the clause on interstellar trade in the United States' Constitution and the lost socks of Daniel Dennett. We can ask the question in an even more provocative way: do witches and atoms have the same reality? I am tempted to say yes, but Rorty's answer is much more nuanced:

> If we drop such representationalist notions as "appearance" and "making true", then we can let numbers and tables, quarks and stars, lost socks and moral values share the same "objective" status. The interesting differences among them will be those made by our (often fluctuating) notions of what is relevant and irrelevant to the truth of beliefs about each different sort of object. These notions will not be responsible to something called "the intrinsic character of the object in question", but only to the ordinary process of reweaving our webs of belief and desire, often in unpredictable ways (as when we begin to think of Riemann's axioms as relevant to interstellar distances or of the origin of the human species as irrelevant to moral values). (Rorty 1998, 106–107)

The ontological status we assign to socks, atoms or numbers has nothing to do with their intrinsic features but with the importance we give them in the discourses they appear. They are the networks of beliefs and desires that weave those centers of descriptive gravity defining in turn the determinations that constitute them and their sense of reality. And certainly the centers of descriptive gravity are rewoven as our networks of beliefs and available discourses change.

In any case, the question we asked above can be rephrased: what is it that makes our beliefs and our discourses change, and consequently the objects and their sense of reality? Convergentism explains these changes in terms of an ongoing process that is guided by the discovery of the intrinsic features of things. The process is progressive to the extent that every time we are closer to the full recognition of such features and, consequently, our discourses are increasingly closer to the truth. As Rivadulla noted, Peirce is a convergentist to the extent that he defines truth and reality in terms of "the end of the inquiry" and Popper is so too because he "maintains that what characterizes science as a rational endeavor is its growing convergence to truth." (Rivadulla 2015, 30 – 31) As can be expected, Rorty's criticism to epistemological and linguistic representationalism leads him to criticize convergentism. (cf. Rorty 2000, 5, 12)

Rorty finds the answer to the question in Dewey when he says that philosophers should abandon the notion of truth and confine ourselves to the *warranted assertibility.* (cf. Rorty 2000, 1–2) That is, we defend some beliefs and some discourses not because they are true but because they have shown the operational force to solve the problematic situations we face, as we explained above. However, as situations change, it may happen that the discourses that once provided solutions no longer provide them, creating even more problems than solutions. In such case there will appear objections to our beliefs, giving rise to situations of doubt, uncertainty, irritation, pain, which we could only overcome by starting a new process that through new vocabularies and discourses, could give rise to new centers of descriptive gravity allowing us to recover the warranted assertibility.

Perhaps it may seem that in all of this there is a remnant of idealism. "For this may seem to entail not saying that objects change not by being battered or moved about or discolored by other objects, but only by our changing our descriptions of them. Further, the suggestion that they change in the latter may seem to go against our intuition that *objects exist independently of thought*, the intuition the idealists tried to put in question." (Rorty 1998, 109) However, it is not possible to maintain idealism if we take Dewey seriously when he says that warranted assertibility is not something that happens in subjectivity but in an objective situation.

10. Reality in a pragmatic sense

Let us go back to the question we attempt to answer in this work: What is real about Augmented Reality? From the standpoint of empiricism, nothing. Augmented Reality is a mere appearance generated in our minds by the action on our senses of a material reality consisting of solid and extensive atoms moving in space and time. But from the viewpoint of empiricism, the reality that appears in our daily experience is also mere mental appearance generated in the same way. The question then is: How to distinguish between everyday reality and Augmented Reality? And the answer we gave is that this will be possible while we be able to distinguish between the affections directly produced on our senses and those produced through the mediation of a technical device. If technology were incorporated into our senses in such a way that this distinction would be made impossible, which is already the case, then we would not be able to separate everyday reality from Augmented Reality.

Analyzing the critique of pragmatism to empiricism we realize that this position is maintained on an ontological dualism, an epistemological representationalism and a linguistic representationalism. Dewey avoids ontological dualism and epistemological representationalism understanding the experience as a complex system of interactions between organism and environment that results in a determined or undetermined situation, and assuming that organisms flee from indeterminate, problematic, confusing, painful, etc. situations. On the work of Dewey, Rorty avoids linguistic representationalism as he defends holism. The result is a notion of reality that is not characteristically based on the existence of intrinsic features in things like primary qualities (strength, size, shape, motion, rest and number), but in terms of the definition in a given vocabulary and in a given discourse on centers of descriptive gravity. The reality attributed to the centers of descriptive gravity depends on the relevance they acquire in the discourse that constitutes them, and the relevance is related to the operational force they show to solve the given problematic situations.

From a pragmatist view, what is real about Augmented Reality? The answer to the question is not about the direct or indirect action on our senses of an alleged material reality, nor about the fact that we can determine the mediation of a technological device between material reality and our senses. The question now has to do with the importance we attach in our discourse to the centers of gravity we define. And the relevance is given in terms of the concrete practical operations that result from our discourses.

Let us give an example. We have the discourse by which we consider as real the landforms we see on other planets through a telescope. That discourse has a high degree of sophistication and has to do with the discourse of physics, optics and astronomy. They allow us to determine what we see as a landform, and such a consideration allows us in turn to solve certain specific practical problems that have to do with the science of our time, but also with our daily lives. Because on them depends the setting of satellites into orbit, our tracking and communication systems, etc. However, the scholastics who managed to open the trial against Galileo understood that what he was watching through his telescope were not landforms, but mere optical appearances generated by the instrument lenses. This was the discourse required by the physics and the ontology of Aristotle, which obviously did not have to face the problem of putting a satellite into orbit, but others of a very different nature.

Will the time come when we say that the reality we see with the Oculus Rift is as real as the one we see with a telescope? It all depends on the problems we could solve through such a discourse. But I bet that, shortly, to say otherwise will pose us more problems than solutions.

References

Dewey, John (1972): "The Reflex Arc Concept in Psychology". In: *The Early Works of John Dewey*, vol. 5, London, Amsterdam, Carbondale and Edwardsville: Southern Illinois University Press, 96–109.

Dewey, John (1988a): *Logic: The Theory of Inquiry*. In: *The Later Works of John Dewey*, vol. 12, London, Amsterdam, Carbondale and Edwardsville: Southern Illinois University Press.

Dewey, John (1988b): "Propositions, Warranted Assertibility and Truth". In: *The Later Works of John Dewey*, vol. 14, London, Amsterdam, Carbondale and Edwardsville: Southern Illinois University Press, 168–187.

Locke, John (1991): *An Essay Concerning Human Understanding*, ed. by Peter H. Nidditch, Oxford University Press.

Newton, Isaac (1779): *Opera Omnia*, vol. IV, London.

Rivadulla, Andrés (2015): *Meta, método y mito en ciencia*, Madrid: Trotta.

Rorty, Richard (1979): *Philosophy and the Mirror of Nature*, Princeton, New Jersey: Princeton University Press.

Rorty, Richard (1998): *Truth and Progress. Philosophical Papers, vol. 3:* Cambridge: Cambridge University Press.

Rorty, Richard (2000): "Universality and Truth". In: Brandom, Robert (ed.), *Rorty and His Critics*, Malden: Blackwell Publishers, 1–30.

Russell, Bertrand (1940): *Inquiry into Truth and Meaning*, New York: Norton and Company.

Shook, John R. (2000): *Dewey's Empirical Theory of Knowledge and Reality*, Nashville: Vanderbilt University Press.

Part 3: **The Epistemology of Augmented Reality**

Spyridon Orestis Palermos

Augmented Skepticism: The Epistemological Design of Augmented Reality

Everything we see hides another thing, we always want to see what is hidden by what we see. There is an interest in that which is hidden and which the visible does not show us. This interest can take the form of a quite intense feeling, a sort of conflict, one might say, between the visible that is hidden and the visible that is present.
(René Magritte on *The Son of Man*)

Abstract: In order to solve the problem of the traditional account of knowledge, according to which justification is the ability to provide reflectively accessible positive reasons in support of one's beliefs, a number of epistemologists have suggested that knowledge is true belief that is the product of cognitive ability. According to this alternative, a belief-forming process may count as a knowledge-conducive cognitive ability if and only if it has been cognitively integrated on the basis of processes of mutual interactions with other aspects of the agents' cognitive system. One of the advantages of this approach is that it allows knowledge and justification to be extended to such artifacts as telescopes, microscopes, smartphones and Augmented Reality systems. Augmented Reality systems, however, rely on deceptive reality augmentations that could significantly deteriorate the epistemic efficiency of users' cognitively integrated natures. This could lead to a form of 'augmented skepticism', whereby it will be impossible to tell augmented from physical reality apart. In order to solve this problem, epistemology should play an active role in the design of future Augmented Reality systems and practices. To this end, this chapter puts forward some initial suggestions, concerning the training of Augmented Reality users and the design of certain reality augmentation features, in order to ensure that everyday epistemic practices won't be disrupted by the introduction of emerging Augmented Reality technologies.

Keywords: Augmented Reality, Extended Cognition, Epistemology, Philosophy of Cognitive Science, Cognitive Integration, Extended Knowledge, Philosophical Engineering, Augmented skepticism.

DOI 10.1515/9783110497656-008

1. Introduction

Weeks after the release of Pokémon Go, Police are offering safety advice to users of the popular online game and reminding players to concentrate on the real world when catching Pokémon. Car accidents, property trespassing, carelessly crossing the road, walking through landmines, and wandering in dangerous areas at inappropriate times of the day have raised a number of concerns, all related to the attention deficiency of overexcited users. Yet failing to concentrate on the real world is not the only and certainly not the most worrying aspect of Augmented Reality.[1]

'Seeing is believing' could so far be hardly doubted in most ordinary contexts. Yet this fundamental aspect of our everyday epistemic life is likely to be soon under serious threat by the advent of Augmented Reality. As Augmented Reality will become ubiquitous, it will likely take over most aspects of our daily interactions with surrounding objects and human beings, making it practically impossible to distance ourselves from this added dimension of future society, much in the same way that most people can no more leave their house without making sure they have their mobile phones on them. There is, no doubt, a great potential in this emerging technology, which promises to enrich our lives beyond imagination. But its users may also be exposed to the serious danger of being unable to tell reality and Augmented Reality apart.

This form of future 'augmented scepticism' cannot be neglected and important steps need to be taken with regards to the design of future Augmented Reality systems as well as teaching users how to employ the emerging technology in order to avoid this looming epistemic threat. By focusing on recent advances within contemporary epistemology and philosophy of mind and cognitive science, and especially the notion of *cognitive integration*, this chapter attempts to address this concern and provide advice that could secure our knowledge of the external world while also allowing our knowledge to be extended beyond our biological capacities, by taking advantage of the opportunities offered by Augmented Reality.

1 Strictly speaking, given how the current version of Pokémon Go works, it is a combination of both virtual and Augmented Reality.

2. Knowledge and cognitive integration

The received epistemological view holds that knowledge is justified true belief. 'Justification', however, is a term of art that can be given a number of different interpretations. According to the traditional account of knowledge, justification is a form of ability to provide explicit positive reasons in support of one's beliefs by reflection alone.[2] This is a familiar demand. We are many times asked to provide explicit reasons in support of our epistemic statements as well as in support of our reasons for claiming that we know such statements and so on. Nevertheless, however common this practice may be, it cannot really represent a universal theory of knowledge and justification as it generates serious problems, both from a theoretical and a practical point of view.

From a theoretical perspective, demanding to always be in a position to offer reasons in support of one's beliefs by reflection alone has the paralyzing epistemic effect of disallowing all perceptual and empirical knowledge. Technically, asking for one to justify one's perceptual and empirical beliefs by reflection alone poses the requirement that there be necessary support relations between one's empirical and perceptual beliefs and one's evidence for holding them. Hume's problem of induction demonstrates, however, that this is impossible.[3]

Similarly, from a practical perspective, there is a number of belief-forming processes, such as vision, hearing and memory, which are supposed to be knowledge-conducive, even though most epistemic agents have no idea how they work

---

2 Within contemporary epistemology, this is known as epistemic internalism. For classical defenses of this view see Chisholm (1977) and BonJour (1985, Chap. 2). See also Steup (1999), Pryor (2001, 3), BonJour (2002), Pappas (2005), and Poston (2008).

3 The problem of induction is well known. We form our beliefs about unobserved matters of fact and the external world on the basis of evidence provided by past and present observations and sensory appearances, respectively. In order for the support relations between our empirical and perceptual beliefs and the evidence offered in their support to be necessary, we also need the further assumptions that the future will resemble the past and that sensory appearances are reliable indications to reality, respectively. The problem is that both of these assumptions rely for their support on what they assert. Consequently, given that circular reasoning is invalid, there are no necessary support relations between our empirical beliefs and the evidence offered in their support. Accordingly, the conclusion that has been traditionally drawn is that our empirical and perceptual beliefs cannot amount to knowledge. For more details on how to reconstruct Hume's skepticism along these lines, see Greco (1999).

or why they are reliable.[4] Accordingly, when we acquire knowledge on their basis, it seems incorrect to require explicit positive reasons in their support.

To solve this long standing problem, several epistemologists have recently suggested that we should give up the aforementioned understanding of justification, and instead embrace a weaker alternative. According to this weaker alternative in order for one's true beliefs to qualify as knowledge, they must simply be the product of a belief-forming process that counts as a cognitive ability.[5] This is known as the *ability intuition on knowledge* and its intuitive appeal comes from the fact that cognitive abilities do seem to be the sort of belief-forming processes that can generate knowledge, even if one has no explicit positive reasons to offer in their support.[6] No one needs to explain why their vision or hearing is reliable when they come to acquire knowledge on their basis, after all.

If this is the way to approach knowledge and justification, however, two central questions need to be further addressed: (1) When does a process count as a cognitive ability and thereby as knowledge conducive, and – depending on how we answer (1) – (2) what is the sense in which one can be justified/epistemically responsible on the basis of one's cognitive abilities, but without requiring to offer any explicit reasons in their support?

In order to answer these two important questions, epistemologists have turned to the concept of *cognitive integration*. Recently, it has been proposed that in order for a process to count as a cognitive ability (and thereby as knowledge-conducive) it must have been *cognitively integrated*, where cognitive integration is a "function of cooperation and interaction, or cooperative interaction with other aspects of the cognitive system" (Greco 2010, 152). Accordingly, the answer to the first question is that a process may count as a cognitive ability (and thereby as knowledge-conducive) so long as it has been cognitively integrated on the basis of processes of mutual interactions with other aspects of the cognitive system.

---

4 This claim may generalize to all epistemic agents. There are no widely received or established views within cognitive science, regarding the mechanisms underlying any of the above belief-forming processes.

5 Within contemporary epistemology, this is known as virtue reliabilism. There is a still weaker alternative conception of knowledge and justification within the literature known as process reliabilism. For an overview of process reliabilism see (Goldman and Beddor 2015). For a number of arguments against the view and why virtue reliabilism is to be preferred see (Greco 1999, 2010, Pritchard 2010; Palermos 2014b).

6 The idea that knowledge must be grounded in cognitive abilities can be traced back to the writings of (Sosa 1988, 1993) and Plantinga (1993*a*, 1993*b*). For more recent approaches to this intuition, see Greco (1999, 2004, 2007, 2010) and Pritchard (2009, 2010a, 2010b, 2010, 2012).

One of the virtues of this approach to knowledge and justification is that it is fairly straightforward: In order for a reliable belief-forming process to count as knowledge-conducive, it must also count as a cognitive ability, and, in order for that to be the case, the relevant belief-forming process must mutually interact with other aspects of the cognitive system. Yet an additional advantage of this approach is that it can also provide a satisfactory response to the second question we posed above – i.e., what is the specific sense in which one can be justified/epistemically responsible on the basis of one's cognitive abilities, even in the absence of any explicit reasons in support of their reliability? The key, again, is to focus on the cooperative and interconnected nature of cognitive abilities: If one's belief-forming process interacts cooperatively with other aspects of one's cognitive system then it can be continuously monitored in the background such that *if* there is something wrong with it, *then* the agent will be able to notice this and respond appropriately. Otherwise – if the agent has no negative beliefs about his/her belief-forming process – he/she can be subjectively justified/epistemically responsible in employing the relevant process *by default*, even if he/she has absolutely no positive beliefs as to whether or why it might be reliable.

For example, in order for agent *S* to responsibly hold the belief that there is man standing in front of her, *S* does not need to offer explicit, positive reasons in support of the reliability of her visual system. Instead, provided that *S*'s visual system is interconnected with the rest of her cognitive system, then, in the mere lack of defeaters against the reliability of her visual perception, *S* can take herself to be epistemically responsible in holding the relevant belief *by default*. Had her working memory alerted her to the fact that the lighting conditions were not good, had she felt extremely tired, had her long term memory reminded her that she is watching a magic show, or had she tried to touch the person without receiving the expected tactile feedback, she would refrain from accepting the visually formed belief, no matter how truth-like it would appear to her. Nevertheless, in the absence of any such negative reasons against her belief, she can take herself to be epistemically responsible in holding the automatically delivered visual belief, *by default* (Palermos 2014b).

This way, we can make sense of the commonly held idiom that 'seeing is believing', or at least, 'seeing is believing, unless there are reasons to believe it is not'.

3. Extended knowledge and cognitive integration

But is this always the case, or just when we perceive the world through our biological equipment? Recent studies at the intersection of epistemology and philosophy of mind and cognitive science indicate that knowledge and justification can be technologically extended (Pritchard 2010c; Palermos 2011, 2014b, 2015, 2016; Palermos/Pritchard 2013; Carter *et al.* 2014).

Over the last two decades, philosophy of mind and cognitive science has become increasingly receptive to the idea that cognition is not head-bound but instead potentially extended to the artifacts we mutually interact with. Broadly known as the current of active externalism, this idea has been expressed under a number of headings by several philosophers and cognitive scientists (Clark/Chalmers 1998, Rowlands 1999, Wilson 2000, Wilson 2004, Menary 2007). One of the most influential formulations – perhaps the most influential – is known as the hypothesis of extended cognition and it holds that "the actual local operations that realize certain forms of human cognizing include inextricable tangles of feedback, feedforward and feed-around loops: loops that promiscuously crisscross the boundaries of brain, body and world" (Clark 2007, sec. 2). A list of examples of interactive, cognition extending equipment would include telescopes, microscopes, GPS systems, even pen and paper when trying to solve complex scientific problems (Palermos 2015) or while performing simple multiplication tasks.

Think about a three-digit multiplication problem such as 987 times 789. It is true that few if any of us can solve this problem by looking at or contemplating on it. We may only perform the multiplication process by using pen and paper to externalize the problem in symbols. Then we can serially proceed to its solution by performing simpler multiplications, starting with 9 times 7, and externally storing the results of the process for use in later stages. The process involves eye-hand motor coordination and it is not simply performed within the head of the person reciting the times tables. It involves intricate, continuous interactions between brain, hand, pen and paper, all the while it is being transparently regulated by the normative aspects of the notational/representational system involved – for instance, that we cannot multiply by infinity, that we must write the next digit under the second to last digit of the number above, what operation we must perform next and so on.[7]

Proponents of the hypothesis of extended cognition note that in such cases we can talk of an extended cognitive system that consists of both biological and technological resources, because the completion of the relevant cognitive task (e.g., performing the multiplication task) involves non-linear, cooperative interactions between the two components. According to dynamical systems theory

7 For the importance of the normative aspects of the external representational systems in explaining cognition see Menary (2007).

(DST) – i. e., the most promising mathematical framework for modeling such dynamically interacting systems – when this is the case we have to postulate an overall coupled system that consists of all the mutually interdependent components at the same time.[8] According to a dynamical interpretation of the hypothesis of extended cognition, when two (or more) components mutually interact with each other in order to complete a cognitive task, they give rise to an extended cognitive system that consists of all of them at the same time.[9]

This brings to the fore the possibility that knowledge-conducive cognitive abilities can be extended to the artifacts we employ. This is because epistemology and philosophy of mind and cognitive science put forward the same condition in order for a process to count as *cognitively integrated*, and thereby knowledge-conducive: Just as philosophers of mind claim that a cognitive system is integrated when its contributing parts engage in ongoing reciprocal interactions (independently of *where* these parts may be located), so epistemologists claim that cognitive integration of a belief-forming process (be it internal or external to the agent's organism) is a matter of cooperative interactions with other parts of the cognitive system.[10] The theoretical wedding of the two disciplines suggests there is no reason to disallow the belief-forming processes of extended or even distributed cognitive systems from counting as knowledge-conducive.

Provided that the relevant system is cognitively integrated on the basis of the mutual interactions of its component parts, it can generate epistemically responsible/justified beliefs, independently of whether it is organism-bound or extended. The ongoing interactivity of its component parts – i. e., its cognitively integrated nature – allows the system to be in a position such that if there is anything wrong with the overall process of forming beliefs, the system will be alerted to it and respond appropriately. Otherwise, if there is nothing wrong, the system can accept the deliverances of its belief-forming processes by default, without the further requirement to provide explicit positive reasons in their support. This is a form of justification/epistemic responsibility that does not belong

---

8 For more details behind this rationale and an extensive defense of this claim see Palermos (2014a). For an introduction to DST, see Abraham *et al.* (1990).

9 By contrast, using a ladder to paint the ceiling, heating food with microwaves, supermarket lists, turning the lamp on to see in a dark room, etc. won't qualify as cases of cognitive extension because in such cases there is no ongoing mutual interactivity between the agent and the involved artifact.

10 Elsewhere (Palermos 2011, Palermos 2014b), it has been argued that both disciplines also put forward the same broad, common sense functionalist intuitions on what is required from a process to count as a cognitive ability. Briefly, both views state that the process must be (a) normal and reliable, (b) one of the agent's habits/dispositions and (c) integrated into the rest of the agent's cognitive character/system.

to any of the component parts but to the relevant system as a whole. The reason is that it does not arise on the basis of any component parts operating in isolation but instead on their ongoing interactivity, which, according to DST, belongs to the system as whole.

For example, it is possible to use the above approach in order to explain how a subject might come to perceive the world on the basis of a Tactile Visual Substitution System (TVSS), while also holding fast to the idea that knowledge is belief that is true in virtue of *cognitive ability* (i.e. the ability intuition on knowledge). A TVSS comprises of a mini video camera attached on a pair of glasses, which converts the visual input into tactile stimulation under the agent's tongue or her forehead. By moving around and on the basis of the associated sensorimotor contingencies,[11] blind patients quickly start perceiving shapes and objects and orienting themselves in space. Occasionally, they also offer reports of feeling as if they are *seeing* objects, indicating that they are enjoying phenomenal qualities very close to those of the original sense modality that is being substituted. In light of DST, seeing through a TVSS qualifies as a case of cognitive extension, because it is a dynamical process that involves ongoing reciprocal interactions between the agent and the artifact. By moving around, the agent affects the input of the mini-video camera, which continuously affects the tactile stimulation she will receive on her tongue or forehead by the TVSS, which then continuously affects how she will move around and so on. Eventually, as the process unfolds, the coupled system of *the agent and her TVSS* is able to identify – that is, see – shapes and objects in space.

---

11 For a recent review on TVSS, see Bach-y-Rita and Kercel (2003). For a full account of how sensorimotor knowledge is constitutive of perception see Noë (2004). "The basic claim of the enactive approach is that the perceiver's ability to perceive is constituted (in part) by sensorimotor knowledge (i.e. by practical grasp of the way sensory stimulation varies as the perceiver moves)" (Noë 2004, 12). "What the perception is, however, is not a process in the brain, but a kind of skillful activity on the part of the animal as a whole" (Noë 2004, 2). "Perception is not something that happens to us or in us, it is something we do" (Noë 2004, 1). Sensorimotor dependencies are relations between movements or change and sensory stimulation. It is the practical knowledge of loops relating external objects and their properties with recurring patterns of change in sensory stimulation. These patterns of change may be caused by the moving subject, the moving object, the ambient environment (changes in illumination) and so on.

4. Augmented skepticism

Given the way Augmented Reality systems work, they have the potential to qualify as *cognitively integrated* and thereby knowledge-conducive extensions of biological cognition.

Most modern Augmented Reality systems combine the input from hardware components such as digital cameras, accelerometers, global positioning systems (GPS), gyroscopes, solid state compasses, and wireless sensors with simultaneous localization and mapping (SLAM) software, in order to track the position and orientation of the user's head and overlay computer data and graphics to her visual field in real time. By moving around with the Augmented Reality system, the user affects the input received by the hardware components, which continuously feeds in to the SLAM software. In turn, the SLAM software keeps constructing and updating a map of the user's unknown environment while simultaneously keeping track of the user's position in the physical world, the way she is pointing the device at and the axis the device is operating in. This constant interplay between the user, the Augmented Reality hardware and the Augmented Reality software allows the system to display computer-generated images on the user's field of perception and allows the user to visually interact with these virtual images while she moves in space as if they were real, physical objects.

In light of epistemology and philosophy of mind and cognitive science, this advanced degree of ongoing mutual interactivity between the user and the Augmented Reality system indicates that Augmented Reality can become a powerful technology for extending our knowledge beyond the epistemic abilities provided by our organismic cognitive capacities. A number of emerging applications across a multitude of disciplines indicate this clearly.

Users can perceive electromagnetic radio waves overlaid in exact alignment with their actual position in space. Augmented Reality can also be used to assist archaeological research, by superimposing archaeological features onto modern landscapes, allowing archaeologists to draw inferences about site placement and configuration. Augmented Reality archaeology applications can assist users reconstruct ruins, buildings and landscapes as they formerly existed. Architects and civil engineers can employ the technology to visualize future building projects. Computer-generated images of buildings can be overlaid into a real life local view of a property before the construction process begins. Architecture sight-seeing can be enhanced with Augmented Reality applications allowing users to virtually see through the walls of buildings and gain access to visual information about interior objects and layout. With recent improvements to GPS accuracy, construction companies are able to use Augmented Reality to visualize georeferenced models of construction sites, underground structures, cables and pipes.

Similarly, there is a number of potential commercial uses. Augmented Reality can enhance product previews such as allowing consumers to view what's inside a product's packaging without opening it. It can also be used in order to facilitate the selection of products from a catalogue or a kiosk. Augmented Reality users could gain access to additional content such as customization options and images or videos of the product in its use. Such technologies are already in use. It is possible, for example, to design printed marketing material so that it can bear certain "trigger" images that, when scanned by an Augmented Reality device, they activate a video version of the promotional material.

Augmented Reality can also make significant contributions to health and safety. Imagine a rescue pilot who is looking for a lost hiker in a forest. Augmented Reality systems can provide geographic awareness of forest road names and locations. As a result, the rescuer can more easily detect the hiker knowing the geographic context provided by the Augmented Reality system. Similarly, Augmented Reality can be used to let a surgeon look inside a patient by combining one source of images such as an f-MRI scan with another such as video.

Augmented Reality can also augment the effectiveness of navigation devices. Directions can be displayed on a car's windshield, while also indicating weather, terrain, road conditions and traffic information as well as alerts to potential hazards. Augmented Reality applications can enhance a user's travel experience by providing real time informational displays of her location and its features, as well as access to comments of previous visitors of the site. Augmented Reality applications can allow archaeological site visitors to experience simulations of historical events, places and objects by overlaying them into their view of a landscape. They can also offer location information by audio, calling attention to features of interest as they become visible to the user.

The above examples make it obvious that Augmented Reality has the potential to permeate and enrich our everyday lives in a variety of ways. As Augmented Reality technologies become less intrusive and more transparent, moving from hand held devices, to Augmented Reality glasses and finally to contact lenses, Augmented Reality will possibly not only penetrate every aspect of our lives but will become a constant, additional layer to physical reality that users will be practically unable to disengage from. Short films *Sight* (https://vimeo.com/46304267) and *Hyper-Reality* (https://vimeo.com/166807261) provide good tasters of how the augmented future might soon look like.

Augmented Reality therefore promises to provide a great opportunity for extending our knowledge in a variety of new and exciting ways. At the same time, however, it also poses the serious threat of obstructing our knowledge of the external world. Contrary to other forms of extended cognitive systems, Augmented Reality is specifically designed to generate and operate on the basis of unreal yet deceivingly truth-like mimicries of the external world in a way that users won't be able to distinguish augmented images from actual images of the world.

Of course, the integrated nature of our cognitive systems may still be in a good position to single out reality augmentations that cannot be easily confused as parts of physical reality. For example, floating prize tags above products or fluorescent navigation arrows in our visual field won't be of particular concern. On the basis of cognitive integration, our previous experience and knowledge of the external world will allow us to perceive such items as reality augmentations. Other aspects of augmented experience, however, are going to be troubling.

Consider, for example, *S*'s mundane experience of visually perceiving that a person is standing opposite her. *S* will be considerably worse off holding such a belief in an epistemically responsible manner while having her Augmented Reality system turned on than when she has it turned off. The possibility of having real-like yet virtual representations being superimposed on one's perception of the physical world will require a much more thorough background check by *S*'s integrated cognitive system before she can believe what she perceives. Normally, the presence of good-lighting and a relatively stable experience, along with the absence of any beliefs regarding the possibility of being tricked by a magician or undergoing drug-induced hallucinations, would be more than enough for *S* to know that there is a person standing opposite her. An Augmented Reality experience, however, would essentially amount to participating in a magic show. As such, believing what one sees would additionally require making haptic checks or being sensitive to additional cues that could potentially warn *S*' cognitively integrated nature to the fact that she is in a context where the presence of Augmented Reality avatars is to be expected.

In the absence of such additional background checks, 'augmented skepticism' would ensue, making it impossible to distinguish between virtually any aspect of augmented and physical reality. Perceiving and interacting with the external world would no more be the same, bringing about a dramatic change to our everyday epistemic practices.[12]

12 Indeed, it could have a destructive effect. One of the most promising ways to avoid the threat of radical skepticism is to note that our everyday beliefs are modally *safe*. However, this strategy works only on the assumption that radical skeptical hypotheses are modally far off from the actual world (see for example, Pritchard 2013, § 2). Practically speaking, this assumption has so far been easy to grant. Nevertheless, the advent of Augmented Reality technologies could make rad-

5. Future use and design

Augmented Reality therefore has the potential to both extend and distract our organismic epistemic capacities. Of course, technology optimists may disregard the above worries as being exaggerated. One could turn their Augmented Reality systems off anytime they liked, thereby eliminating the threat of 'augmented skepticism' at the push of a button. But how realistic is such optimism?

Considering the present-day analogue of owning a smart-phone, how often do we turn them off? Mobile phones are significantly less intrusive and attention-grabbing than future Augmented Reality technologies such as Augmented Reality glasses and Augmented Reality lenses are going to be. Smart-phones require their users to actively look at the screen instead of having information automatically pushed within their visual field. Yet mobile phone addiction has already started posing real life threats:

> In the case of cell-phones, such an addiction may begin when an initially benign behavior with little or no harmful consequences – such as owning a cell-phone for safety purposes – begins to evoke negative consequences and the user becomes increasingly dependent upon its use. Owning a cell-phone for purposes of safety, for instance, eventually becomes secondary to sending and receiving text messages or visiting online social networking sites; eventually, the cell-phone user may engage in increasingly dangerous behaviors such as texting while driving. Ultimately, the cell-phone user reaches a "tipping point" where he/she can no longer control their cell-phone use or the negative consequences from its over-use. (Roberts *et al.* 2014, 255)

Responsible theorizing and future planning and design cannot therefore rest on unsubstantiated optimism, especially when relevant evidence points in the opposite direction. Future Augmented Reality technologies are more likely than not to storm users' visual fields with push-on notifications, advertisements, personalized suggestions and reminders. Such reality augmentations could, in the best-case scenario, obstruct the user's perception of the external world and, in the worst-case scenario, cause severe disorientation with regards to what may be part of actual reality.

Careful planning and design, however, can reduce or even eliminate such risks. The preceding epistemological remarks on the role of cognitive integration can offer significant guidance to this end. Previously we noted that epistemic responsibility and justification rely on the mutual interactivity of the agent's belief-

---

ically skeptical scenarios modally close, thereby seriously questioning our psychological dismissal of radical skepticism on the basis of practical considerations.

forming processes. If there is something wrong with the way the agent is currently forming her beliefs, then it will clash with at least one of the agent's belief-forming processes running in the background, such that the agent will take notice and respond appropriately. Otherwise, if there is nothing wrong, the agent can accept the deliverances of her belief-forming process *by default.*

Given that Augmented Reality overlays augmentations on one's visual field, many of which might be deceptively real, one initial suggestion is to attempt to teach users how to employ the technology in a way that can diminish the ensuing 'augmented skepticism'. While it is difficult to imagine how future Augmented Reality will actually look like, a generic solution to this problem may include the progressive training of Augmented Reality users to recognize and automatically be aware of settings and social contexts in which deceptive reality augmentations are likely to be present. In such cases, users will have to be aware that relying on what they perceive won't be safe. Instead, they will need to employ their cognitively integrated nature more than it is normally required by performing additional background checks that will involve supplementary interactions with the perceived item (e.g., reaching out for the item in order to test whether it will provide the corresponding haptic feedback).

Key to the above solution is that users will be able to tell deceptive reality augmentations from non-deceptive ones apart. It assumes that even though users may be tricked by reality augmentations that look like deceptive representations of physical reality, they can easily spot augmentations that are unlikely to be found in physical reality (e.g., floating price tags above products, or navigational arrows pointing users in the right direction). This ability of our cognitively integrated natures relies on extensive previous experience of interacting with the physical world.

But what happens if the user has never had the opportunity to become thoroughly acquainted with the physical world outside Augmented Reality? Given how attractive digital technologies are to children, this is a developmental danger that future educational systems and upbringing must take into consideration. It may well sound as yet another exaggerated threat, but given the potential prevalence of Augmented Reality in future societies, it may not be easily disregarded as far-fetched. Should that ever become the case, children and students should be encouraged to spend as much of their day interacting with the actual physical world alone, or they may fail to enhance their cognitively integrated nature with the expectations that will be required to tell most instances of augmented and physical reality apart – even if reality augmentations are specifically designed to stand out from physical reality.

Future Augmented Reality users should therefore prime their cognitively integrated nature to identify non-deceptive augmentations as well as the contexts and settings in which deceptive augmentations are likely to appear. Yet despite such measures, users' epistemic standing may still be severely compromised. Not at all unlikely, the contexts and settings in which deceptive augmentations may appear could be widespread or even ubiquitous. If that turns out to be the case, users' ability to perceive the external world would be severely limited and slowed down, due to having to perform a number of additional – presently unnecessary – background checks with every step they'd take. Eventually, their experience would amount to walking through a mirror room.

A solution to this problem would require turning our attention away from the users' practices and towards the design of Augmented Reality. Augmented Reality developers would have to make sure that all augmentations bear features that would allow them to clearly and immediately stand out from the physical elements in the world without the need of unrealistically burdensome checks on the part of the users. The design of future Augmented Reality systems should not pose unrealistic demands on the users' cognitively integrated nature. Reality augmentations should automatically stand out as such, leaving minimal room for confusion or misinterpretation. For example, they should be delineated with fluorescent borders, have a see-through effect or both. In fact, to ensure users' epistemic ease and safety, such Augmented Reality design specifications could even be enforced via public policies and the law.[13]

Instead, a completely immersive experience, where virtual images could be entirely indistinguishable from physical reality could be retained for virtual reality, where the user's awareness of her physical disengagement will allow her to fully and safely enjoy the experience of mediated reality.

6. Conclusion

In order to solve the problem of the traditional account of knowledge, according to which justification is the ability to provide reflectively accessible positive reasons in support of one's beliefs, a number of epistemologists have suggested that knowledge is true belief that is the product of a cognitive ability. According to this alternative, a belief-forming process may count as a knowledge-conducive cognitive ability if and only if it has been cognitively integrated on the basis of processes of mutual interactions with other aspects of the agents' cognitive

13 For further considerations on how the hypothesis of extended cognition might invite a reconceptualisation of current legal theorising and practices, and especially of how we should perceive the right against personal assault, see Carter/Palermos (forthcoming).

system. One of the advantages of this approach is that it allows knowledge and justification to be extended to such artifacts as telescopes, microscopes, smartphones and Augmented Reality systems. Augmented Reality systems, however, rely on deceptive reality augmentations that could significantly deteriorate the epistemic efficiency of users' cognitively integrated natures. This could lead to a form of 'augmented skepticism', whereby it will be impossible to tell augmented from physical reality apart. In order to solve this problem, epistemology should play an active role in the design of future Augmented Reality systems and practices. To this end, this chapter has put forward some initial suggestions, concerning the training of Augmented Reality users and the design of certain reality augmentation features. This is but a first step to ensuring that our everyday epistemic practices won't be easily disrupted by the advent of Augmented Reality technologies. To avoid such threats it is important to not undermine the impact that philosophical engineering (Halpin 2013, Hendler/Berners-Lee 2010, Halpin et al. 2010, Palermos forthcoming), in general, and epistemological design, in particular, can make on the development of emerging technologies.

Acknowledgements

I am very thankful to Duncan Pritchard and Panagiotis Kourtesis for their thoughtful comments on a previous draft of this chapter.

References

Abraham, F. S./Abraham, R. H./Shaw, C. (1990): *A Visual Introduction to Dynamical Systems Theory for Psychology*, Santa Cruz, Ca: Aerial Press.

Bach-y-Rita, P./Kercel, S. W. (2003): "Sensory Substitution and the Human- Machine Interface". In: *Trends in Cognitive Science* 7(12), 541–546.

BonJour, L. (1985): *The Structure of Empirical Knowledge*, Cambridge, Ma: Harvard University Press.

BonJour, L. (2002): "Internalism and Externalism". In P. Moser (ed.), *Oxford Handbook of Epistemology*, Oxford: Oxford University Press, 234–264.

Carter, J. A./Kallestrup, J./Palermos, S. O./Pritchard, D. (2014): "Varieties of Externalism". In: *Philosophical Issues* 24(1), 63–109.

Carter, J. A./Palermos, S. O. (forthcoming): "The Ethics of Extended Cognition: Is Having Your Computer Compromised a Personal Assault?". In: *The Journal of American Philosophical Association.*

Chisholm, R. M. (1977): *Theory of Knowledge*, Englewood Cliffs, NJ: Prentice-Hall.

Clark, A. (2007): "Curing Cognitive Hiccups: A Defence of the Extended Mind". In: *The Journal of Philosophy* 104, 163–192.

Clark, A./Chalmers, D. (1998): "The Extended Mind". In: *Ananlysis* 58(1), 7–19.
Goldman, A. / Beddor, B. (2015): "Reliabilist Epistemology". In: E. N. Zalta (ed.), *The Stanford Encyclopedia of Philosophy*. Retrieved from http://plato.stanford.edu/archives/win2015/entries/reliabilism/
Greco, J. (1999): "Agent Reliabilism". In: *Philosophical Perspectives* 13, 273–296.
Greco, J. (2004): "Knowledge As Credit For True Belief". In: M. DePaul/L. Zagzebski (eds.), *Intellectual Virtue: Perspectives from Ethics and Epistemology*, Oxford: Oxford University Press, 111–134.
Greco, J. (2007): "The Nature of Ability and the Purpose of Knowledge". In: *Philosophical Issues* 17, 57–69.
Greco, J. (2010): *Achieving Knowledge: A Virtue-Theoretic Account of Epistemic Normativity*, Cambridge: Cambridge University Press.
Halpin, H./Clark, A./Wheeler, M. (2010): "Towards a Philosophy of the Web: Representation, Enaction, Collective Intelligence". In: *Proceedings of the WebSci10: Extending the Frontiers of Society On-Line*. Retrieved from http://journal.webscience.org/324/
Halpin, H. (2013). "Does the Web Extend the Mind?". In: *Proceedings of the 5th Annual ACM Web Science Conference*. Retrieved from http://dl.acm.org/citation.cfm?id=2479972.
Hendler, J./Berners-Lee, T. (2010): "From the Semantic Web to Social Machines: A Research Challenge for AI on the World Wide Web". In: *Artificial Intelligence* 174(2), 156–161.
Menary, R. (2007): *Cognitive Integration: Mind and Cognition Unbound*, Basingstoke: Palgrave McMillan.
Noë, A. (2004): *Action in Perception*, Cambridge, Ma: MIT Press.
Palermos, O. (2011): "Belief-Forming Processes, Extended". In: *Review of Philosophy and Psychology* 2, 741–765.
Palermos, S. O. (2014a): "Loops, Constitution, and Cognitive Extension". In: *Cognitive Systems Research* 27, 25–41.
Palermos, S. O. (2014b): "Knowledge and Cognitive Integration". In: *Synthese* 191(8), 1931–1951.
Palermos, S. O. (2015): "Active Externalism, Virtue Reliabilism and Scientific Knowledge". In: *Synthese* 192(9), 2955–2986.
Palermos, S. O. (2016): "Spreading the Credit: Virtue Reliabilism and Weak Epistemic Anti-Individualism". In: *Erkenntnis* 81(2), 305–334.
Palermos. S. O. (forthcoming): "Social Machines: A Philosophical Engineering". In: *Phenomenology and the Cognitive Sciences*.
Palermos, S. O./Pritchard, D. (2013): "Extended Knowledge and Social Epistemology". In: *Social Epistemology Review and Reply Collective* 2(8), 105–120.
Pappas, G. (2005): "Internalist *versus* Externalist Conceptions of Epistemic Justification". In: E. Zalta (ed.), *Stanford Encyclopaedia of Philosophy*. Retrieved from http://plato.stanford.edu/entries/justep-intext/
Poston, T. (2008): "Internalism and Externalism in Epistemology". In: B. Dowden & J. Fieser (eds.), *Internet Encyclopaedia of Philosophy*. Retrieved from www.iep.utm.edu/int-ext/
Pritchard, D. (forthcoming): "Anti-Luck Virtue Epistemology". In: *Journal of Philosophy*.
Pritchard, D. (2009): *Knowledge*, London: Palgrave Macmillan.
Pritchard, D. (2010a): "Knowledge and Understanding". In: A. Haddock / A. Millar / D. H. Pritchard (eds.), *The Nature and Value of Knowledge: Three Investigations*, Oxford: Oxford University Press.

Pritchard, D. (2010b): "Cognitive Ability and the Extended Cognition Thesis". In: *Synthese* 175 (1), 133–151.
Pritchard, D. (2013): *What is This Thing Called Knowledge?*, London and New York: Routledge.
Pryor, J. (2001): "Highlights of Recent Epistemology". In: *British Journal for the Philosophy of Science* 52, 95–124.
Roberts, J./Yaya, L./Manolis, C. (2014): "The Invisible Addiction: Cell-phone Activities and Addiction Among Male and Female College students". In: *Journal of Behavioral Addictions* 3(4), 254–265.
Rowlands, M. (2009): "Extended Cognition and the Mark of the Cognitive". In: *Philosophical Psychology* 22(1), 1–19.
Steup, M. (1999): "A Defense of Internalism". In: L. Pojman (ed.), *The Theory of Knowledge: Classical and Contemporary Readings* Belmont, CA: Wadsworth, 310–321.
Wilson, R. A. (2000): "The Mind Beyond Itself". In: D. Sperber (ed.), *Metarepresentations: A Multidisciplinary Perspective*, New York: Oxford University Press, 31–52.
Wilson, R. (2004): *Boundaries of the Mind: The Individual in the Fragile Sciences: Cognition*, New York: Cambridge University Press.

Bolesław Czarnecki and Tadeusz Czarnecki

Is Augmented Reality a Source of New Types of Knowledge?

Abstract: Some everyday cases of cognition show how computers functioning within Plain Reality give us a new type of knowledge. In contrast, the project of Augmented Reality is epistemologically challenging because it proposes hybrid scenarios which are friendly for cognitive agencies but infuse them with Virtual Reality (VR) overlay that is alienated from reality. Working with the assumption that Augmented Reality is ontologically heterogeneous, as it mixes experiences of individual objects with experiences of models, we examine its cognitive usefulness. We argue that insofar as our cognitive contact with Augmented Reality-based simulations may be even better than the celebrated contact with reality, there is room for extending the notion of knowledge.

Keywords: knowledge-that, knowledge-how, skill, Augmented Reality, model, simulation, registration, instrumental value.

1. Introduction

Pieces of knowledge-*that* may be interpreted as products of cognitive agents who, for example, transform their veridical experiences into true beliefs. Skeptical "Brain in a Vat" (BIV) scenario suggests that a brain totally immersed into Virtual Reality (VR) stands no chance of coming to know because its agency and experiences become illusory. We question whether BIV scenario is consistent if it does not explain how the agency of a brain can be reconstructed on the basis of VR experiences. Granting that agency and "contact with reality" are standard conditions for knowledge-*that* to emerge, we ask what is required to create an environment for a new type of experience which could result in a new type of knowledge. Such an environment should not violate cognitive agency and offer a new type of non-deceptive experience. There are everyday cases of cognition which show how computers functioning within Plain Reality provide us with information which is a new type of knowledge. These cases are easily acceptable because the information respects the requirement that we remain in touch with reality. In contrast, the project of Augmented Reality is epistemologically challenging because it proposes hybrid scenarios which are friendly for cognitive agencies but infuse them with VR overlay that is alienated from reality. Augmented Reality scenarios do not tamper with our senses and essentially extend of our

DOI 10.1515/9783110497656-009

experiences. They provoke, however, the question in what sense VR overlay could be veridical, as it somehow must be in order to support instances of new types of knowledge. We propose that it is helpful to assume that Augmented Reality is ontologically heterogeneous and mixes experiences of individual objects with experiences of models. Models become cognitively useful when they are models of future individuals, and are adequately anchored in reality. If this last condition is satisfied, cognitively advantageous situations may be generated whereby we experience 3D models in the environment of individuals, rather than 2D models in the environment of other 2D models. In this paper, we mainly consider the usefulness of 3D presentations in quite a different context of possible extensions of knowledge-*how*. That is, we analyze the possibility that 3D artificial experiences of an agent are sufficiently multilayered to generate their new manual skills. Though skeptical about it, we try to formulate conditions which augmented experiences should fulfil to generate reliable simulations of new manual skills. We claim that in both areas of knowledge simulation is the crucial component to take into account. We believe that our cognitive contact with simulations may be even better than the celebrated contact with reality. Especially, if simulations are able to diminish the risk of failure when we strive for useful information or useful manual skill in order to obtain practical goals. If we adhere to the idea that problems should precede pieces of knowledge necessary to solve them, then reliable simulations may by indisputably more valuable in solving problems than fully veridical experience. Thus, we finally come to a conclusion that Augmented Reality project gives us perhaps a strategic impulse to extend the basic notion of knowledge and ask on what conditions new types of knowledge can be found in the sphere of computer simulations.

2. Skeptical VR scenario

Epistemologists resign themselves to the idea that cognitive agents fully immersed in Virtual Reality (VR) cannot have knowledge, perceptual knowledge, in particular. Let's try to explain first who are cognitive agents. Minimally, they are meant to be individuals of sufficient cognitive abilities and skills to acquire and sustain their own justified true beliefs. To be an agent requires having cognitive autonomy. A criterion of cognitive autonomy is self-knowledge: an agent has to know who they cognitively are. They need to be cognitively sensitive to their cognitive self. And this seems to involve the agent's knowing what their cognitive skills and capacities are. Another, and more obvious criterion is that to be an agent one to have successful cognitive grasp of reality: an agent has to know to a degree what reality is like and this knowledge should be acquired in virtue of their own skills and capacities. In any case, reliable evaluation of one's cognitive resources is a necessary condition on having knowledge about reality.[1]

The question whether computer simulations could extend one's knowledge may have an affirmative answer if we assume that such simulations (1) do not violate someone's cognitive agency and (2) information that they provide for the agent remains in a way reliably veridical: it systematically maps the reality, or, at least, it is not systematically cognitively deceptive. Here, however, we face a deeper question whether simulations can give us new knowledge. It seems that Virtual Reality opens the possibility of immediate artificial experience which precedes or even predicts future facts and may be in a special sense veridical. Still, the agent must intellectually process the experience to produce cognitively useful beliefs. The intellectual operation of predicting future, which requires special cognitive skills of reasoning, would then change into direct seeing of future facts.

We can easily imagine that the agent is provided with reality-like 3D experience of a new type which was impossible to acquire without computer processing. It surely opens a window of opportunity for new type of knowledge. Now, we want once again to stress the difference between feeding an agent with experiences and formulating by the agents their own beliefs on the basis of these experiences. We will claim that artificial experiences need not to be deceptive if the agent consistently distinguishes between objects of reality and models of reality. Along with that, we assume that ascriptions of cognitive success to someone are fully justified only on the level of their beliefs, not on the level of experiences. For simplicity, we envisage perceptual experiences here as connected with natural capacities had by an agent, i.e., the senses, whereas the agent's perceptual beliefs are connected with something well beyond: skills of interpretation acquired by cognitive training. Agents typically learn how to formulate perceptual beliefs and the strength of their agency is measured by their skills of interpretation.

Epistemologists seem equally fascinated with virtuous and vicious cognitive scenarios involving computer processed information. A "Brain in a Vat" (BIV)

1 These remarks locate our proposal within a vast range of virtue-theoretic approaches, particularly those of Montmarquet (1987), Sosa (1980, 2007, 2015) and Zagzebski (1996), where the multilayered notion of skillful cognitive engagement is central. That said, we will largely remain neutral with respect to other proposals on offer. Where our proposal stands out most clearly, perhaps, is in respect of value-turn aspect of cognitive virtue (see Pritchard 2007).

scenario is of the latter kind.[2] Typical variants of BIV are intended to offer situations of full cognitive deception. An important deficiency of these scenarios, however, is that they contain explanatory gaps that prevent us from understanding what implies full cognitive deception. In effect, we face the question of what it would take for a BIV scenario to constitute a credible BIVR scenario – "Brain in Virtual Reality."[3] As far as standard BIVs are concerned, epistemologists stress (1) the cognitive isolation of the discarnate brain, (2) cognitive cruelty of the mad scientist who manipulates the brain and (3) the unlimited creative capabilities of the computer he uses to feed the brain with artificial experiences. It is then declared that whatever the brain is cognitively fed with depends entirely of the mad scientist who controls the computer which is the only source of the brain's experiences.

But consider, very briefly, problems with two variants of BIV: *envatment of cognitive agency*, which is an instance of full deception, and *doxastic envatment*, whereby beliefs are under threat, even though cognitive agency has not been compromised.[4]

We think that full deception is not an easy task to achieve if one assumes that the brain should be deceived only on the level of its beliefs: the brain would be fully deceived if it acquired false beliefs at the manipulator's will. However, for it to acquire any belief, the brain must retain cognitive agency, which involves the capacity for self-evaluation of its abilities and skills. This requirement may cause unpleasant restrictions on the manipulator's alleged omnipotence. After all, how does it happen that the discarnate brain remains convinced of his intact cognitive agency? How is it made the case that although in no way the brain controls its cognitive processes it is still convinced that it does? Even if the manipulator materially faces a brain, he must cognitively challenge an agent. Here, we think, the manipulator has two options to choose from, and both equally mysterious. Firstly, he may try to reconstruct the original cognitive agency of the brain. How could he know how to do this? How could he have a full access to the original cognitive agency of the brain? Secondly, he could wash the brain and overlay on it a new cognitive agency. Again, what would that mean? Either option leads to the following problem: How is it possible to deceive the brain

2 For the classical formulation see Putnam (2000). For distinct interpretations and treatments see Brueckner (1986) and Warfield (1995). For the most recent assessment of skeptical strategies including BIV, see Pritchard (2016) and Wright (1992).

3 Dennett (1993) outlines a number of concerns in a similar spirit.

4 In a related context of cognitive extension Pritchard (2010) maintains that in the BIV scenario an agent could easily be fed *beliefs* of various types. We contend that *doxastic envatment* is not an easy epistemic situation to achieve.

about its cognitive agency without recreating its cognitive autonomy? We think it is exceptionally difficult to state what processes the recreation should involve to be successful. In effect, we suspect that epistemologists do not quite know what they talk about when they consider cognitive implications of "Brain in a Vat" scenarios.

The *doxastic envatment* variant of the scenario seems a bit simpler. It concerns causal chains resulting in the brain's artificial experiences. Specifically, causal chains resulting in perceptual experience of the brain are always mediated by the computer. For instance, they may begin within the computer and then lead to deceptive experience, or begin within the reality, but then get transformed by the computer in ways that make experience unreliable. Crucially, and this presumably is the most speculative component of the story, deception coming from the scientist *via* the computer mainly consists in their switching at will between falsidical and veridical perceptual experiences to provoke the brain – made to believe to some extent that it is a cognitive agent – to formulate false beliefs about the reality. Whether beliefs turn out true or false does not matter much, since falsidical experience that underpins them is *ex hypothesi* totally worthless, whereas veridical experience is unreliable and, therefore, hardly better. Here again, however, one faces the question: How to engineer a virtual environment (like a real one!) that supports the generation or maintenance of false beliefs about reality without the brain – which is to a significant degree cognitively autonomous – ever forming a belief that its experience is deceptive?

There are no proposals to explain why the brain believes that it is an agent having typical cognitive abilities and special cognitive character; how the manipulator makes the brain think that it has a living body which is perceptually sensitive and skillful in acting, has its own cognitive aims, own practical targets, and so on.

It is not our aim, however, to engage with BIV scenarios in detail, but merely to highlight that they purport to show, one-sidedly, that Virtual Reality is cognitively useless without explaining why. Usually they are imprecise as to whether and how the brain retains its cognitive agency, how it is possible to produce for it a false cognitive agency, how the false cognitive agency is to be fed with experience to make the brain cognitively satisfied, and so on. What matters for our purposes is that radical scenarios end with the pessimistic conclusion, not necessarily well justified, that no VR information in no VR world for no VR agent can become a form of knowledge.

3. Benign scenarios involving computer information

Normally, we take it for granted when using computers that our cognitive agency is impregnable to a sufficient degree. To be sure, the quality of interaction with computers is becoming increasingly agent-like. Nevertheless, as things stand we give our computers no chance to deceive us as to who we are as cognitive agents, and they are frequently reduced to being our sources of information. Crucially, if we see a computer as an independent external object with some information written on its screen, there is often no problem with ascribing a logical value to the information and to decide whether it is reliable enough to provide for us a source of knowledge-that. Similarly, if we watch 2D pictures displayed on a computer screen which is a separate object within our field of view among other external objects, it is often easy enough to decide whether the computer pictures carry true information, e.g., whether they map the reality around us in epistemically salient ways. Whenever that's the case, the basic epistemic problem is just that: What cognitive use are we able to make of the information?

3.1 Operational knowledge-*that*

Let's distinguish between factive knowledge-that, and operational knowledge-that. For example, as a skilled car driver Ela believes that GPS truly shows to her both where she is and where she should go. The first information is factive, whereas the second is operational. If GPS reliably transmits true information, there is no problem with ascribing to her knowledge that she is here-and-so and that she should go there-and-so. Both types of knowledge are interconnected: GPS enables Ela to know where she should drive because it also enables her know where she is. Typically, GPS knowledge is of essential instrumental value, i.e., often one wants to know where one is not because they just want to know where they are but because it helps them to move efficiently; and, in Ela's case, to reach some previously established destination point.

If Ela is a skillful interpreter of GPS visualizations, these help her to remain on the right track towards her final destination. Arguably, this type of knowledge is of a new type because she knows where she is and where to go in the surroundings that are totally unfamiliar to her. Factively, she may be lost, but operationally she is still in control. With this kind of operational knowledge she can move efficiently. In contrast, if she only had factive knowledge where she is and what destination point she wants to reach, this knowledge in unknown surroundings would be useless.

Locally, GPS information may be functionally on a par with information provided by a system of road signs which are all elements of reality. For instance, some signs point Ela in the right direction, so when she sees and follows these, she doesn't need to follow information from GPS. Indeed, GPS has no monopoly on guiding her driving, though usually it guides her more efficiently and, absent technological mishaps, more reliably than road signs. But there are important differences in what the road signs and GPS afford to Ela. First, unlike signs, GPS makes her driving in unknown areas as smooth as her driving in well-known areas. But there is also a robust qualitative difference that goes beyond the degree of efficiency, namely, that GPS opens for Ela a new perspective on moving. Using it, Ela may identify her position and a way to a destination in unknown surroundings: starting in *any* unknown place Ela may move efficiently to *any other* unknown place. She can navigate without first becoming a navigator herself.

Now, we find it vital for our discussion of Augmented Reality to introduce the following enabling condition. When digital information is displayed in such a way that the computer and its screen are invisible to you, and it seems to you that the information is placed immediately in reality which surrounds you, then you find yourself in Augmented Reality. We think an important definitional implication is that when computer-generated information transforms Plain Reality into Augmented Reality, the information enriches your overall experience in a mode that bypasses and, is experientially insulated from, experiences caused by external objects. And if we could precisely define what are the new types of experiences, then we could also define new types of experiential knowledge. As we see it, then, GPS projections on one's mobile phone screen are not yet a part of Augmented Reality, though they easily could be. To satisfy the condition, it is enough to make invisible the screen on which the information is primarily displayed.

Consider the following to be a somewhat more precise elaboration of that condition. So long as a computer screen is a visible external object, and together with other external objects co-creates one's field of view, then what one experiences is treated as part of Plain Reality. Plain Reality transforms into Augmented Reality when one sees information that is displayed on a fully transparent screen which creates new boundaries of one's field of view, but is not itself a part of their field of view. If one has the impression that any pictorial or written information they see is present immediately among external objects, then they face what is called Augmented Reality. Finally, one finds oneself within Mixed Reality, if when equipped with a device containing a transparent screen, they can experience 3D objects which seem to be placed in the fragment of reality that they actually see through the screen. The simplest way of making GPS a part of Augmented Reality is by generating a visible secondary screen within an invisible primary screen. These are basic tricks of Mixed Reality: to generate 3D artificial experience by displaying information on a transparent screen or by displaying new 2D visible secondary screens behind the invisible primary screen.

There are two systematic illusions connected with creating an Augmented Reality. Firstly, even if a screen is necessary to generate projections, it must be so positioned as if there were no screen at all, that is, as if you had an unmediated visual contact only with external objects and *via* unaided eye. Secondly, all 3D projections are illusory in the following sense: Reality remains unchanged, only our artificial experiences change. A question to answer is what can be the cognitive status of 3D projections. If they are virtual, how could they be sources of knowledge-*that?*

3.2 Knowledge-*how* to act

Computer information may be decisive in acquiring knowledge-*how* to act. In particular, simulators when coupled with computer simulations seem highly effective in supporting the acquisition of manual knowledge-*how* to act. For instance, we can significantly deepen our skills of driving a car. Technically, standard simulators involve real tools, such as a driving wheel to manipulate, along with computer simulations projected on a computer screen which visualize predicted results of our manipulations. What is important here is that standard simulation procedures combine real causes, real actions, and predicted unreal results, with our bodies being engaged in manipulating material tools essentially similar to those we will use in performing real actions. For example, we manipulate a wheel which functionally resembles a real driving wheel with the expected final result being a real skill acquired by simulated training. Standard simulators are valuable because they enable us to learn through "trial and error" with no negative results characteristic of real errors: when we make simulated errors no real damage is done. We can learn on errors which have only virtual consequences.

In a special sense, such knowledge-*how* is of a new type because virtual errors are pedagogically as efficient as real errors. At this juncture, an important question arises whether we can go any further in learning by computer simulations and apply Augmented Reality to acquire real manual skills either *via* (1) reversing the order of causes and results, i. e., starting with simulated causes and ending with real effects, or (2) totally breaking the pattern by substituting real causes and effects with simulated caused and effects.

Arguably, when we entirely separate ourselves from reality, we are unable to acquire manual skills. For example, we cannot learn how to drive a car only by making thought experiments, i.e., by imagining that we manipulate a driving wheel in a certain way and imagining that the results we obtain are such and such. An argument supporting this claim would be that these imaginary simulations cannot work because there is no reliable connection between imaginary moving of an imaginary driving wheel and imaginary results of imaginary driving. These imaginary causes and the results are in no way anchored in reality.

Now, a question may be asked whether we can eliminate the drawbacks of thought experiments by simulations made within Mixed Reality. Whether we can learn how to drive a car by applying a virtual wheel of a virtual car in a real scenery or a virtual wheel connected with a virtual secondary screen presenting virtual surroundings. It seems that much would depend on anchoring all the important elements of such augmented simulation in reality. But then still further problems arise. To acquire a manual skill something more is necessary than new visual experiences. We need new bodily experiences such as, for example, new kinaesthetic feelings. Such feelings do not arise without tactile experiences in our body. But it is unclear whether Magic Leap project, for example, has ambitions to equip us with new artificial tactile experiences.[5]

4. Non-standard simulations and new knowledge-*how*

People alone cannot transform stored information about their past natural experiences into the same experiences again: they cannot re-vitalize past experiences. They also cannot see objects they only have thought about or imagined: they cannot pre-vitalize future experiences. In contrast, information stored in computer's memory can be repeatedly transformed into people's artificial perceptual experience. This opens the doors for experiences transcending time. Similarly, people cannot generate visual simulations of objects, events or actions at will, but computers give them this special possibility.

5 Here one may also find it useful to engage more closely with distributed cognition frameworks, particularly those that focus on embodied and enactive character of skill, to then present a case for a new type of tactile cognitive extension through AR.

In some sense standard characterisations of Augmented Reality, following Azuma's (1997) definition which requires that it combine the real and virtual, be interactive in real time and registered in 3D, are somewhat misleading since they may incite the hope that computer technologies are aimed at bringing direct changes in the world. It is obvious that augmentation makes sophisticated hardware appear in the world, but when we speak of the results of augmentation it should be clear that we mean solely changes in our experience caused *by* this hardware. Firstly then, to straighten out the matter of what augmentation may change, it is useful to stress that (1) experience alone does not change the world and (2) the world provides the ultimate point of reference, but in decidedly different ways, both for our natural experiences and artificial experiences generated by computer technologies. Natural experiences are caused by, whereas artificial experiences must be registered with, the world to count for us. The world does not materially change by augmentation though our experience may change immensely, and we augment our experience reasonably when, for example, inspired by instrumental reasoning about means to obtain ends, we decide to make a change in the world and, before we actually make it, thanks to artificial experience we feel well prepared to succeed in making it. We deliberately change the world only by actions, although we may precede the actions with deliberate augmentations.

Thus, the issue of Augmented Reality begins to look serious if we manipulate our experiences motivated by problems we face and our perseverance to solve them. Anyway, here we distinguish between capricious augmentations which are art for its own sake and purposeful augmentations which prepare us to undertake actions to successfully change the world in order to improve our position in it.

From the point of view of epistemology, inspiring are these definitional conditions which require that Augmented Reality be a medium for displaying 3D presentations (1) registered with the world and (2) phenomenally adjusted to the world and the agent who perceives them.[6] These conditions imply, for example, that if some places are chosen in the world as stable points of reference and an agent using Augmented Reality glasses is a mobile point of reference, then the way he is experiencing virtual objects is fully consistent with the way he is experiencing material objects. Experiences of both types should follow the same rules of presentation, or their basic phenomenology should have the same gram-

6 For a characterization of AR as medium rather than a type of technology itself see Craig (2013). For a survey of definitions see Billinghurst *et al.* (2015) and Grubert *et al.* (2016). The latter discuss conditions for *pervasive* Augmented Reality that would offer continuous experience of reality-registered presentations and be context-aware.

mar. That is, if the shape a virtual object is experienced in a particular way by an agent, the shape of its physical counterpart would be experienced by him in the same way.

A desirable property of augmented experiences is their plasticity. Natural visual experiences are not essentially plastic in relation to the agent. To retain veridicality, their content must be determined by external causes, i.e., properties of material objects. Augmented Reality offers the agent an option of controlling the substance of their artificial experiences. And it is fascinating that artificial experience may become interactive in relation to its agents, whereas natural experience is interactive mainly in relation to its objects. The property of plasticity is intellectually promising when manipulations are meant to display, for example, a sequence of possible states of affairs to allow us to make the best choice between them.

A separate question is whether the plasticity of experience is practically promising, i.e., whether by manipulating artificial experiences we can improve our manual skills; whether, in particular, we can acquire new manual skills by manipulating our experiences of manipulating virtual objects, instead of manipulating material objects. It is important whether Augmented Reality technologies can simulate causal connections between, for example, artificial experiences of an agent and bodily skills of the agent. Standard simulators destined for teaching manual skills connect authentic bodily actions engaging physical tools with computer simulations of their results in some virtual surroundings. That is, such simulations predict only the results of actually performed actions: real causes are combined with reliably predicted though unreal effects.

Could we introduce non-standard simulators which would reverse the order of real causes and simulated effects while retaining the reliability of standard simulators (i.e. ones where we begin with virtual causes and reliably end with real effects)? Think, for instance, of a golf stroke simulator that mixes strokes performed with real clubs and balls *with* virtual trajectories of the balls visualized on a screen. Can it allow for the possibility of augmented *strokes?* The person in such a scenario sees their body performing moves characteristic of a stroke, but the stroke is partially augmented as it involves artificial experience of a club. They strike the ball by engaging their real body, in the real surroundings of a golf course, yet its result is artificially visualized in the real space of the course. Could we make such reverse simulations reliable? If we could, we could also improve our game by such simulations. This would mean that we have an unquestionably new source of knowledge-*how* to act.

Thus, we face many questions concerning the possibility of extension both of the methodology of learning how to act and, further, the environment of acting; the possibility that our actions easily switch between Plain Reality and Augmented Reality. The fundamental one is whether it is practically illuminating to mix manual moves of a body with virtual tools and observe their virtual results in the real world. We show below how one could learn intellectually by mixing two worlds of objects, but the question remains whether one can also learn manually by mixing two worlds of actions. Especially, when the learning begins with highly augmented bodily moves and but its aim are real results of the moves.

It seems uncontroversial that augmentation may develop the intellectual aspect of manual actions because spatio-temporal manipulations may turn out sufficiently helpful to decide whether or not one encounters an opportunity to act. We can plan virtually how to make the best use of the skills we already possess. But it is uncertain whether augmentation gives us a chance to improve the skills themselves, or whether it always makes sense to try to improve them by augmentation.

Let's take a closer look at the golf shot case. When one has artificial experience of a golf club, then its location is independent of where one is and how they move. One clearly is the viewer of the virtual club. But can they also be the user of the virtual club? If one's artificial experience of a club were mixed with their natural experience of a golf course, then the experience of the club would be rooted in a hardware, whereas the experience of the golf course would be rooted in reality. There would, then, be two independent causal chains of their intertwined experience, one that hinges on the external world and the other that is enabled by computer stored information. Generally, where virtual objects are involved, these exist imprisoned in a computer, as opposed to the physical world. Optimists about artificial experience may try to persuade us that due to its spatio-temporal registration with the world, the club may be felt present in the world.[7] But spatio-temporal location is only the tip of the iceberg when we try to understand what would be the profile of artificial experience such as to make one feel, and believe, that they are actually producing a golf shot with a virtual club and ball. Minimally, a reliable simulation seems required of one's bodily contact with the ball *via* the club, a reliable simulation of the physical impact of the club on the ball and, finally, a reliable simulation of the result of the impact. If this can be done, Augmented Reality will become a powerful source of knowledge-how. But can this be done? And, further, does it always make sense to produce non-standard simulations?

Apart from its location in the world, a physical club also has dispositional properties that determine its identity as a specific tool. It is in virtue of these properties that the club responds in certain ways to certain bodily actions of

7 See Craig (2013).

the player and can be used purposefully. If we are not mistaken, Augmented Reality technologies at their present stage of development enable one to change the location of a virtual club, however, it is dubious whether they also enable them to use it.

Clearly, one cannot directly strike a physical ball with a virtual club, i.e., with their artificial experience of a club. And this is because there are no direct causal links between one's body, their experiences of virtual objects such as a club, and the target physical object – in our case, the ball. Now, direct causal links would be dispensable if they could be reliably simulated. Could the causal links between one's body and a physical object, which standardly create an action, be reliably simulated when, with their body, one intends to make some use of that object's virtual counterpart? This troublesome question demands a precise answer. And as long as we don't know what types of dispositional properties of virtual objects could be reliably simulated, we also don't know what actions engaging these objects could be simulated.

At present, real objects and virtual objects have very distant grammars of dispositional properties. That is, our interactions with virtual objects are so far one-sided and primitive in comparison with interactions we can have with physical objects in Plain Reality. And it is hard to predict whether this distance will be essentially shortened and which dispositional properties will be selected as worth simulating. Anyway, as we need in advance a list of dispositional properties of physical objects if we want to evaluate their manual utility, similarly, we will need to have a list of respective simulations if we want to act in Mixed Reality effectively and reasonably.

There are, therefore, two limitations to break if we are to acquire new knowledge-*how* while being immersed in Mixed Reality. First limitation pertains to the physical impact that one's body can be simulated to have on virtual objects. The second one concerns the impact that virtual objects can be simulated to have on the physical world, including one's body. So far, it is unclear whether the breaking has been started. Though spatio-temporal registration with the world is undoubtedly a success, something we could call "dispositional registration" would surely outbalance its significance. It would be quite stimulating if we could manipulate dispositional properties of virtual objects, eliminating the undesirable and adding or enhancing the desirable ones. But, again, we don't know when such augmentations will be possible, and so it is difficult to say, for example, which types of simulations we should avoid or accept.

5. Chances of new types of knowledge-*that*

It is said that some 3D virtual objects may have their physical counterparts. This claim is somewhat disputable. If one entertains 3D artificial experience of a golf club which is modelled on a particular club that one actually has, is their real club a counterpart of the virtual club? Is the virtual club one sees an individual? Generally, are 3D virtual objects one sees *via* Augmented Reality headsets individuals? There are reasons to hold they are not.

Firstly, the objects of artificial experience function as, and have properties of, models, i.e., general objects. They are the same for all users of a headset. i.e., the same digital information is processed to produce the same artificial experiences for many people. When they are displayed, all users of headsets of a type enjoy qualitatively the same possibilities of experiences. Objects displayed in Mixed Reality presentations provide, of course, various sorts of models: (1) Models of objects which exist, (2) models of non-existing objects which are intended to exist and, finally, models of the unreal objects which are not intended to exist. And if we were to bet which of them are the right candidates for vehicles of new types of knowledge-*that*, our choice would be that models of intended objects.

By models we mean objects that are neither autonomous nor unique entities: objects that can be perfectly replicated, or repeatedly displayed by many displayers, with no change in their visible properties. Similarly, if models undergo a structural change, the change is determined or initiated externally: they are not sources of their own structural changes and, especially, they do not autonomously evolve. A crucial property of 3D models is that they cannot be changed by direct external impact coming from real objects or agents; especially, from direct impact initiated by bodily actions of human agents.

What more can we get to know from Mixed Reality that we cannot get to know from Plain Reality alone? If we ask this question there is a preliminary demarcation line to draw between projections made for mere entertainment, or for purely mercantile purposes, and those made for serious cognitive purposes.[8] To the extent that computer games are usually made to entertain the consumer, and for financial gain of the seller, we will largely set aside the possibilities of their development. Of course some games escape this qualification, especially when they directly serve educational purposes. In any case, we expect that if serious

---

8 For a roughly similar point on models see Hofmann (2013) who holds that a distinguishing feature of "serious" simulations is their validity, where basic assumptions about what exists, how to come to know, and how to achieve a goal are key determining factors at play.

augmentations of reality entail essential ontological extensions of reality, they should bring original additions to people's bodies of knowledge. If we look through advertisements of Microsoft or Magic Leap technologies, it is often unclear whether they entail such extensions or in what sense they do.[9]

5.1 Seeing models in real surroundings

Mixed Reality (MR) presentations seem sometimes cognitively idle in that they are aimed to make a momentary impression: their programmed result is "Wow!" of the viewer; an exclamation of astonishment. Advertisements of MR equipment offer a lot of cognitively undetermined simulations. That is, when we watch them it is difficult to decide whether they carry any clear message for the viewer as to how to consume them intellectually or practically. As if the ambition of these technologies was restricted only to whether artificial experiences already are, or are not yet, qualitatively indistinguishable from natural experiences; as if nothing more should be required of them beyond the mere capacity to "fool our senses". Fortunately, MR leaders unanimously declare their technologies are intended not to fool us as cognitive agents but, on the contrary, to help us cognitively. How can they help?

One promising development consists in changing the way of designing new objects which are intended to exist. Where the geometry of an object is essential for its future functioning – no matter of what type the object is to be – making spatial models of such objects is indispensable before producing real individuals. The old-fashioned method of designing the geometry of a model consisted in drawing on paper three 2D projections of its intended shape. After which a key turning point came: movable 3D computer projections on a visible computer screen. With recent advancements the question has become: what can we gain when we complete our designs with 3D augmentations, i. e., when we experience a 3D final model of an object in some real surroundings? The answer is that the closer to the reality the model is, the better we know whether the real object will fit the reality. Obviously, we get "perfect" knowledge about fitting only when we see how a real object fits real surroundings. But the second best option is to see a 3D model in real surroundings. Designers acknowledge that the environment of an object is important. For example, architects aim to anticipate whether a house will fit certain real surroundings geometrically and aesthetically; and it is not uncommon that the view of the real object in its real surroundings does not satisfy

9 For an informative discussion of the enigmatic Magic Leap see Kelly (2016).

the expectations of its designer; particularly, the real object sometimes looks worse in real surroundings than its model looked in fully artificial surroundings. Although the profit of MR designing is sometimes minor – as when the model shows the shape but cannot show the functioning of the future object – we undoubtedly gain a new type of knowledge when what we see now is as close to the future as possible.

Importantly, the value of such knowledge-*that* increases if the object and its surroundings form a whole. If in planning a new type of object we must also plan its physical and functional contexts of functioning, and when its functioning tightly depends on other objects' functioning, then it makes a qualitative epistemic difference that we oppose 3D projections and real objects. A reason is that reality is coarse-grained, whereas models are ideal, or finely-grained. It is an unpleasant shock when it turns out that a model embedded in another model fitted perfectly but a real object embedded in real surroundings does not. Typically, old-fashioned designs consisted of models within models: of models of objects embedded in models of their surroundings. From that angle, transition to the model-reality pair is surely advantageous as it makes designing more reliable and more flexible. We may choose what to put into what. Sometimes it is preferable to put a real object into artificial surroundings, sometimes it is preferable to put an artificial object into real surroundings.

5.2 Seeing the inner structure

An identification mark of the old-fashioned designing were 2D cross-sections of models. As 2D projections showed usually the exterior planes of an object, always when it was also necessary to reveal key connections of its interior elements, 2D cross-sections were unbeatable. They were necessary to show that the design was internally consistent, that there were no conflicts between its elements. As a house, for example, includes different installations, wiring, ventilation, gas fittings, among others, and they must be skillfully coordinated, cross-sections were necessary to show that they were. Now, 3D models offer the possibility of seeing the full interior of a designed object in any scale. We can at will see the interior of a future house in its full scale, along with every element in its real dimensions. It is, therefore, tempting to claim that we can perceive now a future house, or even that we now visually know the house although it does not yet exist. Of course, there is a difference between seeing a model and seeing a real house. A lot may happen between having a finished model and having a target real object. But sometimes we are certain that the difference will be negligible. Although the model and object may eventually differ, this will not be because the design was internally defective. And this is, we think, the main criterion of having knowledge-*that:* that one is in possession of information which essentially diminishes the risk of their intellectual or practical failure.

We fail practically, for example, when we cannot predict that an object is mechanically unsound, i.e., is not ready to fulfil its standard function. Hence we must not avoid the question whether experimenting with the geometry of an object is essentially helpful for predicting future mechanics of the object. Does artificial experience help to predict whether, for example, a geometrically sound model is also mechanically sound? It may to a degree, if we know in advance the material properties of its elements and we do not need to experiment with their mechanical adequacy. Nevertheless, evaluating the mechanical soundness of a future object is far more complicated than evaluating its geometrical soundness. At that point, we inevitably return to the question about seeing the future which from the beginning was of special significance: Can MR projections show us also the future mechanics of the designed object, show its future inner mechanism at work, especially, if its work is to be dynamic, involving not only moves of many elements but also their functional interaction. If testing a mechanism is necessary, modeling usually becomes an insufficient endeavor because sooner or later we need something more than a model, namely, a prototype of the designed object. In this way, we come to the question whether MR technologies may equip us with models having characteristics of prototypes, with models, for example, enabling us to test the future work of an intended object; to help us to decide that the model is mechanically sound. It would surely be an epistemic breakthrough if we could now know how an object will work because we can see now a reliable MR simulation of its moves. But we doubt that seeing moves of a model makes us know the future work of a real object. If we know in advance how a real object works, MR presentations may be so designed as to show us how it works. But if we don't know in advance how an object works, MR modeling of its moves will not reliably predict its workings. Thus we need to sharply distinguish between virtual presentations of the mechanics of known objects and virtual tests of the mechanics of newly designed objects. Virtual presentations may be pedagogically useful, but are useless when we need reliable tests to acquire knowledge of a new type. We are uncertain whether MR technologies aim at all at producing simulations of reliable prototypes or reliable testing. But as long as they don't, their presentations are mechanically idle in the sense that although they explain a lot of what we already know, they predict very little. If they don't let us test an unreal object functionally, no new window of epistemic opportunity opens.

5.3 The instrumental value of knowledge

It is hard to decide whether MR experiences are sources of new knowledge until one establishes what to expect from our beliefs. Our view is that beliefs, and perceptual beliefs in particular, provide tools which should be utilized, intellectually or practically. And although we accept the distinction between (1) autotelic value of knowledge-*that* – consisting mainly in its truthfulness – and its (2) instrumental value, we don't care much about the former. To our mind, beliefs become instrumentally valuable if we efficiently process them intellectually to gain a result: a final belief which brings a solution to an intellectual problem. If beliefs become reliably efficient in the service of solving problems, they can be classified as pieces of knowledge-*that*. As we see it, efficiency in solving problems is an interesting criterion of possessing knowledge: beliefs we have are pieces of knowledge if they at least diminish our failures in achieving goals. For example, we make an intellectual use of factual beliefs when we use them in explanations of past facts, or in making predictions of future facts. If the explanations/predictions work, beliefs that contribute to them become pieces of knowledge-*that*. More importantly, perhaps, we view as knowledge also those beliefs that efficiently support solutions to our practical problems; beliefs that help us to decide whether to act or, which is even more crucial, how to act. Shortly, knowledge is what equips its possessors with information that is necessary for them not only to think rationally but also to act rationally and, we should stress, skillfully.

6. Conclusions: The scope of artificial knowledge

The issue we investigated in this paper – i.e., whether 3D presentations may initiate new types of knowledge – provides us with problem solving information which could be generally labelled "artificial knowledge". If we are epistemological conservatives who hold fast to the requirement that knowledge must mean "epistemic contact with reality", then the answer will be negative. Obviously, such conclusion implies that Augmented Reality presentations are not sources of knowledge-*that*. If, however, we switch to instrumentalism, reasons quickly emerge to start speaking about perceptual knowledge-*that* about the future; especially, if artificial experience presents us with models of objects which we have already decided to materialise and the models are (1) sufficiently close to reality and (2) reinforce our positions as agents. It is of course a tricky question whether, for example, one sees now a future house when they see now a 3D model of a house. We suggest that under a special condition the answer should be positive: when the model significantly diminishes the risk of failure when we finally switch to acting in Plain

Reality. If, for example, the soundness of the model had been reliably tested before we turned to producing a real object or perform a real action.

MR visualizations do not bring knowledge-*that* of a new type unless they open for us the future in a new way, i.e., unless the visualized models are registered with reality. We stressed throughout the paper that the registration should take a variety of forms if the range of new knowledge is to qualitatively widen. At the same time, it remains unclear to us which forms of registration could be actualised and, importantly, whether it would make sense to actualise every one that could be.

Even once strong instrumentalism has been adopted, we may still find it difficult to decide the question. After all, does one have perceptual knowledge-*that* when they see pure MR presentation, presentation being no test of soundness? If MR presentations which tested nothing were not cases of perception, we would then have strange cases of handicapped visual experience which cannot turn into perception. Still, we mainly asked with what properties of models we should experiment to profit from artificial experiences and we suggested that experiences testing geometrical soundness are inferior in relation to the ones testing mechanical soundness.

We admit that our ultimate question was whether Augmented Reality allows us to experiment with our agentive soundness, i.e., to test the soundness of our manual skills. Here we did not move beyond speculations. On the one hand, it is obvious to us that reliable simulation is an extraordinary tool for making manual progress. And that it would be superb to have artificial experiences which could create the opportunity of reliable simulation. Given that, we find it quite stimulating to ask questions such as: Can we experiment with manual use of VR models placed in real surroundings, in an essentially similar way to the way we experiment with real objects placed in real surroundings, when we make plain experiments, or at least with real objects placed in unreal surroundings, as when we use standard simulators? It remains unclear to us whether MR technologies create such opportunities.

Although propagandists speak of unlimited capabilities of MR technologies, we find the issue of developing our manual skills within MR uncomfortable for them. If we lack reliable simulations of direct bodily contact with VR-objects, if we do not learn from simulations of touching them, if we do not make any simulated impact on them with our bare hands, then our knowledge-how cannot progress in a new way. Additionally, there are so many possible mutations of manual actions' simulations within MR that it becomes really difficult to decide which mutations are still challenging and which are already absurd. If, for example, a manual action involves an agent, some tools and some surroundings, in some cases it is troublesome not only to decide what may be reliably simulated but also why it should be.

References

Azuma, R. T. (1997): "A Survey of Augmented Reality". In: *Presence: Teleoperators & Virtual Environments* 6(4), 355.

Billinghurst, M./Clark, A./Lee, G. (2015): "A Survey of Augmented Reality". In: *Foundations and Trends® in Human–Computer Interaction*, 8(2–3), 73–272. DOI: 10.1561/1100000049, visited on 13 September 2016.

Brueckner, A. L. (1986): "Brains in a Vat". In: *Journal of Philosophy* 83(3), 148–167.

Craig, A. B. (2013): *Understanding Augmented Reality*, Boston: Morgan Kaufmann.

Dennett, D. C. (1993). *Consciousness Explained.* Penguin: UK.

Grubert, J./Langlotz, T./Zollmann, S./Regenbrecht, H. (2016): "Towards Pervasive Augmented Reality: Context-Awareness in Augmented Reality". In: *IEEE Transactions on Visualization and Computer Graphics*, *PP*(99), 1–1. DOI: 10.1109/TVCG.2016.2543720, visited on 13 September 2016.

Hofmann, M. (2013): "Ontologies in Modeling and Simulation: An Epistemological Perspective". In: A. Tolk (Ed.), *Ontology, Epistemology, and Teleology for Modeling and Simulation*, Berlin and Heidelberg: Springer, 59–87. Retrieved from http://link.springer.com.ezproxy.is.ed.ac.uk/chapter/10.1007/978-3-642-31140-6_3.

Kelly, K. (2016): "The Untold Story of Magic Leap, the World's Most Secretive Startup". Retrieved from https://www.wired.com/2016/04/magic-leap-vr/, visited on 10 September 2016.

Montmarquet, J. A. (1987): "Epistemic Virtue". In *Mind*, 96(384), 482–497.

Pritchard, D. (2007): "Recent Work on Epistemic Value". In: *American Philosophical Quarterly* 44(2), 85–110.

Pritchard, D. (2010): "Cognitive Ability and the Extended Cognition Thesis". In: *Synthese*, 175 (1), 133–151.

Pritchard, D. (2016): "Epistemic Angst". In: *Philosophy and Phenomenological Research*, n/a-n/a. DOI:10.1111/phpr.12280, visited on 5 September 2016.

Putnam, H. (2000): "Brains in a Vat". In: S. Bernecker / F. I. Dretske (Eds.), *Knowledge: Readings in Contemporary Epistemology*, Oxford University Press: Oxford, 1–21.

Sosa, E. (1980): "The Raft and the Pyramid: Coherence Versus Foundations in the Theory of Knowledge". In: *Midwest Studies in Philosophy* 5(1), 3–26.

Sosa, E. (2007): *A Virtue Epistemology: Apt Belief and Reflective Knowledge, Volume One*, Oxford: Oxford University Press.

Sosa, E. (2015): *Judgment and Agency*, Oxford University Press: Oxford.

Warfield, T. A. (1995): "Knowing the World and Knowing Our Minds". In: *Philosophy and Phenomenological Research* 55(3), 525–545.

Wright, C. (1992): "On Putnam's Proof That We Are Not Brains-in-a-Vat". In: *Proceedings of the Aristotelian Society* 92, 67–94.

Zagzebski, L. T. (1996): *Virtues of the Mind: An Inquiry into the Nature of Virtue and the Ethical Foundations of Knowledge*, Cambridge: Cambridge University Press.

Karsten Schoellner

Augmented Reality and Augmented Perception

Abstract: In this paper I argue that the term 'Augmented Reality' as a description of technologies that informationally augment our perception is misleading and possibly harmful. The paper begins with a characterization of the concept of 'reality' and describes three different philosophical phenomena that could be accurately described as 'Augmented Reality'. The first section discusses the poet Wallace Stevens' notion of how the poetic imagination can enrich our reality. The second section looks at the "sensibility theory" of moral and aesthetic value associated with McDowell and Wiggins, which is meant to explain how anthropocentric but objectively real values can enter into a naturalistic world. The third section examines Wittgenstein's notion that someone who ceases laying down conditions upon the world and learns to accept it has enriched their reality. A fourth section then examines the claim of Augmented Reality technologies to be an 'augmentation of reality'. I argue that the term reflects a dangerous confusion. When we see these technologies in contrast with the three different notions of what 'augmenting reality' discussed in the first three sections, we see that while Augmented Reality technologies can be incredibly useful and to that extent valuable, they also threaten to *diminish* our reality. The conflation of truly Augmented Reality with a technological augmentation of our perception is a moral temptation that we should avoid.

Keywords: Augmented Reality, sensibility theory, Wallace Stevens, McDowell, Wiggins, Wittgenstein, minimalist theory of truth.

1. The minimalist conception of reality and poetic invention

I will start by introducing a 'deflationary' or 'miminalist' notion of reality, modelled on the 'deflationary' or 'minimalist' understanding of truth. The minimalist conception of truth starts from the equivalence between *p* and *it is true that p* for any proposition *p*. Someone who says 'it is true that it is snowing outside now' has only told us 'that it is snowing outside now' and added a certain rhetorical emphasis; conversely, anyone willing to assert the proposition 'it is snowing outside now' should be willing to say 'it is true that it is snowing outside now'. The

DOI 10.1515/9783110497656-010

minimalist conception of truth distinguishes itself from other conceptions in that it starts *and ends* with this equivalence. The truth of *p* is just *p*; what speaks in favor of believing in *the truth of p* is just whatever speaks in favor of believing in *p*; there is nothing general to be said about truth. This conception of truth has its roots in Frege; although he did not consistently uphold the minimalist position, he offers an argument against the possibility of any general characterization of truth. Suppose we want to say that truth is correspondence to reality, for example. Then to determine whether it is true that 'it is snowing outside now', we will have to determine whether the proposition 'it is snowing outside now' corresponds to reality; in other words – given the equivalence of *p* and *it is true that p* – we will have to determine whether *it is true* that the proposition 'it is snowing outside now' corresponds to reality. And to determine whether that is true, we will need to determine whether it is true that the proposition 'the proposition "it is snowing outside now" corresponds to reality' corresponds to reality, etc. Hence the correspondence theory of truth fails by opening and endless regress. And Frege writes:

> And every other attempt to define truth collapses too. For in a definition certain characteristics would have to be stated. And in application to any particular case the question would always be whether it were true that the characteristics were present. So one goes round in a circle. (Frege 1999, 87)

The argument may not be convincing exactly as it stands. If 'the proposition "it is snowing outside now" corresponds to reality' just means 'it is snowing outside now', then the determination of the latter will already be a determination of the former and the regress does not begin. But then we have avoided the regress only be retreating to a deflationary understanding of the talk of 'correspondence'; that *p* corresponds to reality just means that *p*. If on the other hand we want to understand 'the proposition "it is snowing outside now" corresponds to reality' as telling us something more substantial than just *that it is snowing outside now*, then the regress will begin. Hence the minimalist theory of truth tells us that there is nothing general *and non-empty* to be said about truth; other theories of truth, such as correspondence, have to be given a minimalist reading of their key terms in order to function.

It was Ramsey (1990, 38–39) who first explicitly presented the minimalist theory of truth, which was also endorsed by Wittgenstein, Ayer and Strawson among others. For example, the notes on Wittgenstein's lectures in the 1930s have him saying:

> The words "true" and "false" are two words on which philosophy has turned, and it is very important to see that philosophy always turns upon nonsensical questions. Discussion of these words is made easier once it is realized that the words "true" and "false" can be done away with altogether. Instead of saying "*p* is true" we shall say "*p*", and instead of "*p* is false", "not-*p*". That is, instead of the notions of truth and falsity, we use *proposition* and *negation*. [...] Let us examine the statement that a proposition is true if it agrees with reality and false if it does not. We must look at language games to see what this agreement and disagreement consist in. There are cases where what is meant by agreement and disagreement is clear. (Ambrose 2001, 106)

It is not quite true that we can do away with the word 'true' altogether, for we need it for what Blackburn (2010, 38) calls "deferred reference". If I wish to say 'everything that she says is true' without using the word 'true', for example, I would have to say 'If she says *p* then *p*, if she says *q* then *q*....etc.' But once we see the function of the concept of truth more clearly, we at least lose any sense of a great metaphysical puzzle about truth. And as Wittgenstein notes in the passage above, this should shift our interest from truth in general to *p*, to what it is to assert *p* and how the conviction in *p* is determined. The proposition *snow is white* is true just in case snow is white, and the proposition, to use one of Blackburn's (2005, 17) examples, that "life, like a dome of many-colored glass, stains the white radiance of eternity" will be true just if life does in fact stain the white radiance of eternity like a dome of many-colored glass. In the second case there still is a philosophical puzzle, but it is not a metaphysical problem about truth in general. Rather we do not know exactly what we are asserting when we assert life's staining of eternity's white radiance, nor, relatedly, do we have any sense of what might ground that assertion, by what mode and manner of thought or perception one might come up with anything that supports it. But if it does become to clear to us through some experience or reflection that life does in fact stain the white radiance of eternity like a dome of many-colored glass, then we will be willing to say that it is *true*. (It is important to note that it is not a consequence of the minimalist theory of truth that our thinking something makes it true; rather, our thinking *p is* our thinking that *p* is true; and here there is no philosophical mystery about the truth of *p* that could not be cleared up by an understanding of *p*.)

A minimalist understanding of 'reality' would likewise understand the reality of *p* to consist simply in *p*, and hold that no more substantial general characterization of reality can be given. Some people, in contrast, feel that reality ultimately only consists in the laws discovered or discoverable in the natural sciences, or more specifically in physics. If we adopt a minimalist understanding of the concept *reality*, it does not exactly compete with the claim that reality is ultimately the reality of the laws of physics; it displays what this claim would amount to. Someone who thinks that reality comprises only the laws of physics would, on a minimalist understanding of reality, be someone who only believes and is willing to assert the laws of physics and nothing else. If they also want to insist that they were wronged by their mugger, then, on the minimalist understanding, they clearly believe in a reality that includes not just the laws of physics but also this wronging. If they cannot abandon their conviction that human dignity is inviolable, then they will believe in the reality of our inviolable human dignity as well.[1] (I am assuming here for the sake of simplicity that these claims cannot be reduced to physicalist terms, and that the claims are in fact propositional, and do not have the underlying form of imperatives or avowals of emotion; in the formulation *It is part of reality that p = that p*, *p* serves as a variable ranging over all *propositions*, not over anything a person might think or say.) What speaks in favor of including an inviolable human dignity in our conception of reality, is simply whatever speaks in favor of believing human dignity to be inviolable; and the only thing that could speak in favor of some bare physical conception of reality would be some set of compelling considerations that undermined every other sort of belief, for example our belief that human dignity is inviolable.

There is a good deal more that could be said about these matters. Here we only need the roughest outlines of a minimalist understanding of reality to begin to consider what it might look like to 'augment' reality. I will begin in this section by briefly canvassing the idea that *poetry* can achieve a greater reality. There is a great different between a reality that only includes bare physical facts, on some understanding of 'bare' and 'physical' – perhaps the concatenations of particles and their forces – and a reality that includes such facts as life's staining the white radiance of eternity. Assuming for now that a conviction that life stains the white radiance of eternity makes sense and is merited, some people have felt that this cannot be something the poet has discovered, that rather this reality is the poet Shelley's achievement, that it was in no sense real prior to the poetic articulation. This was the view of the poet Wallace Stevens (1951, 32), for example, who felt that "[a] poet's words are of things that do not exist without the words." Stevens wrote:

1 My minimalist understanding of "reality" is clearly closely related to Quine's notion of how we incur ontological commitments – we are committed to the existence of anything we find ourselves quantifying over – as well as Taylor's "Best Account" principle, according to which whatever we need to make "the best sense of our lives" after critical reflection is therefore real. (cf. Quine 1964, Taylor 1989, 56–9)

> There is, in fact, a world of poetry indistinguishable from the world in which we live, or, I ought to say, no doubt, from the world in which we shall come to live, since what makes the poet the potent figure that he is, or was, or ought to be, is that he creates the world to which we turn incessantly and without knowing it and that he gives to life the supreme fictions, without which we are unable to conceive of it. (Stevens 1951, 31)

This does not mean that the poet can invent any reality at will. The achievement of poetry is more than an act of will; and not every poetic achievement is possible in every age and culture. Stevens is clear that differing cultural and historical circumstances offer the poet different rages of possibility. In his essay "The Noble Rider and the Sound of Words" Stevens (1951, 6 f.) discusses how certain poetic images of nobility from earlier ages have lost their ability to move us precisely because they have become unreal for us, and "the imagination loses vitality as it ceases to adhere to what is real [...] It has the strength of reality or none at all." And one of Stevens' central concerns in his work is that in our time we have lost the ability to sustain conviction in anything but bare physical reality – what Critchley (2005, 27) calls "an oppressive or *contracted* sense of the real [...] what Hilary Putnam would call 'realism without a human face'" – that with the loss of metaphysical and religious foundations and under the enormous "pressure of reality" nowadays poetry can only lament the loss of a meaningful reality. But at other moments in his work he maintains his hope that poetry can transform reality. We can see this in the opening canto of "The Man with the Blue Guitar":

> The man bent over his guitar,
> A shearsman of sorts. The day was green.
>
> They said, "You have a blue guitar,
> You do not play things as they are."
>
> The man replied, "Things as they are
> Are changed upon the blue guitar."
>
> And they said then, "But play, you must,
> A tune beyond us, yet ourselves,
>
> A tune upon the blue guitar,
> Of things exactly as they are. (Stevens 1964, 165)

The phrase "things as they are" recurs as a refrain of the following thirty-two cantos, and seems to reflect quite different associations and moods in every canto. What underlies these variations is a consistent minimalism, I would argue. The poem cycles back and forth between hope and despair, sometimes giving in the suspicion that the only things we can say honestly and with conviction concern bare physical reality, sometimes rising to the hope that things as they actually are can be meaningful and expressive. Even within this first canto we can see something of this tension. An anonymous audience essentially accuses art of illusion and irreality, saying “you do not play things as they are”. The artist responds: “things as they are are changed upon the blue guitar” – they are not falsified but rather transformed. And at this point the audience voices that wild and unhinged desire verging on incoherence that we all bring to art – that it show us something “beyond us, yet ourselves ... of things *exactly as they are*.” We turn to art to find something more than plain reality, beyond plain reality – but it must also be real or it will not satisfy us. (“It has the strength of reality or none at all.”) We want something more than plain reality, yet not an illusion or empty fantasy; we want a transformed reality, an Augmented Reality. It is helpful here to recall Coleridge’s distinction between *imagination* and *fancy*, a distinction that is of central importance to Stevens – the true poetic imagination is a meditation upon reality rather than a willed recombination of ideas unconstrained by reality[2]. As the philosopher Simon Critchley (2005, 11) writes in his book on Stevens: “the poetic imagination imagines things as they are, but beyond us, turned about, whereas fancy fantasizes about things that are not: unicorns, gods, golden mountains.” As this formulation reminds us, we can also distinguish imagination from *fantasy*, from escapism and self-indulgence. Sometimes self-indulgent escapism is exactly what we want, of course, but this is not what we want from art, which must adhere scrupulously to reality in its own way. We could take a passage from “An Ordinary Evening in New Haven” as Stevens’ ambitions for poetry:

> ......We seek
> Nothing beyond reality. Within it,
>
> Everything, the spirit’s alchemicana
> Included, the spirit that goes roundabout
> And through included, not merely the visible,
>
> The solid, but the movable, the moment,
> The coming on of feasts and the habits of saints,
> The pattern of the heavens and high, night air. (Stevens 1961, 471 f.)

---

2 Coleridge’s discussion of imagination is somewhat obscure, but he describes fancy as “a mode of Memory emancipated from the order of time and space; while it is blended with, and modified by that empirical phenomenon of the will, which we express by the word CHOICE.” (Coleridge 1983, 305)

This is one conception of what it might mean to 'augment reality' – and it is a possibility that only comes into view when we start by conceiving reality minimalistically. If we started with some more substantial conception of reality such as the fundamental entities and laws of physics, it is hard to say what an augmenting of reality might look like. Perhaps if the universe as a whole is growing, or if the total number of particles increases? Otherwise reality could only be augmented from outside by the *unreal*; a conviction in the inviolable dignity of each human, for example, would only be an unreal projection upon the real. If we start with a minimalist conception of reality, then this allows for the possibility that only some domain of bare physical fact is the only thing we can sustain conviction in, but it also allows for the possibility that reality could grow inwards, that reality could multiply inwardly in what Stevens (1964, 486) calls "the intricate evasions of as"[3]. It is important to note that Stevens' view does not *follow* from the minimalist conception of reality; that conception only allows Stevens' view as a possibility. The minimalist conception is not that thinking something real makes it real; the minimalist conception is only that to think something is to think it real, and that what speaks in favor of a belief in the *reality* of any propositional claim *p* is simply whatever speaks in favor of *p*. Hence the poet does not necessarily create reality simply by creating conviction. One could hold the minimalist notion of reality and also at the same time think that poetry only at best *reveals* something real rather than creating the reality, hence that the poet can only augment our *sense* or our *perception* of reality and cannot augment reality itself. This is not Stevens' view, but it's the default view for us nowadays. I think Stevens' view is not as improbable as it might seem. The next section briefly discusses the "sensibility theory" of moral and aesthetic value developed McDowell and Wiggins, which explains how what they call "anthropocentric properties" can emerge from human culture, properties that are fully real and objective and yet also dependent in some sense upon human sensibilities. We can derive from this theory a related notion of what 'augmenting reality' would be that should help to make Stevens' idea of poetry more credible.

---

3 The passage in "An Ordinary Evening in New Haven" reads: " ... A more severe, / More harassing master would extemporize / Subtler, more urgent proof that the theory / Of poetry is the theory of life, / As it is, in the intricate evasions of as, / In things seen and unseen, created from nothingness, / The heavens, the hells, the worlds, the longed-for lands."

2. Sensibility theory and the creation of value

Philosophy has been worried about the reality of color since early modernity; it has been argued that the fundamental reality we live in excludes color. If I am right to say that this table-cloth in front of me is red – it's not, e.g., brown that I'm seeing in a poor light – then on a minimalist conception of reality, the table-cloth *really* is red, and its color is a part of reality. It is not a projection upon something more real. Color is, of course, what Wiggins (1998, 106) calls an "anthropocentric" property – "The category corresponds to an interest that can only take root in creatures with something approaching our own sensory apparatus." Hence color attributions are not available to just any hypothesized rational creature. But as long as we can maintain a distinction between my thinking something red and its actually being red, we do not need to deny their reality.[4] The example of "secondary qualities" such as color, scent etc. is meant to show, for McDowell and Wiggins, that the notions of reality, truth, objectivity, etc. can consort perfectly well with anthropocentricity, with a dependence on human sensibility.

McDowell and Wiggins apply this lesson to moral and aesthetic value. McDowell uses the example of twelve-tone music, which is notoriously hard to hear. A composition of Schoenberg's will contain features – *this* development of the theme, *this* tension, etc. – that are genuinely there in the piece, though they can only be heard by someone who has learned to respond appropriately. Here the parallel to secondary qualities such as color is somewhat imperfect. Certainly these musical properties would not exist without our biologically given human sensibility, but that is not enough. The listener will need to be familiar with the developments of Western classical music leading up to twelve-tone composition. And the 'familiarity' is not a purely intellectual matter; the listener must have learned to respond emotionally in appropriate ways, to affectively participate in the music. The tension will simply not be accessible to someone who cannot actually feel tense upon hearing certain sound sequences. So these musical properties require not just our universally human sensibility, but a community of listeners who have internalized certain responses of pleasure, desire, tension, agitation, etc. Though composers are constrained by musical reality and do not create arbitrarily, the musical reality cannot be prised apart from a historically and culturally contingent sensibility that was created over time. And yet

4 McDowell (1998, 175, 185) writes that the notion of objectivity only requires that there be a difference between being right and seeming right.

the musical properties are truly there in the music, and individuals can be mistaken about what is actually there.

McDowell (1998, 85) offers a roughly parallel view of the values and moral demands that a virtuous person sees due to their upbringing, which shapes the person's sensibility or "second nature". "In moral upbringing what one learns is not to behave in conformity with rules of conduct, but to see situations in a special light, as constituting reasons for acting". He writes that "the relevant conceptions are not so much as possessed except by those whose wills are influenced appropriately" (McDowell 1998, 54), whose practical intellect has a "certain determinate non-formal shape." (McDowell 1998, 184 f.) In fact:

> In acquiring one's second nature – that is, in acquiring *logos* – one learned to take a distinctive pleasure in acting in certain ways, and one acquired conceptual equipment suited to characterize a distinctive worthwhileness one learned to see in such actions, that is, a distinctive range of reasons one learned to see for acting in those ways. (McDowell 1998, 188)

Within any established second nature or ethical sensibility, there is the possibility of individual error – someone could misread a situation. Hence the sensibility entails standards by which individual actions and characters are to be judged; something is not morally or aesthetically true just because I think it true. And yet McDowell (1998, 194) concedes that "[a]ny actual second nature is a cultural product." Thus McDowell ultimately seems to think that a moral reality can be culturally produced.

Wiggins, who defends a very similar view and is often grouped together with McDowell, is more upfront about how the reality of value emerges through human history. He is comfortable tentatively adopting what he calls a "Humean" story of how value enters the world, a story that begins with nothing more than the natural world and humans' various affective responses to it. On the story Hume tells in the *Enquiry Concerning the Principles of Morals*, we begin with quite divergent sets of emotional responses to the world, until we begin to rub off on each other. The fact that we can talk to each other about the responses we share, tends to reinforce those shared responses; and our ability to see ourselves from the perspectives of others is another mechanism that tends to create a shared reality. On the story that Hume tells in "Of the Standard of Taste", this process can be accelerated on the individual level by critics, who seek to broaden and at the same time deepen their own capacity for response by sampling works from as many different cultures from distant places and ages as possible. Wiggins (1998, 196) adds a bit more to the Humean story, but the important point is only that we can imagine some completely naturalistic, metaphysically innocuous story of cultural development that eventually brings us to the point where "a system of anthropocentric properties and human responses has surely taken on a life of its own. Civilization has begun."[5] There is at some point a reality of value that we live in just as we live in the physical world, that is no longer purely *subjective* in being a matter of merely personal whim.

We could describe the way that culture accumulates increasingly intricate and subtle realities as a process of *augmenting reality*. When we create the culture of Western music up to twelve-tone compositions, then there is that much reality, there is that much there to be heard in those pieces; we have Augmented Reality to that extent. When we create a new culture of culinary appreciation, then there is that much reality to be appreciated in the food, etc. And this picture of how value enters the world consorts well with a form of non-naturalist realism that is prevalent in contemporary metaethics, represented by authors such as Scanlon, Nagel, Parfit, Dworkin, Putnam, Charles Taylor and others. In this brand of non-naturalist realism, the question of realism for any domain of thought and discourse – ethics, aesthetics, mathematics, etc. – hinges not on any metaphysical problems but simply and solely on whether we have the resources in our first-order thought in that domain to unequivocally support specific assertions. If we have the resources within our moral thought to show that murder is wrong and that there is nothing else to think, then we have shown that murder is *really* wrong. Or as Nagel (1997, 125) writes: "we can defend moral reason only by abandoning metatheory for substantive ethics."

None of this is meant to be individualistic or to imply that we can create reality by believing different things or that the individual can make something real by willing it. These augmentations of reality pull us out of ourselves more, and come to serve as a standard by which to judge and correct our individual wants and desires and feelings. Hume emphasizes that we have to overcome our own merely idiosyncratic responses at two different levels. Firstly, we rub off on each other and come to see ourselves from a shared and impartial viewpoint; and in raising our children within an existing moral and aesthetic culture we give them this impartial viewpoint on themselves. Secondly, for certain forms of aesthetic reality to exist there must be individual artists and critics who practice a more demanding self-discipline. I have been emphasizing here that we can see moral or aesthetic reality as collectively and historically created while at the same time being truly objective and not subject in any way to individual whim.

5 For Wiggins' various descriptions of this developmental process see "Truth, Invention, and the Meaning of Life" and "A Sensible Subjectivism?", both in Wiggins (1998), as well as Wiggins' "Moral Cognitivism, Moral Relativism and Motivating Moral Beliefs", where he supposes that our moral sensibility perhaps "has its first origin in a primitive system of responses scarcely more differentiated than *boo* and *hurrah*." (Wiggins 1991, 69 f.)

McDowell and Wiggins might both nonetheless be uncomfortable with any hint that these realities are created in any way. Both are opposed to the metaphor of a 'projection' of value upon an initially value-neutral reality; and Wiggins in particular is concerned to preserve some space for the idea that values are discovered rather than invented. For the individual, this is how it works. But at a more macroscopic level, neither McDowell nor Wiggins give any foundational role to moral of aesthetic facts existing prior to human sensibility and justifying the cultures that emerge; they only wish to insist that the reality that *has* emerged serves as a check on individual human sensibilities. Hence would say that on their sensibility theory it appears that we humans have *augmented reality* with additional layers of reality through the course of human history.

3. "The world must become quite another"

I would like to briefly introduce another conception of 'augmenting reality' before turning to the issues raised by 'Augmented Reality' technologies. I will begin by looking at Raimond Gaita's discussions of the idea – which is of course not an idea he invented, but a long-standing theme of moral philosophy – that each and every human being is absolutely unique and irreplaceable and thus of absolute value, incommensurable with anything else: "that human beings are individuals in the way nothing else in nature is." This sense of individuality is essential to our moral life and "is internal to our sense of what it is to wrong someone", he writes (Gaita 1990, 125). I turn to Gaita's development of this idea because, firstly, he makes it absolutely clear that no human being is in any empirical sense especially unique or irreplaceable. Insofar as I am the bearer of useful capacities or other properties, there are surely other people who could replace me. We see individual people as absolutely irreplaceable through the experiences of love and remorse, Gaita (1990, 126) writes, or rather through experiencing "the power of human beings to affect one another in ways they cannot fathom." This does not mean that we can only acknowledge the absolute value of those we love; but seeing the absolute value of a stranger would be impossible "unless we also saw him as the intelligible object of someone's love." (Gaita 1990, 132) We can see each person as a world in themselves only if we can see how each person could be loved, i.e. could be the whole world to someone else.

Gaita's concern is with our typical failure to see others fully, or as he puts it, to fully acknowledge their humanity; he writes about "the ways human beings are sometimes invisible, or only partially visible, to one another." (Gaita 2002, xx) Racism is a particularly clear example of this, at least as he interprets the phenomenon. He discusses a woman he knew who had lost one of her children, watching on TV "a documentary on the Vietnam War which showed the grief of Vietnamese women whose children were killed in the bombing raids. After a few minutes the woman remarks: 'But it is different for them. They can simply have more.'" (Gaita 2002, 57) In Gaita's view, racism does not need to involve any false empirical claims about the othered race, though it often does – that they are less intelligent, less trustworthy, etc. – but racism always involved a failure to attribute the same 'depth' to the othered race. "'They' can do and feel almost everything we can except not as we do, not as deeply we do. We grieve, but they 'grieve', we are joyful, they are 'joyful', we love and they 'love', we feel remorse, they feel 'remorse' and so on." (Gaita 2002, 63) The racist might not deny any of the facts of the fully human lives of the other race, but fail to response to them in the same way; this is, it seems to me, a failure of imagination and empathy and self-awareness. An example of McDowell's works quite similarly; he imagines someone saying, "You don't know what it means that someone is shy and sensitive", noting however that "[f]ailure to see what a circumstance means, in the loaded sense, is of course compatible with competence, by all ordinary tests, with the language used to describe the circumstance." (McDowell 1998, 86) If the minimalist scheme holds that *the reality that p* is simply *that p*, we see now that this scheme can easily mask a difference in the reality experienced by two different people who are differently involved in the proposition *p*. If *p* is the fact of someone else's suffering, this might be very real to one person, and a rather meaningless fact to another. Insofar as we can rely on the notes to Wittgenstein's "Lectures on Religious Belief", it would seem that he felt this situation quite typical of religious belief; although an atheist might seem to be denying some proposition *p* asserted by a believer, it is unclear whether they mean the same, and "[t]he difference might not show up at all in any explanation of the meaning". (Wittgenstein 1966a, 53)

I can know that someone is in fact a human, a person with an independent life, but this could be more or less real to me, depending upon how much work I am willing to do on the quality of my attention to others. The same could be said of the natural world, or of anything in the world at all; sometimes we are stuck in our own heads, and only our own narrow concerns are very real for us; and sometimes we wake up and are shocked at how real the world independent of our concerns is. In Wittgenstein's "Lecture on Ethics" he wrote that the paradigmatic experience of absolute ethical value for him was the experience where he was inclined to say: "how extraordinary that anything should exist!", which he also described as the experience of seeing the world as a miracle. (Wittgenstein 1993, 41–3) It has been a frequent theme of poets like Whitman, and of Christian mystics like Meister Eckhart, that our attention to everything is half-hearted and conditional, that we should be more alive to the reality of everything. Wittgenstein (1966b, 185) wrote in 6.43 of the *Tractatus* that the "ethical will" cannot change anything in the world, "it can only change the limits of the world [...] the world must thereby become quite another, it must so to speak wax or wane as a whole. The world of the happy is quite another than that of the unhappy."

This is another context where one might naturally speak of 'augmenting reality'. It arguably involves a somewhat subjective use of the terms *world* or *reality*; the person whose world enlarges will likely feel that they have discovered this larger world that was there the whole time, so to say that 'their world' or 'their reality' is larger really means that *their sense of reality* has been augmented, while of course reality itself remains unchanged. People naturally tend towards this subjective characterization, I think, precisely because they are describing an experience where nothing has changed except everything. They have not discovered any new facts; all facts now appear to them in a changed light. Thus it is not anything *in the world* that has changed for them; and they will naturally want to say that only the world itself has changed. Though this involves a subjective use of the terms *world* or *reality*, nonetheless we can see this experience as an achievement of greater objectivity, since this enlarged sense of reality is only possible for people who put in the effort to overcome their own self-involvement and transcend their own narrow concerns. And it should be possible to combine this notion of augmenting reality with the notion of augmenting reality I sketched in the preceding sections, according to which the development of culture is the creation of new anthropocentric realities. We might want to say that each person already is an absolute value, that this is revealed to anyone who can put in the work of imagination and empathy that is needed to overcome their own self-involvement; and we might at the same time want to say this reality of absolute value only exists as a creation of culture, and that to sustain this reality a sufficient portion of the people must always be exerting themselves sufficiently to acknowledge each other's humanity. But to argue for this would take be far beyond the scope of this paper.

4. Augmented perception technology and Augmented Reality

I have worked out three closely related notions of what 'augmenting reality' might look like. Of course the technologies that have come to be known collectively as 'Augmented Reality' differ. 'Augmented Reality' refers, for example, to the capability of various devices such as iPhones to incorporate information about our surroundings into our perception of those surroundings. In what sense is this an *augmentation* of *reality?*

We should first bear in mind that the word "reality" in the phrase "Augmented Reality" as applied to informational technologies can be read in contrast to *virtuality*. In a paper from 1994 the engineering professor Paul Milgram proposed understanding "Augmented Reality" and "virtual reality" as counterparts on a spectrum of "mixed realities". Milgram (1994, 283) defines one end of the spectrum as the unmixed or unaugmented reality of the "real environment", which is "any environment consisting solely of real objects." On the other end is the "virtual environment" unmixed with any reality, which Milgram (1994, 283) defines as an environment "consisting solely of virtual objects, examples of which would include conventional computer graphic simulations, either monitor-based or immersive". 'Augmented Reality' is situated just right of "the real environment" and just left of "augmented virtuality" – it is an environment comprised mostly of "real" objects, augmented by some "virtual objects".

This distinction is intuitively clear in a sense, but it tends to drive certain quite important philosophical distinctions out of sight. Consider a Heads-Up Display (HUD) built into a car windshield that displays the speed I'm driving at. If the product is worth anything, the number it shows me will be the speed that I *really* am driving at. In Milgram's conceptual scheme, the "real" would presumably include the other cars on the road, the road itself, road signs, etc. and the visual information about my speed would be not real but virtual. As Milgram's intuitive distinction shakes out in practice, essentially only physical objects count as part of reality. But this blurs a very important distinction: the Augmented Reality display should display my *real* speed, and not a falsehood or a fiction; it should only augment 'my reality' with more information *about reality*. A dysfunctional Heads-Up Display would give me a falsehood, and a virtual reality display would give me a fiction; but a properly functioning Augmented Reality display is entirely constrained by reality and nothing else. To put it quite simply: nothing about the speedometer or the speed that the speedometer measures becomes any *less real* when we move it from the dashboard to the windshield.

The essentials of Milgram's understanding of "Augmented Reality" have been repeated by others; for example, Marcus Tönnis (2010, V, my translation) has written that "in contrast to VR, in Augmented Reality the actual reality surrounding the user is augmented with three-dimensional visual elements." Bimber and Raskar (2005, 2) write that "in contrast to traditional VR, in Augmented Reality the real environment is not completely suppressed; instead it plays a dominant role. Rather than immersing a person into a completely synthetic world, Augmented Reality attempts to embed synthetic supplements into the real environment."

There are some examples of technological works labelled 'Augmented Reality' that are in fact fictional, such as Helen Papagiannis' "AR pop-up book", "Who's Afraid of Bugs."[6] But the vast majority of technologies that are labelled 'Augmented Reality' are meant to be informational rather than fictional, which is what makes "tracking" one of the fundamental challenges of this technology. (cf. Bimber and Raskar 2005, 4) Augmented Reality devices typically explore reality, we might say, while VR devices typically explore fantasy; at any rate Augmented Reality devices do not aim to augment reality with irreality. The philosopher Ortega y Gasset (1942, 26; my translation) characterized reality as the "counter-will", as "that which we must reckon with, whether we want to or not", and this comes out clearly in the HUD case: I want the display to show the speed I'm actually driving, whether I want to or not. Of course I might also want to be driving a certain speed and then adjust my speed until the desired number appears in the display; nonetheless the display is only serving its purpose if it not under the direct control of my will but rather controlled only by the reality of my actual speed.

It is important to keep this in mind, since the enthusiasts and evangelists of Augmented Reality often describe the potentialities of Augmented Reality technology in terms of greater control and freedom, for example: "We're only at the beginning of the journey right now to help give people full control of their world." (Choi 2016) There is some truth to this, and I will return to the point in a moment; to put it succinctly: Augmented Reality technology promises to give us more control over the sorts of information about reality that our perceived environment displays and over the format of that display. But there is an absolute distinction to be made between technologies that allow us to control the content of those perceptions, that make the content a function of the will of the user or the designer and hence ultimately a product of whim or fantasy – virtual reality technologies – and technologies which are only successful if the content is not in the control of anyone's will but rather tracks an independent reality. (We might say that what Augmented Reality technologies really offer is *augmented perception*; what VR technologies offer is *augmented fantasy.*)

In section one of this paper I outlined one notion of what 'augmenting reality' would look like, and section two described a related notion of 'augmenting reality' that can be derived from the "sensibility theory" of McDowell and Wiggins. In that sense of 'augmenting reality', Augmented Reality technologies do not augment reality at all. My car is really moving at a certain speed anyways

6 Papagiannis' projects can be seen at http://augmentedstories.com/projects/, accessed 17 February 2016.

– the HUD simply delivers the information about that speed in a new way. No new domain of reality has emerged. Of course if Augmented Reality devices become far more advanced and their use far more common and widespread, it will inevitably shape our culture in unforeseeable ways, and it is possible that rich new cultural forms will emerge that truly augment reality in the way that the development of our musical sensibility has Augmented Reality. For reasons that should emerge in what follows, I think this is somewhat overoptimistic.

Augmented Reality technology might be usefully compared to the other sense of 'Augmented Reality' I outlined in the third section, in which we can wake up out of our own self-involvement and see our whole 'world' expand suddenly and every aspect of reality become, in a certain sense, more 'real'. It can be argued that the phrase 'Augmented Reality' as a description of Augmented Reality technologies involves a subjective use of the term "reality", just as we are speaking subjectively when we say that the 'reality' of the happy person is different than the 'reality' of the sad person. I had said that the distinction between "real objects" and "virtual objects" is an intuitive one. When I am driving, the other cars, the road, etc. are the real objects, and the display of my speed is the virtual object. Of course the virtual object is also ultimately a real object – the display of pixels actually does exist in the windshield and is not an optical illusion. The distinction between real and virtual is perhaps clearer in the case of simulations, for example when Augmented Reality technology allows a surgeon to see the position of the organs underneath the skin of a patient, through the visual projection of the organs onto the patient's skin. Here again the virtual object is in one sense a real object – the projection of light onto the skin is a real part of the real environment. And in a sense the surgeon is really seeing the position of the organs – if the technology works well and the projection is faithful and accurate. But the real object that is the projection of light, and which allows the surgeon to see where the organs really are, is not really the organs. The projection of light by itself is not "virtual" in contrast to something that is more "real", like the organs; the projection of light and the organ are both real parts of the real environment. But the projection of light simulates something that it is not, and that simulated content could usefully be called a "virtual object" in contrast with the "real object" that it simulates.

All this is a long way of getting to the point that the term 'reality' is being used subjectively here: it is the reality available from the perspective of the user that is being augmented, not reality itself. When I put on Augmented Reality glasses, 'my reality' is augmented, in a twofold sense. Firstly, I simply have easier access to more information; if I know more facts about my environment when wearing the glasses, then in a sense 'my reality' is larger. In this sense however I also "augment reality" whenever I look something up in Wikipedia, or even in a regular printed encyclopedia. Secondly, the information presented by Augmented Reality devices is seamlessly integrated into my perception, such that it seems like the objects themselves are informing me about themselves, as if the whole world were more gregarious all of a sudden. If we leave aside the subjective uses of 'world', 'reality' etc., what is really happening is this: information that is already known or in principle knowable is integrated in a particularly convenient way into my perception. Subjectively, however, we might say: we have given the world speech; now reality readily answers every question I ask it.

This subjective use of terms is clear in Milgram's use of "environment" – in his terms, when I wear Augmented Reality glasses, I have added something virtual to the real environment. With the glasses I might be able to see what temperature my coffee is before I drink it, but this does not add anything to the real environment, objectively speaking – the temperature of the coffee was already a part of the real environment. At most we have added the glasses to the real environment, but in this sense I am adding something to the environment of my kitchen whenever I go grocery shopping. The glasses do however add information to 'my environment', to my perception of my surroundings. As Augmented Reality designer Helen Papagiannis (2011) says, Augmented Reality technology allows us "be able to see different information layered on top of our reality." The same could be said of Wittgenstein's use of 'world' in the closing sections of the *Tractatus.* If I wake up out of my egocentric rut and notice the outside world, objectively speaking nothing has been added to the environment – it was all already there – but it is still intelligible if I speak as if *everything* has been added to *my* environment, to my world, my reality, where before there was very little. It is perhaps odd and verging on paradoxical that though the experience is one of coming out of oneself and one's narrow and self-centered concerns and *discovering* the outside world, and is in that sense an experience of achieving greater objectivity, it is nonetheless natural to express the experience in entirely subjective terms as an enlargening of one's world.

The typical Augmented Reality technologies are objectively speaking no augmentations of reality at all; they deliver an informationally augmented *perception* of reality rather than any true augmentation of reality. I don't think this objection is *entirely* pedantic. We have seen that the intuitive distinction between 'real objects' and 'virtual objects' involves a tendency to include only physical and solid objects under the heading of the 'real', carrying with it the suggestion that everything else is *unreal*, including "the movable, the moment, / The coming on of feasts and the habits of saints", etc. This is already a tendency of our materialistic and scientistic age, and it seems to me that the tendency is bad for us spiritually and morally. The term "Augmented Reality" as applied to Augmented Reality technologies does not need to necessarily confuse us, but I believe it encourages a certain confusion or at least reflects it. Moreover this sense of 'the real' as solid physical objects tends to obscure the working practices of Augmented Reality engineers and designers, who are of course perfectly aware that temperature, for example, and speed, are quite real and must be *accurately* measured and displayed by the end products. The designation of Augmented Reality technologies as "Augmented Reality" also encourages a subjective understanding of "reality", which again strikes me as a potentially quite harmful conceptual innovation, and moreover one that obscures rather than illuminating the working practices of Augmented Reality engineers and designers, who want their devices to *really* work, which means tracking *real* phenomena. (VR designers of course also want their devices to *really* work and are to that extent interested in objective reality.)

Let us accept this subjective use of 'reality' and ask: do Augmented Reality technologies "augment reality" in the sense outlined in section three of this paper – do they enrich the user's *sense* of reality? This also strikes me as unlikely and misguided. Augmented Reality technologies deliver more information to the user's perception – information about the facts of the user's surroundings. But Gaita and Wittgenstein both emphasize that greater factual knowledge is irrelevant here. If I fail to acknowledge the humanity of others, this means that their independent lives are not real to me. But that other people exist and lead lives independent of me, and have cares and concerns and projects independent of mine, is not a fact I am unaware of. I am aware of the fact, but I discount it for the most part. We might say that even though I know that other people exist, I don't see it for the most part; the fact that they lead lives of their own remains a bit of background information that is largely irrelevant to my concerns, and I see them only in terms of my own concerns. Now there is no technology that will fix this. You could not invent Augmented Reality glasses that show me people as real, such that I suddenly see beyond my own egocentric rut when I wear them. No matter how many facts we assemble, the quality of our attention to the facts and our involvement in those facts remains an ongoing problem for us, a problem that cannot be solved by the addition of new facts. And when Wittgenstein suggests that the happy person inhabits a larger world than the unhappy person, he does not mean that the happy person knows more. The happy person accepts the world; the unhappy person places demands on the world, she accepts it only insofar as it meets the conditions she lays down. Now Augmented Reality technologies do in a sense increase our control over the world we perceive, as I suggested above – they increase our control over the form and scope of our perception. They aim to increase this control and they encourage a desire for greater control. To this extent, they seem to encourage a personal development diametrically opposed to that recommended by

Gaita and Wittgenstein; in the terms I've developed here, these technologies would tend to diminish our reality. There is such a thing as an 'information junkie' or a 'news junkie', someone who obsessively seeks out more and more facts; in one sense this person would have a very broad knowledge of their world, but in another sense this is obviously a kind of escapism, and they are failing to get out of their own head and attend to the world around them. In fact, Stevens, McDowell, Wiggins, Gaita and Wittgenstein all emphasize in their various ways the need to get beyond our own will, our own need to possess and control, in order to augment reality; as does Hume in his own way, and Coleridge when he contrasts imagination with fancy and defines fancy as a function of choice.[7]

I also do not think that this is an entirely pedantic objection – I am not saying that Augmented Reality technologies fail to achieve something they are not trying to achieve, measuring them against a completely foreign standard. The term 'Augmented Reality' is clearly meant to be inspirational. I suspect that the term itself, and the enthusiasm for the technologies grouped under that term, reflect a spiritual longing for a transformation of our experience. I have been arguing that technology will not deliver this, precisely because and to the extent that it seeks to enhance our control over our experience[8]. The possibilities of augmented perception that Augmented Reality technology promises could *occupy* our attention endlessly, while distracting us from the task of improving our attention to the world as a whole. Augmented Reality technologies are perfectly positioned to seduce us – since we do long for a transformation of our experience, but we do not want to do the constant work on ourselves this would actually require, and would much rather just buy a machine that could do it for us. This is the harmful but seductive fantasy that Kierkegaard continually warns us against:

> From the external and visible world there comes an old adage: "Only one who works gets bread." Oddly enough, the adage does not fit the world in which it is most at home, for imperfection is the fundamental law of the external world, and here it happens again and again that he who does not work does get bread, and he who sleeps gets it even more abundantly than he who works. [...] It is different in the world of the spirit." (Kierkegaard 1983, 25)

---

7 See footnote 2.

8 This is perhaps not entirely true; technology in a loose sense might be able to help us. There are techniques for overcoming self-involvement in the Christian and Buddhist traditions at least; and arguably psychoactive inventions such as LSD or ayahuasca can help someone as well. However, these techniques and technologies are helpful only to the extent that they override our need for control; they do not place more of our experience under our control, as Augmented Reality technology promises to do, but rather actively subvert our control.

The sense in which Augmented Reality glasses could be said to make the world expressive, to make all the things of the world responsive to us, is close to the vision presented in Whitman's poetry, for example; it is a false (because overly literal) semblance of the transformation we truly desire.

Insofar as Augmented Reality technologies are useful, there is exactly that much to be said for them: they are useful. If Augmented Reality technology can make surgery more accurate and airplane flights safer, that is good. They can be useful in integrating information into our visual field. Insofar as the term 'Augmented Reality' reflects some spiritual longing for a transformation of our ordinary experience, we are cheating ourselves if we buy the idea. Augmented Reality technologies are not necessarily bad for us (time will tell), but thinking of them as 'augmenting reality' is bad for us. As humans we are prone to certain temptations, ways of living that are easier in the moment but ultimately unsatisfying, and informational technology has been feeding these temptations for some time now. We all know what *screen addiction* is, addiction to staring into one's computer or phone. It is one of the more powerful forms of our perennial temptation to escapism, to always being away, getting out of the present moment. This is brought out beautifully in a scene in the episode "The Entire History of You" (2011) from the TV series *Black Mirror*, which imagines a world where people can replay their experiences in their own minds through a computational device implanted in their brains. When the husband and wife are having sex, the man is replaying in his mind his experience of a different time they were having sex. He is not even fantasizing about a different woman – he is sexually attracted to his wife – but he simply cannot be in that moment and yield to it. Because a distraction is available, he takes it. The danger of Augmented Reality technologies, insofar as they go beyond a specialized usefulness and are seen as a constant accompaniment to our experience, is that they will in this way diminish our reality.

References

Ambrose, Alice (ed.) (1979): *Wittgenstein's Lectures 1932–1935*, Amherst, NY: Prometheus Books.

Bimber, Oliver/Raskar, Ramesh (2005): *Spatial Augmented Reality*, Wellesley, MA: A K Peters.

Blackburn, Simon (2005): *Truth*, Oxford: Oxford University Press.

Blackburn, Simon (2010): *Practical Tortoise Raising*, Oxford: Oxford University Press.

Choi, Charles Q. (2016): "Fine-Tune the World with 'Augmented Reality' Earbuds", http://www.livescience.com/53599-augmented-reality-here-earbuds.html, accessed 17 February 2016.

Coleridge, Samuel Taylor (1983): *Biographia Literaria*, vol 1, London: Routledge & Kegan Paul.

Critchley, Simon (2005): *Things Merely Are*, NY: Routledge.

Gaita, Raimond (1990): "Ethical Individuality". In: Raimond Gaita (ed.), *Value and Understanding*, London and New York: Routledge, 118–148.
Gaita, Raimond (2002): *A Common Humanity*, London and New York: Routledge.
Ortega y Gasset, José (1942): *Ideas y Creencias*, Madrid: Revista de Occidente.
Kierkegaard, Søren (1983): *Fear and Trembling; Repetition*, Princeton, NJ: Princeton University Press.
McDowell, John (1998): *Mind, Value, and Reality*, London and Cambridge, MA: Harvard University Press.
Milgram, Paul (1994): "Augmented Reality: A Class of Displays on the Reality-Virtuality Continuum". In: *SPIE* Vol. 2351, Telemanipulator and Telepresence Technologies.
Nagel, Thomas (1997): *The Last Word*, Oxford: Oxford University Press.
Papagiannis, Helen (2011) "Augmented Reality and the Power of Imagination". http://augmentedstories.com/ted-talks/, accessed 17 February 2016.
Quine, Willard Van Orman (1964): "On What There Is". In: *From a Logical Point of View*. Cambridge, MA: Harvard University Press, 1–19.
Ramsey, Frank (1990): "Facts and Propositions". In: D. H. Mellor (ed.), *Philosophical Papers*, Cambridge: Cambridge University Press, 34–51.
Stevens, Wallace (1951): "The Noble Rider and the Sound of Words". In: *The Necessary Angel*, London: Faber and Faber Limited, 3–36.
Stevens, Wallace (1964): *The Collected Poems of Wallace Stevens*, New York: Alfred A. Knopf.
Taylor, Charles (1989): *Sources of the Self*, Cambridge: Cambridge University Press.
Tönnis, Marcus (2010): *Augmented Reality. Einblicke in die erweiterte Realitat*, Heidelberg: Springer.
Wiggins, David (1990): "Moral Cognitivism, Moral Relativism and Motivating Moral Beliefs". In: *Proceedings of the Aristotelian Society*, New Series, 91: 61–85.
Wiggins, David (1998): *Needs, Values, Truth*, Cambridge MA and Oxford: Basil Blackwell.
Wittgenstein, Ludwig (1966a): *Lectures and Conversations on Aesthetics, Psychology and Religious Belief*, Oxford: Basil Blackwell.
Wittgenstein, Ludwig (1966b): *Tractatus Logico-Philosophicus*, London: Routledge & Kegan Paul Ltd.
Wittgenstein, Ludwig (1984): *Werkausgabe*, vol. 1. Frankfurt on Main: Suhrkamp.
"The Entire History of You". *Black Mirror*. Aired 18 December 2011. Television.

Part 4: Negative Knowledge Through Augmented Reality

Jaana Parviainen

"Imagine Never Not Knowing": An Epistemological Framework for Understanding Negative Knowledge in Augmented Reality

"The most profound technologies are those that disappear."
Mark Weiser, 1991

"Imagine true Augmented Reality. Imagine a world of knowledge in front of your eyes. Imagine never not knowing, always having your hands free. Imagine SmartEyeglass."
Sony Mobile Communications Inc., 2015

Abstract: Using the apps and devices of Augmented Reality technologies when walking down the street, we are part of epistemological processes in which acquiring information and forming knowledge are involved in visual, aural, and kinesthetic sensations. This paper approaches Augmented Reality in the context of the smart city, considering questions of information materialism related to social epistemology and the phenomenology of the body. Exploring Augmented Reality as an embodied medium rather than a bunch of technologies, the purpose of the paper is to foster a broader look at Augmented Reality, discussing notions of "non-knowing" and "negative knowledge". Drawing on recent sociological discussions of ignorance, I consider negative knowing as an epistemological phase where "we know that we don't know". Karin Knorr Cetina's notion of liminality offers an epistemological framework to understand how augmented technologies provides contextual information by supplementing or replacing human senses. The paper proposes that the technologies of Augmented Reality promise to bring us new information of our physical world while simultaneously concealing information from us.

Keywords: Negative knowledge, non-knowledge, pervasive computing, phenomenology, social epistemology, embodiment, urban environment.

DOI 10.1515/9783110497656-011

1. Introduction

Motivating ideas behind the development of interactive technology have been to make our lives convenient and comfortable and to reduce physical action and cognitive load. Following in the footsteps of Mark Weiser's vision of *calm computing* (cf. Weiser 1991, Weiser/Brown 1996), the user interface should be an experientially transparent, quiet and invisible servant. So instead of using a hand for giving commands to the device via gestural input, the device itself can experientially become an extension of our hand, seamlessly augmenting the enactive sense-making of the user. Weiser's central thesis was that we should be attuned to interfaces without attending to them explicitly or consciously (e.g. Rogers 2006). With computers embedded everywhere in our environments and even in our bodies, Weiser and Brown (1996) argued that interfaces better not overburden our cognition in our everyday lives.

Weiser's vision of ubiquitous computing has had an enormous impact on the directions that ubiquitous computing and Augmented Reality have taken over the past 15 years. Digital devices have shrunk continuously with the consequence that digital applications are no longer "black boxes", but they set invisible distributed processes. Thus, technology has become increasingly an inseparable aspect of embodied experience such as bodily movements (Parviainen *et al.* 2013). Proactive computing was put forward as an approach to determine how to program computers to take the initiative to act on people's behalf. The environment has been augmented with various computational resources to provide information and services. Sensors embedded in the physical environments and biosensors as wearable fabrics and accessories within our bodies provide data about our movements, health, and changes in our everyday activities.

Critical research on digital technology (e.g. Rogers 2006, Savat 2013) has suggested that we need to rethink the value and role of calm and proactive computing as main driving forces. The very idea of calm computing has also raised a number of ethical and social concerns. In particular, is it desirable to depend on computers to take on our day-to-day decision-making and planning activities? Will our abilities to learn, remember, and think for ourselves suffer if we begin to rely increasingly on the environment to do them for us? Furthermore, how do designers decide which activities should be left for humans to control and which are acceptable and valuable for the environment to take over responsibility for? Rogers (2006) argues that it is difficult to build calm computing systems because algorithmic solutions are never neutral but inherently political. When they include some choices they exclude others. This requires determining how to make intelligible, usable, and useful the recordings of science, medicine, etc., which are streaming from an increasing array of sensors placed throughout the world. It also entails figuring out how to integrate and replay, in meaningful and powerful ways, the masses of digital recordings that are being gathered and archived such that professionals and researchers can perform new forms of computation and problem-solving, leading to novel insights.

This paper approaches Augmented Reality in the context of the smart city, considering questions of information technology through the lenses of social epistemology and from the phenomenological point of view. The concept of the smart city can be viewed as recognizing that amid the rise of new Internet technologies and the use of smartphones and sensors, the critical infrastructure components and services of cities – which include city administration, education, healthcare, public safety, and transportation – can be more intelligent, interconnected, and efficient (e.g. McQuire 2008, *Townsend 2013)*. Social epistemology refers to a broad set of approaches that emphasizes social and collective dimensions of knowledge, including questions of technology and embodiment (e.g. Braidotti 2007). Drawing on phenomenological methodologies of technology (e.g. Kozel 2007) and notions in critical technology studies (e.g. Savat 2013), I assume that our being and embodiment can never be separated from the technology. Embodied beings, things, and technology form an assemblage, and it is their interaction that determines what thoughts and actions are possible. However, the technological co-presence has intensified in our bodies in a given milieu, so we will discuss Augmented Reality related to technological unconsciousness. Using Clough's (2001) term *technological unconsciousness,* Thrift (2004, 177) means by it "... the bending of the bodies-with-environment to a specific set of addresses without the benefit of any cognitive inputs ..." According to Thrift, we are entering a new phase of the technological unconscious where everyday activities, such as the simple coordination of the body required by mobile phones, are affected by complicated "invisible" software in the background. When our interaction with computers becomes more and more mundane, automatized, and embodied, we apparently no longer "use" devices, but our being and acting becomes part of their functions. This implies that we generally do not understand or sometimes ignore systems of computers and devices. Opening up such infrastructure and its dynamics is a challenge, as the scale of these systems is much bigger than has been considered in traditional human-computer interaction (cf. Haddadi *et al.* 2013).

Algorithms have been developed to process data so that computers could automatically make inferences for people. Data is increasingly being used to automate mundane operations and actions that we would have done in our everyday worlds using conventional knobs, buttons, and other physical controls. For example, our favorite music or TV show that we like to hear or see when exercising can be automatically played as we step on a treadmill in the gym. Sensed data is also being used to remind us of things we often forget to do at salient times, such as detecting the absence of milk in the fridge and messaging us to buy a carton when passing the grocery store.

When algorithmic systems are designed to read, interpret, and act upon people's moods, intentions, and desires, they also steer our actions in the everyday context. Their "interpretations" of our intentions are sometimes frustrating and irritating, for example, when a system decides to switch on a light because we do not move in the room in 10 minutes. These algorithmic inferences are likely to be unnerving and extremely annoying, especially if they are persistently wrong. Pervasive technologies become increasingly flexible in scope for providing new solutions to "sense", monitor, and detect people's movements, bodily functions, etc., in ways not possible before. There is a danger, however, that such techniques may probe too far into the lives of less-able people, resulting in – albeit unintentionally – "extreme" forms of recording, tracking, and monitoring that these people may have no control over (e.g. Rogers 2006).

Exploring Augmented Reality as a medium rather than a bunch of technologies, my purpose is to reach beyond describing technologies required to support Augmented Reality. My aim is to foster a broader look at Augmented Reality and its epistemological implication, discussing knowing and "non-knowing" – or "negative knowledge" – in terms of Augmented Reality. Before I introduce the notion of negative knowledge, I clarify what I mean by Augmented Reality and how it differs from the notions of virtual reality and mixed reality.

2. Augmented Reality as medium

The vision for Augmented Reality dates back to at least the 1960s with the work of Ivan Sutherland. In the visionaries of virtual reality, virtual environments were often used to describe systems that attempt to replace much or all of the user's experience of the physical world with synthesized 3D material such as graphics and sound (Feiner *et al.* 1993). For instance, John Perry Barlow wrote "A Declaration of the Independence of Cyberspace" to resist a proposed United States law that would impose limits on online communications. "I declare the global social space we are building to be naturally independent of the tyrannies you seek to impose on us ... [Cyberspace] is an act of nature it grows itself through our collective actions ... Our identities have no bodies, so, unlike you, we cannot obtain order by physical coercion." (Barlow 1996, cited in Kendall 2002). In Barlow's view, cyberspace constitutes an organically separate, sovereign realm that is characterized by the absence of bodies. For many like Barlow, much of the hype of cyberspace and virtual reality resides in its sovereignty and separation from "real life." Instead of blocking out the real world, Augmented Reality and ubiquitous computing offer new layers of reality and the physical world.

Virtual reality technologies completely immerse a user inside a synthetic environment, and while immersed, the user can no longer see the real world around him or her. In contrast, Augmented Reality takes digital or computer-generated information – whether images, audio, video, and touch or haptic sensations – and overlaying them in a real-time environment. Augmented Reality refers to systems that combine real and virtual objects in a real environment, run interactively and in real time, and align real and virtual objects with each other (cf. Azuma *et al.* 2001). Unlike virtual reality, Augmented Reality allows the user to see the real world, with virtual objects superimposed upon or composited with the real world. Milgram and Kishino (1994) use the term "mixed reality", which includes the "virtuality continuum", to cover a spectrum of different forms of mixed reality from purely physical, real environments at one extreme to purely virtual environments at the other. In between these two extremes lies Augmented Reality, which signifies physical environments that are overlaid with digital information. On the other side lies augmented virtuality, in which virtual environments are overlaid with physical information (Benford/Giannachi 2011, 2).

Technically, Augmented Reality can be used to enhance all five senses, thus, Augmented Reality supplements reality, rather than completely replacing something in the environment. The following three characteristics are needed for the definition of Augmented Reality: 1) combines real and virtual information, 2) is interactive in real time, and 3) operates and is used in a 3D environment. A common example is a heads-up display (HUD), which gives a fighter pilot a digital overlay showing an artificial horizon, digital speed, and other information while looking out the cockpit window (Kipper/Rampola 2013). Calo and his colleagues (Tech Policy Lab 2015) define Augmented Reality as "... a mobile or embedded technology that senses, processes, and outputs data in real-time, recognizes and tracks real-world objects, and provides contextual information by supplementing or replacing human senses."

Augmented Reality is the combination of several technologies that work together to bring digital information, more commonly, into visual, haptic, or aural sensations. This system is seen to have a lot of economic potential for service development in urban areas. For instance, Augmented Reality technologies are used to enhance sightseeing experiences and navigation in tourism industries. Augmented Reality systems–based city guides help people find places to eat, drink, and shop, giving users real-time visual directions to and graphic information about places they are looking for. In the entertainment and gaming industries, Augmented Reality is thought to have tremendous potential even if few game applications have been designed to be used in specific locations. Though Augmented Reality has been under development for more than four decades, 2009 is widely considered the year that Augmented Reality technology became mainstream. The hype surrounding this technology was similar to previous tech hypes in the past, such as virtual reality during the 1990s.

When our phones, trackers, cars, and other devices are increasingly reactive to the environment around us, in this type of interaction, the distinction between display and environment will be easily blurred. Today, a number of companies are investing heavily in the development of Augmented Reality devices and technologies. Some specific examples of Augmented Reality technologies being marketed or developed today include: Sony's Smart Eyeglass, Google Glass, Microsoft's HoloLens, Meta's Space Glasses, Magic Leap, Navdy Automotive, Across Air, and Word Lens (Tech Policy Lab 2015). These systems have the potential to deliver numerous new applications including hands-free instruction and training, language translation, obstacle avoidance, advertising, gaming, and museum tours.

These systems do not only generate data and information for us, but they also collect various forms of data about us as users: our locations, intentions, and desires. The sensors of Augmented Reality may include video (e.g., depth cameras, cameras worn on the body), audio, haptic input (i.e., detecting physical touch), location (e.g., GPS, GSM triangulation), motion, or wireless signals (e.g., WiFi, Bluetooth) (Tech Policy Lab 2015). Information gathered and processed by the system will generally be overlaid on the user's usual perception of the world; this is unlike virtual reality, which replaces the user's setting with an entirely new environment. The information provided by the system to the user is contextual and timely, meaning it will relate to what the user is currently experiencing.

The systems of Augmented Reality make it possible for individuals to perceive the same environment differently. One person may perceive an environment in an augmented state, while a person without the technological solutions has a different impression of the world. Moreover, two people using the same device and application may both experience an augmented space, but their versions may consist of different information overlays. Furthermore, people do not experience Augmented Reality in the same way, because its sensory information can be perceived and felt differently. For some individuals – notably, those living with disabilities – Augmented Reality may partially replace a sense. Thus, for instance, an assistive technology may vibrate as people or objects approach or convert auditory information to visual stimuli (Tech Policy Lab 2015). Those living with disability may come to rely upon these signals, such that their sudden interruption could create an inconvenient or even dangerous sensory deficit.

Augmented Reality systems may prove both empowering and disabling for a certain group of people. For example, Augmented Reality could empower children by providing a wider range of educational experiences. For instance, they are able to view and experience a site from several social perspectives and view its structure and uses across different historical layers. Similarly, though Augmented Reality can reveal, distract, and imperil people in new ways, it can also empower them by permitting them to record their surroundings, communicate with others, and gain information while keeping alert.

As stated above, Augmented Reality systems overlay information onto the world in real-time. These systems blend information with everyday activities in ways that can blur the distinction between real and perceived environments and potentially cause physical harm and risks. For instance, Augmented Reality can make objects appear that are not there, and make objects that are there disappear. If users rely on this information in error, or if the information distracts a user, then it may also cause injuries or lead to their making wrong conclusions about given situations. Understanding in this system or medium is intuitive, so users usually instantly relay information delivered by the systems of Augmented Reality. This could lead to a new category of product liability at the intersection of information and object.

Since Augmented Reality is not limited by today's technology and new applications, I will consider Augmented Reality as a *medium* rather than a bunch of technologies, to explore Augmented Reality from the epistemological point of view. However, I will illustrate my approach using Sony's SmartEyeglass and its advertising to concretize and contextualize what kind of promises that technology companies make to their customers regarding the user experience and usability of Augmented Reality technologies. I recall here the citation on Sony's SmartEyeglass in an advertisement presented as an opening phrase in the beginning of this article. It declares: "Imagine true Augmented Reality. Imagine a world of knowledge in front of your eyes. *Imagine never not knowing*, always having your hands free. Imagine SmartEyeglass." The phrase implies that before SmartEyeglass and Augmented Reality technologies, we lived in the world in which knowledge was hidden from us, in a state of "non-knowing." Now, through SmartEyeglass, all the knowledge of reality is in our hands. This is hardly true, but it opens up an interesting perspective about how this medium is expected to reveal to us the "hidden" knowledge and information that is an inherent part of our physical infrastructure. Interestingly, this advertisement implies that the technologies of Augmented Reality can turn our "non-knowledge" into something that can be available only through this technology. Since the technologies of Augmented Reality are recognized in the context of non-knowing, I will examine in more detail how the notions of "non-knowledge" and "negative knowledge" can be understood in the discussions of social epistemology.

3. Negative knowledge in the epistemological context

Over the past two decades, we have witnessed dramatic changes in information and knowledge production. These changes are not only associated with developments in information technologies and infrastructures, but the social, material, technical, and political relations of knowledge production have changed through digitalization of data and virtualization of social networks. To explore the notion of negative knowledge, it is necessary to link this discussion to the more general epistemological question: What does it mean to "know" in an age of information technology, when we have access to "bigger," "wider," "longer," "faster," and "augmented" information? One crucial epistemological question is: How is knowledge generated, maintained, revised, and spread through this information? And even more importantly: Does information overload really lead to better opportunities to form knowledge, or does it in fact refer to the opposite, difficulty in finding relevant knowledge? Paradoxically, an increasing amount of data available on the Internet can make us even more ignorant.

During the past two decades, the focus on notions of ignorance (e.g. Smithson 1989, Sullivan/Tuana 2007, Proctor/Schiebinger 2008, Firestein 2012, Gross/McGoey 2015), non-knowledge (e.g. Simmel 1992, Beck 2009), nescience (e.g. Kerwin 1993), negative knowledge (e.g. Minsky 1994, Knorr Cetina 1999), negative expertise (Parviainen/Eriksson 2006, Gartmeier *et al.* 2011), and unknown processes (e.g. Gross 2007) have become increasingly important in theorizing about modern society and the production of knowledge in the 21st century. Many of these terms are used to denote certain states of epistemological attitudes whether these attitudes precede knowing something or they are stubborn resistance to some evidence. The debate over non-knowledge and ignorance goes back at least to Socrates, who famously observed "I know one thing, that I know nothing." His wisdom is seen to lay in knowing what he did not know, occasionally referred to as non-knowledge (cf. Jaspers 1951). In other words, to know something, we must realize first that we don't know something. In this sense, "not-knowing" is vital for human existence because without this state we are not able to create new knowledge.

According to Gross (2007), non-knowledge does not necessarily mean a lack of knowledge, but rather, as Tacke (2001, 295) put it, "a social construction, which is dependent on knowledge as its respective flip-side." Experts, for instance, need to know what they do not know, to understand the limits of their own expertise. In this stream of thought, non-knowledge is regarded as the other side of "positive" knowledge, and consequently as the other half of a distinction (Japp 2000). In trying to outline different connotations in sociological and philosophical usage of these concepts, I attempt to simplify and integrate these epistemological concepts.

Exploring the notions of non-knowledge, negative knowledge, and ignorance, it is fruitful, first, to introduce the notion of "metacognition awareness". *Metacognition awareness* refers to one's awareness concerning one's own cognitive processes (cf. Flavell 1979, Schraw/Dennison 1994). Metacognition concerns the actor's awareness about his or her own thoughts and cognitions (cf. Dunlosky/Metcalfe 2009). To further illustrate metacognition in the context of social epistemology rather than as a psychological term, we find different "attitudes" toward knowing; we are aware of some of them, but some go beyond our capabilities or awareness. Image 1 describes four major and robust components of metacognition awareness: 1) we know that we know, 2) we don't know that we know, 3) we don't know that we don't know, and 4) we know that we don't know. The first one, positive or *declarative knowledge* is composed of facts, beliefs, and episodes that we can state verbally and hence are accessible to conscious awareness. It means that "we know that we know". The second, implicit, procedural, or *tacit knowledge* refers to nonconscious processing of forming knowledge and developing cognitive or embodied skills. Tacit knowledge means that "we don't know that we know". The next two categories are more problematic, and there are several different interpretations of them.

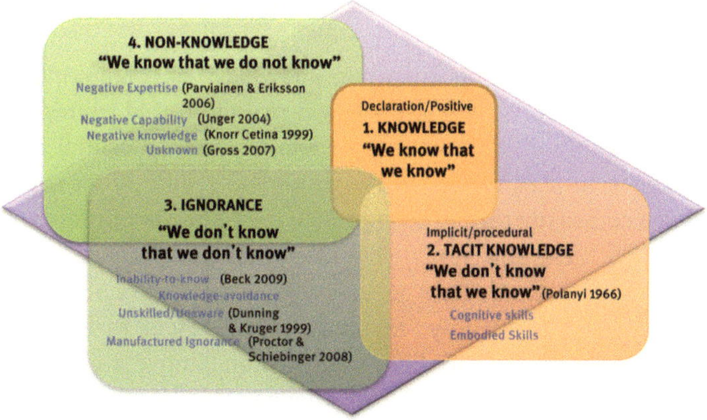

Fig. 1: Four major epistemological atttitudes

Following Gross' (2007) formulation, I suggest that the English term "ignorance" should function as a kind of cover term that generally points to intentional and unintentional bracketing out of knowing and skills. The third epistemological category in my formulation, ignorance, refers to a situation when "we are not aware that we don't know". Actors who falsely believe they are knowledgeable will not seek out clarification of their beliefs, but rather rely on their ignorant position (cf. Dunning/Kruger 1999). Thus, ignorance can stifle learning, when the ignorant actors believe that they are not ignorant. However, ignorance is not necessarily something we can evaluate as a voluntary or involuntary activity. Proctor and Schiebinger (2008) talk about "manufactured ignorance," asking, "What keeps ignorance alive, or allows it to be used as a political instrument?" In their edited book *Agnotology*—the study of ignorance—provides theoretical perspectives to understand "Why don't we know what we don't know?"

According to Gross (2007), the word *nescience*, which was incorrectly used as a translation of Simmel's *Nichtwissen*, should rather be seen as a prerequisite for a total surprise beyond any type of anticipation. Nescience, as a total lack of knowledge, at first sight comes close to what Kerwin (1993, 179) and Beck (2009, 8–9) has termed "unknown unknowns", things not known that they are not known. It can also be seen as synonymous with Wynne's definition of indeterminacy when applied to environmental policy. It could also fill the place of Beck and Wehling's (2012) description of a complete unawareness of non-knowledge, since this unawareness can only be made "visible" in sociological analysis, when, like knowledge, its social utterances, constructions, or negotiations can be registered (Gross 2007). However, nescience can be seen as belonging to the same epistemic class as ignorance, even if nescience can only be detected in retrospect as Böschen (2009) has shown in his study on CFCs, DDT, and Dioxin.

The main categorical difference between non-knowledge and ignorance is that in the former case we are conscious of unknown realms so that we register the possibility of being ignorant. We then can decide to frame potential non-knowledge and ignorance in a certain way. The empirical reality often shows that positive knowledge can easily turn into ignorance if we stick to our false beliefs. So, in this sense, all these epistemological categories are connected, and their boundaries are fragile.

The fourth epistemological category, non-knowledge, refers to situation when "we know that we don't know". "We know that we don't know" can be considered as a starting point to forming new knowledge. The creation of new knowledge always includes a big paradox: how to strive toward something about which one cannot know anything. Unlike Firestein (2012), I consider that there is no direct access from ignorance to "positive knowledge" without acknowledgement and awareness that we don't know something. So in this sense, non-knowledge and the "unknown", rather than ignorance, drive researchers to puzzle over thorny questions or inexplicable data.

So, non-knowledge is used here as an epistemological term that concerns attitudes toward several different epistemological aspects, including its literal translation of the German *Nichtwissen,* which is also the original usage in classical sociological language, especially that of Georg Simmel (1992). This term points to a kind of symmetry between "positive" knowledge (*Wissen*) and its natural flip side (*Nichtwissen*) to denote that there can be knowledge (*Wissen*) about what is not yet known. As Gross (2012) suggests, this aspect is not captured in the English word "ignorance". Non-knowledge as "unknown" (Gross 2007) is a kind of subcategory that includes active consideration into a certain direction that might be important. This subcategory may lead to the development of new or "extended knowledge", based on planning, tinkering, or researching with new phenomena. The new extended knowledge can reveal, for instance, that earlier ideas about reliable and accepted knowledge must be reinterpreted. Gross (2007) considers that negative knowledge is a subcategory of ignorance, but I assume that it belongs to "non-knowledge."[1]

I follow here Knorr Cetina's (1999, 63–71) formulation of negative knowledge, in which negativity concerns "liminal" phenomena, things that are neither empirical objects of positive knowledge nor effects in the formless regions of the unknowable, but something in between. Departing from Ulrich Beck's view on "inability-to-know," Knorr Cetina (1999, 64) means by negative knowledge "... knowledge of the limits of knowing, of the mistakes we make in trying to know, of the things that interfere with our knowing, of what we are not interested in and do not really want to know". The importance of Knorr Cetina's approach lies in the fact that in the analysis of scientific decisions, the limits of knowing are admitted by bracketing out certain areas of knowledge and non-knowledge. This strategy can also lead to an acknowledgement of non-knowledge that so far has been neglected, but is suddenly taken seriously and may even be seen as fundamental.

In my formulation of negative knowledge, I follow Knorr Cetina's notion of *liminality,* stressing the idea that ambiguity and uncertainty are inherent aspects

1 Martin Gartmeier and his fellows (2011) conceptualize negative expertise as the professional's ability to avoid errors during practice due to certain cognitive agencies. In their study, negative knowledge refers to knowledge about what is wrong in a certain context and situation. In this sense, their notion of negative knowledge is related to (positive) knowledge rather than to the category of non-knowledge.

of negative knowledge As Knorr Cetina (1999, 63) suggests, *limen* means "threshold", "doorstep", and "entrance" in Latin. It is a type of knowing in which we enter things indirectly, as seeing a photo through its negative, guessing how things really are when we see only the opposite. In a negative approach, we outline phenomena without ever confronting them directly but based on half-knowledge (Adlam 2014) or just following hints and traces, guessing at what these phenomena might look like. In this sense, they are inherently "liminal" phenomena, things which are neither empirical objects of positive knowledge nor effects in the formless regions of the unknowable, but something in between. Knorr Cetina (1999, 64) describes negative knowledge by reference to Christian theology and its approach called negative or *apophantic theology*. The God is not prescribed in terms of what *He is* but what *He is not* because positive assertions could not be made about His essence. The negative approach is needed because all descriptions or definitions, if attempted, are ultimately false, thus conceptualization should be avoided. In a similar way, some phenomena in physics, as Knorr Cetina suggests, are needed to approach with the negative tools, by delimiting the properties and possibilities of the objects. By making errors and mishaps in studying these phenomena, they gradually reveal some parts of them to us but not necessarily entirely. Knorr Cetina (1999, 65) emphasizes, however, that it is quite remarkable how much one can do by mobilizing negative knowledge.

Discussing negative knowledge in terms of Augmented Reality, in this indirect accessibility–described embodiment and spatiality, is given a central role. Ubiquitous computing embeds large numbers of computers and displays in the world so they become an inextricable and socially invisible part of our surroundings. "Seeing through" or "hearing through" mobile or wearable displays, we can craft an Augmented Reality whose user interface is not restricted to the displays and interaction devices embedded in the surrounding world or held in the user's hands but concern the whole body and transition in environment. Next, I consider how the negative approach as forming knowledge of augmented environments is connected to our embodiment, kinesthesia, movement, and transition in space.

4. Negative knowledge in urban environments

According to my definition above, Augmented Reality supplements reality, rather than completely replacing something in the environment. By shifting to a more widespread use of digital devices, digital technologies are vastly expanded and affect more and more aspects of our life. We are no longer captured at home or in offices within digital devices, but the use of digital media grows in urban environments such as in cafes, shops, railway stations, and city parks. The solutions of Augmented Reality technologies have contributed to the expansion of urban cultures. People in cities live their daily lives "on the move" as they traverse the city from one stopping point to another, moving around the city from their homes or places of work or study to shopping, recreations, and social events.

When people are constantly moving through the city, following habitual paths with stopping points at their destination sites, this network of "stopping points" can be seen to be interconnected by trajectories (e. g. Benford *et al.* 2009, Mellish 2012, Gabrielli *et al.* 2013). *Movement trajectories* refer here to people's daily travels and moves around the city between home, work, and social events, as well as their everyday bodily movements and embodied practices. These movement trajectories are supported or intervened by technical vehicles and digital devices. These everyday habitual trajectories form personal and collective choreographies in cities when people move from home or place of work or study to having lunch or shopping.

Kinesthetic sensations while walking on the street can be partly shaped by detailed advertisements and information renderings that pervade urban environments. Although responding to different sensibilities, there are striking similarities among these various registers of everyday experiences of the street. The digital means of production of street imagery – never delivering a clear end product and always circulating between material and virtual networks – allows potential consumers only fleeting glances as they walk on the street (cf. Savat 2013). It seems that what is most important in these visual advertisements is not so much the content of the imagery as their *immediacy*. Mathematically dexterous algorithms that can calculate the geometry of three-dimensional spaces and recognize specific objects are being developed and used widely in urban settings. The abilities of Augmented Reality will move beyond the planar, expanding the "storytelling canvas" to the complexities of any given room, location, and environment. For instance, SmartEyeglass is lightweight, binocular eyewear that enables three-dimensional Augmented Reality experiences. Text, symbols, and images are superimposed onto your sensual field of view. This development requires new concepts, theories, and research methods that would combine close analyses of the image with the study of the practices of production, circulation, and consumption of the image, and the diverse set of social, cultural, affective, and performative implications of it in everyday life.

According to Thrift (2004), we have entered a new phase of technological unconsciousness in which everyday activities, such as the simple coordination of the body required by mobile phones, are affected by complicated "invisible" software in the background. Unlike the Freudian or Lacanian notions of unconscious, this conscious is not "in" the body, but in the very signifying process it keeps us in the loop of technological infrastructure. When interacting with computers and their information, what they produce for us becomes more and more mundane, automatized, and embodied. Traditional ways of acquiring "propositional" information becomes more embodied. In the previous chapter, we illustrated how positive or declarative knowledge "we know" is composed of facts and justified true beliefs that we can state verbally and hence are accessible to conscious awareness. However, using the apps and devices of augmented technologies, we are part of epistemological processes in which acquiring information and forming knowledge involves visual, aural, and tactile perceptions – even kinesthetic sensations like walking on the street.

Friedrich Kittler is one of the pioneers of what might be called *media materialism* – an approach that prioritizes analysis of the material structures of technology over the meanings of these structures and the messages they circulate (cf. Gane 2005). This approach emphasizes material components of the communication system: Information infrastructures are both material and immaterial. Kittler's approach to "information materialism" addresses the ways in which information and the communication system here merge into one, meaning that information is "transformed into matter and matter into information." (Kittler 1997, 126) Kittler fleshes out these arguments through a series of detailed historical analyses of media technologies dating from the late 18th century onward. Information materialism moves from information theory to an analysis of the physical components of communication systems, drawing on discussions of new materialism (e.g. Coole/Frost 2010). In Kittler's approach, there is no attempt to prioritize corporeality and embodiment, because the boundaries between bodies and machines blur – "The age of media... renders indistinguishable what is human and what is machine ..." (Kittler 1999, 146) However, my approach, which is based on a phenomenological notion of embodiment, emphasizes movement and kinesthesia as a primary source as access to information in an urban environment.

In the context of science and technology studies, Edwards (2010) defines *knowledge infrastructure* as "robust networks of people, artifacts, and institutions that generate, share, and maintain specific knowledge about the human and natural worlds." Under this definition, knowledge infrastructure includes the ensembles of individuals, organizations, information technologies, routines, shared norms, and practices (Edwards et al. 2007). Infrastructures are not systems in the sense that they are fully coherent, deliberately engineered, end-to-end processes. Rather, infrastructures are ecologies or complex adaptive systems; they consist of numerous actants, each of which has unique origins and goals. They are made to interoperate by social practices, norms, and individual behaviors that smooth out the connections among them. This adaptive process is continuous, as individual elements change and new ones are introduced – and it is not necessarily always successful. The current situation for knowledge infrastructures is characterized by rapid change in existing systems and introduction of new ones, resulting in severe strains on those elements with the greatest inertia.

In these transitions between places, the body, movements, and social interaction within technological devices are what making happen in synchrony of everyday life. Augmented Reality technologies are closely linked to this combination of being and doing. What constitutes infrastructural support and control, then, is not just the technological gadgets, as these are simply material components, but also the entire set of practices within our bodies and technological needs and interest they serve (Guattari 1995, 36; Mumford 1995, 305). From such a perspective, as bodily beings we are always part of some *technological ensembles* and their infrastructural control. When digital technologies, action, and materiality intertwine, our gestures and movements become one actor of a larger assemblage or choreography. Augmented technologies in urban environments tend to become part of our "tacit background" and no longer require engagement with them or the development of skills (Dreyfus 2001, Coeckelbergh 2015). Using Polanyi's (1966) conceptual distinction between tacit and focal awareness, wearing SmartEyeglass requires no focal engagement but becomes part of our tacit orientation in the urban environment. Focal or cognitive engagement is needed only when a user attempts to interpret information on the screen.

We are increasingly being tracked in urban settings by sensors that register our bodies, such as the use of facial recognition technology in billboards. Architectural elements of physical space, as well as social architectures, often frame and cue actions – some very minute and instantaneous. However, in the case of facial recognition technology, our mere physical bodies, without even any cognitive effort, can certainly become actors that generate the code. The more wired the world becomes, the more code bodies will generate, including on the biological level. It is important to consider that smart fabrics within their algorithms easily cross the line between private and public places. Companies often promote the illusion that algorithmic processes and data-driven systems are purged from human bias and based on neutral and objective decisions (cf. Ajana 2015). However, the algorithms reflect choices, among others, about data, connections, inferences, interpretation, and thresholds for inclusion that advance a specific purpose. Classification systems are neither neutral nor objective; they reflect the explicit and implicit values of their designers. Data collected through search engines can be saved and later on analyzed, opening up the potential for profiling everyday rhythms or family relationships in the home environment.

Given the rise of digital technologies within social networking and the ever-increasing digitalization of leisure and daily activities, the quantity of data being generated today has reached an unprecedented scale. As Pentland (2013) suggests, we live in the "data-driven" society. People no longer "use" devices but interact with a mundane and embodied knowledge infrastructure, which they generally do not understand or even recognize. In this infrastructure, technologies and objects are treated as active members of networks, transacting themselves, circulating ideas, and affecting actions through relationships. In this sense, we are involved in an ensemble of techniques, a knowledge infrastructure (cf. Ajana 2015). It means that people interact with an apparently mundane knowledge infrastructure that they generally do not understand and would rather ignore.

Non-knowledge as unknown is an epistemological subcategory that includes active consideration to think further in a certain direction that might be important. In the case of wearing SmartEyeglass, when texts and images are superimposed onto a user's field of view, the user might become aware of new aspects of his or her environment. Augmented Reality as a "liminal space" (Sheery *et al.* 2014) can potentially provoke individuals to attain fresh understanding of different aspects of their environment. This reminds us of Knorr Cetina's notion of liminality that refers to the zone of ambiguity and uncertainty, including simultaneously the potential to explore unknown and invent new ideas. Augmented Reality technologies can liberate individuals from their normative and traditional use of spaces, so they might develop deeper and more personalized ways to attain their environment. Furthermore, educational potentials of Augmented Reality may lead to the development of new or "extended knowledge", based on planning, tinkering with, or researching new phenomena. The new extended knowledge can reveal, for instance, that earlier ideas about reliable and accepted knowledge must be reinterpreted. In this sense, Augmented Reality has potential as creative technology to support educational purposes and to challenge stereotyped notions of our environment.

Equally, the use of Augmented Reality devices has potential to promote ignorance. Previously, we defined ignorance as a condition when "we don't know that we don't know". It can mean that we are not aware that we don't know something. As suggested above, in urban settings, people interact increasingly with a mundane knowledge infrastructure whose function they do not necessarily understand. For instance, people are not aware what kind of data that the systems of Augmented Reality are tracking in their everyday behavior in urban settings. These systems generate and collect various forms of data about the users, including their locations, intentions, and desires. Information gathered and processed by these systems is hidden from the user's usual perception of the world. Furthermore, regarding the perceptual world, the technological solutions of Augmented Reality can make objects appear in our field of view when the purpose is, for instance, to create entertaining fictional worlds for people in live-action role-playing games in urban environments. If users rely on this information in error, or if the information distracts a user, then it may also cause injuries or lead to the user reaching wrong conclusions about given situations. Most people who attend to urban pervasive games are, of course, aware of their fictional nature, but such events in a public space may cause problems and confusion for innocent bystanders who might be accidentally engaged in game.

Turning back to Knorr Cetina's (1999) notion of negative knowledge, in using technologies of Augmented Reality such as SmartEyeglass, new information that interferes with our consciousness can be relevant for us, but can also introduce information we are not interested in and do not really want to know. Whether we are watching a live game or concert, touring a new city, or carrying out a job, our experience can be supported by the context-specific extra data and information. The importance of Knorr Cetina's approach to negative knowledge lies in the fact that placing new information in our hands simultaneously brackets out certain areas of the real world. This strategy can also lead to a situation in which information revealed to us through Augmented Reality technologies may even be seen as fundamental and suddenly taken seriously. While this technology can offer us an access to "hidden" information in the physical location, it can make some relevant objects and information disappear. In this way, Augmented Reality can reveal, distract, and imperil people in new ways.

Furthermore, another relevant question is whether we are capable of processing all the information that augmented technologies superimpose onto our perceptual field. The advertisement of SmartEyeglass sensors wants to assure us that we never remain in the state of "non-knowing", putting all possible information about our physical world in our hands. The advertisement suggests that the user can access numerous sensor data using the built-in camera or the sensors available on the phone. We should be able to process all this information while moving from one place to another. The SmartEyeglass shows text and bitmaps on the user's display, while users need to concentrate on the stream of information in the real world to avoid crashing into objects and other people in the urban environment. New unintended side effects thus develop via a widening rift between real-world information and augmented information.

The development of augmented technologies means that people's habitual trajectories can be utilized via applications such as location "check-in" information to find the nearest restaurant and its menu. Fenster (2005) noticed that the kinesthetic experiences of everyday walking and the knowledge accumulated while doing so enabled the development of "belonging and attachment" to the urban environment. The development of new apps for the devices of Augmented Reality tend to focus on subjects and their movements while "in transit" between places or certain important locations such as railway stations, theaters, museums, etc. (e.g. Mellish 2012). When digital technologies, action, and materiality intertwine, our gestures and bodily movements become one actor of larger assemblage that crosses the line between private and public places. This type of knowledge infrastructure makes it difficult for us to select which information is relevant for us and which we should disregard. We have difficulty ignoring irrelevant information and staying in a state of "non-knowing."

Paradoxically, when the technologies of Augmented Reality promise to bring us new information about our physical world, they also simultaneously conceal information from us and perhaps superimpose some irrelevant information onto our perceptual field. Companies can expand but also limit our view of the world through new apps and devices. The technologies of Augmented Reality can be considered as filters that drill some information while covering up other information. For without the needed procedural transparency and access to adequate information, individuals remain in the dark with regard to what kind of data are being collected about them, how these data are being processed, and for what purpose. When interfaces of augmented technologies have begun to overburden our cognition in everyday life, it is obvious that some part of the perceptual world remains in shadow.

Acknowledgement

I would like to *thank Martin* Gartmeier and José María Ariso for providing valuable comments on this paper.

References

Adlam, John (2014): "Going Spiral? Phenomena of 'Half-knowledge' in the Experiential Large Group as Temporary Learning Community." In: *Pedagogy, Culture & Society* 22(1), 157–168.

Ajana, Btihaj (2015): "Augmented Borders: Big Data and the Ethics of Immigration Control." In: *Journal of Information, Communication and Ethics in Society* 13(1), 58–78.

Azuma, Ronald/Baillot, Yohan/Behringer, Reinhold/Feiner, Steven/Julier, Simon/MacIntyre, Blair (2001): "Recent Advances in Augmented Reality." In: *Computer Graphics and Applications* 21(6), 34–47.

Beck, Ulrich (2009): *World at Risk*, Cambridge: Polity Press.

Beck, Ulrich/Wehling, Peter (2012): "The Politics of Non-knowing: An Emerging Area of Social and Political Conflict in Reflexive Modernity." In: Fernando D. Rubio/Patrick Baert (eds.), *The Politics of Knowledge*, London and New York: Routledge, 33–57.
Benford, Steve/Giannachi, Gabriella (2011): *Performing Mixed Reality*, Cambridge: The MIT Press.
Benford, Steve/Giannachi, Gabriella/Koleva, Boriana/Rodden, Tom (2009): "From Interaction to Trajectories: Designing Coherent Journeys through User Experiences." *Conference Proceedings CHI 2009* held at Boston, Massachusetts, USA 4–9 April 2009.
Böschen, Stefan (2009): "Hybrid Regimes of Knowledge? Challenges for Constructing Scientific Evidence in the Context of the GMO Debate." In: *Environmental Science and Pollution Research* 16(5), 508–520.
Braidotti, Rosi (2007): "Feminist Epistemology after Postmodernism: Critiquing Science, Technology and Globalization." In: *Interdisciplinary Science Reviews* 32(1), 65–74.
Clough, Patricia T. (2001): *Auto Affection: Unconscious thought in the Age of Technology*, Minneapolis: University of Minnesota Press.
Coeckelbergh, Mark (2015): "Care Robots and the Future of ICT-mediated Elderly Care: A Response to Doom Scenarios." In: *AI & Society: Knowledge, Culture and Communication*. DOI 10.1007/s00146-015-0626-3.
Coole, Diana H./Frost, Samantha (eds.) (2010): *New Materialisms: Ontology, Agency and Politics*, Durham: Duke University Press.
Dreyfus, Hubert (2001): *On the Internet*, 2nd edition, London and New York: Routledge.
Dunlosky, John/Metcalfe, Janet (2009): *Metacognition*, Los Angeles, CA: Sage.
Dunning, David/Kruger, Justin (1999): "Unskilled and Unaware of It: How Difficulties in Recognizing One's Own Incompetence Lead to Inflated Self-assessments." In: *Journal of Personality and Social Psychology* 77(6), 1121–34.
Edwards, Paul N. (2010) *A Vast Machine: Computer Models, Climate Data, and the Politics of Global Warming*, Cambridge, MA: MIT Press.
Edwards, Paul N./Jackson, Steven J./Bowker, Geoffrey C./Knobel, Cory P. (2007): *Understanding Infrastructure: Dynamics, Tensions, and Design*, Ann Arbor, MI: Deep Blue.
Flavell, John H. (1976): "Metacognitive Aspects of Problem Solving." In: Luren B. Resnick (ed.) *The Nature of Intelligence*, Hillsdale, NJ: Erlbaum, 231–236.
Feiner, Steven/MacIntyre, Blair/Seligmann, Dorée (1993): "Knowledge-based Augmented Reality." In: *Communications of the ACM*, Special Issue on Computer Augmented Environments: Back to the Real World, 36(7), 53–62.
Fenster, Tovi (2005): "Gender and the City. The Different Formations of Belonging." In: Lise Nelson/Joni Seager (eds.), *A Companion to Feminist Geography*, Oxford: Blackwell, 242–256.
Firestein, Stuart (2012): *Ignorance: How It Drives Science*, Oxford: Oxford University Press.
Gabrielli, Lorenzo/Rinzivillo, Salvatore/Ronzano, Francesco/Villatoro, Daniel (2013): "From Tweets to Semantic Trajectories: Mining Anomalous Urban Mobility Patterns." In: Jordi **Nin**/Daniel **Villatoro** (eds.), *Citizen in Sensor Networks*, Heidelberg, New York, Dordrecht, London: Springer, 26–35.
Gane, Nicholas (2005): "Radical Post-humanism Friedrich Kittler and the Primacy of Technology." In: *Theory, Culture & Society* 22(3), 25–41.

Gartmeier, Martin/Lehtinen, Erno/Gruber, Hans/Heid, Helmut M. (2011): "Negative Expertise: Comparing Differently Tenured Elder Care Nurses' Negative Knowledge." In: *European Journal of Psychology of Education* 26(2), 301–302.
Gross, Matthias (2007): "The Unknown in Process. Dynamic Connections of Ignorance, Non-knowledge and Related Concepts." In: *Current Sociology* 55(5), 742–759.
Gross, Matthias (2012): "'Objective Culture' and the Development of Nonknowledge: Georg Simmel and the Reverse Side of Knowing." In: *Cultural Sociology* 6(4), 422–437.
Gross, Matthias/McGoey, Linsey (2015): *Routledge International Handbook of Ignorance Studies*, New York, London: Routledge.
Guattari, Felix (1995): *Chaosmosis: An Ethico-Aesthetic Paradigm*, Trans P. Bains/J. Pefanis, Sidney: Power Publication.
Haddadi, Hamed/Mortier, Richard/McAuley, Derek/Crowcroft, Jon (2013): "Human-data Interaction." In: *Technical reports* 837, University of Cambridge Computer Laboratory. http://www.cl.cam.ac.uk/techreports/ (accessed 19, 10, 2015).
Japp, Klaus P. (2000): "Distinguishing Non-knowledge." In: *Canadian Journal of Sociology* 25 (2), 225–38.
Jaspers, Karl (1951): *Way to Wisdom: An Introduction to Philosophy*, New Haven, CT: Yale University Press.
Kendall, Lori (2002): *Hanging out in the Virtual Pub: Masculinities and Relationships Online*, Berkeley and Los Angeles, CA: University of California Press.
Kerwin, Ann (1993): "None too Solid: Medical Ignorance." In: *Knowledge: Creation, Diffusion, Utilization* 15(2), 166–85.
Kipper, Gregory/Rampolla, Joseph (2013): *Augmented Reality: An Emerging Technologies Guide to AR*, Amsterdam, Boston: Syngress.
Kittler, Friedrich A. (1997): *Literature, Media, Information Systems*, Amsterdam: G+B Arts.
Kittler, Friedrich A. (1999): *Gramophone, Film, Typewriter*, Stanford, CA: Stanford University Press.
Knorr Cetina, Karin (1999): *Epistemic Cultures: How the Sciences Make Knowledge*, Cambridge, MA: Harvard University Press.
Kozel, Susan (2007): *Closer: Performance, Technologies, Phenomenology*, Cambridge, MA, and London: The MIT Press.
McQuire, Scott (2008): *The Media City. Media Architecture and Urban Space*, Los Angeles, CA: Sage.
Mellish, Liz (2012): "Dance Movements and Urban Trajectories across and in the City: A Romanian Case Study." In: *Nar. Umjet.* (Croatian Journal of Ethnology) 49(1), 131–145.
Milgram, Paul/Kishino, Fumio (1994): "A Taxonomy of Mixed Reality Visual Displays." In: *IEICE Transactions on Information Systems*, E77-D12, 449–455.
Minsky, Marvin (1994): "Negative Expertise." In: *International Journal of Expert Systems* 7(1), 13–19.
Mumford, Lewis (1995): "Technics and Human Development." In: Donald L. Miller (ed.), *Lewis Mumford Reader*, Athens, GA: The University of Georgia Press.
Parviainen, Jaana/Eriksson, Marja (2006): "Negative Knowledge, Expertise and Organisations." In: *International Journal of Management Concepts and Philosophy* 2(2), 140–153.
Parviainen, Jaana/Tuuri, Kai/Pirhonen, Antti (2013): "Drifting down the Technologization of Life: Could Choreography-based Interaction Design Support us in Engaging with the

World and Our Embodied Living?" In: *Challenges* 4(1), 103–115. DOI: 10.3390/challe4010103.
Pentland, Alex S. (2013): "The Data-driven Society." In: *Scientific American* 309, 78–83. DOI: http://dx.doi.org/10.1038/scientificamerican1013-78.
Polanyi, Michael (1966): *The Tacit Dimension*, Garden City, NY: Doubleday Anchor.
Proctor, Robert/Schiebinger, Londa (eds.) (2008): *Agnotology: The Making and Unmaking of Ignorance*, Stanford: Stanford University Press.
Rogers, Yvonne (2006): "Moving on from Weiser's Vision of Calm Computing: Engaging UbiComp ex-periences." In: Paul Dourish/Adrian Friday (eds.), *Conference Proceedings*, UbiComp 2006: Ubiquitous Computing: 8th International Conference, UbiComp 2006 Orange County, CA, USA, September 17–21, 2006, 404–421.
Savat, David (2013): *Undoing the Digital: Technology, Subjectivity and action in the Control Society*, London: Palgrave.
Schraw, Gregory/Dennison, Rayne S. (1994): "Assessing metacognitive Awareness." In: *Contemporary Educational Psychology* 19, 460–475.
Sheely, Kieron/Ferguson, Rebecca/Clough, Gill (2014): *Augmented Education: Bringing Real and Virtual Learning Together*, New York: Palgrave.
Simmel, Georg (1992): *Soziologie: Untersuchungen über die Formen der Vergesellschaftung*, Frankfurt on Main: Suhrkamp.
Smithson, Michael (1989): *Ignorance and Uncertainty: Emerging Paradigms*, New York: Springer.
Sony Mobile Communications Inc. (2015): http://developer.sonymobile.com/products/smarteyeglass/developer-tools/#seg-header (accessed 4, 11, 2015).
Sullivan, Shannon/Tuana, Nancy (eds.) (2007): *Race and Epistemologies of Ignorance*, S. Albany, NY: State University of New York Press.
Tacke, Veronika (2001): "BSE as an Organizational Construction: A Case Study on the Globalization of Risk." In: *The British Journal of Sociology* 52(2), 293–312.
Tech Policy Lab (2015): "Augmented Reality: A Technology and Policy Primer". http://techpolicylab.org/wp-content/uploads/2015/10/Augmented_Reality_Primer.pdf (accessed 4, 11, 2015).
Thrift, Nigel (2005): *Knowing Capitalism*, Thousand Oaks: Sage.
Townsend, Anthony (2013): *Smart Cities. Big Data, Civic Hackers, and the Quest for a New Utopia*, New York: W. W. Norton & Company.
Unger, Roberto (2004): False Necessity: Anti-Necessitarian Social Theory in the Service of Radical Democracy, London: Verso.
Weiser, Mark (1991): "The Computer for the 21st Century." In: *Scientific American* 265(3), 94–104.
Weiser, Mark/Brown, John S. (1996): *The Coming Age of Calm Technology Xerox PARC.* www.ubiq.com/hypertext/weiser/acmfuture2endnote.htm (accessed 6/25/2015).

Martin Gartmeier, Charlotte Jonasson and Maria Solomou

Negative Knowledge in Virtual and Game-Based Environments

Abstract: Negative knowledge is experiential knowledge about what is wrong, about what not to do and about limitations in one's own knowledge, skills or cognition. Such knowledge is primarily acquired through learning from errors. Virtual environments, like simulations and games, afford altered conditions for what constitutes errors and for how and why learning from errors occurs. This leads to the notion of negative knowledge being substantially altered in such contexts: First, simulations afford ideal conditions for practicing critical, error-prone tasks and for developing relevant negative knowledge. Second, an aspect of the rewardingness of games is their potential to enact counter-moralities. Third, progressing in games can be thought of as continuously transforming negative into positive knowledge. Fourth, because games limit an individual's possibilities for acting, they provide an experientially rewarding platform due to the elimination of complexities and ambiguities inherent in real-world contexts.

Keywords: negative knowledge; learning from errors; game learning; video games; simulations.

In many situations of life, it is utterly helpful to have a sound idea about what not to do under all circumstances. An example: In a Nepalese hospital, a local doctor confronts visiting physicians with "seven easy ways to kill a new-born infant (without even trying)" – e.g. feeding infants with buffalo milk or not washing hands prior to examining infants (Oser/Spychiger 2005, 66). In this example, a physician's actions are described which would seriously endanger the life of a newly born infant. For the local doctor welcoming visiting colleagues, it makes much sense to describe these strategies for several reasons: Firstly, the visiting physicians may not be familiar with the special challenges and circumstances that pertain to the work-context they are about to enter. Secondly, the explication of these strategies may increase the chance that the visitors are able to pursue a knowledge-based strategy for avoiding (serious) errors.

The hints given in the example are helpful to understand the concept of negative knowledge (Gartmeier et al. 2008, Oser/Spychiger 2005, Parviainen/Eriksson 2006). Such knowledge is focused on *what is wrong* or on *what not to do* under all circumstances in a particular situation in order to avoid errors. In

DOI 10.1515/9783110497656-012

other words, negative knowledge hints to actions or outcomes of actions that lie beyond boundaries separating "right" from "wrong". The example above describes actions which are beyond the boundary of what is medically "right" (in the sense that it is beneficial for the well-being of a particular individual, in this case, a new-born). In that sense, negative knowledge holds information, e.g., about what actions lead to such boundaries being crossed in negative and detrimental ways.

Let's now imagine the initial example being part of a computer-based simulation of a Nepalese hospital including virtual doctors and simulated patients whose treatment is part of the simulation. The key question raised in the present chapter is how negative knowledge and the learning processes through which it is developed are affected when being situated in virtual environments. We assume that games have the potential to generate "anomalous states of knowledge" (Harviainen 2012, 509), meaning they alter the conditions for acquiring knowledge, for applying knowledge and, more generally, for thinking and theorizing about knowledge. As the educational potential of virtual environments is more and more recognized (Paraskeva et al. 2010), it is relevant to analyse which conditions they offer for learning from errors and, respectively, for developing negative knowledge. We argue that virtual environments have the potential to *substantially* and *fruitfully* change the conditions for making and learning from errors compared to real world situations (Milne 2013). Consequentially, there are profound effects on the idea of negative knowledge applied to virtual contexts: Generally, the idea of knowledge being "positive" or "negative" is deeply connected to certain standards of what is "wrong" or "right" (appropriate/inappropriate, desirable/undesirable, legal/illegal, ethical/unethical, possible/impossible etc.) that pertain to a particular context (Heid 1999). Virtual contexts can offer very different sets of standards compared to "real" world settings. One substantial difference is that in some virtual environments, e.g. in games or simulations, grave, even fatal errors can be made without having any real, tangible consequences – a notion which opens up rich opportunities for learning. This is because in virtual environments, actors can restart and continue acting within the virtual space even after they have failed a particular task. In virtual spaces, different types of contexts can be simulated, from game-like scenarios to serious simulations designed to allow for improving professional competencies, e.g. of pilots or surgeons. This allows for analysing the conditions for the development of negative knowledge in virtual environments from multiple perspectives. This chapter explores the interdependence between contextual conditions, error-related learning processes and (negative) knowledge resulting from these. The main backdrop of the present analysis is educational science, with references to psychology, philosophy and media science. In the following, we will firstly introduce the concept of negative knowledge. Then, we will characterize our idea of computer-based virtual environments in focus of this analysis and explore the altered conditions these environments offer for developing negative knowledge. In the discussion, we will outline directions for future research.

1. Negative knowledge

One key assumption made by the theory of negative knowledge (Gartmeier et al. 2008, Minsky 1997, Oser/Spychiger 2005, Parviainen/Eriksson 2006) is that in individuals' knowledge, negations exist which have relevance for cognitive processes, like reflection or decision making, and (professional) competencies: A concise way of defining knowledge is seeing it as a *system of justified true beliefs* (Lehrer 2000). On the one hand, this definition acknowledges the idiosyncratic character of knowledge through describing it as a system of *beliefs*. Unlike facts or information, beliefs are embedded in individuals' cognitive structures. Consequentially, they are closely tied to individual attitudes, orientations and views of the world. Therefore, the above definition stresses the importance of individual experience for learning (Kolb 1984) and, consequentially, for acquiring knowledge. On the other hand, describing knowledge as *justified* refers to processes of *justification*. As constructivists have stressed, the key criterion in the construction of knowledge is its viability (von Glasersfeld 1991), i. e., its usefulness for achieving goals.

With regard to the concept of negative knowledge, the key point here is that negations can very well fulfil the described criteria: They might be relevant as *beliefs* which individuals have found to be useful when making experiences and when learning from these. To give examples for useful functions that negative knowledge serves, we draw upon the general purposes that have been related to negativity (Koch 2005), i. e., indicating non-existence *("This shop doesn't exist anymore, it was closed a week ago")*, non-identity (*"A whale is no fish"*), factual wrongness (*"Johannesburg is not the capital of South-Africa"*), unallowedness (*"You are not allowed to cross this border without a visa"*) or adverseness (*"If you travel to Hawaii, don't forget your sunscreen"*).

Many of these very brief examples represent two perspectives: Firstly, a perspective focused on past experiences and on processes of summarizing lessons learned from these. Essentially, this idea is expressed in the theories of learning from experience (Kolb 1984), more specifically, through learning from errors (Bauer 2008). The second perspective expressed in the given examples relates to actions which are currently planned and are supposed to be undertaken at some point in the future. This notion is expressed in the theory of negative knowledge, which assumes that such knowledge is related to conscious error-avoidance strategies. In the following, we will give a more detailed description of how the idea of negative knowledge has evolved.

1.1 Negative morality and knowledge

Labelling knowledge as "negative" may initially evoke misleading associations, such as a perception that this is "detrimental" or "harmful" knowledge (Gartmeier et al. 2008). Yet, "negative" is used as a descriptive, not as a judgmental-term here, similar to referring to "negative" numbers. This is also the case in earlier conceptions of negative knowledge in the context of moral education (Oser 1996) and relating to the idea of negative expertise (Minsky 1997).

In context of his seminal work on the development of morality, Oser (1996) advanced the idea that an individual's experience of shame and regret may induce the development of knowledge about immoral behaviour. On the one hand, such negative moral knowledge holds information about *what not to do.* On the other hand, it is deeply connected with emotional impressions and with an individuals' episodic memory. Oser argues that such knowledge can have a valuable function in that is serves to prevent similar wrongful behaviours in the future in having the function of a contrastive element to the "right" behaviour. Imagine, e. g., a child being caught stealing by his parents. There may be a subsequent blustering by the parents resulting in the child's feelings of guilt and shame about the wrongdoing. Oser's concept of negative moral knowledge hypothesizes such an emotionally impressive momentum to be a crucial aspect of the intention not to repeat the experience. This example helps to clarify why a statement like "You shall not steal!" can sometimes be more than a random sentence containing a negation: If understood as being episodically grounded and related to basic moral categories of "right" and "wrong", negative knowledge can represent an individual's insights into a variety of aspects. Firstly, into standards or guidelines for behaviour which are relevant in order to avoid errors. Secondly, such knowledge may also possess a very personal character. This is because it is related to a person's insights into own weaknesses, limitations or lacks of knowledge.

1.2 Functional view of negative knowledge

In pursuing a similar idea within a different conceptual framework, Minsky advanced the notion that any expert in a professional field "must know both how to achieve goals and how to avoid disasters" (Minsky 1997, 517). What is stressed here is a more *functional* notion of negative knowledge: Previous conceptions focused upon negative knowledge featuring behavioural guidelines being encoded in *moral* categories. Similar guidelines may, however, relate to categories like *efficacy* or *quality* of (work) products or processes. In this respect, Minsky advances that – besides taking positive measures – another very plausible way to avoid accidents and mistakes is by forbearing actions that are known to cause trouble. Two points are made here: Firstly, a negative way to conceptualize expertise is to regard experts as persons who are able to deliberately avoid grave errors. Secondly, one plausible prerequisite of this ability is experts' negative knowledge.

According to Minsky, negative knowledge can be conceived as a meta-cognitive resource helping to monitor action at work by reminding the actor of what to avoid. To illustrate this notion, human cognition is hypothesized as being split in two parts: While brain A is connected to the outside world, brain B is solely monitoring and controlling brain A. For brain B, many instances are plausible where a negative regulative influence seems very useful: "If A is not making progress toward its goal, force it to review that goal / If A is occupied with too much detail, then make it take a higher level view / If A is not being specific enough, then make it focus on more details" (Minsky 1997, 519). These examples indicate a notion of B being a metacognitive instance that is aware of how not to solve certain problems and of influencing actual behaviour accordingly.

As they are key aspects in our further reflection on the role of negative knowledge in virtual environments, the following sections will cover the acquirement of negative knowledge through learning from errors as well as its application.

1.3 Acquisition of negative knowledge through learning from errors

Although in formal educational settings, actors may be taught what to avoid in the performance of a task, we argue that personal experience is the powerful way to acquire negative knowledge (Oser/Spychiger 2005). Hence, negative knowledge basically can be seen as a special form of experiential knowledge (Kolb 1984). An experience may serve as a starting point for the acquisition of negative knowledge especially in cases which raise an actor's awareness of having wrong assumptions or applying wrong strategies for solving a problem at hand. Typically, errors are experiences that meet this description (Gartmeier et al. 2008). Errors are conceptualized as a category of adverse events that produce "stress, accidents, inefficient human-machine interaction, quality and performance problems, and a bad climate" (Rybowiak et al. 1999, 528). Nevertheless, errors provide opportunities to reflect on their causes and thereby gain insights that may allow the avoidance of similar errors in future practice. While conducting error-related learning activities, actors may become aware of having inadequate conceptions, such as lacking particular problem-solving strategies (Bauer 2008). The results of such reflective processes contribute to building a body of negative knowledge, on the one hand, about what should be avoided in a given class of situations. On the other hand, such negative knowledge might also be focused upon own or upon other individuals' limitations (Gartmeier et al. 2010).

1.4 Application of negative knowledge

We argue that negative knowledge can be regarded as a valuable cognitive resource in contexts of goal-directed action because of its focus on wrong assumptions or courses of action which lead to errors. Besides, a more self-focused aspect of negative knowledge has been described, e.g. as knowledge about one's own limitations in terms of skills, knowledge or competencies (Gartmeier et al. 2008, Oser/Spychiger 2005).

As was foreshadowed above, experiential learning entails learning through acting, reviewing the outcomes of actions and finally evaluating what works and what does not. Especially in situations which are connected to insights into what does not work, experiential learning is connected to acquiring negative knowledge. One rarely explicated premise of the relationship between errors, learning from them and the resulting negative knowledge lies in the fact that the term "error" is one of meta-language (Heid 1999). This means, labelling a phenomenon as *error* is the result of a subjective, socially negotiated and context-dependent process of applying abstract criteria to a certain phenomenon. This again means that errors, learning from them and the resulting (negative) knowledge can only be analysed in their contextual embeddedness, e.g. in a specific professional, local or cultural context.

In brief, to apply negative knowledge means to avoid detours in thinking and acting, to avoid doubts and rumination and, consequentially, to avoid making errors. This of course depends upon the familiarity of an actor with the conditions prevailing within a certain context. As has been advanced (Minsky 1997,

Gartmeier et al. 2011), a negative view on expertise is to analyse how high-performing professionals are reliably able to avoid errors.

In the above sketched self-reflective understanding, negative knowledge is connected to individuals' self-perception of own abilities, potentials and knowledge. It can be understood as insights which are the result of internal cognitive discursive processes and which describe one's own limitations. A realistic image of where the boundaries of one's own skills and knowledge are is functional, e. g. for being able to understand needs for learning, to know when to ask for help or when to seek for lacking information. Deficiencies in one's self-reflective knowledge may be related to constant over- or underestimation of abilities or potentials, both of which are not functional and potentially disadvantageous.

2. Virtual environments

Before we explore the relationship between negative knowledge and virtual environments, we characterize which attributes of such environments make investigating this interrelation an interesting endeavour.

Innovations in the field of ICT-technology have spawned the development of environments which represent "virtual", "enhanced" or "augmented" versions of reality as we know it (Steuer 1992). In its original meaning, virtual reality describes a certain kind of hardware or media, like televisions or computers. However, when speaking of virtual environments in context of the present analysis, we put a stronger focus on the "particular type of experience" (Steuer 1992, 77) connected to specific uses of virtual reality environments that are entirely computer-based and share various characteristics, namely *telepresence*, *vividness*, and *interactivity. Telepresence* describes the sense of being immersed in an environment. It is caused by various sensual impressions from visual or auditorial channels and by the opportunity to interact with the virtual environment. So, a "virtual reality" is defined as "a real or simulated environment in which a perceiver experiences telepresence" (Steuer 1992, 80). A further important characteristic of virtual environments is *vividness* which is defined in terms of "sensory breadth (number of sensory dimensions simultaneously presented) and sensory depth (resolutions within each perceptual channel)" (Steuer 1992, 80). Vividness can be seen as a precondition for the notion of telepresence as it is a critical factor for the notion of being immersed in a virtual environment. Moreover, the most commonly known aspect is *interactivity* which describes "the extent to which users can participate in modifying the form and content of a mediated environment in real time" (Steuer 1992, 87). These features entail the potential of virtual environments to realistically simulate certain scenarios or aspects of reality and for creating immersive virtual worlds (Thomas/Brown 2007).

Emphasizing the experiential nature of our interaction with media technologies, especially with virtual environments, media use is described as mimesis (Laurel 1997) (a form of artistic imitation typically applied in dramatic contexts), a term which likens the relationship between user and technology to the notion of action in a play. Moreover, the importance of encouraging the user of a technology to develop a first-person, rather than third-person, relationship with his or her mediated environment is emphasized. Engagement, which is described as a primarily emotional state with cognitive components (Laurel 1997), serves as a critical factor in engendering such a first-person feeling. In order to analyse the relationship between negative knowledge and virtual environments, it is essential to take these altered conditions into account which are offered in such environments.

3. Negative knowledge and virtual environments

Certain conditions that apply to virtual reality environments are in particular focus here: Firstly, in many virtual environments, e.g. in most computer games, there is some form of goal which is supposed to be reached by the player. In order to reach the game goals, different strategies may lead to success (Salen Tekinbaş/Zimmerman 2003). In relation to these goals, it is possible to judge each action undertaken by a player for how well it contributes to the attainment of this goal, according to the chosen strategy. This provides a quality criterion upon which to judge the outcomes and consequences of any action performed in a game. This means, actions can be described with labels like "successful" or "effective" (Salen Tekinbaş/Zimmerman 2003). Secondly, it matters for the actor whether, overall, his/her performance in the VR-environment is labelled as *successful* (or any other evaluative term). This is relevant because if a person uses a VR-environment only for the sake of the experience itself – e.g. for wandering through and exploring a beautifully designed virtual landscape – without pursuing any specific goals (in the narrower sense), the question after errors and learning from errors is pointless. This is not too different to the real world: Slumbering through a park on a Sunday afternoon is not a specifically goal-oriented action, so any path to take through the park might be a good one. Basically, there are no errors to be made (except, maybe, to get lost in the park and not finding the way back before dawn). In our notion of games, a player within a digital game does not necessarily have the same abilities as in the real world, but may have extraordinary skills, like the ability to fly, to travel through space etc. This means, there is a loose connection to the real world. However, most games provide some sort of "fictional realism", meaning that within the framework of rules they provide, they also provide restrictions, e. g. that actors cannot penetrate walls.

With these properties of game based environments in mind, we will hypothesize how the above introduced concept of negative knowledge can be conceptualized, understood and operationalized within these environments in the following. Thereby, we adopt a pragmatic approach. This means, the vantage points of our analysis are not strictly derived from a particular theory, but represent points of crystallization which have emerged through our own reflection on the topic at hand. We have labelled these points in a pointed way as *cause-effect correspondence, contextual morality, boundary stones to unknown terrain,* and *limitation as liberation.*

3.1 Cause-effect correspondence

We argue that the degree of correspondence between the real world and virtual scenarios is positively correlated to the degree to which negative knowledge is relevant and transferable between these. This is especially relevant in simulated environments, like e. g. in flight simulators: They are designed to realistically recreate the experience of flying an aircraft. Flight simulators are virtual reality environments designed to provide a 1:1 simulation of an airplane pilot's experience (Hays et al. 1992, Ron et al. 2006). In recent years, similar tools for other professional tasks have been developed, e. g. in the area of medicine, for simulating surgical interventions (Brown-Clerk et al. 2011, Ron et al. 2006). The didactic idea of simulators lies in their potential to realistically re-create complex situations in which (professional) actors have to solve difficult and challenging tasks. Simulators are created with a very concrete idea in mind about what a person shall learn while using a simulator. This means, firstly, actions in a simulator are clearly goal-oriented. Imagine, a task in a simulator is to land a plane on a very difficult landing strip in conditions of bad weather. The ultimate goal clearly is to land the plane safely. Each single action a pilot undertakes can be weighed in its appropriateness with regard to its contribution to this specific goal. Secondly, there is an attempted 1:1 connection between a simulation and the corresponding real-world environment which is simulated. This means, any knowledge acquired in a simulator, ideally, corresponds to the conditions in the real world. The same 1:1-relationship holds true for the role of the individual in a flight simulator.

We argue that this combination of circumstances is ideal for developing relevant negative knowledge which may well be applied to real world settings: Flight simulators provide ideal opportunities for reflecting upon errors (Bauer 2008). An error can be re-played in slow-motion and analysed in depth after the action sequence. Depending upon the technical circumstances at hand, this may even be possible through recording an individual's performance in a simulator, (re)viewing it and through thoroughly reflecting upon courses of action and erroneous aspects of these. This corresponds to structured learning-processes which have been described in the literature as after-event-reviews (Carroll 1995, Ron et al. 1996). This is

> a learning from experience procedure that gives learners an opportunity to systematically analyse the various actions that they selected to perform a particular task, to determine which of them was wrong or not necessary, which should be corrected, and which should be reinforced (Ellis 2012, 215).

The description highlights several aspects of how negative knowledge can emerge from simulators: A simulator allows a pilot that undergoes training to realistically experience which courses of action may lead to crashing an airplane. This means, there is an opportunity to perform an in-depth analysis of errors, also very severe ones, and of their causes and to memorize these for future action. This relates to the idea of procedural negative knowledge as knowledge about *which situations should be avoided* and about which actions lead to such situations (Gartmeier et al. 2010). In addition, the design of the flight simulator training may also involve opportunities of exploring negative knowledge through working with problem-*posing*. Problem posing means giving learners the opportunity to formulate problems which they find both, relevant and challenging for their own learning and to work on the solution of these problems (Chang et al. 2012). The implementation of problem-posing has been found to enhance problem-solving abilities through clarified conceptualization of the subject matter. The posing of relevant problems also rests on negative knowledge about an individuals' limitations in problem-solving abilities. Hence, simulations offer the opportunity to create scenarios which very specifically target the boundaries of an actors' knowledge and skills (Chang et al. 2012, Gartmeier et al. 2008).

Due to their potential to realistically recreate conditions in a real cockpit, flight simulators provide good circumstances for transferring knowledge – of course given the usual conditions and limitations for transfer (Gegenfurtner et al. 2013). The latter aspect relates to what is described in the literature as proceduralization of knowledge during expertise development. Describing this process may contribute to a deeper understanding of the role of negative knowledge during flight simulator training. On the other hand, a substantial difference between a real plane and a simulator lies in the fact that crashing the simulated plane does not lead to loss of human life, money etc. This might be critical for what has been described above as an *emotionally impressive momentum* (Oser/Spychiger 2005) in the context of learning from errors: If erroneous behaviour has no real consequences, learning from errors might not take place due to a lack of a feeling of urgency and relevance.

3.2 Contextual morality

Computer games provide enhanced immersive possibilities as compared to personal phantasies, books or movies. Dynamics, interactivity, involvement of sound and language and sometimes even haptic elements together make up the character of games as "interactive fiction machines" (Milne 2013, 2). Games have the potential to liberate a player not only from physical, but also from moral boundaries which exist in the real world: In games, killing human beings, even eradicating civilizations, might just be the most plausible and normal thing to do in order to reach the goal of a particular game. Hence, computer games are fertile grounds for enacting *fictionally immoral attitudes*. Relating this to negative knowledge, the notion brings a lustful element to the foreground: Playing with what is forbidden, living dark sides, feeling free from boundaries are aspects of computer games that thrive on the fact that our world puts so seemingly narrow chains of efficacy and rationality around us. This ties in strongly with the idea of negative knowledge being related to moral categories, such as *allowed/unallowed* or *ethical/unethical*. In contrast, games can create conditions which reward immoral behaviour and, as such, allow the pursuing of fundamentally different moral-systems compared to those that underlie our everyday lives. So, if thinking of negative knowledge as cognitive agency executing preventive, inhibitive or corrective functions, how rational and plausible does it seem to lustfully break down these boundaries and become consumed by games as *interactive fiction machines*. This also corresponds to description of games as *psychologically intelligible* and *self-illuminating* imaginative experience (Kieran 2003) – in particular, if this experience leads to the adoption of what's fictionally an immoral attitude.

As was advanced above, negative knowledge can be viewed as a crystallisation of our own limitations on the level of knowledge, like a cognitive representation of everything that is beyond our own knowledge, skills or power. These limitations exist, e. g. due to natural laws *(we cannot fly or rewind time)*, or social norms *(robbing banks is illegal).* We argue that one aspect of what makes virtual worlds experientially rewarding is that they allow turning established personal epistemologies upside down. This corresponds to the notion of *liminal spaces* which are located "a step outside mundane reality, yet exist in continuity with it" and are characterized by the fact that "systems of logic or ethics may not apply, as they are replaced by temporary new ones" (Harviainen 2012, 508). The epistemically interesting aspect here lies virtual worlds representing "upside down" spaces, where one steps outside mundane reality replacing normal rules and norms with new ones (Turner 1969). Hence, liminality may bring with it cause for a novel perspective, re-consideration of the rules and norms defining mundane reality and might even be connected to learning experiences:

> Further, given that imaginatively adopting an immoral attitude might deepen our understanding of why certain immoral actions are pursued, imaginatively developing an immoral attitude out of which we ourselves fictionally act might, additionally, deepen our understanding of how it feels to freely act thus and to acknowledge one's responsibility for such actions (Milne 2013, 5).

In that sense, games allow a player to adopt an idiosyncratic *counter-morality.* The intrinsically rewarding nature of this lies in its limited adoptability in real life, at least according to established civic and legal standards (Kieran 2003). In other words, "imaginative experiences that get us to take up fictionally immoral attitudes can enhance our understanding of something in otherwise unavailable ways" (Milne 2013, 4).

This idea might be developed further drawing upon the concept of negative knowledge in comparing it to a system of mental warning signs which prevent individuals from going beyond what is (ethically, legally or otherwise) reasonable (Oser/Spychiger 2005). But what if an actor simply does not accept such moral standards or feels a (maybe irrational) urge to trespass them? Not only can violating standards (like e.g. road speed limits) involve joyous sensations. As was stressed above, the idea of negative knowledge connects individual cognition to externally established and internally accepted systems of standards. Finding an arena – like computer games – in which to abandon these standards might be rewarding on the emotional level, through a feeling of freedom and immersion and on the cognitive level, by a change of perspective. Such a change of perspective developed by confronting e.g. delinquent youth with various consequences of violating practices could encompass learning opportunities for understanding the need for new courses of action.

Interestingly, though, games and virtual worlds correspond to real world contexts (e.g., to workplaces) in that they are also not free from (informal) rules and boundaries which are socially constructed by the community of players (and not by the creators of the game or virtual world itself). One example are online forums that correspond to particular games. These are characterized by restrictive norms forum users adhere to regarding which game-related information is to be made accessible for inexperienced players – and which information should be kept unrevealed (Harviainen 2012).

3.3 Boundary stone to unknown terrain

Playing games is rewarding due to their potential to immerse individuals into an alternative environment (Dunleavy et al. 2009). We argue that this, in part, is due to the idea of learning from mistakes being very important in games as it describes a key mechanism for a player to improve and make progress through a game. In that sense, negative knowledge marks the boundary of own skills in a game. Interestingly, Knorr Cetina (2002) also uses the *liminality*-term to describe such boundaries, but in a different sense than Harvainen (2012) – cf. previous section. In Knorr Cetina's view, *liminal* phenomena are "neither empirical objects of positive knowledge nor the formless regions of the unknowable, but something in between" (Knorr Cetina 2002, 94). This notion can be applied nicely to jump and run games where a player moves in a linear way through some landscape (e.g., like Super Mario World). Every stage and sequence in such a game poses specific challenges to the player. These may be connected to a player's skills or knowledge about the circumstances at a specific spot (e.g. about suddenly appearing enemies). Usually, a player is more or less reliably able to master all challenges in such a game up to a certain point – which could be described as the area of positive knowledge, in Knorr Certina's terms. Then, there is a point which the player has not yet crossed, the new level or new challenge in the game. Having tried and failed to get past this point several times, the player may possess negative knowledge about what not to do and what is wrong there – but no knowledge about how to master the specific challenge. This is the liminal area or, in other words, the zone of negative knowledge. Over several trials, a player accumulates more and more knowledge about *how not to move* beyond this point, but not how to do so successfully. Beyond that point, eventually, lies unexplored terrain. So, negative knowledge marks the boundary to be crossed, the threshold of the unknown (Knorr Cetina 2002).

In many computer games, there is only one correct way for how to solve certain problems or to survive particular situations. In contrast, there are very many courses of action which lead the player's character to get killed. One could say, game based worlds are full of negative knowledge about how not to solve certain problems. This is unlike in the real world, where, one the one hand, there mostly are several ways to come to the correct goal. On the other hand, an actor may choose not pursue a specific goal any more, but aim for another one. In many games which are characterized by a linear logic, such options do not exist.

In games which are characterized through a player's continuous trial-and-error around the threshold of the unknown, making progress through the game can be described as gradually fine-tuning to the limitations of the environment (Gibson/Pick 2000, Linderoth/Bennerstedt 2007). This fine-tuning of skills to situations and their challenges corresponds to processes of refining professional competencies, e. g. on the level of professional vision (Goodwin 1994, Linderoth/Bennerstedt 2007).

3.4 Limitation as liberation

Finally, we explore the notion of *limitation as liberation* in game based environments. One aspect here is that the limitation of options in games can be regarded as liberation from complexity and ambiguity inherent in real world contexts. This commonality between virtual and real games which is nowhere as plastically visible as in many sports disciplines, e. g. in football or tennis: Such forms of social practice take place within a clearly marked rectangular field which, for instance, consists of white lines on green lawn (or red sand) and is characterized by a set of comparatively few clearly defined rules. Compared to real life, this represents a strong reduction of complexity. We argue that limiting the scope of complexity in such a drastic way is plausibly perceived as liberation and relief from the real world challenges and ambiguities. Based on this notion of *limitation as liberation* (Gee 2003), it is argued that computer games solve a dilemma: They somehow manage to get people to learn how to master challenges which are very long and hard and, at the same time, find enormous joy in this endeavour. This relates to a basic duality: On the one hand, limitations of the real world can be left behind in computer games. However, there are new rules and constraints which restrict what can be done and what not. So, mastering a computer game, in many cases, is a story of failing repeatedly, of overcoming the failures and, if the game is completed and no failures are made any more, of starting from scratch with another game. In that sense, negative knowledge is essential to finish the game because only when knowing exactly what to avoid in any in-game situation, one can manage to pass through all levels. On the other hand, it is not enough to know what not to do in certain situations, but to find out how to actually solve certain problems. Hence, the motivation for moving on to new challenges (and failures) in novel games may lead players to engage in experiential and error-based learning processes (Kolb 1984).

An aspect of learning from errors, however, which is also visible in games is that such learning is stressful as it is connected with displeasing, even painful (Oser/Spychiger 2005) insights into one's own fallibility: Many features have been established in games which help a player making progress, e. g. focusing the player's attention to a specific point in the virtual environment. This means, the computer system provides support "by visually showing the affordances that need to be acted on in order for the game to progress" (Linderoth 2012, 53). Other strategies for cheating typically involve the use of online search engines to find solutions for specific problems which a player faces in a specific computer game. The question arises to which degree such support strategies actually compromise the failing and trying again aspect of computer games. As was already foreshadowed, learning from errors has been characterized as *painful* (Oser/Spychiger 2005), mainly because it involves insights into ones fallibility. From this viewpoint, it is easy to understand why players don't approach a game with a mastery orientation, i. e., they do not primarily strive for developing their own skills as far as possible. Instead, they seek to progress through the game as smoothly as possible or, in other words, without experiencing too many situations where they primarily accumulate negative knowledge about how *not* to overcome certain obstacles. So, for game designers, it seems critical to regulate the learning from errors-aspect of games by making it harder or easier for a player to overcome obstacles. Computer games "can be designed to facilitate both the exploratory and performatory mode of action" (Linderoth 2012, 58). The more the focus rests upon the performatory aspect, the less negative knowledge a player has to deal with regarding the limits of own skills. This points towards the need to find the right degree of limitation in games in order to optimally foster a player's notion of being liberated from real world boundaries.

4. Concluding thoughts

Computer games and virtual environments substantially change the conditions for theorizing about acquiring and applying negative knowledge as compared to non-virtual contexts. This is because they provide opportunities for both, *imitation* and *alteration* of non-virtual contextual conditions regarding cause-effect relationships, moral standards and contextual boundaries. In the present analysis, the interplay between learning from errors, negative knowledge and virtual environments was analysed from various perspectives. Two concluding points highlight the relevance of these relationships: First, for designers of virtual environments, it seems important to reflect upon the epistemological potential inherent in the platforms they create. Virtual environments allow for making learning from errors a joyful and rewarding experience. It is hence plausible that this aspect also contributes to the feeling of immersion and enjoyment experienced in such environments. Second, we argue that the present contribution is particularly relevant in the discussion around the epistemology of games and virtual environments (Connoly et al. 2012). As we hopefully could show, even games which are not epistemological (or educational or serious) games in the narrower sense, should be analysed from an epistemological perspective in order to develop a more thorough understanding of the nature of experience connected to being immersed in virtual environments.

References

Bauer, Johannes (2008): "Learning from Errors at Work: Studies on Nurses' Engagement in Error-related Learning Activities". http://epub.uni-regensburg.de/10748/1/diss_veroeff_end-version.pdf, visited on 4 March 2016.

Brown-Clerk, Bernadette/de Laveaga, Adam E./LaGrange, Chad A./Wirth, Laura M/Lowndes, Bethany R/Hallbeck, Susan M. (2011): "Laparoendoscopic Single-Site (LESS) Surgery versus Conventional Laparoscopic Surgery: Comparison of Surgical Port Performance in a Surgical Simulator with Novices." In: *Surgical Endoscopy* 25(7), 2210–2218.

Cannon-Bowers, Janis A./Bowers, Clint A. (2012): "Synthetic Learning Environments: On Developing a Science of Simulation, Games, and Virtual Worlds for Training." In Eduardo Salas/Steve Kozlowski (eds.), *Learning, Training, and Development in Organizations: The Oxford Handbook of Organizational Psychology, Volume 1,* Oxford: Oxford University Press, 229–255.

Carroll, John (1995): "Incident Reviews in High-Hazard Industries: Sense Making and Learning Under Ambiguity and Accountability." In: *Organization & Environment* 9(2), 175–197.

Chang, Kuo-En/Wu, Lin-Jung/Weng, Sheng-En/Sung, Yao-Ting (2012): "Embedding Game-based Problem-solving Phase into Problem-posing System for Mathematics Learning." In: *Computers and Education* 58, 775–786.

Connolly, Thomas M./Boyle, Elizabeht A./MacArthur, Ewan/Hainey, Thomas/Boyle, James M. (2012): "A Systematic Literature Review of Empirical Evidence on Computer Games and Serious Games." In: *Computers & Education* 59, 661–686.

Dunleavy, Matt/Dede, Chris/Mitchell, Rebecca (2009): "Affordances and Limitations of Immersive Participatory Augmented Reality Simulations for Teaching and Learning." In: *Journal of Science Education and Technology* 18(1), 7–22.

Ellis, Shmuel (2012): "Learning from Errors: The Role of After-Event Reviews." In Johannes Bauer/Christian Harteis (eds.), *Human Fallibility: The Ambiguity of Errors for Work and Learning*, Dordrecht: Springer, 215–232.

Gartmeier, Martin/Bauer, Johannes/Gruber, Hans/Heid, Helmut (2008): "Negative Knowledge: Understanding Professional Learning and Expertise." In: *Vocations and Learning* 1(2), 87–103.

Gartmeier, Martin/Gruber, Hans/Heid, Helmut (2010): "Tracing Error-Related Knowledge in Interview Data: Negative Knowledge in Elder Care Nursing." In: *Educational Gerontology* 36(9), 733–752.

Gartmeier, Martin/Lehtinen, Erno/Gruber, Hans/Heid, Helmut (2011): "Negative Expertise: Comparing Differently Tenured Elder Care Nurses' Negative Knowledge". In: *European Journal of Psychology of Education* 26(2), 273–300.

Gee, James P. (2003): *What Video Games Have to Teach Us about Learning and Literacy*, New York: St. Martin's Griffin.

Gegenfurtner, Andreas/Veermans, Koen/Vauras, Marja (2013): "Effects of Computer Support, Collaboration, and Time Lag on Performance Self-Efficacy and Transfer of Training: A Longitudinal Meta-analysis." In: *Educational Research Review* 8, 75–89.

Gibson, Eleanor/Pick, Anne (2000): *An Ecological Approach to Perceptual Learning and Development*, Oxford: University Press.

Goodwin, Charles (1994): "Professional vision." In: *American Anthropologist* 96(3), 606–633.

Harviainen, J. Tuomas (2012): "Ritualistic Games, Boundary Control, and Information Uncertainty." In: *Simulation and Gaming* 43(4), 506–527.

Hays, Robert T./Jacobs, John W./Prince, Carolyn/Salas, Eduardo (1992): "Flight Simulator Training Effectiveness: A Meta-analysis." In: *Military Psychology* 4(2), 63–74.

Heid, Helmut (1999): "Autorität. Über die Verwandlung von Fehlern in Verfehlungen." In: Wolfgang Althof (ed.), *Fehlerwelten. Vom Fehlermachen und Lernen aus Fehlern*, Opladen: Leske und Budrich, 129–136.

Khalifa, Mohamed/Shen, Ning (2004): "System Design Effects on Social Presence and Telepresence in Virtual Communities." International Conference on Information Systems (ICIS), Washington, USA.

Kieran, Matthew (2003): "Forbidden Knowledge: The Challenge of Immoralism." In: Jose Luis Bermúdez/Sebastian Gardner (eds.), *Art and Morality*, London: Routledge, 56–73.

Knorr Cetina, Karin (2002): *Wissenskulturen: Ein Vergleich naturwissenschaftlicher Wissensformen*, Frankfurt am Main: Suhrkamp.

Koch, Lutz (2005): "Eine pädagogische Apologie des Negativen." In: Dietrich Benner (ed.), *Erziehung, Bildung, Negativität. Zeitschrift für Pädagogik, 49. Beiheft*, Weinheim: Beltz, 88–104.

Kolb, David A. (1984): *Experiential Learning: Experience as the Source of Learning and Development*, Englewood Cliffs: Prentice Hall.

Laurel, Brenda (1997): "Interface Agents: Metaphors with Character." In: Batya Friedman (ed.), *Human Values and the Design of Computer Technology*, Cambridge: Cambridge University Press, 207–219.

Lehrer, Keith (2000): *Theory of Knowledge*, Boulder: Westview Press.

Linderoth, Jonas (2012): "Why Gamers Don't Learn More: An Ecological Approach to Games as Learning Environments." In: *Journal of Gaming & Virtual Worlds*, 4(1), 45–62.

Linderoth, Jonas/Bennerstedt, Ulrika (2007): "This is Not a Door: An Ecological Approach to Computer Games". Conference Proceedings DIGRA 2007 Situated Play Conference, Tokyo, 600–609.

Milne, Daniel Alexander (2013): "Developing Fictionally Immoral Attitudes: Spaces of Moral and Narrative Possibilities in Computer Games". Conference Proceedings Philosophy of Computer Games Conference, Bergen. http://gamephilosophy2013.b.uib.no/files/2013/09/milne_Paper_DFIA_Final.pdf, visited on 4 March 2016.

Minsky, Marvin (1997): "Negative expertise." In: Paul J. Feltovich/Kenneth M. Ford/Robert R. Hoffman (eds.), *Expertise in Context: Human and Machine*, Cambridge: AAAI/MIT Press, 515–521.
Oser, Fritz (1996): "Learning From Negative Morality." In: *Journal of Moral Education* 25(1), 67–74.
Oser, Fritz/Spychiger, Maria (2005): *Lernen ist schmerzhaft. Zur Theorie des negativen Wissens und zur Praxis der Fehlerkultur*, Weinheim: Beltz.
Paraskeva, Fotini/Mysirlaki, Sofia/Papagianni, Aikaterini (2010): "Multiplayer Online Games as Educational Tools: Facing New Challenges in Learning." In: *Computers & Education* 54 (2), 498–505.
Parviainen, Jaana/Eriksson, Marja (2006): "Negative Knowledge, Expertise and Organisations." In: *International Journal of Management Concepts and Philosophy* 2(2), 140–153.
Ron, Neta/Lipshitz, Raanan/Popper, Micha (2006): "How Organizations Learn: Post-flight Reviews in an F-16 Fighter Squadron." In: *Organization Studies* 27(8), 1069–1089.
Rybowiak, Volker/Garst, Harry/Frese, Michael/Batinic, Bernad (1999): "Error Orientation Questionnaire (EOQ): Reliability, Validity, and Different Language Equivalence." In: *Journal of Organizational Behavior* 40(4), 527–547.
Salen Tekinbaş, Katie/Zimmerman, Eric (2003): *Rules of Play: Game Design Fundamentals*, Cambridge: MIT Press.
Steuer, Jonathan (1992): "Defining Virtual Reality: Dimensions Determining Telepresence." In: *Journal of Communication,* 4(24), 73–93.
Thomas, Douglas/Brown, John Seely (2007): "The Play of Imagination: Extending the Literary Mind." In: *Games and Culture* 2(2), 149–172.
Turner, Victor W. (1969): *The Ritual Process: Structure and Anti-Structure*, Chicago: Aldine.
von Glasersfeld, Ernst (1991): "An Exposition of Constructivism: Why Some Like It Radical." In George Klir (ed.), *Facets of Systems Science*, New York: Springer, 229–238.

José María Ariso

How to Increase Negative Self-Knowledge by Using Cognitive Restructuring Through Augmented Reality: A Proposal and Analysis

Abstract: One of the main problems in implementing cognitive restructuring lies in the resistances experienced by the client when trying to use this technique even though, paradoxically, it had previously produced good results for him. Besides feeling too lazy to start putting this technique into practice, the client often gets easily distracted when he has already began carrying it out: stated otherwise, he often hardly shows interest in dismantling those very self-criticisms which are tormenting him. I argue that Augmented Reality can constitute an effective recourse for resolving these and similar problems by increasing what I call 'negative self-knowledge', a concept that I present and analyze in this article.

Keywords: cognitive restructuring, negative knowledge, self-knowledge, conceptual self, Augmented Reality glasses, self-criticism, locus of control, resistance.

1. Introduction

Let us imagine the case of an individual with a tiring, time-consuming and poorly paid job. After preparing himself during years of study and great sacrifices to get a better employment, he finally finds it in another company. It is expected that this new brings him great joy, as he had made tremendous efforts to get a better occupation, which may entail consequences as favorable as a salary increase, greater social and familiar recognition, and a more tolerable or even pleasant lifestyle. But it is also conceivable that he might receive the new with great regret, to the extent that he could even get depressed by it. He might think, among other things, that he is not really prepared for such a position, that it will be impossible for him to resist pressure from his workmates and chiefs, that he will therefore not be welcome in the new company, and that this job will thus become tortuous for him: as a necessary consequence of this, he may also think that he will become unemployed, abandoned by his family, and mentally destroyed until his dying day. This is a clear example of how the same event may be experienced very differently by a given individual depending

DOI 10.1515/9783110497656-013

on the thoughts he may have at each time. By themselves the mentioned news are neither good nor bad: strictly speaking, they are simply news. Depending upon the thoughts someone has at a given moment, a piece of news can be regarded either as a blessing or as a tragedy. Proof of this can be seen in the fact that, if the individual's catastrophist thoughts become rewarding, his mood may improve to the point that he could end up considering enthusiastically the idea of enjoying his new position.

Our thoughts can take the form of unspoken monologues, isolated sentences or even mere visual images. Even though we may be aware of these thoughts, they often happen to us without our being conscious of them. It is precisely then, when we cannot control them, that their influence on us is greater. It is due to such thoughts that, without our knowing why, we often feel happy or sad, optimistic or pessimistic, safe or unsafe, to the extent that the predominance of a certain kind of thoughts may become a habit that can condition our mood and even our very life. Unfortunately, these thoughts are sometimes very negative and affect an individual who may have hardly been aware of them for a very long time, resulting in the chronification of negative appraisal biases regarding virtually all events that happen to him. Some decades ago, Beck and colleagues developed a broad approach called 'cognitive restructuring', which has since been used in cognitive behavioral therapy and rational emotive therapy for helping clients learn to identify, dismantle and modify maladaptive thoughts which generate psychological disturbance (cf. Beck 1987, 1996; Beck/Emery 1985; Beck et al. 1979, 2009). It is often difficult to detect these thoughts because we are so accustomed to them that we are hardly aware of how and when they affect us. That is why it is important to resort to self-monitoring and note such disturbing thoughts as soon as we feel they are affecting us. Once we have recorded a number of thoughts, we will be in a position to detect one or more core beliefs which reflect our expectations of and convictions about ourselves, so that these beliefs will also lie at the heart of the thoughts we have written down. By way of example, someone can experience great anxiety about a particular task and become convinced that he will fail: in this case, he may be at the mercy of his core belief 'I must be perfect', which leads him to believe he is stupid because he can never live up to his exorbitant self-demand. As a result, it is possible that the fact of facing such a task triggers thoughts like 'People are realizing I am very nervous', 'They are looking at me as if I were to fail', 'They know I am stupid', 'This cannot turn out OK', etc. In such instances, the subject who resorts to cognitive restructuring must start by detecting which thoughts on himself and his environment grab him when he feels pessimistic, identifying core beliefs which underlie those thoughts, drawing upon his own previous experience to verify that those beliefs are inaccurate, concluding which appraisals and expectations are the most hopeful, positive, reasonable and realistic to match a given situation, and daring to act according to them.

Cognitive restructuring consists of three main components (cf. Clark 2014). The first element is what Beck et al. (1979) called collaborative empiricism, that is, a therapeutic relationship in which client and therapist work together on establishing treatment goals as well as the session agenda, and negotiating homework assignments; but in such a way that none of them has more responsibility than the other for the direction of therapy. It will be particularly evident that this collaboration is empiricist when the therapist uses Socratic questioning in order to ensure that the client analyses long-held beliefs and attitudes not by trying to convince him of whether a given belief is appropriate, but by inviting him to check his beliefs and attitudes in the light of his own personal experience. If collaborative empiricism is effective, clients will be more predisposed to attribute their improvement to their own efforts rather than external factors (cf. Tee/Kazantzis 2011). *Verbal interventions* constitute the second element. In order to modify maladaptive thoughts and beliefs, cognitive behavioral practitioners have proposed a number of strategies: the most common ones consist in gathering evidence, analyzing costs and benefits, identifying cognitive errors, and proposing alternative explanations. Other strategies consist in distancing by taking an observer stance, reattributing the causes of his difficulties, etc. Nevertheless, all these strategies require that the client is previously willing to seriously analyze his thoughts, consider the possibility that they are inaccurate and counterproductive, and adopt new perspectives. In fact, clients will not be amenable to cognitive restructuring if they are convinced that their maladaptive beliefs constitute immutable facts. The third and last element is *empirical hypothesis-taking* understood as "planned experiencial activities, based on experimentation or observation, which are undertaken by patients in or between cognitive therapy sessions" (Bennett-Levy et al. 2004, 8). These behavioral experiments may vary depending on the disorder. Regarding anxiety disorders, such experiments may consist in exposure to fear triggers but preventing escape and avoidance (cf. Clark/Beck 2010). As regards psychosis, behavioral experiments should be designed so that the client not only verifies that his interpretations of reality are inaccurate, but also improves his coping strategies to deal with delusions and hallucinations (cf. Beck et al. 2009, Kingdon/Turkington 2005).

In this article, I explain how cognitive restructuring can be implemented through Augmented Reality. As seen above, cognitive restructuring has been successfully used for anxiety disorders and psychosis, but its efficiency has also been proven in depression (cf. Dozois et al. 2009, Garratt et al. 2007), obsessive-compulsive disorder (cf. Whittal et al. 2008, McLean et al. 2001), borderline personality disorder (cf. Linehan 1993), post-traumatic stress disorder (cf. Tarrier/Sommerfield 2004), panic disorder with agoraphobia (cf. Bouchard et al. 2007), social phobia (cf. Taylor 1997), gambling addiction (cf. Jiménez-Murcia et al. 2007), bulimia (cf. Cooper et al. 2007), and internalization of locus of control among older adults (cf. Wolinsky et al. 2010) as well as secondary school students (cf. Tony 2010). However, I will not focus on the way in which the application of cognitive restructuring may be efficient to treat a specific disorder; instead, I will explain how and why this technique may have added advantages if it is applied through Augmented Reality. Specifically, I will clarify how the use of cognitive restructuring through Augmented Reality may contribute to generate a kind of knowledge I will call 'negative self-knowledge'. To expose this concept, I will take as a reference the terms 'self-knowledge' and 'negative knowledge', which will enable me to show why cognitive restructuring is particularly useful to foster negative self-knowledge. Subsequently, I will describe in detail how cognitive restructuring can be applied through Augmented Reality by showing the advantages of this combination over the isolated use of cognitive restructuring.

2. What is negative self-knowledge?

Taking as a basis the form of information which underlies self-knowledge, Neisser (1988) distinguishes five kinds of selves characterized by different origins, developmental histories, what each of us knows about them, the pathologies that can affect them, and their contribution to human social experience. These selves are the following. Firstly, the *ecological* self is the self which can be perceived above all through kinetic information; however, this self does not necessarily coincide with the biological body, for it also includes any controllable object that moves within the individual's point of observation. Secondly, the *interpersonal* self is also perceived on the basis of perceptual information, but it exists only when the individual is interacting with other people. While attending only to mere ecological information, without considering the interpersonal, may lead to treat other people as non-human objects, the interpersonal self is molded and even confirmed by the partner's expressive gestures, thus giving rise to a fluent intersubjective relationship. Thirdly, the *extended* self is modeled by our memories and expectations, so that it refers to the self just as we remember it in the past and as it is expected to be in the future. Hence, this self can be comprised or shown in a life-narrative made up of remembered experiences. Fourthly, the *private* self is composed of all those conscious experiences which are considered as 'inner' inasmuch as they cannot be directly shared by anyone else. Indeed, other people can receive information about my pains and dreams, but

I am the only person who can feel my pain and dream my own dreams. Fifthly and most importantly, the *conceptual* self – also called 'self-concept' – refers to the concept each one has of himself. This concept is based on self-theories that originate from socially established ideas assimilated by the individual through his life, but above all during childhood. Since self-theories are not based on objective information, they are often inaccurate although they shape our social behavior and our very interpretations of private experiences. Within the context of this article, it is particularly important to highlight a specific kind of sub-theory comprised in the conceptual self: I am referring to trait attributions, which consist in internal models of ourselves which condition our social roles. If one believes, for example, to be funny or boring, clever or stupid, such a belief will condition his interaction with other people and his expectations towards himself.

As cognitive restructuring is intended to identify and modify the theories and beliefs which determine our view of ourselves through the utterance of blurred thoughts that often go unnoticed, it is focused above all on the conceptual self. Yet we should not forget, as Neisser (1988) pointed out, that the other four kinds of self-knowledge are represented in one way or another in the conceptual self, so the modifications of the conceptual self will also affect the other forms of self-knowledge. One important point to consider at this stage is that self-knowledge generated by cognitive restructuring is of a negative nature, for it does not reveal what we are like, but *what we are not like.* To shed light on this issue, it is appropriate to bring up now the term 'negative knowledge', which was defined by Oser and Spychiger (2005) as knowledge about what something is not, as opposed to what it is; how something does not function, as opposed to how it functions; which strategies do not allow to solve complex problems, as opposed to those that allow to do so; and why some connections do not work, as opposed to why others work. Yet Parviainen and Eriksson (2006, 144) warned that "negative" should not be considered in this context "as the mere empty opposite to the 'positive'", as the adjective "negative" has here "its own independent arena". Therefore, Gartmeier et al. (2010, 2) defined negative knowledge as "experientially acquired knowledge about wrong assumptions that tend to be considered true". This conception of negative knowledge fits very well with the sort of knowledge generated by cognitive restructuring. For, as seen above, cognitive restructuring is efficient when clients acquire knowledge based on their own experience regarding wrong assumptions about themselves – or more specifically, about their conceptual self – that they regarded as true.

Keeping this in mind, I propose the term 'negative self-knowledge' to make reference to the kind of knowledge provided by cognitive restructuring. To be precise, I consider negative self-knowledge as the knowledge, drawing on one's own experience, that some assumptions, theories or beliefs one had on himself are inaccurate. Showers (1992) had already used the expression 'negative self-knowledge', but in a different way. According to Showers, global self-views do not depend so much on the fact that one's knowledge about his self is positive or negative as on the way in which this information is organized. Self-knowledge is categorically organized in positive and negative self-aspects which can be rated or perceived as more or less important depending on each individual. Thus, when someone regards positive self-aspects as important, compartmentalization turns out to be very rewarding because that self-aspect will contain only positive knowledge about the self. Yet when priority is given to negative self-knowledge, it is preferable to form self-aspects not compartmentalized but mixing positive and negative self-knowledge. Showers adds that these patterns may be very useful to treat those patients, like those suffering from depression, whose negative self-knowledge greatly debilitates them. In fact, she concludes that "negative knowledge about the self need not necessarily be changed or denied" (Showers 1992, 1048). Therefore, she points out that if a depressed person's negative knowledge turns out to be realistic (cf. Allan et al. 2007, Ackerman/DeRubeis 1991), it is better to reorganize it than to change it in order to improve self-evaluation. I find Showers' conclusion very interesting, yet it is important to make clear that her conception of negative self-knowledge is different from mine. Indeed, Showers regards self-knowledge either as positive or as negative depending upon its affective or evaluative valence. Thus, a student's knowledge about himself as a mathematics student will be positive if he perceives himself as brilliant or skilled, but negative if he sees himself as bad or terrible in that field. Conversely, my conception of negative self-knowledge consists in someone's knowing *what he is not like*. Starting from the classification of different kinds of negative knowledge carried out by Gartmeier et al. (2010), what I have called 'negative self-knowledge' could be contemplated as a sort of declarative negative knowledge, which consists in knowing how something is not. Furthermore, it has some relationship with self-reflective negative knowledge, which consists in knowing about one's own limitations. Nevertheless, my conception of negative self-knowledge does not fully coincide with any form of self-reflective negative knowledge, for this knowledge concerns the limitations of one's own realm of influence (cf. Sparbel/Anderson 2000) as well as the deficiencies of one's knowledge and skills (cf. Parviainen/Eriksson 2006).

An important aspect to be considered at this point is that my conception of negative self-knowledge seems to refer to a very superficial and, what is worse, unreliable sort of knowledge; after all, it could be objected that someone's knowledge of what he is not like might be easily confused with his believing or wanting to believe some sources whose reliability remains to be proven. By way of example, someone might be strongly inclined to take a specific belief on himself either as appropriate or inappropriate not because he has contrasted it with his previous experience, but simply because it turns out to be easier or more comfortable for him. Such biased use of cognitive restructuring will take place mainly when it is not rigorously implemented because the patient is not sufficiently motivated to dismantle his self-criticism. Therefore, in these cases there are usually distractions, lack of contrast with previous experience, and insincere conclusions when accepting that the belief to be dismantled no longer exerts its pernicious effect. Yet it should be noted that those thoughts which are usually detected through cognitive restructuring are not vague and imprecise ideas which cannot be clearly contrasted with previous experience. Indeed, they are often formulated in absolute terms – 'always', 'never', 'everything', 'nothing', etc. – regardless of whether such thoughts concern facts or the individual himself: thus, it is clear what would count as a refutation of each thought. As an example, when the belief 'I am stupid' seizes an individual, especially when he is not aware of it, he may end up becoming convinced of being absolutely and completely stupid, in all circumstances and without any possibility of ceasing to be stupid. As previously stated, such individual seems not to be amenable to cognitive restructuring because, at least in principle, he appears to be convinced that his maladaptive belief is an immutable fact. But in such cases cognitive restructuring, especially when it is applied through Augmented Reality, allows one to draw on one's own experience avoiding distractions in order to verify that one has often acted in a number of ways which do not fit with the mentioned belief. Where this is done, it is not intended that the patient develops a false, tainted or sweetened view of himself: far from such a thing, it is simply expected that the client becomes aware of what he is not like, but without trying to convince him that he is better in a given dimension than he really is – although, in so doing, his self-concept and even his self-esteem were enhanced.

3. Implementing cognitive restructuring through Augmented Reality

My proposal does not consist in explaining in detail how to design an application that allows the user to easily and successfully apply cognitive restructuring without the assistance of a therapist. Instead, I simply intend to clarify how and why Augmented Reality could enhance the application of cognitive restructuring *in situ*, that is, in every situation – outside the therapist's office – in which the patient starts experiencing a strong self-criticism and intense pessimism. The therapist would continue to play a pivotal role, as my proposal is not intended to substitute him, but to present a tool whose adaptation to the client and later monitoring would be carried out by the therapist. To this should be added that my proposal can be implemented with relative ease through Augmented Reality glasses, for it does not require much more than recording some video and audio files as well as scheduling some voice commands. It is true that the current models of Augmented Reality glasses are still expensive and are at the developmental stage. Nevertheless, the usage of Augmented Reality glasses that I will suggest is so elemental that it should be no problem to implement my proposal in models such as Epson Moverio BT-20, Sony SmartEyeglass or Vuzix M100 Smart Glasses, in addition to other models which will soon be available like Microsoft HoloLens, Recon Jet or the new edition of Google Glass. Having said this, I now turn to present my proposal.

To begin with, it is essential that the interface is as simple and intuitive as possible. It must be taken into account that, just when it is necessary to apply cognitive restructuring, that is, when the client begins to suffer the effects of self-criticisms, he often feels especially reluctant to apply any resource that might help him to address his tendency towards negativity. Even if the client has successfully used cognitive restructuring in many cases, resistances to improvement may cause him very often to forget either the existence of this therapeutic tool or the occasions in which it worked great: in short, it is highly likely that he will simply fall prey to the enormous laziness he may experience when considering the mere possibility of using cognitive restructuring. Since a complex interface will not help the patient to apply this tool, it would be desirable to design the interface in such a way that it encourages him to use it as soon as he needs it. To this end, the word 'Help' might appear flashing in one of the upper corners in the size, design and color which the client considers to be the most stimulating and attractive to initialize the application either through voice activation or touchpad. It is important to count on both options because it may be more convenient for the client to use one or the other depending on the circumstances and his own mood. By way of example, when the individual is in a situation in which it is advisable to remain silent, it may be inappropriate to suddenly say 'Help'; likewise, there are contexts in which it may seem strange or out of place that the client is using the touchpad, so that a quick and discreet voice activation may constitute a better option. In any case, it would be desirable for the patient to discuss with the therapist how the initiation mechanism should be triggered in order for it to be activated with no doubt when needed.

As far as possible, the application itself should encourage and motivate the client to the extent that, after having initiated it, he has the feeling of having entered into an intense and absorbing dynamic from which he does not even consider escaping or evading until having dismantled the self-criticism that torments him at that moment. If, once initialized, the application turns out to be bland and facilitates that the client's attention wanders or, still worse, that he starts thinking whether to go on using it, then it is not well designed. Once again, it will be up to the client to decide which resources of the interface he finds more stimulating to encourage the application of cognitive restructuring until the end of the process. As a rough guide, the application may offer several possibilities, e.g. a few and forceful words in audio, video or both, like 'You don't feel good. Let's solve it!' A formula of this kind may be of great help because, on the one hand, it clearly utters the discomfort sensation experienced by the patient without trying to hide it or replace it by a more sweetened view of the situation, and on the other, it strongly urges to seek a solution to the problem. Furthermore, someone who is felt especially motivating by the client might record the formula in video and audio. At this stage, the therapist should help the patient to find the formulas and resources which he considers more stimulating.

The fact that the application, once initialized, must capture the client's attention does not mean that it must necessarily offer an interface overloaded with contents, for a large volume of information makes it difficult to search for targets as well as understanding the information delivered by Augmented Reality (cf. Li/Been-Lirn 2013, Stedmon et al. 1999). The effort of paying attention not only to the real world scene, but also to each and every content which appears in the interface, may cause difficulties to use it: in such cases it is very likely that the patient will fall prey to thoughts like 'You are stupid', 'You are not able to use the application', 'With every passing day, you are more and more useless', etc. It should be noticed that the client would resort to this application just when he feels more vulnerable from the psychological standpoint. Hence, it is fundamental that guidelines are clear, motivating, and as minimal as possible.

The next task which should be carried out by the therapist consists in helping the patient to choose the four or five self-criticisms which most often disturb him. It is important that their formulations are brief, clear and do not overlap with each other. Such formulations should also be perceived by the client as the unequivocal expressions of a self-criticism he has already experienced many times. It may be objected that four or five self-criticisms could prove insufficient, yet there are two reasons for not suggesting more options. On the one hand, it is frequently noted that patients' self-criticisms are limited to a few. Regardless of whether contexts and sensations vary, therapists and patients often agree that self-criticisms can be reduced to a short number of formulations. On the other hand, it would be possible to show more formulations of self-criticisms, to the extent that they could be exposed in screens which are easy to scroll at a single touch. Nevertheless, this would mean twice the effort because the patient should scroll through screens and sharpen his attention to choose from a greater number of options. Both tasks may seem simple and do not require a great deal of effort, but we should not forget that the client will use the application just when he perceives serious difficulties to overcome negativity and laziness. Keeping this in mind, it is advisable that, just after a formula of the kind 'You don't feel good. Let's solve it!', the patient finds simultaneously shown on display four of five options among which it is easy to choose. It is true that the patient will necessarily have to choose an option, but such task will be much simpler than the identification and utterance of a self-criticism without having any reference, as it would be the case if he could not rely on the application.

To give some examples, I will mention some self-criticisms which may be selected by therapist and client to appear in the interface. A very common self-criticism is 'I am a total failure'. Of course, this formulation may vary slightly, as it would also be possible to opt for other expressions like 'I am stupid', etc. In any case, the patient is very often convinced, above all in moments of negativity and pessimism, that he has always been, is and will be a loser, a complete failure. If the client opts for this self-criticism, a video should be immediately played in which someone – the therapist, a subject who is respected and admired, or the client himself – affirms briefly – between fifty and eighty words – and unequivocally that, even though he had often made a certain kind of mistake, he had also achieved some great things and, moreover, he is loved and appreciated by different people. This enables the client to avoid a task which just at that moment may be as tiring and stressful as trying to dismantle the self-criticism by actively developing his own thoughts. This video will be more likely to succeed if it has previously been prepared with the therapist by choosing the speaker, elaborating the text, repeating the recording if needed, etc. Furthermore, it may be useful to add some pictures which clearly evoke for the client the idea of having done in the past things that make him proud of himself. The second self-criticism may be 'This is ruined'. It can arise when the client is afraid that something will necessarily go wrong because it has not started well. In this frame of mind, it may be helpful to record a video in which the patient himself firmly states, to give an example, that he once made a mistake when taking for granted a fatal diagnosis as a result of a clinical analysis because he believed there were signs of such prognosis everywhere. This will enable the patient to realize that his negative predictions are often wrong and based on very biased interpretations. The third self-criticism might be 'No woman can be interested in me'. Perhaps he is convinced that he cannot be successful with women because they find him ugly and boring. In such a case, the video might start by noting that the fact that he is neither handsome nor funny does not mean that no woman could be interested in him. In fact, some woman could state in the video that if a man takes for granted that no woman could be interested in him, his attitude and behavior will neither contribute to encourage such interest nor enable him to recognize it if it ended up arising. The fourth self-criticism may be of the kind 'I am obliged to get the maximum grade at every exam'. This desire for perfection may prevent the client from noticing that such attitude would lead him, above all, to become a kind of obsessive recordman of academic qualifications. In this case, it might be considered whether it would be useful to record a short video in which allusion is made to some people who rose to prominence although they never belonged to those with the highest grades or, better yet, although they sometimes did not get the maximum grade.

Finally, I would like to pay special attention to the fifth self-criticism. I am referring to a thought like 'I can do nothing to remedy this'. At first sight, this self-criticism is very similar to the others, but there are subtle differences which may lead the client to choose a specific one at a given moment: that is why it is so important that the interface contains several options. It should be noticed that the first self-criticism – 'I am a total failure' – constitutes a global attack against the client's self-concept; hence, a strong resistance against focusing on specific details is expected, as a superficial analysis might suffice to exert significant impact on the patient. The second – 'This is ruined' – is characteristic of those cases in which the appraisal of an event and its development focuses on overstating negative information, while discarding any positive information as irrelevant. The third – 'No woman can be interested in me' – illustrates how deeply the client may be convinced of knowing not only what other people think about him, but also that their opinion in this regard is very negative. The fourth – 'I am obliged to get the maximum grade at every exam' – produces exorbitant objectives that may result in significant frustration if they are not achieved. By contrast, the fifth self-criticism – 'I can do nothing to remedy this' – highlights the fact that the client is convinced of the impossibility of solving a specific problem, yet this conviction often conceals an external locus of control. Whilst individuals who have an internal locus of control perceive reinforcement as contingent upon their behavior or traits, 'externals' or people with an external locus of control do not perceive events in their lives as a consequence of their actions. Hence, they tend to attribute their successes to good luck or other people's benevolence, while their failures are attributed to external human and contextual factors (cf. Rotter 1966, Gierowski/Rajtar 2003). Of course, there will be many situations which cannot be modified in any way by the patient, yet the individual who is overwhelmed by self-criticisms, especially if he is an external, is often faced with situations which he can remedy in some way or another even though he is not able to get a glimpse into how to do it just because of his mood and expectations for himself. In certain circumstances, such as some cases of bullying or cyberbullying, the individual may be convinced that he has no alternative but to withstand the attack of his stalker. The therapist should then help the client to become aware of options he had not previously considered (cf. Gerson/Rappaport 2011) until he is able to regard a distressing "scenario as a challenge, in which the victim is free to choose an efficacious response, as opposed to feeling helpless and hopeless" (Ariso/Reyero 2014, 102). If the therapist concludes that the patient is an external, he should develop the client's capacity to find possible solutions to a problem, above all in those situations which entail a great emotional toll for him.

Immediately after watching the video prepared to dismantle a given self-criticism, the client must re-evaluate if the disturbing thought is still perceived as true. If he has really ceased to experience the tormenting influence of the self-criticism, even temporarily, he should leave the application through an utterance like 'I won!' or 'Overcome!', whereupon he might watch in a short closing video how one or several persons that are important to him – and even he himself – exultantly congratulate him. The effectiveness of this procedure will depend to a large extent on whether the client is absolutely sincere in acknowledging that the self-criticism was truly unwarranted. As it is expected that the usage of the application will not always enable the patient to overcome a given self-criticism, it should be programmed to encourage him to try it again. If he ultimately cannot dismantle the self-criticism, he should have the option to exit the application through an utterance such as 'Out'. If an escape is not offered to the client, he will be forced to leave the application by affirming that he has dismantled a self-criticism, even if it is not true. When the usage of the application is not successful, it will be necessary to analyze the problem in the therapist's office and make adjustments in the application if necessary. A further eventuality to be considered is that, after having overcome a given self-criticism, the client can return to the self-criticisms menu in order to choose a new one, as he may then experience the influence of another one. In any case, it is fundamental that the client does not use the application passively or without being sure about what he really aims to achieve with it, as its usage will then be associated with apathy, confusion and inefficiency. Instead, such usage should be linked with high concentration and, above all, the firm intention of overcoming a specific self-criticism determinedly and without allowing the slightest distraction.

In order to adapt the application to the client's characteristics and necessities, it would be advisable to add some resources. One of them could consist in visibly displaying at the side an option called 'Laugh' to gain access to a joke or something similar which, unfailingly, makes the client laugh. It should not be forgotten that no one can maintain a negative attitude while he is laughing heartily, for his attention cannot then be focused on something negative like a self-criticism. Therefore, if the patient laughs at a joke or an anecdote, his mood will greatly and quickly improve, so that it will be easier for him to dedramatise certain conflicts, which will in turn increase the likelihood of applying cognitive restructuring successfully. A further idea is to seek a specific person to utter the self-criticisms. Just like a respected and appreciated subject was chosen to express the rebuttal of every self-criticism, the person who utters the self-criticisms should be someone he does not like, to the extent that such person automatically encourages the client to react and not to let himself be overcome by him. This resource may be especially useful when the client seems to be poorly motivated or does not react strongly enough to self-criticisms. Furthermore, if the client has overcome a self-criticism but lacks initiative in acting, it could be useful for him to watch a short video in which he himself acts properly in that very situation. To this end, there are procedures to cut out his silhouette against the real world scene which the patient is seeing at that moment. Of course, the recorded image or silhouette is not intended to fit perfectly in the real scene, but it can be a good aid to move the client to start acting, for inaction may lead him to doubt and relapse into self-criticism.

As can be seen, the personal adaptation of the application would require a considerable amount of previous work in the practice. It would be necessary not only to record videos and audios, but also to begin testing the use of the application in imaginary situations. This would make it possible to gradually adapt different aspects of the application for maximum effectiveness. Moreover, it can be particularly advisable to record every use the patient makes of the application, and later on consider commenting it in the practice. The recording may be a very useful resource because the fact of watching again the real scenes through the interface may help the client to remember and explain in detail his train of thought, in particular if the next appointment will be before long. A further possibility is that, in some specific case, the therapist is not only watching in real time the same scene that the client is seeing through his glasses, but also providing indications along the way if they are needed. Nevertheless, the possibility that the therapist may assist the client in this way at a given time should not lead us to think the implementation of cognitive restructuring through Augmented Reality is not aimed at fostering his autonomy. Indeed, it is of the utmost importance that the client dominates the use of cognitive restructuring by himself to the point that he ends up being able to overcome self-criticisms without using the application after treatment has finished. While the patient is still using the application, and depending on his progress, some steps like the initial message of encouragement or the videos can be reduced. Afterwards, the menu of self-criticisms should also be overlooked, as the patient should be able to identify and overcome them by himself, without using the application.

4. Conclusion

It is obvious that the implementation of cognitive restructuring through Augmented Reality, at least in the way exposed in this article, would entail some changes in the therapist's role. For he should also become a specialist not only in elaborating brief and convincing videos, but also in helping the client to find the most appropriate configuration of the application for him without ceasing to adjust it along the way if needed. The therapist must train the client to use this tool autonomously in order to face his disturbing thoughts by appealing to his own experience and common sense. Ultimately, the patient should learn to apply cognitive restructuring spontaneously and without aid. In order to master its use, Augmented Reality can be of great help. As seen above, the application presented in this article provides support outside the practice, just in those situations in which the client needs to use cognitive restructuring but cannot count on the therapist's supervision. This support is especially helpful in overcoming resistances which the client, just when starting to apply cognitive restructuring, will often experience as terrible laziness, astonishing forgetfulness, lack of mental agility, as well as disappointment with the technique and even with the therapist although cognitive restructuring had produced satisfactory results so far. Moreover, the application can be progressively adapted to facilitate the spontaneous use of cognitive restructuring without the support provided by Augmented Reality glasses. The result of all this should be twofold. On the one hand, the patient will learn to become free from his self-criticisms as soon as they start tormenting him. On the other, the patient's self-knowledge will increase. We might say it will be positive knowledge in an accumulative sense, that is, inasmuch as the patient will know more and more about himself; but it will really be negative knowledge because the characteristic procedure of cognitive restructuring consists in knowing increasingly better what one is not like without being able to reach a full and complete knowledge of what one really is like. Let us see this more slowly.

While participating in a discussion aiming at comparing different arts and elucidating which should be regarded as the most sublime one, Leonardo da Vinci (1835) noted a relevant distinction between painting and sculpturing. Whilst painting proceeds *per via di porre* or by putting on, that is to say, by placing heaps of paint on a blank canvas, sculpturing works *per via di levare* or by taking away, I mean, by extracting the work of art out of the stone block in which it was contained. Several centuries later, Freud (1953) brought up this comparison to illustrate the difference between his psychoanalytical therapy and the suggestive technique. Specifically, he pointed out that this technique proceeded *per via di porre*, whilst his psychoanalytic technique worked *per via di levare*. In this way, he aimed to highlight that suggestive technique resorts to suggestion in order to prevent the expression of the pathogenic idea, while his psychoanalytic therapy is not intended to add anything but to take away: that is why it is focused on merely understanding patient's resistances that result from the unconscious conflicts which are converted into psychopathological symptoms. Yet I think this way of proceeding *per via di levare* also resembles cognitive restructuring and, by extension, the conception of 'negative self-knowledge' presented above. By ruling out inaccurate theories and beliefs on himself not through dogmatic arguments but by means of his own experience, the client progressively gets to know what he really is not like. This task would be like taking away those pieces of stone which seemingly distorted his real figure or what we might call the most adjusted self-concept he could have of himself, with the particularity that, in this case, the problem is not restricted to the fact that residual stone hindered the view, for this stone – understood as theories and beliefs – also generates an inaccurate model of oneself which sometimes has a very influential and pernicious impact on the individual. However, this residual stone can never be completely extracted, as we will always have some theories and beliefs which will determine our view of ourselves. We can reach a less and less distorted self-concept, but the approach to an alleged last and true self will always be asymptotical because it is not even clear what such direct knowledge of our own self would be or what it would be like. Nevertheless, this will not diminish the relevance of cognitive restructuring, as it is designed in such a way that generates negative self-knowledge which, in turn, allows us to reduce the effect of harmful self-criticisms.

References

Ackermann, R./DeRubeis, R. J. (1991): "Is Depressive Realism Real?" In: *Clinical Psychology Review* 11(5), 565–584.

Allan, L. G./Siegel, S./Hannah, S. (2007): "The Sad Truth about Depressive Realism." In: *The Quarterly Journal of Experimental Psychology* 60(3), 482–495.

Ariso, J. M./Reyero, D. (2014): "Reconsidering the Scenario of Cyberbullying: Promoting the Internalization of the Locus of Control in Adolescents through Cognitive Restructuring." In: *Adolescent Psychiatry* 4(2), 98–103.

Beck, A. T. (1987): "Cognitive Models of Depression." In: *Journal of Cognitive Psychotherapy* 1, 5–37.

Beck, A. T. (1996): "Beyond Belief: A Theory of Modes, Personality, and Psychopathology." In P. M. Salkovskis (ed.), *Frontiers of Cognitive Therapy*, New York: Guilford Press, 1–25.
Beck, A. T./Emery, G. (1985): *Anxiety Disorders and Phobias: A Cognitive Perspective*, New York: Basic Books.
Beck, A. T./Rector, N. A./Stolar, N./Grant, P. (2009): *Schizophrenia: Cognitive Theory, Research and Therapy*, New York: Guilford Press.
Beck, A. T./Rush, A. J./Shaw, B. F./Emery, G. (1979): *Cognitive Therapy of Depression*, New York: Guilford Press.
Bennett-Levy, J./Westbrook, D./Fennell, M./Cooper, M./Rouf, K./Hackmann, A. (2004): "Behavioural Experiments: Historical and Conceptual Underpinnings". In J. Bennett-Levy/G. Butler/M. Fennell/A. Hackmann/M. Mueller/D. Westbrook (eds.), *Oxford Guide to Behavioural Experiments in Cognitive Therapy*, Oxford: Oxford University Press, 1–20.
Bouchard, S./Gauthier, J./Nouwen, A./Ivers, H./Vallieres, A./Simard, S./Fournier, T. (2007): "Temporal Relationship Between Dysfunctional Beliefs, Self-efficacy and Panic Apprehension in the Treatment of Panic Disorder with Agoraphobia." In: *Journal of Behavior Therapy and Experimental Psychiatry* 38, 275–292.
Clark, D. A. (2014): "Cognitive Restructuring." In: D. Dozois (ed.), *The Wiley Handbook of Cognitive Behavioral Therapy*, Volume I, Chichester: John Wiley & Sons, 1–25.
Clark, D. A./Beck, A. T. (2010): *Cognitive Therapy of Anxiety Disorders: Science and Practice*, New York: Guilford Press.
Cooper, M./Todd, G./Turner, H./Wells. A. (2007): "Cognitive Therapy for Bulimia Nerviosa: an A-B Replication Series". In: *Clinical Psychology and Psychotherapy* 14, 402–411.
da Vinci, Leonardo (1835): *A Treatise on Painting*, London: J. B. Nichols and Son.
Dozois, D. J. A./Bieling, P. J./Patelis-Siotis, I./Hoar, H./Chudzik, S./McCabe, K./Westra, H. A. (2009): "Changes in Self-schema Structure in Cognitive Therapy for Major Depressive Disorder: A Randomized Clinical Trial." In: *Journal of Consulting and Clinical Psychology* 77, 1078–1088.
Freud, S. (1953): "On Psychotherapy." In: J. Strachey (ed.), *The Standard Edition of the Complete Psychological Works of Sigmund Freud*, Volume VII (1901–1905): A Case of Hysteria, Three Essays on Sexuality and Other Works, London: The Hogarth Press and the Institute of Psychoanalysis, 257–270.
Garratt, G./Ingram, R. E./Rand, K. L./Sawalani, G. (2007): "Cognitive Processes in Cognitive Therapy: Evaluation of the Mechanisms of Change in the Treatment of Depression." In: *Clinical Psychology: Science and Practice* 14, 224–239.
Gartmeier, M./Gruber, H./Heid, H. (2010): "Tracing Error-related Knowledge in Interview Data: Negative Knowledge in Elder Care Nursing." In: *Educational Gerontology* 36, 1–20.
Gerson, R./Rappaport, N. (2011): "Cyber Cruelty: Understanding and Preventing the New Bullying." In: *Adolescent Psychiatry* 1, 67–71.
Gierowski, J. K./Rajtar, T. (2003): "Chosen Factors Influencing the Locus of Control in Perpetrators of Criminal Acts." In: *Problems of Forensic Sciences* 3, 129–138.
Jiménez-Murcia, S./Álvarez-Moya, E. M./Granero, R./Aymami, M. N./Gómez-Peña, M./Jaurrieta, N./Sans, B./Rodríguez-Marti, J./Vallejo, J. (2007): "Cognitive Behavioral Group Treatment for Pathological Gambling: Analysis of Effectiveness and Predictors of Therapy Outcome." In: *Psychotherapy Research* 17, 544–552.

Kingdon, D. G./Turkington, D. (2005): *Cognitive Therapy of Schizophrenia*, New York: Guilford Press.
Li, N./Been-Lirn, H. (2013): "Cognitive Issues in Mobile Augmented Reality: An Embodied Perspective". In: W. Huang/L. Alem/M. A. Livingston (eds.), *Human Factors in Augmented Reality Environment*, New York: Springer, 109–135.
Linehan, M. M. (1993): *Cognitive Behavioural Treatment of Borderline Personality Disorder*, New York: Guilford Press.
McLean, P. D./Whittal, M. L./Thordarson, D. S./Taylor, S./Söchting, I./Koch, W. J./Paterson, R./Anderson, K. W. (2001): "Cognitive versus Behavior Therapy in the Group Treatment of Obsessive-compulsive Disorder." In: *Journal of Consulting and Clinical Psychology* 69, 205–214.
Neisser, U. (1988): "Five Kinds of Self-knowledge." In: *Philosophical Psychology* 1(1), 35–59.
Oser, F./Spychiger, M. (2005): *Lernen ist schmerzhaft. Zur Theorie des Negativen Wissens und zur Praxis der Fehlerkultur*, Weinheim and Basel: Beltz.
Parviainen, J./Eriksson, M. (2006): "Negative Knowledge, Expertise and Organizations." In: *International Journal of Management Concepts and Philosophy* 2(2), 140–153.
Rotter, J. B. (1966): "Generalized Expectancies for Internal versus External Control of Reinforcement." In: *Psychological Monographs: General and Applied* 80, 1–28.
Showers, C (1992): "Compartmentalization of Positive and Negative Self-knowledge: Keeping Bad Apples out of the Bunch." In: *Journal of Personality and Social Psychology* 62(6), 1036–1049.
Sparbel, K./Anderson, M. A. (2000): "Integrated Literature Review of Continuity of Care: Part I, Conceptual Issues." In: *Journal of Nursing Scholarship* 32, 17–24.
Stedmon, A. W./Kalawsky, R. S./Hill, K./Cook, C. A. (1999): "Old Theories, New Technologies: Cumulative Clutter Effects Using Augmented Reality". 1999 IEEE International Conference on Information Visualization, London.
Tarrier, N./Sommerfield, C. (2004): "Treatment of Chronic PTSD by Cognitive Therapy and Exposure: 5-Year Follow up." In: *Behavior Therapy* 35, 231–246.
Taylor, S./Woody, S./Koch, W. J./McLean, P./Paterson, R. J./Anderson, K. W. (1997): "Cognitive Restructuring in the Treatment of Social Phobia." In: *Behavior Modification* 21, 487–511.
Tee, J./Kazantzis, N. (2011): "Collaborative Empiricism in Cognitive Therapy: A Definition and Theory for the Relationship Construct." In: *Clinical Psychology: Science and Practice* 18, 47–61.
Tony, T. S. K. (2010): "Locus of Control, Attributional Style and Discipline Problems in Secondary Schools." In: *Early Child Development and Care* 173, 455–466.
Whittal, M. L./Robichaud, M./Thordarson, D. S./McLean, P. D. (2008): "Group and Individual Treatment of Obsessive-Compulsive Disorder Using Cognitive Therapy and Exposure plus Response Prevention: A 2-year Follow up of Two Randomized Trials." In: *Journal of Consulting and Clinical Psychology* 76, 1003–1014.
Wolinsky, F. D./van der Weg, M. W./Martin, R./Unverzagt, F. W./Willis, S. L./Marsiske, M./Rebok, G. W./Morris, J. N./Ball, K. K./Tennstedt, S. L. (2010): "Does Cognitive Training Improve Internal Locus of Control among Older Adults?" In: *Journal of Gerontology: Psychological Sciences* 65B(5), 591–598.

Part 5: **Educational Applications and Implications of Augmented Reality**

Juan Luis Fuentes

Augmented Reality and Pedagogical Anthropology: Reflections from the Philosophy of Education

Abstract: Philosophy of education, as applied philosophy, deals with educational issues from a philosophical point of view, including those raised by modern technology. Being a form of social interaction, education is probably one of the experiences most altered by technology; through ICTs, it has gained a myriad of options not only for accessing knowledge but also for human development. In this chapter, I will analyze some challenges that Augmented Reality presents in philosophy of education, paying particular attention to its ramifications for pedagogical anthropology. To be specific, I will explore the following human traits: lack of instincts and its influence on the development of initiative; human precariousness in the environment and ability to adapt; ontological knowledge of reality, through transmediation, and Zubiri's concept of the human being as an "animal of realities;" and, finally, leisure understood as a non-vital human need.

Keywords: Augmented Reality, pedagogical anthropology, philosophy of education, human initiative, human precariousness, ontological knowledge, transmediation, leisure.

1. Introduction

One of the most thought-provoking dialogs in Lewis Carroll's famous story *Alice's Adventures in Wonderland* goes like this:

> Alice: Would you tell me, please, which way I ought to go from here?
> The Cat: That depends a good deal on where you want to get to.
> Alice: I don't much care where ...
> The Cat: Then it doesn't matter which way you go.
> Alice: ...so long as I get somewhere.
> The Cat: Oh, you're sure to do that, if you only walk long enough. (Carroll 2001, p. 87)

A range of reflections could arise from this brief conversation. Noddings (2002) believes that it has considerable didactic value in teaching formal conversation – the philosophical type of discourse that is useful in teaching the norms of

DOI 10.1515/9783110497656-014

proper discussion. My own interest, from a pedagogical standpoint, lies in calling attention to a particular reflection it inspires vis-à-vis the aims of education – that the goal dictates the path to be taken. In other words, not all roads lead to the same place, and to determine the best route or best means to employ to get where we want to go, we must first know *where* we want to go. In pedagogical terms, this means that, preliminary to all educational actions, an approach must be chosen based on the type of person we want our educational endeavors to produce (Escámez/García López 1998) – which refers us, of necessity, to anthropological thinking on education.

Comparing the *human development approach*, elaborated through the efforts of Martha Nussbaum and Amartya Sen, with the *economic development approach* will elucidate this idea. The latter approach, because it equates 'progress' with 'economic development', has major implications for the organizational structure of a society or country, in general, and the educational system, in particular. Among the most consequential of these is the weighting of the curriculum toward certain competencies and content. Under the economic development model, for example, a society would place special emphasis on mathematical skills, technological and financial know-how, and marketing strategies as the foundation of literacy – the ultimate objective being to make that society more competitive in the free market (Nussbaum 2012). This means that other subjects, such as History, Art, Literature, and Philosophy would become subordinate, along with skills like critical thinking and democratic dialogue. Thus, depending on the model a society aspires to create, it is not difficult to shape one type of person vs. another type of person by the choice of curriculum content.

This is nothing new in the history of education; since the days of ancient Greece, educational thought has been linked, more or less explicitly, with anthropological thought. Today, however, owing to modern technology's impact on basic aspects of human life, we find ourselves in a situation that could bring about a significant departure from previous thinking. Thanks in large part to technological advancements, changes are taking place in the realms of employment, communications, friendship, love, responsibility, privacy, and education, leading us to ponder certain areas in need of an update for the digital age. This major, categorical change in the anthropological conception has even prompted some authors to start inquiring into the possibility of a new stage in human evolution and introducing concepts such as *post-humans* (Bostrom 2008, Cortina/Serra 2015). Biologists like Wilson (2014) maintain that we are in the midst of another Enlightenment that puts us in position to abandon the logic of natural selection in favor of artificial selection based on human will and intelligence. Genetic manipulation would enable us to live longer and to have more robust memory, better eyesight, etc. and, in this day and age, the Humanities would have to yield to Science and allow technology to address questions about the meaning of our existence. Philosophers like Bostrom (2009) argue that technological advances have the power to alter the human condition or human nature itself by endowing individuals with capabilities that were once unimaginable. In this panorama, there seems to be new meaning in Nietzsche's Superman; as the German thinker once declared, "Man shall be just that to the Superman: a laughingstock or a painful embarrassment" (Nietzsche 2000, 8).

Not only does technology enable us to do more things but the things we can do are quite different from what we used to do, and we are capable of functioning in new, quite diverse areas. As far as education is concerned, this means updating didactic methods, of course. First, however, abiding by the logic in the dialog between Alice and The Cat, we must take the anthropological model into consideration so that what we do makes sense and does not become frantic activity driven by the pressure of empty and meaningless innovation (Barrio 2015). In other words, if anthropology and education are not in harmony on this matter, we risk becoming like a chicken with its head cut off, running around aimlessly.

In this chapter, I will use the prism of Philosophy of Education to analyze the relationship between technology and the way we view the human being – focusing, in particular, on Augmented Reality. My point of departure will be the characteristics that certain philosophical and educational anthropologists have identified in the human being.[1] Although these characteristics are interrelated and impossible to understand in isolation from each other, we will view them separately for purposes of this analysis. These characteristics are the *lack of instincts*, *human precariousness in the environment*, the *capacity for ontological knowledge of reality and for devising realities not present*, and the *human need for leisure.*

1 A glance at the history of thought reveals that it is not possible to speak of a unified philosophical conception of the human being, for this idea has changed with the different trends and authors. Furthermore, as Scheler (2000) has stated, for some years now, we have found ourselves in a time of profound difficulties in anthropological study. Since it is not the purpose of this chapter to list them all, we will choose those that we believe are most relevant to the characteristics of today's digital technology, in general, and of Augmented Reality, in particular.

2. Key anthropological aspects of the relationship between education and technology

Education simply would not be possible if we, as individuals, did not have certain specific traits in common – a set of characteristics that allow us to speak of a transformative influence on the reality of an individual or group of individuals. This is one of the reasons that, traditionally, the word 'education' has not been used in connection with species other than human beings; concepts such as training or instruction are used instead. Let us identify some of the major anthropological traits that are relevant to technology, adhering to the proposals of certain scholars in pedagogical anthropology (Wulf 2008, Barrio 2000, Escámez/García López 1998). While anthropology has been of interest to philosophers since its inception, *pedagogical* anthropology – from an educational perspective – is a discipline that did not systematically evolve until the latter half of the twentieth century, especially in Germany and the United States (Bouché *et al.* 1995).

2.1 The lack of instincts and its impact on initiative

Strictly speaking, human beings do not have instincts that would cause them to behave at all times in a specific, stereotypical manner – this being, most likely, the result of phylogenetic evolution and brain development. This may be better understood through comparison with other animal species. Whereas the members of an animal species will all be similar to each other in their behavior, owing to immutable, pre-determined genetic parameters, human beings show great complexity in their behavior. This limits our ability to ascertain the shared genetic traits that would enable us to understand a species as a whole. Thus, although it is accepted, nowadays, that genetics has an influence on human behavior, we can say that this behavior does not follow a strict pattern; rather, there are individual patterns created over a lifetime through personal initiative and with varying degrees of originality. Even mimetic abilities – an inherently human trait – should be understood as the individual embodying something he/she has observed and not just imitating a model; in other words, it is creating, not just copying (Wulf 2008). Here we have the outcome of that lack of instincts – here, where the ability to make decisions is rooted not in genetics but in the individual's own will, contextualized in the here and now. Rationality and affectivity are two elements that have an influence on this will of the individual by adding a wide array of variables that impact decision-making. Along with this, the specific context exerts a not inconsiderable influence on the individual. Thus, in response to a given stimulus, human behavior cannot be characterized as predictable, for that response is mediated by many factors that impact the decision-making process.

This is highly relevant to the development of modern technology and, most especially, to its applications in education. With every advancement in hardware and software, there appears to be a corresponding increase in the centrality of the user's role in applying the technology. The transition from Web 1.0 to Web 2.0 has been, perhaps, technology's most significant conceptual shift, qualitatively speaking, for it signaled a revolution in the individual's role – from being just an information viewer and recipient to being an information author and creator participating in the information production process. It is no longer just a small group of computer technicians who are building the Internet; roles are now distributed through a sort of digital democratization that, in a sense, reinforces the cultural democratization process that has unfolded in recent decades. A tremendous array of possibilities for human development has opened up, owing to the ease of sharing information and, in many cases, creating innovative applications that offer new forms of expression, behavior, and human interaction in cyberspace. This scenario appears to be more suitable for the anthropological trait of lack of instincts than earlier technological schemes, in that it affords open space for human singularization. Viewers seated in front of a screen that sends all viewers the same information would seem to be consistent with a closed, deterministic anthropological conception, with no space for the initiative required. In contrast, growing technology-mediated participation has expanded the opportunities for human agency in responding to stimuli and has improved human's ability to make decisions and to create – not mere variations on a melody which, according to Scheler (2000), pertains to animals, but rather entirely new melodies, which puts fulfillment as a 'being of action' within reach (Escámez/García López 1998).

From an educational standpoint, there are two major consequences of this approach. First, the prevailing technological paradigm opens up opportunities for individual initiative and, therefore, achievement rooted in a basic anthropological trait. In addition, this initiative has, increasingly, a second dimension that is highly relevant to education. Technology opens up not only avenues for individual expression but also the opportunity to participate in creating those avenues of expression. In other words, it creates opportunities to participate in designing both technological devices and applications (Prensky, 2008) – designs that often include educational and Augmented Reality activities, as occurs with *studio-based learning*, through games or research into the surroundings (Wu *et al.* 2013). Second, it facilitates the designing of individualized educational pathways, which represents a fresh appreciation of human singularity and humans' specific learning needs.

It would be fitting, however, to present two thoughts on these contributions. On the one hand, excessive openness in creative spaces could lead us to encouraging what Thomas (1995) referred to as post-industrial society's "self-actualization through creativity", the major consequences of which include an increasing narcissism and a false socialization of creativity, which aspires to a reinvention and persistent originality resulting, paradoxically, in massification and social homogenization. On the other hand, in today's educational milieu – and despite the paradigm shift – we still find technology-mediated schemes that severely limit this human capability. In effect, aspiring to make educational actions more systematized, efficient, and scientific has often led to technology being used as a control mechanism, as seen today in certain systems, such as certain MOOCs (Carver/Harrison 2013, Margaryan *et al.* 2015) and even *learning analytics* and Augmented Reality itself (Wu *et al.* 2013).

ICTs have not brought about the educational transformation they promised, one reason being, most likely, that the organizational changes required did not follow the investments in equipment. Among those changes, one of the most crucial is student interaction and student participation in the learning process (Akbiyik 2010), which entails modifying not only the technology but also the instructional design. While changing the tools is hardly simple and straightforward, changing the model is far more complex.

2.2 Human precariousness in the environment and technological transformation

As a characteristic specific to humans, some anthropologists, such as Arnold Gehlen and Adolf Portmann, have pointed out that humans are poorly suited, biologically, to their environment. The most obvious manifestation of this is the fact that humans need adult supervision and upkeep during the first years of life and are limited in terms of biological specialization. Conversely, however, humans have not only the ability to care for and nurture their young but also the extensive intellectual development that makes it possible for them to adapt the environment to their needs. Humans are at a considerable advantage in that they are not bound to a specific ecosystem, which endows them with great versatility and enables them to live in a variety of surroundings (Aselmeier 1983). The means we employ to live in those surroundings are what we refer to as *culture*.

Technological advancement is the product of this intellectual capacity together with that culture. Therefore, so is Augmented Reality – demonstrating, simultaneously, a further step in transforming the environment. Augmented Reality gives us a privileged vision of reality that could be referred to as a *heightened sensory experience*, so to speak, for it is a more advanced vision than we could get through our senses alone. The valuable information we obtain in real time enables us to make a more comprehensive and, therefore, more accurate assessment of the situation which, in turn, will facilitate effective decision-making.

Augmented Reality introduces several innovations, however, with reference to the traditional human experience of understanding reality. First, the transforming of the environment takes place on a level prior to the present reality itself, where there is not necessarily any direct impact on the environment. In other words, the intervention is carried out on the channel through which the environment is observed but does not modify what is observed – at least not initially. What is modified, actually, is the observer's intellectual experience, and this greatly multiplies social-cognitive opportunities – or, to put it another way, the learning opportunities for a group of individuals. If the observers are spared the work of modifying the environment, they may each have a more intense subjective learning experience.

Second, as we were pointing out, even though humans' intellectual capacity enables them to modify the environment without having to modify themselves significantly or to develop specialized defense or survival organs, there is a feedback effect that happens with Augmented Reality. This is because the human intellect is capable of generating new, augmented ways of understanding the environment that enhance the options for adapting it to human needs. In short, if my intellectual ability makes it easy for me to understand the environment, I will be better able to transform it and adapt it to my needs. But if my intellectual ability develops new ways of understanding the environment that are qualitatively superior to the traditional ways, I will be able to act upon the environment even more efficiently and more intelligently. This was demonstrated with the previous point, which enables me to act upon it and obtain knowledge of it without ever modifying it, through subjective experiences I share with several individuals.

Third, while *heightened sensory experience* refers to seeing and hearing, mainly, it is worth stressing that there is a growing interest in including other senses that would provide a well-rounded experience. For example, we now have theaters where movies are projected in four dimensions, including thermal effects, wind, heat and cold, even rain and various scents, like wet earth or flowers that appear in a meadow before us, a freshly baked cake, big city smog, etc. The sense of touch deserves special mention, especially in light of the upsurge in

3D printers, which can produce and reproduce objects that can be not only viewed like a picture or photograph but also handled.

Human beings are a reality open to the world and remain that way throughout their existence. Of the conditions that make learning and education possible, this is the most obvious – known also as malleability, unfinishedness or, in a more specific sense, educability. Along this line, Barrio (2000) has stated that the more human beings know, the more they grow as individuals; what's more, they incorporate what they know in such a way that it becomes part of them. This, in turn, implies that the potential for growth is determined by the opportunities for learning and understanding which, to a great degree, depend upon the context in which the individual is found. An environment where new information that could become knowledge is lacking and where there is little opportunity to access resources or interact with people would be an environment that is not very favorable to human development. In contrast, a milieu rich in information networks, with connections to different resources and a variety of people, constitutes a situation very favorable to steady growth.

Augmented Reality is located in the latter type of environment, which is enriched because it supplies not only information – which, generally speaking, the Internet also supplies – but also specific information linked with the structuring of the information the user receives. Even though the individual chooses where to cast his/her eyes in a mixed observation of reality, there is, in fact, a pre-established architecture that arranges the hyperlinks and connections. The upshot of this pre-set design is a mediated navigation that could deprive individuals of autonomy; they should be aware of this and develop what Burbules (2004) has called *critical hyper-reading*. Once we accept, however, that there is no net neutrality, the Augmented Reality experience may be thought of as training in evaluation of online content – which is precisely one of the principal things Education demands of the Internet (Esteban/Fuentes 2015).

2.3 Ontological knowledge and the animal of realities

The philosopher Xavier Zubiri (1986) attributes to human beings, vis-à-vis their relationship to reality, a number of unique characteristics that distinguish them from other living beings. We will point out two of these here. On the one hand, he states that humans are capable of a far deeper understanding of the environment than animals, for animals perceive the environment only in terms of stimuli, whereas humans are able to grasp its true reality. As Barrio (2000) puts it, this is an ontological type of knowledge, in that humans are able to grasp and comprehend the entire scope of their reality. Augmented Reality enhances this ontological knowledge, and that has major ramifications for education.

When we visit a city and access information about a building that can be acquired only through Augmented Reality, we are enriching our knowledge of the environment. The same happens when we visit a museum where we see paintings and, simultaneously, access information about the artists, the society in which they lived, the meaning of the symbols and colors they used in their work, etc., thereby enhancing both the experience and our knowledge. Likewise, this is how we turn the viewing of a painting into a transmedia learning experience (Fuentes 2015), for we can not only view it but also listen to an audio narration about its context; read a text; watch a video; compare it with other works by the same artist or other artists of that period, thus comparing two schools of painting; and even debate perceptions of the painting with other people. We can listen to the music that the artists listened to or that inspired them while they were painting; we can have an interpretive guide for each part of a painting. All of this contributes to our ontological knowledge of reality in that it enables us to comprehend more fully what the painting means, its socio-historical context, and even the perspective that influenced how the artist proceeded with the work.

Transmediation also finds a connection with the two anthropological traits previously mentioned – specifically, heightened sensory experience and initiative. The opportunity to participate and interact, in particular, is one of the basic features of transmedia narratives (Fuentes *et al.* 2015; Jover *et al.* 2015) – mainly those defined as *framework or open transmedia* (Pence 2012), which are freely created by multiple users producing visions of a particular world, as opposed to *experience or closed transmedia*, which are produced by a single agent. In this regard, as spaces suitable for transmediation – largely because of their association with mobile devices (Rojas 2013) – Augmented Reality schemes must take into account the setting in which it is desired that they be implemented; in the educational sphere, consistent with the anthropological trait of lack of instincts, this calls for a greater degree of openness to user creation and participation.

On the other hand, Zubiri defines the human being as an 'animal of realities' in that individuals are capable of devising a reality that transcends their immediate environment. In other words, humans can have a cosmovision without having to be physically present in all the places that shape it – or, to put it another way, can shift from one scene to another without actually having to appear in any of them. This anthropological trait is more evident in the context of technology. Let us consider two examples. First, communication with people far away is possible when the speaker is contextualized. It is not enough just to receive the message; a coherent contextualization – the environment where the message originated, the circumstances that gave rise to it, etc. – is required to understand the message properly. As Polaino (2008) explains, this is why, when we have a cell phone conversation, we usually start by asking, 'Where are you?' – simply because we need to situate or contextualize the other person. When we call a known landline, this is obviously not necessary because contextualization precedes the call. What makes this possible, as Zubiri describes, is our ability to grasp several realities simultaneously without the need to be physically present in them.

The second example has to do with Augmented Reality, through which we sidestep the actual reality and shift to other realities not present that, though not exactly the same, are associated with the reality we are seeing; they are other superimposed realities that complement the original one. This ability to shift, however, is temporal as well as spatial; using Augmented Reality devices, a twelfth-century castle's dimensions and features throughout its history may be projected onto the actual view of it, including the peculiarities of the different cultures and the wishes of the various generations who have resided there. In this sense, the human being is not only an 'animal of realities' but also an 'animal of times'. Naturally, we could think of this ability as being prior to Augmented Reality, for both the memory that attends conscious existence itself and the narrative of History – in books, films, art, and other formats – enable us to be conscious of different temporal realities. There is no doubt, however, that Augmented Reality can play a very important role with regard to the confluence of multimedia narratives and the actual physical presence of a natural or artistic object.

Another angle on this anthropological trait that is worth considering from a pedagogical standpoint is the spaces and times for education, in the institutional sense of the word – formal schooling, in other words. Cuendet *et al.* (2013) have sounded a warning about the restrictions placed on school spaces to accommodate Augmented Reality designs, recommending that these be tested in both a laboratory and in an actual school environment to ensure their effectiveness. It is also worth reflecting upon the opposite, however – that is, if a human being is an animal of different realities and times, and if modern technology like Augmented Reality exaggerates this trait, then there is the possibility of ubiquitous learning (Burbules 2012), and we would call into question the physical restrictions of formal schooling and, therefore, call attention to how this would effectively limit the development of a basic anthropological trait and the opportunities for human progress that technology offers.

2.4 Leisure as a non-vital human need

One dimension of the human being that is scarcely addressed in pedagogical anthropology but is of growing interest in today's societies and closely associated with technology and with education is the human need for leisure. Heidegger has made us more aware of the fact that individuals are temporal beings whose existence is measured not only in terms of years, months, and days but also in terms of their activities. Since human beings have physical and mental limitations, work cannot take up all of their available time. So, they have free time, as well – periods when there are no obligations, no requirements, and no particular activity associated with it – in conjunction with which we have *leisure*, explained some years ago by Pedró (1984) as constituting a specific activity of an invigorating nature, with no financial, utilitarian, or proselytic aims, the purpose of which lies solely in happiness- and pleasure-oriented activities. This simple definition, however, places serious restrictions on activities that we routinely engage in but mistakenly think of as leisure. A weekend outing to the mountains, for example, could erroneously be considered leisure, if the goal is to recover physical or emotional strength after a stressful week. In this case, the rest or recuperation of energy is for the purpose of returning to work, which harks back to Marxist logic in which leisure is nothing more than the motor force of productivity. The wealth of examples of this type that we could mention should be cause for reflection – and such reflection should also be applied to the innumerable continuing education activities we undertake and categorize as leisure. The seemingly harmless confusion on this point highlights a characteristic of today's society – it's extreme utilitarianism, which has a major impact on how the human being is understood.

It appears that the human need for leisure and its relationship first to technique and later to technology have existed in most societies since prehistoric times. According to Pedró (1984), we have evidence of ludic activities in widely diverse cultures going back 6,000 years. However, it was not until the development of farming and ranching techniques – a major technical advancement – that a sedentary life was possible. Then, when some were producing more than they needed for themselves and others could spend less time working, leisure got a significant boost. This excess production of subsistence foods also led to the emergence of social classes, however, with a minority in possession of most of the goods contracting with the majority to perform the work. This pattern – a minority free to spend time on non-productive activities with a specific purpose, in and of itself, and no obligations attached – was destined to be repeated in many later eras. Starting with the Athenians' array of recreational, philosophical, artistic, and sports activities that enjoyed the support of philosophers like

Aristotle, who viewed leisure as a superior activity, it continued with Rome, where the games democratized ludic activities, in a sense, but the elite still had a much more refined, much less cruel and bloody leisure than the Roman games, which were also critiqued by philosophers, like Seneca, for their political component and for being 'bread and circuses' entertainment for the masses. The Middle Ages and the Renaissance left a similar pattern, with various specificities; during the Industrial Revolution, working hours were established – quite lengthy at first and later reduced – which allowed the idea of free time to spread to the entire population and opened up opportunities for leisure.

Even though extending leisure to most of the population was a major innovation, leisure still retains some of its more negative features from previous periods in history that make it difficult to see it as such. First, the strong differentiation of social classes is also marked by leisure, which represents an inherent contradiction. Leisure activity, which has no purpose other than enjoyment, in and of itself, is used as a means of distinction and not as pure enjoyment. Second, the 'escape' nature of leisure is two-sided, in that it is for alleviating stress but would also be used, Roman-style, to escape social and political reality. The proliferation of low-cost leisure harks back to the free games in the Coliseum, as portrayed in *The Hunger Games*. Moreover, in this series of novels and films, the methods that make leisure possible are improved, thanks to technological advances and to the culture of spectacle – elements that are connected in that the latter feeds on the grandiose products of the former. Lastly, capitalist logic, rooted in infinite economic growth, has had a two-fold impact on leisure: a) it has integrated leisure into its structure, whether as rest that is absolutely necessary for the activity we were mentioning above or as activity that entails a financial cost – low, in some cases, but a cost that helps to sustain the mercantile system – and b) it has stretched the concept of usefulness to extraordinary limits, thus reducing the anthropological vision of the human being to its *homo faber* dimension.

In contrast, leisure supports a much more comprehensive vision of the human being (Dumazedier 1968) by reinforcing the concept of *homo faber* – not in the foregoing sense but in the sense of craftsmanship production. The final result of this may be thought of as a work in itself, where the singular contribution is observed and one is distracted from the feeling of being part of the mechanism of a system that Chaplin masterfully portrayed in *Modern Times*. It also strengthens the *homo ludens* dimension, alluding to *play* as a key but not unique aspect of leisure – and not limited to children but available to the entire population. Leisure also makes it possible to speak of an imaginary man as a sign of the present-day rationalist insufficiency and the need that humans have to spice up their monotonous existence by visualizing dreams. It brings to life a dimension of *homo sapiens* that is related to accessing information for no reason other than a desire to know and the enjoyment of learning, and where the Internet and social networks play a vital role. Lastly, leisure allows us to speak of a *homo socius*, in that leisure has a significant social and community-oriented component.

Still, with human beings, leisure has a specific and even more profound role – wherein lies its primary educational benefit. This is revealed through a philosophical analysis addressing the concept of usefulness. Pieper (2006) noted this in a study of festivities as an element of leisure, recognizing festivities as a way to decompress from menial labor and an absence of the 'for what' or 'for whom' in this type of human activity that imparts meaning to a full life.

These reflections on leisure highlight its importance in today's world that is striving to put into practice Nussbaum's economic development model, in which autotelic activities are considered useless. Technological innovations can delve more deeply into this way of understanding reality while, at the same time, affording an opportunity to rethink leisure. Augmented Reality, in particular, should be viewed not just in terms of its role in education or instruction but also as a way to enjoy a properly-understood leisure. Bearing this in mind, Augmented Reality cannot be used simply as a self-paced method of accessing more information more quickly; rather, it should help one to experience reality in a more leisurely manner. Experiencing it this way has to do with contemplation, which involves a non-interventionist, non-manipulative, attentive attitude that enables one to acknowledge what is observed exactly as it is, with no intention of transforming it. Only in such tranquility can one discover the profound reality of things – the ontological knowledge we were mentioning in the previous section – and to move on from a relative vision to a broader, more general perspective (Pieper 2006); otherwise, augmenting reality could become just another pointless, superficial activity.

This does not contradict what has been said previously, when we were speaking of human initiative and the lack of instincts, where participation and interactivity were recognized as positive. On the contrary: in human beings, contemplation and intervention should be recognized as complementary activities. Moreover, this transforms leisure itself to an educational activity, given that education is the humanizing of the person, in Kant's terms, and leisure allows that humanity to be made reality – which goes beyond financially-motivated production. In other words, education strengthens the idea of *person*, also part of Kant's conception, which envisions the non-exploitable dimension of persons and calls for them to be treated not only as a means but also as an end in themselves.

As we have seen, technological advances made leisure possible at the beginning of human history and remain at its core today, for the majority of leisure activities involve technology. There is one very important role that leisure plays in education, however, and it has to do with the individual's ethics education. An anthropology that makes no reference to ethics is a half-baked anthropology (Millán-Puelles 2007); and, as Da Vinci wrote (1995, 264), "The man who does not control his instincts lowers himself to the level of beasts". This is the reason for calling attention to the ethical potential of leisure, properly understood, for it facilitates integrating the non-exploitative treatment of other people into the understanding of reality. Individuals who are in pursuit of financial gain across their entire range of behavior will be capable of pursuing advantage only for themselves – not for other individuals around them. The contemplative aspect of leisure also allows other individuals to be recognized as reality, thus precluding manipulative attitudes. This means accepting others as something good, and this suppresses transformative attitudes destined, inevitably, to become actions (Thomas 1995).

One clarification should be made here, for education is usually understood – particularly by the socio-critical paradigm – as a tool for social transformation. Nothing can be built, however, without identifying something of value upon which to build. If hope is education's engine, confidence is its indispensable ally.

Also, as Unamuno (1967, 73) showed, education is not just method, nor does it achieve its objective with "barometers, thermometers, rain gauges, wind gauges, dynamometers, maps, diagrams, telescopes, microscopes, spectroscopes: for wherever you look, your eyes are steeped in science". Education is also love, and love is an essential component of leisure, for without love neither contemplation nor enjoyment, in and of themselves, would make sense. In short, Augmented Reality designs can help to promote this ethical-educational concept of leisure, insofar as, technologically, they occupy a good portion of people's free time. Schools and educators have a key role in this, consisting of not limiting its use in the natural sciences and also exploring the wide world of opportunities afforded by the social sciences and the humanities. This will also prevent another of the negative effects that have attended leisure throughout history: that it distinguishes social classes, with the lower classes of society being denied high culture. To be specific, some current studies have shown that there is a digital divide separating young people who are in social difficulty from other social groups and that it results from the former having no access to high-quality content and uses such as Augmented Reality (Melendro *et al.* 2016), their use of technology being extremely limited and of very little educational value. But if the educational system aspires to become society's elevator, it must ensure that all students – especially those most vulnerable – have access to the highest forms of culture, which put us closer in touch with our most human side (Steiner/Lajdali 2006) and, in the words of Schopenhauer (2015), comfort, alleviate, and strengthen us, which may help us to transform Augmented Reality into *cultivated reality.* The ninth ability on the list suggested by Nussbaum (2011) names enjoyment and play as elements that impart value to a human life. Although none of the other abilities involve the use of technology, the author's openness to updating makes it reasonable to suppose that an ability of that type will soon be added to the list. That would have some major ramifications for education, in that it is dependent upon the State as advocate for public policies.

3. Conclusions

The case of South African athlete Oscar Pistorius may cause us to reflect upon the paradox of human progress through technological advancement. While his prosthetic legs were evidence of achievements in the evolution of human thought in one of its dimensions, the fact that his fiancé Reeva was murdered by four shots fired in his own home shows that the concept of human improvement must go beyond the study of applied technology and is directly related to educational action, as a valid strategy for shaping the ethical aspect of the individual.

Like a general analysis of technology, a pedagogical analysis of Augmented Reality should lead us to consider whether using it will get the result that Kant attributed to education – humanization – particularly when some philosophers like Bostrom (2009, 551) are saying that, even beyond natural disasters, "[t]he most severe existential risks of this century derive from expected technological developments".

In this chapter, we have attempted to contribute to these reflections beginning with four anthropological elements that are key to education: the lack of instincts and its impact on initiative, which plays a crucial role in the current technological model; human precariousness and the ability of humans to adapt the environment, which takes on a peculiar form in Augmented Reality, in that the environment is not substantially modified and offers a privileged perspective with feedback on intellectual capacity; the ontological knowledge of reality through information obtained and the opportunity for interaction and transmediation; and leisure, which maintains strong ties to technology, facilitates a comprehensive vision of the human being, and plays a major role in human ethical education – because of which it should be taken into account for Augmented Reality designs, especially those in the social sciences and the humanities.

The complexity of human beings and the importance of their relationship with technology are matters that call for ongoing, in-depth study exploring other significant anthropological traits. Among these, sociability stands out, for we have known since Aristotle's day that humans need other people – not only to survive but also to live humanely. Likewise, as a cultural element, technology represents a joint endeavor. To be more specific, far from being limited to experiences afforded by visual devices for individual use – and in keeping with the social nature of the Internet – Augmented Reality is coming to be used more and more on a group and shared basis, which is of great educational value, as well.

As we educators and pedagogues tackle the challenges of using technology in our daily endeavors, there will be many questions we cannot avoid. Among them, and in connection with the subject of this chapter, the following seem pertinent to me: Are robotized human beings the anthropological ideal? Should education switch to mechanization as its path to human development? Could we stop using technology so that we can *be* technology? As on many occasions, literary and audiovisual narratives help to light the path to the answers. In a chapter of the series *Black Mirror*, certain issues are raised with regard to coexistence in a future when ocular implants enable us to record everything that passes before our eyes – thus tremendously expanding our memory capacity, along the lines of what some authors have suggested as a characteristic of post-humans. Pedagogical anthropology, along with philosophy and ethics, must address questions not only about the possibility of changing the term 'human being' but also about whether that would take us closer to what we wish to be as a species.

References

Akbiyik, C. (2010): "¿Puede la informática afectiva llevar a un uso más efectivo de las Tecnologías de la Información y de la Comunicación (TIC) en la Educación?" In: *Revista de Educación* 352, 179–202.

Aselmeier, U. (1983): *Antropología biológica y pedagógica*, Madrid: Alhambra.

Barrio, J. M. (2015): "La Universidad en la encrucijada." In: F. Gil/D. Reyero (eds.), *Educar en la universidad de hoy. Propuestas para la renovación de la vida universitaria*, Madrid: Encuentro, 13–33.

Barrio, J. M. (2000): *Elementos de antropología pedagógica*, Madrid: Rialp.

Bostrom, N. (2008): "Why I Want to Be a Posthuman When I Grow Up." In: B. Gordijn/R. Chadwick (eds.), *Medical Enhancement and Posthumanity*, Dordrecht: Springer, 107–137.

Bostrom, N. (2009): "The Future of the Humanity." In: J. K. B. Olsen/S. A. Pedersen/V. F. Hendricks (eds.), *A Companion to the Philosophy of Technology*, Malden and Oxford: Wiley-Blackwell, 551–556.
Bouché, H./Fermoso, P./Larrosa, J./Sacristán, D. (1995): "La antropología de la educación como disciplina: Proyecto de diseño." In: *Teoría de la Educación: Revista Interuniversitaria* 7, 95–114.
Burbules, N. C. (2004): "La red como un lugar retórico." In: I. Sneyder (ed.), *Alfabetismos digitales: comunicación, innovación y educación en la era electrónica*, Archidona: Aljibe, 115–128.
Burbules, N. C. (2012): "Ubiquitous Learning and the Future of Teaching." In: *Encounters in Theory and History of Education* 13, 3–14.
Carver, L./Harrison, L. M. (2013): "MOOCs and Democratic Education." In: *Liberal Education* Fall, 20–25.
Cortina, A./Serra, M. A. (2015): "Introducción." In: A. Cortina/M. A. Serra (eds.), *¿Humanos o posthumanos? Singularidad tecnológica y mejoramiento humano.* Barcelona: Fragmenta.
Cuendet, S./Bonnard, Q./Do-Lenh, S./Dillenbourg, P. (2013): "Designing Augmented Reality for the classroom." In: *Computers & Education* 68, 557–569.
Da Vinci, L. (1995): *Cuadernos de notas*, Madrid: M. E. Editores.
Dumazedier, J. (1968): *Hacia una civilización del ocio*, Barcelona: Estela.
Escámez, J./García López, R. (1998): "Antropología y Educación." In R. Gil (ed.), *Filosofía de la Educación hoy*, Madrid: Dykinson, 451–463.
Esteban, F./Fuentes, J. L. (2015): "La educación universitaria virtual: una reflexión en torno al cultivo de las virtudes." In: *Teoría de la Educación. Revista interuniversitaria* 27(1), 103–118.
Fuentes, J. L. (2015): "Narrativas transmedia ¿qué son y para qué nos sirven en la educación?" In: *Harvard Deusto. Learning & Pedagogics* 3, 6–11.
Fuentes, J. L./Esteban, F./Caro, C. (2015): *Vivir en internet: retos y reflexiones para la educación*, Madrid: Síntesis.
Jover, G./González, M. R./Fuentes, J. L. (2015): "Exploración de nuevas vías de construcción mediática de la ciudadanía en la escuela: de Antígona a la narrativa transmedia." In: *Teoría de la Educación. Revista interuniversitaria* 27(1), 69–84.
Margaryan, A./Bianco, M./Littlejohn, A. (2015): "Instructional quality of Massive Open Online Courses (MOOCs)." In: *Computers & Education* 80, 77–83.
Melendro, M./García Castilla, F. J./Goig, S. (2016): "El uso de las TIC en el ocio y la formación de los jóvenes vulnerables." In: *Revista Española de Pedagogía* 74(263), 71–89.
Millán-Puelles, A. (2007): *Ética y realismo*, Madrid: Rialp.
Nietzsche, F. (2000): *Así habló Zaratustra*, Madrid: Alba.
Noddings, N. (2002): *Educating Moral People: A Caring Alternative to Character Education*, New York: Teachers College Press.
Nussbaum, M. (2011): *Creating Capabilities: The Human Development Approach*, Cambridge (MA) and London: Harvard University Press.
Nussbaum, M. (2012): *Not for Profit: Why Democracy Needs the Humanities*, Princeton and Oxford: Princeton University Press.
Pedró, F. (1984): *Ocio y tiempo libre: ¿para qué?*, Barcelona: Humanitas.

Pence, H. E. (2012): "Teaching with Transmedia." In: *Journal of Educational Technology Systems* 40(2), 131–140.
Pieper, J. (2006): *Una teoría de la fiesta*, Madrid: Rialp.
Polaino, A. (2008). *Aprender a escuchar. La necesidad vital de comunicarse*, Barcelona: Planeta.
Prensky, M. (2008): "Students as Designers and Creators of Educational Computer Games: Who Else?" In. *British Journal of Educational Technology* 39(6), 1004–1019.
Rojas, E. (2013): "Dispositivos móviles y el audiovisual social." In: *Revista Comunicación* 30, 111–116.
Scheler, M. (2000): *El puesto del hombre en el cosmos*, Barcelona: Alba Editorial.
Schopenhauer, A. (2015): *Sobre la lectura y los libros*, Madrid: Sequitur.
Steiner, G./Ladjali, C. (2006): *Elogio de la transmisión*, Madrid: Siruela.
Thomas, H. (1995): "Bürgerliche Arbeitsgesellschaft oder nachindustrielle Freizeitgesellschaft: Entfremdung ist der Verlust des Festes." In: F. Bydlinski/T. Mayer-Maly (eds.), *Die Arbeit: ihre Ordnung, ihre Zukunft, ihr Sinn*, Vienna: Wilhelm Braumüller Universitäts-Verlagsbuchhandlung, 159–176.
Unamuno, M. (1967): *Amor y pedagogía. 3 novelas ejemplares y 1 prólogo*, Madrid: Magisterio Español.
Wilson, E. O. (2014): *The Meaning of Human Existence*, London: W. W. Norton & Company Ltd.
Wu, H./Wen-Yu, S./Chang, H./Liang, J. (2013): "Current Status, Opportunities and Challenges of Augmented Reality in Education." In: *Computers & Education* 62, 41–49.
Wulf, C. (2008): *Antropología. Historia, cultura, filosofía*, Barcelona: Anthropos.
Zubiri, X. (1986): *Sobre el hombre*, Madrid: Alianza.

Almudena Castellanos and Carlota Pérez

New Challenge in Education: Enhancing Student's Knowledge through Augmented Reality

Abstract: The evolution of Augmented Reality has been fast and global, and as it could not be otherwise, its potential in education has begun to be explored. Indeed, we truly believe this technology could be especially valuable in the classroom. First of all, it allows teachers to show virtual objects in the real-world environment which otherwise would be impossible to show. On the other hand, it can also be used to enhance collaborative tasks, as well as encourage socializing and inclusive activities for people with special needs. This chapter gives a brief overview of how the implementation of Augmented Reality can be improved in the school environment not only by showing its versatility and possibilities, but also by describing a number of proposals for applications in different educational levels.

Keywords: Augmented Reality, Mobile Augmented Reality, Educational Technology, Pedagogy, Learning, Didactical Methodologies.

1. Introduction

The 2005 Horizon Report (Johnson et al. 2005), which foresaw the technologies expected to have a major impact on educational context in the next five years, spoke about Augmented Reality for the first time as an instrument capable of offering additional information to individuals about their physical environment and providing enriching learning experiences; moreover, this report predicted the implementation of this emerging technology in the educational context around the years 2009 – 2010. Though the 2006 Horizon Report repeated that the widespread implementation of Augmented Reality technology in the educational system should take place within four or five years (Johnson et al. 2006), while the Horizon Reports 2010 and 2011 (Johnson et al. 2010, 2011) delayed later the generalized implementation of Augmented Reality in the educational field until 2012 – 2014, the fact is that the forecast remains unfulfilled. In this chapter we aim to show that the use of Augmented Reality technology in schools should be encouraged, as it improves the teaching-learning process and, by extension, students' acquisition of knowledge. Thus, we will begin by explaining

DOI 10.1515/9783110497656-015

why this technology is still not a mainstream technology in education. Subsequently, we will present a series of resources which allow that even the layman can create Augmented Reality applications. Lastly, we will describe many uses made of Augmented Reality technology in different educational stages and curriculum areas.

2. Definition of Augmented Reality

According to Lee (2012), the term 'Augmented Reality' was coined in the 1990's by Tom Caudell. To date, Augmented Reality technology has been used in many fields, such as medicine (Kilgus et al. 2015), architecture, clinical psychology (Chicchi et al. 2015), and education, among others. As previously stated, in this chapter we will draw attention to the possibilities that Augmented Reality opens up in the process of learning, for they have already been highly appreciated by educational experts and researchers (Bower et al. 2014, Lee 2012, Nincarean et al. 2013, Wu et al. 2013).

However, although studies on Augmented Reality have intensified during the last few years, the term 'Augmented Reality' has been defined in different ways. Thus, we will begin by clarifying this concept. We will not focus on the technology needed for using Augmented Reality, but on its characteristics and possibilities. It can therefore be stated that, even though Augmented Reality is based on the technology that makes it possible, its conceptualization cannot be restricted to such technology. From this point of view, Augmented Reality could be regarded in a wider context as any technology capable of combining real and virtual information in a meaningful way (Klopfer/Sheldon 2010). To shed light on this point, Milgram et al. (1994) referred to a Reality-Virtuality Continuum that ranges from the purely real context to a purely virtual one. If we move away from the poles of this continuum, we can find mixed reality, which is defined as the joint presentation of objects of the real world and objects of the virtual one. Mixed reality is thus composed of Augmented Reality and augmented virtuality (AV). Specifically, Augmented Reality results from combining the virtual world with the real one, with the particularity that the latter is presented to a larger extent that the former. By contrast, AV consists in adding real world objects to a virtual context, but the information provided to the user is mostly virtual.

> Within this framework it is straightforward to define a generic Mixed Reality (MR) environment as one in which real world and virtual world objects are presented together within a single display, that is, anywhere between the extrema of the RV continuum. (Milgram et al. 1994, 283)

This concept of mixed reality is illustrated by a simplified representation of the Reality-Virtuality Continuum in Figure 1:

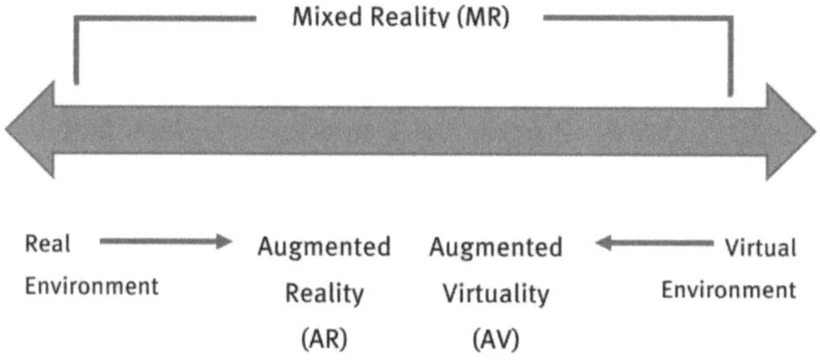

Fig. 1: Reality-Virtuality (RV) Continuum. Milgram et al. (1994, 283).

3. Augmented Reality Technologies: From QR codes to immersive virtual reality

We apply the term 'Augmented Reality' to all those technologies that make possible to superimpose in real time virtual images, markers or information upon real-world scenes (cf. De Pedro/Martínez 2012, Durlach/Mavor 1995, Fombona et al. 2012, Fundación Telefónica 2011). The result is an enriched or Augmented Reality which is obtained by overlaying digital information onto the physical reality perceived through our five senses: in other words, it is a new lens through which we can see a more complete picture of the world (Fundación Telefónica 2011).

Computers with Internet connection have allowed us to live in an interconnected world, but the fact that connectivity has been extended to other devices such as smartphones, tablets, watches and even eyeglasses, makes it possible to receive the information we need in a very natural, easy and fast way. Indeed, we no longer need to wait for the moment when we can isolate ourselves by sitting down in front of a computer. Just as the human being got a broader view of the world when standing upright than when walking stooped, we also have a broader view of reality by using computers. Thanks to devices like smartphones, Augmented Reality is being increasedly used (Fundación Telefónica 2011), for its scope has been extended to include entertainment, marketing, tourism, education and health.

The term 'Augmented Reality' is also applied to a set of technologies more sophisticated than those mentioned above, as they enable us to reproduce three-dimensional images, recreate virtual worlds, and manipulate virtual objects: this is what is known as immersive virtual reality (Fundación Telefónica 2011). Keeping in mind the increasing complexity of the technology used in Augmented Reality, authors distinguish a series of levels (Prendes 2015):

Level 0. Physical World Hyper Linking. In this level, codes – of bars or two-dimensional ones like the QR codes – are activated and connected to associated contents such as hyperlinks and simple images, texts, audios or videos (see figure 2).

Fig. 2: QR Code. Wikimedia (https://commons.wikimedia.org/wiki/File:Codigo_QR.svg)

There exist different resources that make possible the personalized creation of this type of codes which is currently used in the educational and other fields. Here are some examples: Kaywa (http://qrcode.kaywa.com/), Visualead (http://www.visualead.com/), QR Stuff (http://www.qrstuff.com/) o GOQR.me (http://goqr.me/).

Level 1. Marker Based AR. Markers are black and white geometrical shapes – usually squares – which contain simple and asymmetrical designs that allow three-dimensional objects superposition and recognition (see figure 3).

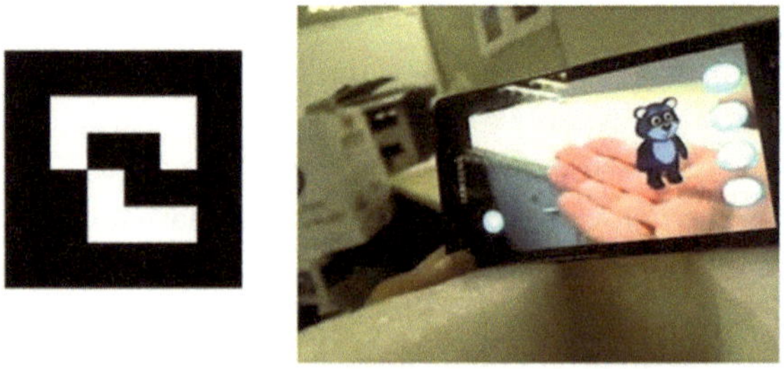

Fig. 3: Marker. Wikimedia (https://en.wikipedia.org/wiki/Augmented_reality)

Level 2. Markerless Augmented Reality. This technology makes possible the superposition of information on a physical world scene by using either images as activators, or objects and persons that activate virtual information even through the use of GPS technology without the need for markers (see figure 4).

Fig. 4: Markerless AR. Wikimedia (https://commons.wikimedia.org/wiki/File:MediatedReality_on_iPhone2009_07_13_21_33_39.jpg)

Level 3. Immersive Virtual Reality or Augmented Vision. In comparison with other levels, this is a disruptive technology inasmuch as computer and mobile device screens are replaced by eyeglasses, lenses or special sensors that immerse us in three-dimensional worlds (see figure 5)

While technology involved in Augmented Reality systems is becoming more complex, their use is also increasingly expanding. According to a recent report (see Research and Markets 2015), the installed base of actively used mobile Augmented Reality apps will increase from 135 million in 2014 to 2.2 billion by 2019;

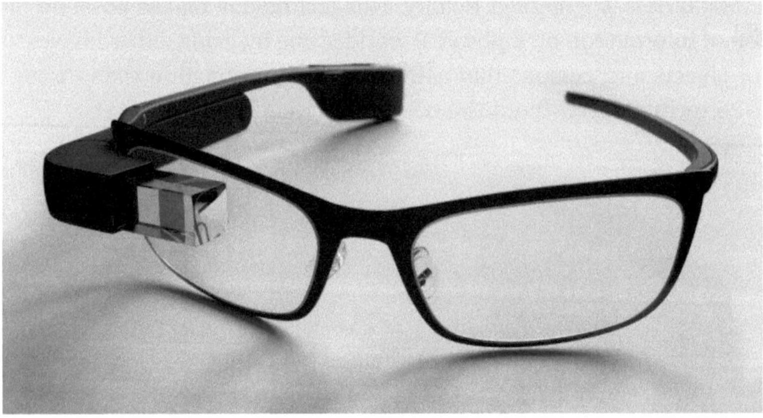

Fig. 5: Augmented vision. Wikimedia (https://en.wikipedia.org/wiki/Google_Glass)

moreover, this growth might create a market of $1.6 billion for mobile Augmented Reality apps in 2019.

4. Augmented Reality in the educational environment

Although the use of Augmented Reality involves increasingly sophisticated devices and tools, the question we are particularly interested in analyzing is how this technology makes learning more meaningful or, in short, improves the learning process. As Bower et al. (2014) pointed out, the superposition of diverse multimedia items to physical world scenes makes Augmented Reality a cognitive support in understanding and performing complex tasks. In this sense, Wu et al. (2013) list a series of contributions of Augmented Reality to the educational field:

A. Projection of specific concepts in three dimensions, which will no doubt facilitate students a better understanding of such concepts.
B. An ubiquitous and collaborative learning through mobile devices and geo-location systems that enable users to be wireless connected at any time and place.
C. The student's feeling of presence, immediacy and immersion in virtual environments, which ends up generating virtual learning communities.
D. Visualization of the invisible, for example, by making it possible to represent concepts like magnetic fields or air currents.

E. Connection between formal and informal learning, as Augmented Reality awakes students' interest in the learning process.

Augmented Reality technologies generate experiences that stay in students' memory longer than if teachers use other resources like traditional or even digital books, slide presentations or video views (García 2014, Jabr 2014, Sommerauer/Müller 2014, Zhang et al. 2014). Furthermore, when digital information in two or three dimensions is added to the pictures of world scenes provided by a Smartphone or a tablet, attention is often automatically drawn to the screen (García 2014), which should be kept in mind when designing didactic resources. After all, it has also been proved that Augmented Reality helps increase students' motivation and improves their academic results (Wei et al. 2015, Bower et al. 2014, Di Serio et al. 2013, Chen/Tsai 2012).

A further advantage of Augmented Reality has to do with the fact that the more senses are involved in a given experience, the better it is retained (García 2014). To this should be added that Augmented Reality makes it possible to manipulate information as if it were an object in space, which increases our knowledge of specific issues. Thus, Augmented Reality can be of great help for the brain when organizing quickly scattered information (Fundación Telefónica 2011). Indeed, when we overlay supplementary items onto physical world scenes, we are already giving meaning to disjointed information by relating it to our prior knowledge. Related to this, Augmented Reality enables students to modify the scale in which virtual objects are shown, so that they can manipulate them in order to better understand characteristics and relationship of objects that are too small – for example, molecules – or too big – for instance, heavenly bodies (Johnson et al. 2010). Sheehy et al. (2014) called this way of learning 'Augmented Learning' to highlight the process in which the real or physical world joins the virtual one through diverse technological devices that enrich our knowledge with new data and experiences.

Like other emerging technologies, Augmented Reality can constitute a strong partner in inclusive education. Indeed, Augmented Reality has already proven to be effective in treating people with autism spectrum disorder. Specifically, Augmented Reality has been useful in capturing their attention and helping them understand non-verbal clues, which created problems in interpreting emotions and facial expressions (Chen et al. 2015, 2016). Augmented Reality has also been used with students with physical disabilities. By way of example, software Scratch 2.0 designed by the Media Laboratory at MIT (http://scratch.mit.edu) was used together with a webcam to catch movements. Participants could watch the computer screen in front of them, while two speakers were put on the floor. Thus, when participants did the correct foot lifting, they received dynamic pictures and sounds as feedback (Lin/Chang 2015).

It can be stated that Augmented Reality technology fits perfectly with those emerging pedagogies that are intended to overcome traditional pedagogy (Muñoz 2014). Traditional schools are characterized by rigid and overloaded curricula as well as the classic figure of the teacher as the unique holder of knowledge which is taught through oral presentations to passive pupils who must learn by heart in a classroom too distant from daily life. Innovative teachers who are aware of this bad practice stand by the principles of the Escuela Nueva (New School) and implement a teaching-learning process through which students learn by doing, as they must construct autonomously their own learning while the teacher orientates and motivates them. That is why we teachers and educational researchers currently talk so much about problem- and project-based learning, multiple intelligences, competences, experiential education, gamification, flipped and flexible learning, among others (Adell/Castañeda 2012). In the last years, terms like 'learning by doing', 'action learning' or 'experience learning' are often used: although they are not synonymous, for each one presents different nuances, they all emphasize the importance of experience, contact with the surrounding reality, and practical applications, so that they can be framed within what has generally been called 'active learning'. This educational trend can be traced back to the figure of John Dewey (1938), who stressed the relevance of experience in formal learning as well as the necessity of relating teaching-learning processes to daily life. Other eminent specialists like Piaget, Bloom, Freire, Gardner or Lewin have also highlighted the importance of experience for achieving learning goals. Nowadays almost nobody casts doubt on the students' need of experimenting and learning to do. We are increasingly aware of the necessity of connecting contents and activities, theory and practice, processes and results, without falling in the sterile activism.

A common feature of all of these pedagogical models is that the student plays an active role, to the extent that he becomes the protagonist of his own learning. By the way, this student's central role is also characteristic of Augmented Reality applications in the educational field (Muñoz 2014). As stated above, Augmented Reality facilitates ubiquitous learning by helping the student learn at any time and place. Thus, Augmented Reality fits with these active pedagogies inasmuch as it makes possible that students from all educational levels and in all subject areas learn comprehensively by doing, investigating, and developing their creativity. In fact, Kesim and Ozarslan (2012) remarked that Augmented Reality combines aspects of the ubiquitous (present anywhere all the time), tangible (clearly perceptible) and social (as it promotes collaboration) technology. In a nutshell, Augmented Reality is fully compatible with a number of pedagogical approaches like the following ones (Bower et al. 2014):

- Constructivist learning. Augmented Reality facilitates that students immerse themselves in their tasks and make more profound and lasting connections in their knowledge framework by using diverse kinds of information.
- Situated learning. Augmented Reality places the student in an actual learning context by incorporating daily life into the classroom.
- Game-based learning. These Augmented Reality games submerge the student in a virtual narrative in which he must play a given role that prepares him to deal with daily life.
- Enquiry-based learning. Augmented Reality makes it possible to experiment with virtual models that are immersed in real world scenes.

5. Reluctances to the application of Augmented Reality in the educational field

As we have seen, the benefits of applying Augmented Reality to the educational field are obvious; however, Augmented Reality is still far from being a mainstream technology in education. To shed light on this issue, we turn now to expose some reasons.

To begin with, innovations that turn out to be rather disruptive – and which thus require changes in very consolidated habits – are much more difficult to accept than those which simply involve a mere quantitative change in what we already know (Moore 2015). Such is the case of Augmented Reality – and also of the Internet as well as of personal computers when they were first introduced – as it entails a new way of contemplating the world, accessing information, interacting with other people, and, by extension, of learning and knowing. Hence, teachers need time to adapt to this technology and to be able to value its potential advantages. The same could be said about parents, for research has proven that many parents are still reluctant to accept Augmented Reality technology as a vehicle for their children's learning (Cheng/Tsai 2016).

Besides problems resulting from the lack of technical knowledge required to elaborate Augmented Reality applications (Kerawalla et al. 2006), there is a shortage of tools specifically designed for the educational field (Martin et al. 2011), which has hampered the successful and generalized use of Augmented Reality in the educational environment. These technical constraints are actually being overcome thanks to the use of some specific applications and others which, as we will see next, allow teachers and students to create Augmented Reality contents even without displaying a high level of technical knowledge. However, teachers are often inadequately prepared to deal with technical problems that may arise at any moment. Of course, such technical training would be necessary in order to avoid that the design of Augmented Reality applications always lies in the hands of computer scientists and technicians who lack pedagogical knowledge or, in other words, are not acquainted with didactic aspects that should be considered when elaborating Augmented Reality educational contents (Billinghurst/Duenser 2012).

Lastly, students who use Augmented Reality applications frequently may become cognitively overburdened due to the vast amount of information they find, the multiple technological devices they must use, and the complex tasks they have to perform (Wu et al. 2013).

6. Uses of Augmented Reality in the educational field

Regarding uses of Augmented Reality in the educational environment, there are some fields and resources worthy of attention (Fundación Telefónica 2011):

- Books: There are currently books with codes, such as the QR, which make it possible to visualize three-dimensional objects and watch videos with the help of an application installed in a technological device.
- Games: Some games show three-dimensional scenarios that can be watched through any mobile device, while others allow players to create virtual objects or people.
- Object modeling: This technology empowers users, amongst other things, to create virtual objects in order to manipulate them, detect anomalies, explore their properties, and interact with other objects.
- Use of standard applications for teaching purposes: A clear example of this is Google Skymap, an open source application that not only allows to see the stars by focusing the camera of a mobile device on them, but also overlays relevant digital information onto their physical image.

New Augmented Reality applications with teaching purposes increasingly emerge throughout the world. Here are some examples:

- Word Lens (http://questvisual.com) serves to translate in other languages words that are focused on by a smartphone camera. Hence, this could be a supporting resource for teaching languages.

- Zooburst (http://zooburst.com) makes it possible for students to create their own digital stories in three dimensions by combining images, texts and audios.
- LearnAR (http://learnar.org) provides a package of ten applications to acquire knowledge about biology, physics, mathematics and diverse languages.

3DU is an Augmented Reality technology that allows users to interact and learn in a virtual university (Estopace 2015).

Particularly noteworthy are those systems like AURASMA (http://aurasma.com), Junaio (http://junaio.com), Layar (http://layar.com) or BuildAR (http://buildar.com) that allow teachers and students to create their own Augmented Reality scenes with images, videos and three-dimensional objects. These systems present very intuitive and simple drag-and-drop interfaces for non-programmers, which greatly simplifies the process of creating Augmented Reality scenes: thus, it is not necessary to be a computer programmer or expert in order to make designs with Augmented Reality. However Cubillo et al. (2015) have developed an easy-to-use application for teachers called UNED ARLE (National University for Distance Education – Augmented Reality Learning Environment), aiming to overcome some constraints that are often encountered when using the above-mentioned applications. As they put it:

> It is not usual that they support interaction or more complex behaviors such as modification of the displayed content, evaluation of content, contextualization of contents. To achieve that, some level of programming is necessary, for example, in Layar, where videos, images, and multimedia content can be inserted; however, to add new 3D objects requires some knowledge of programming languages. There are tools like Aurasma, Augment, Zooburst where interaction is easy and intuitive but limited. Aurasma, the positioning and scaling of objects cannot be modified in real time, while in the case of Augment, which allows real-time interaction, it has limited the number of models in its free version to 2, regarding to Metaio, after purchasing the Metaio Creator application, teachers can connect 3D content, videos, audio, and web pages to any form of printed medium. After careful consideration of the features of the most important tools for developing applications or experiences of AR, the decision was made to develop an authoring tool with the power of tools for programmers, which is as easy to use as tools for non-programmers. A specialized tool for learning would be included, allowing representation of virtual content and interaction with it. The evaluation of acquired contents would be made available through "augmented" questions (MCQs), they enable to increase the interest of students in what they are observing, and all of them are characteristics taken into account in the development of UNED ARLE. (Cubillo *et al.* 2015, 780)

After having made reference to these resources and applications, we would like now to describe a series of current uses of Augmented Reality applications in different curriculum areas and educational stages, which could inspire readers with this new way of educating.

6.1 Early childhood education (3 – 6 years old)

The use of Augmented Reality in early childhood education is increasingly widespread, so that we can find many examples at international level that illustrate the extent to which teachers are trying to implement this technology in the students' learning process. Augmented Reality has been applied very creatively in this educational stage to reinforce playful learning. Let us see three brief examples of this. Firstly, Yilmaz (2016) combined the use of Augmented Reality technology and toys to create an application that empowered teachers to overlay cartoons, three-dimensional objects and flash animations onto toys in order to teach concepts related to animals, fruits, vegetables, vehicles, objects, professions, colours, numbers and forms. Secondly, Tomi and Rambli (2013) explained how storybooks aided by Augmented Reality technology improved the process of learning to read in Malaysia (Tomi/Rambli 2013). Thirdly, Huang et al. (2015) have recently used in Hong Kong kindergarten applications like coIAR for early art education, and informed that the assessments of pupils, teachers as relatives were very positive.

Once said this, we will now expose some activities carried out through Augmented Reality technology in early childhood education:

- Become acquainted with the life and work of historical figures through QR codes. On the occasion of International Day of Peace, students in kindergarten had an initial approach to Nelson Mandela's life through videos and images activated by codes. Children had already received a very special postal card containing different QR codes that could be transformed through the application AURASMA into information about a given figure: for instance, where she was born, or which important things she did (see http://lospequesdemicole.blogspot.com.es/2016/01/mensajero-de-paz-nelson-mandela.html).
- Create interactive city maps. The Project Around the world with Willy Fog was intended for 3 years-old students to discover different countries and cultures. To this end, they could use QR codes to activate videos created by them (see http://lospequesdemicole.blogspot.com.es/2014/07/earthquest-la-vuelta-al-mundo-de-willy.html).
- Design and learn geometrical forms. A robot called Bee Bot is programmed to capture QR codes that are transformed into geometrical forms. In this way, children learn basic mathematics and computer skills (see http://lospe

quesdemicole.blogspot.com.es/2015/12/cuerpos-geometricos-robotica-y-realidad.html).

- Convert objects and pictures into Augmented Reality markers by adding virtual layers of videos that were also created by children themselves. Students made a scale model of the human eye with papier-mâché, recorded videos explaining what they had learned, and linked them to their model of the eye through the application Thinglink (see http://lospequesdemicole.blogspot.com.es/2015/06/maqueta-3d-del-ojo.html).
- Recognize and analyze three-dimensional teaching contents. To become acquainted with the human circulatory system, students used a marker that activates the heart, the veins and arteries as three-dimensional objects in order to manipulate and analyze them (see http://lospequesdemicole.blogspot.com.es/2015/04/el-corazon-las-venas-y-arterias-con-ra.html).
- Stimulate and enrich interactive activities like Webquest and Earthquest. A growing number of teachers are designing this kind of activities based on constructive learning. Students usually enjoy when they must discover the solution of diverse problems by using Internet, but they take an even greater interest in these activities if they are combined with the use of Augmented Reality (see http://lospequesdemicole.blogspot.com.es/2015/03/iniciamos-webquest-del-universo.html).
- Reach other students and classrooms. New technologies are becoming widely used to twin classrooms and schools within a single country or even from different continents. In this sense, Augmented Reality may be of great help when working together on joint projects, as it facilitates that students share videos and images (see http://lospequesdemicole.blogspot.com.es/2015/01/queremos-conocer-un-aula-hospitalaria.html).
- Develop reading and writing skills in a creative way. By way of example, the written form of letters can be converted in markers in order to associate them with the spelling and gesture that each student will have previously recorded (see http://lospequesdemicole.blogspot.com.es/2013/11/nos-iniciamos-en-la-lectoescritura.html).
- Create audiovisual contents to provide information on specific objects, or to send greeting cards which include videos recorded by the students themselves (see http://infantic-tac.blogspot.com.es/2013/12/navidades-digitales.html).
- Turn diverse school areas into interactive learning spaces. When a specific issue is tackled at school, QR codes with digital content elaborated by the students may be placed on walls and doors.

- Bring students' pictures to life. There are applications like Quiver (see http://quivervision.com/) which make it possible to colour drawings that are then transformed into three-dimensional objects.
- Acquire basic concepts such as volume. Thanks to applications like Chromville, students can play in virtual three-dimensional worlds (see https://chromville.com/).
- Know the surrounding environment. Students may go out on the street with their teachers to discover the environment by gathering information from QR codes through devices like Smartphones or tablets (see http://enmiaula deinfantil.blogspot.com.es/2016/01/nuevo-proyecto-y-que-hacemos.html).

6.2 Primary education (6 – 12 years old)

As could be expected, Augmented Reality technology has also been used in primary education. Here are some examples:

- First approach to basic musical principles. There are applications like AR learning that allow students to visualize musical instruments in three dimensions, listen their characteristic sound, write notes on a staff, and become acquainted with sound qualities such as pitch, intensity and tone (see http://www.slideshare.net/citecmat/aumentame-edu-2015?ref=http://www.aumenta.me/node?page=5).
- The Aurasma software (https://www.aurasma.com/) empowers teachers and students to project videos where musicians play those very instruments that students are beginning to use. In this way, students have a model to follow while their motivation increases (Roscorla 2013).
- Modern dance practice through programs like Just Dance, thanks to which students can develop their corporal expression following models projected with Augmented Reality technology (see http://www.slideshare.net/cit ecmat/aumentame-edu-2015?ref=http://www.aumenta.me/node?page=5).
- Library 2.0. It consists in placing QR codes on library and classroom books to enrich them with videos, podcasts or three-dimensional objects (see http://infantic-tac.blogspot.com.es/2013/08/receta-2o-biblioteca-digital-libros-con.html).
- Treasure hunting. This type of playful activity becomes even more interesting for students when they can use QR codes as clues to find the treasure in an amusing yet instructive way (see http://infantic-tac.blogspot.com.es/2013/10/feliz-halloween_24.html).
- Learn linguistic structures through tales. Students can improve their written expression by creating stories which may also be illustrated with pictures

that can be transformed into three-dimensional designs thanks to applca-tions like ChromVille (see https://docs.google.com/presentation/d/1ihhPQqXDk8joYS8jd8fIWJ3gxCYaVlyu-4n1jnak3eA/edit?pref=2&pli=1#slide=id.g9af23b72d_0_0).
- Get a more realistic view of natural phenomena. With the help of programs like K-Solar System, students can contemplate a three-dimensional reproduction of the solar system as well as analyze the interactions among its elements (see https://docs.google.com/presentation/d/1ihhPQqXDk8joYS8jd8fIWJ3gxCYaVlyu-4n1jnak3eA/edit?pref=2&pli=1#slide=id.g9c3b410b2_0_57).
- Elaborate tourist guides. After taking photographs and recording videos to make presentations of emblematic places, students can create QR codes in order to geolocate all those materials on a map (see http://enmiaulade infantil.blogspot.com.es/2015/07/proyecto-de-centro-con-codigos-qr.html).
- Children with autism can learn to recognize parts of their body through applications like Pictogram Room (see http://www.pictogramas.org/proom/init.do?method=gameTab).
- Learn history with geolocalized information related to legends and historical ruins, among other things (see https://prezi.com/nnz_gh-w6r4b/aumentame-2014-granada-17-de-mayo).
- Encourage healthy eating habits. Students can learn through QR codes about the fruits and vegetables that they find in the market (see https://www.youtube.com/watch?time_continue=41&v=sdRksbuVvtg).

6.3 High school and professional development (12 – 18 years old)

We can also find examples of learning activities based on Augmented Reality in high school and professional development:
- Guided tours to museums. Visits to museums are part of annual schools programs and are usually arranged by teachers with the aim of students taking full advantage of the visit. Bearing this in mind, students can use Augmented Reality technology not only to gather information on what they will see, but also to read QR codes which are already available in many museums and galleries (see http://www.aumenta.me/node/255).
- Virtual museums in three dimensions. After presenting in three dimensions objects exposed in different museums, students can analyze them in detail

and interact with them (see https://www.youtube.com/watch?time_continue=154&v=Gbb9DR8bRN8).
- Geolocated routes. Students can take advantage of applications like Layar to create their own routes through Augmented Reality in order to know the architectural styles of a city, fauna and flora of a region, and works of a particular artist (see http://www.aumenta.me/node/259).
- Create a laboratory at school or at home. Augmented Reality helps students develop scientific skills, as they may test hypotheses and perform calculations (see https://docs.google.com/presentation/d/1ihhPQqXDk8joYS8jd8fIWJ3gxCYaVlyu-4n1jnak3eA/edit?pref=2&pli=1#slide=id.g9c3b410b2_0_12).
- Process simulation. Students can enhance knowledge on electronics by designing electronic schemes and simulating their functioning (see http://www.slideshare.net/bernatllopis/ponencia-ardutronica-aumentame-2014?ref=http://www.aumenta.me/node?page=13).
- Study on an experimental basis subjects such as chemistry (see https://www.youtube.com/watch?v=2kpFr0XFgFA).
- Study of geometry. Students develop their mathematical competence by interacting with three-dimensional figures created by themselves (see http://www.slideshare.net/citecmat/presentacion-ar-mat-35051813?ref=http://www.aumenta.me/node?page=13).
- Augmented reading workshop. Books read in this workshop may contain codes like QR to visualize three-dimensional objects, watch videos or listen podcasts elaborated either by the students themselves or by publishers (see https://www.youtube.com/watch?v=EzHld8vRRAo).
- Make augmented books. By way of example, students can make a book that shows front, lateral and top view of geometric figures in three dimensions (see http://victormorenocaceres.wix.com/axonometriaenra).
- Construction of three-dimensional prototypes. Students may design models of dwellings adapted for handicapped people thanks to the application Sketchup (see http://www.aumenta.me/node/252).
- Create scenarios to submerge into them through Augmented Reality glasses like the Cardboard visor. In this way, students can implement current teaching principles, e. g. learning by doing (see https://www.youtube.com/watch?time_continue=5&v=5I5JqbfQpsY).
- Improve oral fluency in different languages. Since Augmented Reality can be used to choose an image as marker and associate it with a video, students can talk in different languages about a number of topics or objects in a motivating and funny way overcoming their initial embarrassment (see https://docs.google.com/presentation/d/1ihhPQqXDk8joYS8jd8fIWJ3gxCYaVlyu-4n1jnak3eA/edit?pref=2&pli=1#slide=id.g9c3b410b2_0_57).

- Enrich and support students' presentations. Students should learn to use Augmented Reality as an innovative and useful tool when explaining issues and facilitating that other people understand one's own argument (see http://labtic.org/emigrandoentremares/).
- Recreations. Students can recreate the classical world by using videos recorded by themselves (see http://illargonauta.blogspot.com.es/).
- Recovery of cultural heritage. The European Union funds a program of international cooperation thanks to which students from seven countries can design innovative Augmented Reality applications to recover cultural heritage, promote tourism, and exchange these informations (see http://www.slideshare.net/xsune/googleglass-aumentame14?ref=http://www.aumenta.me/node?page=12).

6.4 University

Last but not least, research shows that Augmented Reality technology is and can be successfully applied in universities (Tampieri 2015). To give an example, Augmented Reality has a great potential to offer educational and realistic experiences to health sciences students, above all when it is not possible for them to practice in real contexts due to security, cost or viability reasons (Kamphuis et al. 2014, Zhu et al. 2014). Indeed, Augmented Reality technology has proven to be very effective in studying fields as important to medical training as anatomy (Thomas et al. 2010). Here are further applications of Augmented Reality technology to learning activities in higher education:

- Engineering students improved their visuospatial skills by analyzing abstract concepts through three-dimensional representations (Martín-Gutiérrez et al. 2010).
- Teacher training students learnt techniques to teach art through Augmented Reality technology (see https://www.youtube.com/watch?v=cC9UDkHWG3A&feature=youtu.be).

7. Conclusion

Although Augmented Reality technology was not initially designed with educational purposes, its applications on education are getting further relevance. Proof of this can be found in the diverse experiences and initiatives presented in this chapter for different educational stages and curricular areas. Unquestionably, Augmented Reality provides a blended learning experience that enriches reality with digital technology. This allows students not only to build broader and deeper knowledge, but also become acquainted with their future works. After all, major companies are heavily investing in this technology to promote that employees work together in groups, develop a more meaningful learning and increase their motivation, among other things (Johnson et al. 2016). Since technological development progresses steadily and keeps producing devices that are increasingly cheaper and easier to handle, it is expected that Augmented Reality will acquire greater relevance in teaching-learning processes. However, we still cannot state that Augmented Reality has already been widely adopted in schools: in our opinion, at the very least two or three years will be needed for such implementation (Johnson et al. 2016).

References

Adell, Jordi/Castañeda, Linda (2012): "Tecnologías emergentes, ¿pedagogías emergentes?". In: José Hernández/Massimo Pennesi/Diego Sobrino/Azucena Vázquez (eds.), *Tendencias emergentes en educación con TIC*, Barcelona: Asociación Espiral, 13 – 32.

Billinghurst, Mark/Duenser, Andreas (2012): "Augmented Reality in the classroom". In: *Computer* 7, 56 – 63.

Bower, Matt/Howe, Cathie/McCredie, Nerida/Robinson, Austin/Grover, David (2014): "Augmented Reality in education – cases, places and potentials." In: *Educational Media International* 51(1), 1 – 15.

Chen, Chien-Hsu/Lee, I-Jui/Lin, Ling-Yi (2015): "Augmented Reality-based self-facial modeling to promote the emotional expression and social skills of adolescents with autism spectrum disorders." In: *Research in Developmental Disabilities* 36, 396 – 403.

Chen, Chien-Hsu/Lee, I-Jui/Lin, Ling-Yi (2016): "Augmented Reality-based video-modeling storybook of nonverbal facial cues for children with autism spectrum disorder to improve their perceptions and judgments of facial expressions and emotions." In: *Computers in Human Behavior* 55, 477 – 485.

Cheng, Kun-Hung/Tsai, Chin-Chung (2012): "Interactive Augmented Reality system for enhancing library instruction in elementary schools." In: *Computers & Education* 59, 638 – 652

Cheng, Kun-Hung/Tsai, Chin-Chung (2016): "The interaction of child-parent shared reading with an Augmented Reality (AR) picture book and parents' conceptions of AR learning: Child-parent shared Augmented Reality book reading." In: *British Journal of Educational Technology* 47(1), 203 – 222.

Chi, Hung-Lin/Kang, Shih-Chung/Wang, Xiangyu (2013): "Research trends and opportunities of Augmented Reality applications in architecture, engineering, and construction." In: *Automation in Construction* 33, 116 – 122.

Chicchi, Irene Alice/Pallavicini, Federica/Pedroli, Elisa/Serino, Silvia/Riva, Giuseppe (2015): "Augmented Reality: A brand new challenge for the assessment and treatment of psychological disorders." In: *Computational and Mathematical Methods in Medicine*, 2015, 1 – 12.

Cubillo, Joaquín/Martin, Sergio/Castro, Manuel/Boticki, Ivica (2015): "Preparing Augmented Reality learning content should be easy: UNED ARLE—an authoring tool for Augmented Reality learning environments." In: *Computer Applications in Engineering Education* 23 (5), 778–789.

De Pedro, Javier/Martínez, Carlos Luis (2012): "Realidad Aumentada: Una Alternativa Metodológica en la Educación Primaria Nicaragüense." In: *IEEE-RITA* 7(2), 102–108.

Dewey, John (1938): *Experience & Education*, New York: Kappa Delta Pi.

Di Serio, Angela/Ibáñez, María Blanca/Delgado, Carlos (2013): "Impact of an Augmented Reality system on students' motivation for a visual art course." In: *Computers & Education* 68, 586–596

Durlach, Nathaniel I./Mavor, Anne S. (eds.) (1995): *Virtual Reality: scientific and technological challenges*, Washington, D.C: National Academy Press.

Estopace, Eden (2015): "Augmented Reality apps for education win top prize in Philippine Hackaton." Open University (http://libezproxy.open.ac.uk/login?url=http://search.proquest.com.libezproxy.open.ac.uk/docview/1659810189?accountid=14697, visited on 28 February 2016).

Fombona, Javier/Pascual, María Ángeles/Madeira, María Filomena (2012): "Realidad Aumentada, una evolución de las aplicaciones de los dispositivos móviles." In: *Píxel-Bit. Revista de Medios y Educación* 41, 197–210.

Fundación Telefónica (2011): *Realidad aumentada: una nueva lente para ver el mundo*, Madrid: Fundación Telefónica.

García, Fernando (2014): "Fundamentos psicológicos de la realidad aumentada." In: *Revista Comunicación y Pedagogía* 277–278, 67–72

Huang, Yujia/Li, Hui/Fong, Ricci (2016): "Using Augmented Reality in early art education: a case study in Hong Kong kindergarten." In: *Early Child Development and Care* 186(6), 879–894.

Jabr, Ferris (2014): "Por qué el cerebro prefiere el papel." In: *Investigación y Ciencia* 449, 83–93.

Johnson, Larry/Adams Becker, Samantha/Cummins, Michele/Estrada, Victoria/Freeman, Alex/Hall, Courtney (2016): *NMC horizon report: 2016 higher education edition*, Austin, Texas: The New Media Consortium.

Johnson, Larry/Smith, Rachel S./Levine, Alan/Stone, Sonja (2011): *The 2011 horizon report*, Austin, Texas: The New Media Consortium.

Johnson, Larry/Smith, Rachel S./Levine, Alan/Stone, Sonja (2010): *The 2010 horizon report*, Austin, Texas: The New Media Consortium.

Johnson, Larry/Smith, Rachel S./Levine, Alan/Stone, Sonja (2006): *The 2006 horizon report*, Austin, Texas: The New Media Consortium.

Johnson, Larry/Smith, Rachel S./Levine, Alan/Stone, Sonja (2005): *The 2005 horizon report*, Austin, Texas: The New Media Consortium.

Kamphuis, Carolien/Barsom, Esther/Schijven, Marlies/Christoph, Noor (2014): "Augmented Reality in medical education?" In: *Perspectives on Medical Education* 3(4), 300–311.

Kerawalla, Lucinda/Luckin, Rosemary/Seljeflot, Simon/Woolard, Adrian (2006): "Making it real: exploring the potential of Augmented Reality for teaching primary school science." In: *Virtual Reality* 10(3–4), 163–174.

Kesim, Mehmet/Ozarslan, Yasin (2012): "Augmented Reality in education: Current technologies and the potential for education." In: *Procedia – Social and Behavioral Sciences* 47, 297–302.
Kilgus, Thomas/Heim, Eric/Haase, Sven/Prüfer, Sabine/Müller, Michael/Seitel, Alexander/Fangerau, Markus/Wiebe, Tamara/Iszatt, Justin/Schlemmer, Heinz-Peter/Hornegger, Joachim/Yen, Kathrin/Maier-Hein, Lena (2015): "Mobile markerless Augmented Reality and its application in forensic medicine." In: *International Journal of Computer Assisted Radiology and Surgery* 10(5), 573–586.
Klopfer, Eric/Sheldon, Josh (2010): "Augmenting your own reality: Student authoring of science-based Augmented Reality games." In: *New Directions for Youth Development* 128, 85–94.
Lee, Kangdon (2012): "Augmented Reality in Education and Training." In: *Techtrends: Linking Research & Practice To Improve Learning* 56(2), 13–21.
Lin, Chien Yu/Chang, Yu Ming (2015): "Interactive Augmented Reality using Scratch 2.0 to improve physical activities for children with developmental disabilities." In: *Research in Developmental Disabilities* 37, 1–8.
Martín-Gutiérrez, Jorge/Luís Saorín, José/Contero, Manuel/Alcañiz, Mariano/Pérez-López, David C./Ortega, Mario (2010): "Design and validation of an augmented book for spatial abilities development in engineering students." In: *Computers & Graphics* 34(1), 77–91.
Martin, Sergio/Díaz, Gabriel/Sancristobal, Elio/Gil, Rosario/Castro, Manuel/Peire, Juan (2011): "New technology trends in education: Seven years of forecasts and convergence." In: *Computers & Education* 57(3), 1893–1906.
Milgram, Paul/Takemura, Haruo/Utsumi, Akira/Kishino, Fumio (1994): "Augmented Reality: a class of displays on the reality-virtuality continuum". In: *Proceedings the SPIE: Telemanipulator and Telepresence Technologies*, 2351, 282–292.
Moore, Jeoffrey. A (2015): *Cruzando el abismo*, Barcelona: Planeta.
Muñoz, Juan Miguel (2014): "Realidad Aumentada, una oportunidad para la nueva educación." In: *Revista Comunicación y Pedagogía* 277–278, 6–11.
Nincarean, Danakorn/Alia, Mohamad B./Halim, Noor D. A./Rahman, Mohd H. A. (2013): "Mobile Augmented Reality: The potential for education." In: *Procedia – Social and Behavioral Sciences* 103, 657–664.
Prendes, Carlos (2015): "Realidad Aumentada y educación: análisis de experiencias prácticas." In: *Píxel-Bit* 46, 187–203.
Research and Markets (2015): "Global Augmented Reality for mobile devices 2015: Gaming and entertainment, marketing and advertising, information, education and toys, retail and e-commerce, and industrial applications." In: *Business Wire*, 20 March 2015. http://libezproxy.open.ac.uk/login?url=http://search.proquest.com.libezproxy.open.ac.uk/docview/1664738326?accountid=14697, visited on 29 February 2016.
Roscorla, Tanya (2013): "Augmented reality meets music education." In: *McClatchy – Tribune Business News*, 22 August 2013. http://libezproxy.open.ac.uk/login?url=http://search.proquest.com.libezproxy.open.ac.uk/docview/1427327809?accountid=14697, visited on 29 February 2016.
Sheehy, Kieron/Ferguson, Rebecca/Clough, Gill (2014): *Augmented education: Bringing real and virtual learning together*, New York: Palgrave Macmillan.

Sommerauer, Peter/Müller, Oliver (2014): "Augmented Reality in informal learning environments: A field experiment in a mathematics exhibition." In: *Computers & Education* 79, 59–68

Tampieri, Laura (2015): "Innovating the didactical methodologies applied in universities through Second Life and Practice Firm: case study". In: *Technology, Innovation and Education* 1(1).

Thomas, Rhys G./John, Nigel W./Delieuc, John M. (2010): "Augmented Reality for anatomical education." In: *Journal of Visual Communication in Medicine* 33(1), 6–15.

Tomi, Azfar B./Rambli, Dayang R. A. (2013): "An interactive mobile Augmented Reality magical play-book: Learning number with the thirsty crow." In: *Procedia Computer Science* 25, 123–130.

Wei, Xiaodong/Weng, Dongdong/Liu, Yue/Wang, Yongtian (2015): "Teaching based on Augmented Reality for a technical creative design course." In: *Computers & Education* 79, 59–68.

Wu, Hsin-Kai/Lee, Silvia/Chang, Hsin-Yi/Liang, Jyh-Chong (2013): "Current status, opportunities and challenges of Augmented Reality in education." In: *Computers & Education* 62, 41–49.

Yilmaz, Rabia (2016): "Educational magic toys developed with Augmented Reality technology for early childhood education." In: *Computers in Human Behavior* 54, 240–248.

Zhang, Jia/Sung, Yao-Ting/Houc, Huei-Tse/Chang, Kuo-En (2014): "The development and evaluation of an Augmented Reality-based armillary sphere for astronomical observation instruction." In: *Computers & Education* 73, 178–188.

Zhu, Egui/Hadadgar, Arash/Masiello, Italo/Zary, Nabil (2014): "Augmented Reality in healthcare education: an integrative review." In: *PeerJ* 2, e469.

María Elena Alva, Teobaldo Hernán Sagastegui, Vicente García, Jordán Pascual and Rubén González

Teaching Augmented Reality

Abstract: In this chapter, we present a brief description of the concepts that delimit the teaching/learning process of the subject of Augmented Reality and Accessibility, a subject provided in the degree of Computer Engineering at the University of Oviedo (Spain). This includes the requirements needed to achieve a better comprehension and the competences established by the students, a description of the methodology used in this dynamic and participatory process by the student and the technological support used to achieve the goals of the course, based on Bloom's model. Finally, it is also presented the model used for the evaluation process applied in this course, which combines both individual and group assessment activities, with cooperative evaluation from the teacher and the students.

Keywords: Educative models, assessment, evaluation and feedback, Augmented Reality, accessibility and usability, Interaction and Multimedia, mobile device.

1. Introduction

There is no doubt that Computer Science has become a part in our everyday lives making it more comfortable, practical and efficient. Computer science has made work and communication a lot easier since it is complicated to find a field where Computer Science is not present. It has even changed some of the behavior of society, as seen by the social media. The Internet has also shaken up the way of making several daily activities, from reading the news, looking for information of interest, communicating with other people, checking flights, timetables, completing formalities, to obtaining complementary information about some component from the real world, etc.

In addition, the increasing evolution of technology has allowed to convert mobile devices into powerful handheld minicomputers like smartphones and tablets, that nowadays offer big services such as faster access to the Internet, powerful photo and video cameras, instant communication, chat and many other features that make them sensible to the context such as location, motion, direction, compass, etc.

Therefore, the access to technology is a decisive factor when designing or developing an application, however, it has also established the possibility of de-

DOI 10.1515/9783110497656-016

signing and developing simpler applications making the most of the potential of the output devices.

In just a few decades, the supply and demand of applications has substantially evolved; from typical desktop applications in the 80s – students then were prepared to build computer programs so that one user interacts with it. During the 1990s, this scenario changed into web applications based on server, that is, many users doing the same tasks at the same time – students then were educated to build applications that would support large amount of users at the same time, transactions, distributed computing, etc. Nowadays, with the web 2.0 challenge of concentrate the applications in the user, the student must be prepared to develop applications to reach its proper display, use and access through different devices – improved applications that take advantage of the potential of the output device.

The development of Augmented Reality applications is included in this scenario, that is, applications sensitive to the context with capabilities of identifying locations, of recognizing and monitoring markers, images and real places, in order to adapt the display of digital elements of information – text, images, 2D, 3D, videos, etc. – within a specific situation of the user's context and location, adapting it to the user's environment and vision.

The study programs of courses in the Computer Science degree have had to go hand-in-hand with technology's evolution. The acknowledgement of this scenario meant a constant challenge to adapt and update the study programs in order to include new contents in the courses. That is the case of the subject of Augmented Reality and Accessibility, which emerges precisely in this evolution process, planned to educate students in the design, implementation and assessment of applications that would incorporate rich artificial content in real-world scenarios, and them are both usable and accessible, providing students with timeless structural contents, but at the same time encouraging their interdisciplinary skills and making them aware of the need to design applications focused on improving universal access, that is, including those with any physical and/or cognitive limitation.

2. The Subject

The subject of Augmented Reality and Accessibility is part of the study area of Interaction and Multimedia, and is taught in the fourth year of Software Engineering degree at the University of Oviedo as part of the Computer Training and Complementary Technologies module.

The course has two main goals: that students would gain long-lasting knowledge about the fundaments of the course as well as other related aspects, and that they would acquire skills to select tools and technologies that would allow them to design and develop small projects planned to promote the access to additional information. This additional information would improve the experience and life of the users in general, especially to those with cognitive limitations or those with any disability. It would offer the necessary support to these users so they would have actual equal opportunities, that would consider adaptation processes and techniques to their needs, and would add digital elements that would allow them to easily access additional information – computer-generated elements: text, images, videos, etc., resulting in a sense of coexistence of the real environment with the virtual world (cf. Wichrowski 2013) – more adapted to their needs.

The subject of Augmented Reality and Accessibility is designed so students would not only gain basic structural knowledge – concepts, features, algorithms, designs principles, different options of implementation, etc. – and elements of associated knowledge – accessibility topics, cognitive theory, natural interaction, usability and responsive design, etc. –, but so they would have a dynamic and participatory role in the teaching-learning process – designing, producing small projects, assessing and evaluating their tasks –, which means, giving them the opportunity to reinforce and go into detail about the contents of the course and applying them in the development of the activities planned for it.

The course is planned for a total of 150 hours, equivalent to 6 ECTS – European Credit Transfer and Accumulation System – that establishes 25 hours per credit according to the European Higher Education Area. These hours would be distributed as follows: 60 teaching hours – lectures or seminars, workshops, practices, tutorials and evaluations – and 90 hours of personal research – self-learning, study and the student's tasks and projects.

To measure the achievement of the proposed goals for the course, a set of competencies – that the student should acquire – were established on the verification report of the degree and documented in the teaching guide of the course:

1. Methodological competences: design of solutions to human problems; capacity of abstraction, analytical capacity and ability to synthesize.
2. Individual competences: a positive attitude to new situations and technologies, ability to work effectively.
3. Systematic competences: planning and organizational capacity, a preferential attitude to people with cognitive disabilities and/or limitations.
4. Common competences: analysis, design, construction and maintenance of applications capacities in a strong, safe and efficient way, with capacities

to choose the most suitable paradigm and programming language, and the ability to design and assess.

Furthermore, the guide establishes some learning results that the students should achieve by the end of the course, which are the following:
1. To analyze, design, build, adapt and/or test support technologies that would allow the users with some kind of disability to access the information technology.
2. To design and conduct research experiments to complete the scientific knowledge of the special needs from the user's interaction and from the cognitive models.
3. To build accessible and usable user interfaces from the requirements provided by the client and use the current legislation and regulations, which is applied to the development of user interfaces understanding, also, the importance of natural interaction and the integration of support technologies for users with requirements for special requirements.
4. To apply usability and accessibility evaluation techniques.

With regard to the 60 hours of the teaching work, there have been planned five types of work sessions to develop the teaching-learning process and achieve the competences and results suggested in the guide:
1. *Lectures and/or seminar sessions* – to acquire basic knowledge,
2. *Workshop Sessions* – to study cases or particular problems related to the studied matter or the studied unit, carried out individually or by organizing work group,
3. *Practical sessions* – carried out in computer rooms, where students would strengthen the acquired knowledge by a series of guided practice tasks that would require individual work or collaborative work in groups,
4. *Evaluation sessions* –assessment and review of the students' tasks and works carried out by the teachers and by their own classmates
5. *Tutorial sessions* – planned to give support to a student or a group of student's particular needs on the comprehension of the subject or performed task and a determined session in the planning for the whole class, generally to solve questions from the final project of the course.

To reach the established goals – competences and results – we have based out learning process on the model proposed by Bloom (1971). These sessions will be expanded on the following section.

Regarding the work hours for the students, the following sessions have been planned (Figure 1):

1. Self-learning sessions: carried out through readings and review of material related to the study subject and/or through the search for information, which is necessary know so it can be used in the planned activities at the practice and workshop sessions.
2. Self-assessment: there had been prepared a series of self-assessment tests, which are available at the end of every study unit.
3. Surveys – related to a specific study or to a particular study case: execution of tasks and development of small projects, that can be done individually or in groups.

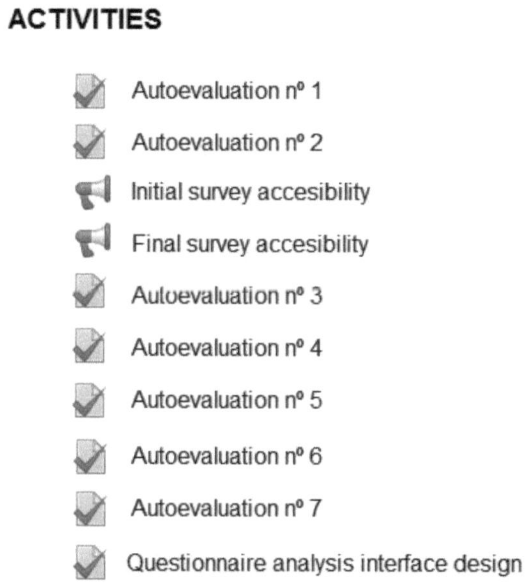

Fig. 1: Activities summary

The topics, through which the students are expected to gather knowledge and skills, are distributed in four main units:

1. *Augmented Reality and Accessibility fundamentals:* This section is focused on letting the students know about the tenets of cognitive theory and the different cognitive issues that could affect the use of an application – definitions, features, types – as well as their identification and negative consequences when experiencing an application. It is also focused on the study of guidelines and proposals to improve the design of interfaces for the different cases presented.

2. *Accessibility principles:* This section looks in the foundation of usability and accessibility on the design of interfaces – concepts, tenets, guides. We make a review of the existing national and international regulations and standards. These should be taken into account when designing an application. In addition, we also review the tenets of responsive design and natural interaction.
3. *Augmented Reality:* In this section, we study the basic knowledge, on which Augmented Reality is based – introduction, basic concepts, features, evolution, types, etc. – and the key principals of Augmented Reality – localization, recognition, monitoring, focus, context, points of interest, markers, etc. We also review the available technologies for the implementation of Augmented Reality applications such as mobile devices and Augmented Reality browser features, Toolkit, and languages that would allow us to introduce Augmented Reality solutions – e.g. Java, C++ and marker languages such as KML and ARML.
4. *Augmented Accessibility:* This section is focused on the study of the user's experience with Augmented Reality applications, their valuation and assessment; as well as, the research of recent studies on this matter, and the impact of natural interaction in this area.

In this way, we attempt to make the student reach the planned goals and the indicated competences on the previous section.

3. Teaching method

The course is planned to have teaching-learning sessions based on Krathwohl's (2002) proposals, who, after reviewing Bloom's taxonomy, established the learning levels in the following order: remember, understand, apply, analyze, evaluate and create.

Bloom's (1971) work is still valid in spite of the passing of time. He proposed a taxonomy of the learning goals, well defined in six major categories in the cognitive domain: Knowledge, Comprehension, Application, Analysis, Synthesis, and Evaluation. As can be seen, Krathwohl's work not only changed the order of the levels but also renamed them. To that end, he used verbs instead of nouns, so that these desired goals would be better understood.

Although the model establishes the goals in the cognitive domain, we believe that is important to distinguish that the adopted model not only suggests to reach the cognitive goals – knowledge – but also strengthen and/or improve the affective – attitudes – and psychomotor – abilities to develop – aspects.

We take Krathwohl's (2002) proposal, adapting it to the course in particular, we take into account the digital tools available as a support for the model, and we considered them within the three established domains.

In the cognitive domain of knowledge, we focus on the learning goals, looking at providing information to the students, through direct teaching – lectures, texts, additional material – with the intention of making the students acquire the basic knowledge that would allow them to develop different tasks during the course. This domain should allow the students to be able to:
1. Remember, list and localize concepts, regulations, guides,
2. Understand, summarize and classify issues related to the UI, mobile devices and Augmented Reality applications that confront users in general, and especially those with cognitive problems. Analyze the most outstanding features or those with major impact in the proposed study cases or in the carried out projects,
3. Apply techniques or technologies; select those more appropriate to complete tasks or assigned projects,
4. Analyze, compare different solutions to the study cases, search and organize relevant and necessary information to propose solutions.
5. Judge, value and assess their own tasks and work or from other classmates in a critique and objective way. Carry out self-learning and value it through self-assessment with the digital resources available. Evaluate their proposed interfaces and applications by using tools in contrast to national and international regulations.
6. Develop the proposed tasks, plan and build small applications.

In the affective domain, the objectives are focused on strengthening the student's attention and active participation throughout the training process. In this domain, the student should be able to:
1. Come to an agreement with their fellow classmates in group activities,
2. Participate in debates and discussions to a suggested problem,
3. Participate, collaborate and share knowledge in group activities. This way, the students not only acquire basic knowledge, but also strengthen and/or improve their personal skills to carry out the tasks suggested to reach an effective work.

In the psychomotor domain, the goal is mostly focused on promoting and improving the verbal communication skills and oratorical abilities to explain their own ideas that were suggested during the group tasks; their progress throughout the performed tasks and projects; as well as, their ability to plan and organize both the development of the suggested tasks and their presentation.

Figure 2 shows the summary of Krathwohl's (2002) improved model, adapted to our own needs and goals.

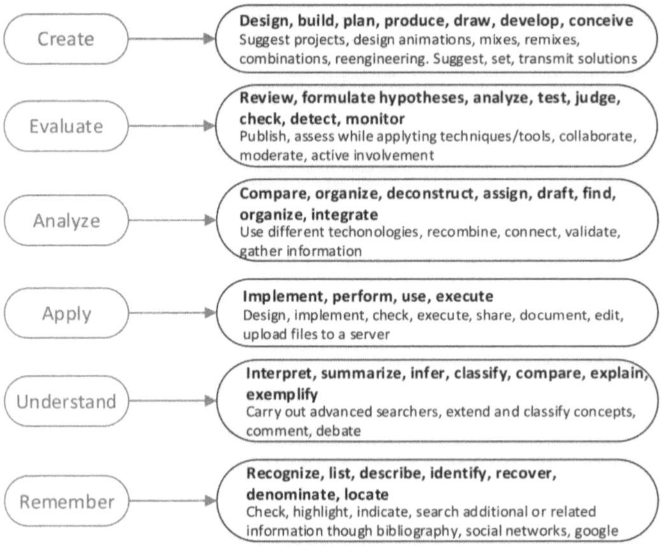

Fig. 2: Adaptation of Bloom model for the aims of the subject of ARA

The described learning model is put into practice throughout the different work sessions proposed for the course – that were mentioned in the previous section.

We will describe now in detail the first three types: lectures/seminars, practice and workshop sessions, leaving out the fourth one – evaluation – that will be further explained separately, because of its magnitude and importance in the evaluation of the expected learning results. The tutoring sessions are not included in this section because they were sufficiently described in the previous section.

1. Lectures and seminar sessions: We encourage the students to review the study material, and search for additional information through bibliography, by using not only both the provided material and links to material within the formal means of learning – University's own Moodle – but also through informal means of learning, and using the Internet as a support tool – through Goggle or other specialized search engines. In these sessions, the goal is to enhance the acquired knowledge and develop abilities in order to highlight and identify concepts and key ideas, and/or promote a debate about them.

2. The practice sessions – which take place in the computer room – are focused on the review and learning of the different guides, techniques and technologies available to perform the given tasks and develop the proposed projects. The goal is to obtain investigation, exploration and interaction skills in the students with the appropriate techniques and technologies. Through these activities, we would manage to make the students read, search, discuss, document and debate about the proposed experimental activities. These activities are organized as follows:
   a. Initial sessions dedicated to research, review and document the design tenets based on studies of cognitive problems, and valid usability guidelines, regulations and accessibility standards.
   b. Sessions dedicated to implement small projects based on the acquired knowledge from previous courses and the knowledge obtained from the research performed in previous sessions. The objective of these sessions is to identify the students' background on markup languages, such as HTML, Java and CSS3 sheets; and script languages, like JavaScript, in order to establish the feedback necessary for subsequent sessions.
   c. Review sessions of Augmented Reality technology based on localization and identification of markers. In these sessions, the student performs small tasks by using the available technologies.
   d. Development sessions of guided mini-projects using programming to implement them. By using both the acquired knowledge and the support material, the students should be able to perform mini-projects. The activities planned for these sessions will be carry out using Java for Android platforms, giving the students the liberty to work in the IDE they know best. Through these activities, we expect that the students would be able to implement, execute and share previously acquired knowledge about techniques/technologies and programming languages needed.

   In this regard, it should be noted that the course does not include the learning of programming languages, but it uses and strengthens the knowledge that the students already have at the beginning of this course. Therefore, the students are provided with some examples, so they would learn from those examples to deal with the given problems and suggest solutions.

   Furthermore, through these activities the students would become familiar with the assessment and evaluation of techniques and tools in the tasks and projects performed; and with the feedback received from the active participation from fellow coworkers and classmates in the assessment and evaluation of their work, that would allow them to make redesign decisions, that could also be reengineering decisions. These activities should be carried out

during the hours of personal research that the student dedicates to the course.
3. Through the workshop-seminar sessions done at the end of every unit, we present situations related to them in order to promote the critical analysis, to encourage the students to discuss and debate (individually or in groups) to reach a common opinion about the problems, study cases or the criteria, on which the students base the choice of some technique or technology, and suggest better alternatives or solutions.
   To ensure the highest level of learning, we present a series of controlled tasks to the students for their empirical study. In some cases, we give them the option to select topics of their own interest.

4. Evaluations

As the course is taught in the fourth year of the degree, the students are expected to have, apart from the required knowledge – knowledge of languages such as Java, JavaScript, HTML, CSS and tools like development contexts, editors, etc. – a certain level of maturity in order to successfully perform the development of the planned activities of the course. On these assumptions, we consider that, more than just doing a final exam, it is important to evaluate the acquired competences through the development of a series of tasks and work during the course, based on the imparted and assimilated knowledge through the different activities programmed for it.

The evaluation process applied to assess the students' competences centers them in the middle of the learning process (cf. Prince 2004) to reach not only the learning outcomes but also their active participation through a series of analytical, evaluation tasks and small-scale projects development. These tasks are carried out through:

1. *Analytical and evaluation activities:* through the different work sessions not only theoretical principles are provided, but the critic and independent thinking is also encouraged:
   a. In the analysis and discussion of the suggested problems or study cases and the proposal of solutions. The students should briefly summarize their proposal and explain it. Examples of this work are: investigation and analysis of support technologies for users with some kind of a concrete disability, investigation and/or determination of specific needs in the user's interfaces to cognitive problems, etc.
   b. Impartial and objective assessment of their fellow classmates' proposals to the performed tasks and projects – to achieve this, the student as-

sumes the role of user and bases his judgement on assumptions established by the teacher, not just as a mere observer.

The cognitive, affective and psychomotor domains are evaluated through these activities.

2. *Practical activities:* Within them, investigation, design, small applications development and/or expansion of some given are included. These activities are evaluated through individual and group tasks:
   a. *Individual practices*, the objective of these activities is to evaluate the acquired competences individually through the resolution of cases and extension of small-size projects.
      For instance, the students receive an application and they will be asked to make some changes/adjustments needed to adjust them to a particular audience, to improve the accessibility and usability, or reach a more natural interaction. They could be also asked to evaluate the accessibility/usability of a given application using different tools suggested by the professor or other suggestions made by him and based on the results, the student would propose changes and upgrades.
   b. *Group practices*, this activities evaluate the student's ability to work in groups – involvement, collaboration and communication (cf. Sánchez 2014) – in the development of Augmented Reality projects specially intended to people with cognitive problems and with some disability. To this end, the class will be divided in small groups – of 2 or 3 students – and they will be asked to suggest a solution, which they should reach in the group together in consensus; after that, one of the members is selected by draw to make a presentation of that solution to the rest of the class. They should explain to their fellow classmates what they did, which problem they would solve, whom is that solution for and which problems did they have.

At both analytical and evaluation activities and at the practical activities, the students' proposals to a problem or study case are analyzed and evaluated by their classmates. These activities allow the student not only to think, analyze and evaluate other proposals, but also help them to focus on ideas and knowledge, and at best, to consider reengineering their own works when analyzed by their classmates. This allows them to be aware of their mistakes and their classmates' misunderstandings resulted from their explanation. Listening to other students correct them would also contribute to a better comprehension. Furthermore, in order to get the attention of the rest of the class, a random classmate would be asked to sum up what they understood of some particular aspect of the presentation and their own point of view – either if they agree or disagree and why). Each student or group –

depending on the case – would assess the presentation and the solution suggested using a scale of five points.

3. *Submission of papers:* The goal of these activities is to assess the students' investigation, analysis and written communication competences and skills, the resolution of crossed questions – between students, between teacher and students – and production of documents related to the tasks and projects (cf. Amengual/Marqués 2013, Marqués *et al.* 2013) that must be defended and debated. These activities will help the students in their own assessment and correction of their work, providing knowledge and ideas while improving the learning process. These are not long documents; and in some cases, they must be presented in a particular format, because they pursue the student to apply their synthesis skills to present the most important ideas.

5. Conclusions

Augmented Reality has grown and evolved by the hand of the new technologies. This matter challenges both teachers and students to look at the development of applications from a new perspective.

This challenges teachers to adapt the contents of the course to the study programs to emphasize the long-lasting structural contents, and it also challenges students to develop applications mainly for mobile platforms – smartphones, tablets, etc. – taking into account that they should reach applications that would offer better access to information than what reality may show and that people with cognitive disabilities and limitations must be included in the development process.

Furthermore, the success of the teaching-learning process of the course depends on the transversal coordination of the contents of previous and/or parallel courses that guarantee the required competences to achieve the expected goals.

Finally, the applied method guarantees a high amount of participation from the students at both an individual level and as a group, preparing them not only to defend their individual and group ideas and suggestions but also to carry those ideas out successfully, and also to train them for debates and discussions that could come up in their presentation, so they would be able to satisfy their audience, who will assess them.

References

Amengual, J. C./Marqués, M. (2013): "Evaluación de la competencia transversal de comuncación oral y escrita mediante la realización de debates". *JENUI 2013*, Castellón.
Bloom, B. (1971): *Handbook on Formative and Summative Evaluation of Student Learning*, New York: McGraw-Hill.
Krathwohl, D. R. (2002): "A revision of Bloom's Taxonomy: An Overview." In: *Theory and Practice: Revising Bloom's taxonomy* 41(4), 212–218.
Marqués, M./Badía, J. M./Martínez, E. (2013): "Una experiencia de autoevaluación y evaluación por compañeros". *JENUI 2013*, Castellón.
Prince, M. (2004): "Does Active learning work? a review of the Research." In: *Journal of Engineering Education* 93(3), 223–231.
Sánchez, P. (2014): "Evaluación individual de resultados producidos por grupos". *JENUI 2014*, Oviedo.
Wichrowski, M. (2013): "Teaching Augmented Reality in Practice: Tools, Workshops and Students' Projects". *MIDI '13 Proceedings of the International Conference on Multimedia, Interaction, Design and Innovation*, New York.

Notes on Contributors

Maria Elena Alva
Industrial Engineer (Industrial Engineering School, Trujillo University, Peru, 1986), Master Information System (UPAO-Peru & I.T.S.M-Mexico, 1988), PhD (Oviedo University, Spain, 2005). Professor for Programming Languages at the Engineering Faculty of the U.P.A.O University in Peru (1990 – 2005). Currently, she is Professor for Programming Languages and Computer Systems at the Oviedo University. Her research interests include web usability and accessibility, web engineering, natural interaction and augmented reality.

José María Ariso
José María Ariso has studied philosophy at the Complutense University of Madrid. After obtaining his PhD in 2003, he spent some research stays in Norwegian (Bergen) and German (Leipzig, Kassel, TU-Berlin and Frankfurt) universities. Since 2011 he is an assistant professor in the Department of Education at the International University of La Rioja. He has published books, several chapters in edited volumes and a number of articles in international journals. His main line of investigation is the analysis of Wittgenstein's later work, but his research interests also cover the fields of philosophy of education, philosophy of psychiatry, philosophy of technology, theory of knowledge and Spanish contemporary philosophy.

Almudena Castellanos
Assistant Professor at the Educational Faculty of the International University of La Rioja. A specialist in educational technology, her research revolves on educative technology, new pedagogical models and personalized education. Actually, her research developed within a research group in EDUC-04 Personalized Education in the Digital Age, whose objective is to study what is the best method to personalize education and improve academic results and student motivation.

Bolesław Czarnecki
Bolesław Czarnecki (PhD) is an associate research member of Eidyn Research Centre and an academic network facilitator for the History of Distributed Cognition Project at the University of Edinburgh. Working at the intersection of epistemology, philosophy of mind and theory of action, he has published on knowledge-how, epistemology of intelligence, and cognitive extension. He is a son of Tadeusz Czarnecki.

Tadeusz Czarnecki
Tadeusz Czarnecki (PhD, Dr. hab.) is an associate professor at the Institute of Philosophy of the Jagiellonian University. Having worked on Wittgenstein and skepticism for over 20 years (*Moore i Wittgenstein: niekartezjańskie rozwiązania problemu pewności*), he has since directed towards practically-oriented epistemology, focusing primarily on the relationship between knowledge-that, practical reasoning and knowledge-how in a wide context of purposeful practices. On a few occasions, Tadeusz has also ventured into political philosophy (*Osiem pouczeń dla obywatela: między demokracją a totalitaryzmem / Acht Unterweisungen für den Staatsbürger*).

Juan Luis Fuentes
European PhD in Pedagogy and Professor in the Theory and History of Education Department at Complutense University of Madrid. He has been a visiting scholar at Eastern Washington University (US), Roehampton University (UK), and Free University of Berlin (Germany). Member of the "Educational Endeavors as Action" research group at Universidad Internacional de La Rioja (UNIR) and of the "Civic Culture and Educational Policies" research group at Universidad Complutense de Madrid. His research is centered on theory and philosophy of education, intercultural education, and the use of ICTs in the educational sphere.

Vicente García
Dr. Vicente García Díaz is an associate professor in the Computer Science Department of the University of Oviedo. He has a PhD from the University of Oviedo in computer engineering. His research interests include model-driven engineering, domain specific languages, technology for learning and entertainment, mobile computing, internet of things, software development processes and practices.

Martin Gartmeier
Martin Gartmeier, PhD, is Postdoctoral Research Fellow at the Chair for Empirical Educational Research (Prof. Dr. Manfred Prenzel), TUM School of Education, TU Munich. His research interests are professional learning, learning from errors, negative knowledge, teacher education and communication between teachers and parents. He earned his PhD at the University of Regensburg (Prof. Dr. Hans Gruber). Its topic was "Error-friendliness at work: Positive attitudes towards errors and negative knowledge as resources of professional behaviour". He has published peer-reviewed articles in *Instructional Science, Vocations and Learning, Teaching and Teacher Education, Human Resource Development International,* and other journals. Contact: martin.gartmeier@tum.de

Thomas Gil
Thomas Gil has been Professor of Philosophy at the Technical University of Berlin since 1998. He has held teaching appointments at the Universities of Cologne, Stuttgart, Brussels, State University of New York at Albany and St. Gallen. He is the author of several books and articles on ethical judgments, scientific research, practical reasoning, human action and rationality ("Ethik", "Die Rationalität des Handels", "Actions, Normativity, and History", "Scientific Reasoning" and "Mind Functions").

Rubén González
Dr. Rubén González has a PhD in Computer Science Engineering. Currently he is Dean of School of Engineering and Technology of UNIR and Director of the AENOR (Spanish Association for Standardization and Certification) Chair in Certification, Quality and Technology Standards. He is advisory board member for the Ministry of Education at Colombia and evaluator from the National Agency for Quality Evaluation and Accreditation of Spain (ANECA). He is member of different ISO committees.

Charlotte Jonasson
Charlotte Jonasson, PhD, is an Assistant Professor at the Department of Psychology and Behavioral Sciences, Aarhus University, Denmark. She works within the combined research areas of educational and work and organizational psychology and has conducted qualitative

field studies in both private and public organizations. Her current research interests are vocational training and learning from errors, student and employee engagement, organizational changes and distributed leadership. She has published articles in *British Journal of Sociology of Education, Vocations and Learning and Organization Studies.* Contact: charlotte@psy.au.dk

Steffen Lepa
Dr. phil. Steffen Lepa, born 1978, is a media and communication scholar living in Berlin, Germany. He studied psychology, communication studies, media technology and media studies at Braunschweig (HBK/TU) and Hannover (HMT). He received his PhD in 2009 from the Faculty of Educational and Social Sciences at the University of Oldenburg. Presently, he is a postdoc researcher at the Audio Communication Group, Institute for Language and Communication, TU Berlin. Additionally, he holds teaching appointments for statistics, digital media change and sound design at different universities. His current key research areas comprise Mediatization research, media reception and use (with a special focus on sound and music), and empirical research methods.

Klaus Mainzer
Klaus Mainzer studied mathematics, physics, and philosophy. After professorships at the universities of Konstanz and Augsburg, he became professor for philosophy of science and technology (since 2008), director of the Carl von Linde-Academy (2008–2015), and 2012–2014 founding director of the Munich Center for Technology in Society (MCTS) at the Technical University of Munich. Since 2016, he is TUM Emeritus of Excellence. His research fields are foundations of mathematical sciences and computational modeling, philosophy of engineering and its societal impact. He is member of several international academies and author of books on the foundations of mathematical and computational sciences and their technological and societal impact.

Spyridon Orestis Palermos
Spyridon Orestis Palermos' research focuses primarily on how technology and the web can transform individuals' and communities' means for acquiring knowledge. He is currently a postdoctoral fellow at Edinburgh's Eidyn Centre, where he also leads the Group Knowledge pilot project. His research has appeared in *Synthese, Erkenntnis, American Philosophical Quarterly, Philosophical Psychology, Journal of American Philosophical Association* and other world-leading journals of analytic philosophy. Orestis also holds a BSc in Chemical Engineering from the National Technical University of Athens.

Jaana Parviainen
Jaana Parviainen is a senior researcher in the School of Social Sciences and Humanities at the University of Tampere (Finland). She received her doctorate in philosophy from the University of Tampere. Her research interests include phenomenology and social epistemology especially relating to embodiment and information technology in the post-industrial economy. Her research has been published in *Consumption, Markets and Culture, Scandinavian Journal of Management, Mobilities* and *European Journal of Cultural Studies.*

Jordán Pascual
Dr. Jordán Pascual Espada is a research scientist at the Computer Science Department of the University of Oviedo. PhD. from the University of Oviedo in Computer Engineering. His

research interests include the Internet of Things, exploration of new applications and associated human computer interaction issues in ubiquitous computing and emerging technologies, particularly mobile and web.

Carlota Pérez
Assistant Professor at the Educational Faculty of the International University of La Rioja. A specialist in educational technology, her research revolves on educational innovation and the application of information and communication technologies in the classroom. Actually, her research developed within a research group in EDUC-01 CYBERBULLYING (CB-OUT) whose objective is to contribute to a great understanding of the phenomenon cyberbullying concentrates on educational analysis, prevention and intervention.

Teobaldo Hernán Sagastegui
Mathematician (Sciences School, Trujillo University, Peru, 1990); Master in Computing Science (Cantabria University, 1993), PhD. (Oviedo University, Spain, 2015). He was Professor at the Mathematical School, Trujillo University in Peru (1985–1992). Since 1991, he is Professor of Programming Languages in the Engineering Faculty of the UPAO University (Peru). His research interests include knowledge society, e-learning, collaborative and analytics learning and Augmented Reality.

Karsten Schoellner
Karsten Schoellner is a freelance translator and proofreader based in Berlin. He has studied literature and philosophy at Stanford University, the Humboldt University in Berlin and the University of Potsdam and published on contemporary metaethical issues as well as Wittgenstein and Ortega y Gasset.

Maria Solomou

Maria Solomou, Ph.D. is a Learning Scientist at the Department of Communication and Internet Studies, Cyprus University of Technology and the Lead Instructional Designer researcher at CARDET. She works on pedagogical design and assessment of learning programs, curricula and materials for online learning spaces, esp. design and evaluation of interactive trajectories in 2D and 3D social online spaces. She manages several European-funded projects. Specializing in game design, she researches ways of intentionally designing learning trajectories for critical, active and reflexive participation and ways of enabling communities function as learning organizations. For that, she has developed a framework of elements for designing within online social, gaming spaces. Contact: msolomou.cut@gmail.com

Pirmin Stekeler-Weithofer
Pirmin Stekeler-Weithofer studied Philosophy, German Literature, Linguistics and Mathematics in Konstanz, Berlin, Prague and Berkeley. Since 1992, he is Professor for Philosophy at the University of Leipzig. He was Visiting Research in Campinas (1988), Swansea (1997–1998), Pittsburgh (1990–1992 and 2006), New York (2002) and Paris (2012).

Juan Antonio Valor
Juan Antonio Valor Yébenes is a Professor at the Faculty of Philosophy of the Complutense University of Madrid. His main research fields are the history and philosophy of science

(especially the philosophy of physics) as well as American pragmatism. He has published the book *Metodología de la Investigación Científica* (Biblioteca Nueva, 2000) and edited *Introducción a la Metodología* (Antonio Machado, 2002), *Pensando la naturaleza desde las universidades europeas* (Editorial Complutense, 2005) and *A Philosophical and Scientific Dialogue on Nature* (Editorial Complutense, 2005). He has published about 40 papers in specialized journals and collective books.

Javier Vilanova

Javier Vilanova Arias is Associate Professor in the Department of Logic and Philosophy of Science at the Complutense University of Madrid, where he started to work after receiving his Philosophy PhD from the University of Santiago de Compostela in 1996. His research interests include logic, philosophy of logic, philosophy of language, theory of argumentation, metaphilosophy and epistemology. His book *Al menos sé que sé algo. Estrategias argumentativas para fundamentar el concimiento* (*At least I know that I know something. Argumentative strategies for founding our knowledge*) was published by Escolar y Mayo in 2015. Sometimes he feels that reality is diminishing.

Stefan Weinzierl

Prof. Dr. Stefan Weinzierl, born 1967, is head of the Audio Communication Group at the Berlin Institute of Technology (TU Berlin). With a diploma in physics and sound engineering, he received his Ph.D. in musicology from TU Berlin. His activities in research include musical acoustics, room acoustics and virtual acoustics, his publications include handbooks on musical acoustics and audio technology as well as more than 100 original contributions in the above mentioned fields. He is currently coordinating research consortia on virtual acoustics (SEACEN, DFG), on the development of digital musical instruments (3DMIN, Einstein Foundation) and on the Semantics of Music (ABC_DJ, H2020, ICT19a). At TU Berlin, he is coordinating a master program in Audio Communication and Technology.

Author index

Subject index

Bei Fragen zur Produktsicherheit wenden Sie sich bitte an:
If you have any questions regarding product safety,
please contact:

Walter de Gruyter GmbH
Genthiner Straße 13
10785 Berlin
productsafety@degruyterbrill.com